THE AGE OF EXPERIENCES

BENJAMIN KLINE HUNNICUTT

THE AGE OF EXPERIENCES

Harnessing Happiness to Build a New Economy

With a Foreword by B. Joseph Pine II,
co-author of *The Experience Economy*

TEMPLE UNIVERSITY PRESS
Philadelphia • Rome • Tokyo

TEMPLE UNIVERSITY PRESS
Philadelphia, Pennsylvania 19122
tupress.temple.edu

Library of Congress Cataloging-in-Publication Data

Names: Hunnicutt, Benjamin Kline, author.
Title: The age of experiences : harnessing happiness to build a new economy /
    Benjamin Kline Hunnicutt ; with a foreword by B. Joseph Pine II, co-author
    of The Experience Economy.
Description: Philadelphia : Temple University Press, 2020. | Includes bibliographical
    references and index.
Identifiers: LCCN 2019014204 (print) | LCCN 2019022395 (ebook) |
    ISBN 9781439917091 (cloth) | ISBN 9781439917107 (paper) | ISBN 9781439917114
    (ebook)
Subjects: LCSH: Happiness. | Experience.
Classification: LCC BF575.H27 H865 2020 (print) | LCC BF575.H27 (ebook) |
    DDC 152.4/2—dc23
LC record available at https://lccn.loc.gov/2019014204
LC ebook record available at https://lccn.loc.gov/2019022395

Printed in the United States of America

9 8 7 6 5 4 3 2 1

Contents

Foreword

Outside my own small partnership, the only company I ever worked for after college was IBM, starting way back in its heyday in the 1980s. I absolutely loved working there, far more than I ever could have imagined back in school. But after I became a manager and accepted a particularly troublesome assignment—far too much work to get done for what the schedule permitted—there was a time when work really got to me. As the pressure mounted, I started losing first sleep and then my appetite. It was the first time I understood that work was not always enjoyable, and of course, for many people, it is never or almost never so.

Ever since I left IBM, over twenty-five years ago, I have been writing, speaking, teaching, and consulting—all of which I love doing even more. Sure, there have been pressures, deadlines, and less-than-scintillating assignments, but I gained true joy out of working and still do to this day. In fact, I don't ever plan on retiring (as long as there are still ideas to research and write about in the world of business—and clients willing to hire me). I just plan on changing the ratio of work to golf and on somewhat transitioning my intellectual pursuits from business to theology. (Meanwhile, my wife, Julie—who left IBM at the same time I did—doesn't know how she ever fit work in before, so busy is she with all her endeavors. She's also still not sure if our departures from IBM are going to work out for us.)

I know that I am not alone but also that my situation is rare. I know that most people must work very hard for low pay just to take care of themselves and their families. Professor Benjamin Hunnicutt has a true heart for such workaday people and wants more than anything for them—for all of us, really—to be able to have more leisure time and, especially, to gain real value from that time that would be to their benefit, that makes them better people. What a thought!

Benjamin has almost singlehandedly kept alive the early-1900s "shorter-hours movement," notably twinning it with the notion of "higher progress" in his earlier book, *Free Time: The Forgotten American Dream*.[1] Now, with *The Age of Experiences* the good professor doubles down on the desire—make that the need—for people to enhance their lives through leisure.

Truth be told, I don't remember ever hearing of Walt Whitman's term "higher progress" until I read *Free Time*. But it fits in well, as Ben makes clear, with my own thinking and writing, particularly in *The Experience Economy*. The fundamental contribution of my partner Jim Gilmore and mine to the academic and economic literature was to identify experiences as a distinct economic offering, as distinct from services as services are from goods (and as physical goods are from fungible commodities). We have shifted into the Experience Economy, in which people desire experiences—memorable events that engage them in an inherently personal way—more than the other economic offerings.

A key to what makes an offering an experience is that it *engages* customers, and as we pointed out, people can be engaged emotionally, physically, intellectually, and spiritually. Within that quadrumvirate lies a lot of leeway, and different pockets of humanity will try everything under the sun at one time or another from trivial amusements to weighty explorations, from the merely diverting to the immensely meaningful, and from the deleterious to the edifying. Within those bounds lies a lot of room for higher progress.

And of course everyone can partake in all such experiences completely on their own, without purchasing them from companies, as has been the case forever. But the history of economic progress is one of charging a fee for what once was free. In 1776, over 90 percent of the citizens in the self-proclaimed United States of America worked on farms; now that the Agrarian Economy is long past, over 97 percent of us pay for others to grow our food. At the height of the Industrial Economy over a hundred years ago, close to half the working population toiled in factories. Today, all our physical goods are produced with less than 8 percent of workers. And so it is going with services as well, as we increasingly pay others for activities we used to do for ourselves, such as cutting our hair, cleaning our clothes, or changing the oil in our cars. From the perspective of businesses, all this leads to the increasing commoditization of goods and services.

In fact, consumers *want* goods and services to be commoditized[2]—bought at the cheapest possible price and greatest possible convenience—so they can spend their hard-earned money and their *harder-earned time* on the experiences they value, purchases of which research shows make us happier than buying things. So as economies become richer and consumers desire higher-level offerings, companies will create such offerings in ways better than almost all of us could do for ourselves.

But this Progression of Economic Value, as we call it, doesn't stop there. There's one more step, for even experiences can be commoditized (as witnessed by the phrase "been there, done that"). And that next and final level encompasses those life-transforming experiences that leave us better in some significant way—better emotionally, physically, intellectually, or spiritually—and help us achieve our aspirations in some fundamental dimension of self. Such *transformations* are also a distinct economic offering, one that puts the "higher" in "higher progress."

Many have accused us of taking the company view of economic progress, and as just this short recap indicates, it is a valid criticism. And it's one reason why *The Age of Experiences* is such a valuable contribution. This book balances our business view of economic progress with a much-needed human view of higher progress.

But there is a constraint to such progress, one that both we and Ben have noticed and commented on: time is limited. We can experience life only twenty-four hours a day, seven days a week (and we have to fit sleep in there somewhere). We've long pointed to how laborsaving devices (i.e., tangible goods) and time-saving activities (i.e., intangible services) have freed up the time to partake in experiences and undergo transformations. (A great companion to this book, for the economically minded, would be Stanley Lebergott's *Pursuing Happiness*.[3]) There is, however, one other huge fount of time that could be freed up for people to experience more, to aspire to more, to progress in our own being. And that is the time we spend *working*.

I had never even considered work as a source of time, but it is something Ben makes so very clear in this book as he forcefully juxtaposes higher progress with the shorter-hours movement—and even more importantly with a beautiful view of human flourishing. The intellectual dance that Ben weaves together from these and many other concepts is precisely why *The Age of Experiences* is so well worth *your time* to read. With the arrival of the Experience Economy and the coming Transformation Economy, it makes perfect *economic sense* that more and more people will choose to give up money for time, hours worked for hours at leisure, and seek to spend that time in pursuits that offer time well spent (experiences) and time well invested (transformations). As Ben points out, the opportunity costs of working—what we miss out on as human beings by spending so much time at work instead of in experiences and undergoing transformations—are becoming simply too high. As he puts it in Chapter 9, all this "would be realized through the free marketplace. The experience and transformation economies may be understood as harnessing the profit motive to the production and marketing of new liberated and liberating experiences, increasing the demand for free time." Ben's point of view is wonderfully provocative, one that I also had not considered before, and one that will become true for more and more people as these new economies grow and deepen.

But the Experience and Transformation Economies do not denote a simple shift from work to leisure, *for there is an essential dignity to work*. In the spirit of Ben's use of the Sabbath as a model for this age of experiences, note that work first appears in the Bible as a curse—the penalty for Adam and Eve's rebellion against God was to leave the idyllic experience that was Eden and instead work the ground for their sustenance. But it is also clear that work is, or at least can be, a blessing. The apostle Paul worked as a tentmaker so as not to be a burden on the churches to which he ministered and to set an example to others on having a good work ethic that did not make one, whenever possible, dependent on others.

So the answer to freeing up time for experiences and transformations is not a guaranteed annual income—a favorite these days for those who think automation in general and artificial intelligence in particular will cause massive unemployment. Nor is it in treating work as a religion (a subject Ben covers well) and toiling so hard that we cannot enjoy the lives we lead or engage in higher pursuits, like those Paul used his tent making to support. No, as Aristotle pointed out, the virtue lies between two vices.

As you may have gathered from my opening paragraphs, with fleeting exceptions I have always enjoyed my work, at IBM and now as an author, speaker, and management advisor. So much so that I have to say that, for me, work is a *joy*. I am blessed to get to do what I do, even if it means spending countless hours on airplanes (no joy there, but at least there is good reading time) and sometimes working from dawn until long past dusk. For work can be an experience as well, and one that truly transforms.

Ben well recognizes this and pulls such edifying work and enriching leisure together with his concept of *intrinsically motivated productive consumption* (IMPC). Such consumption comprises experiences and transformations that are both work (productive economic activity) *and* leisure (freely chosen gratifying activity). Ben illustrates this with the story of his and his wife's love of cooking. Over the years they have purchased foodstuffs from which to make meals (commodities); cooking books and tapes for recipes and learning as well as appliances, pots and pans, dinnerware, and utensils for cooking (goods); restaurant meals from which to gain ideas (services, some of which were certainly experiences); tours of agricultural meccas and movies about food for inspiration (experiences); and cooking schools and instruction to gain skills (transformations). They have, in short, been transformed through all this economic activity and have become chefs in their own kitchen! The Hunnicutts' *love* of cooking tells you it's intrinsically motivated; their eating and sharing of their cooking tells you it's productive consumption. (By the way, you can get all five of the economic offerings related to Italian cooking at what I think is the best new retail format to emerge in years: Eataly.)

So work and higher progress are not incompatible. Their merging into intrinsically motived productive consumption is in fact the natural consequence of today's Experience Economy and tomorrow's Transformation Economy. This shift is fundamentally about time, about choosing experiences that again offer time well spent, and about transformations that offer time well invested—investments in the higher progress of your current and future self.

You know what else is about time? It's about time you read and enjoyed *The Age of Experiences*. My one hope for this Foreword is that it motivates you to do so. I know you will find it highly productive consumption.

B. Joseph Pine II
Cofounder, Strategic Horizons LLP
February 12, 2019

Preface

Whereas the seeds were old and imported from distant places, this book is largely a product of the environment in which it grew.

After graduating from the University of North Carolina at Chapel Hill in the mid-1970s and finding no history jobs available, I made a lateral move, accepting a position at the University of Iowa in the department of leisure studies. Finding myself one of the few historians in this field, I set about trying to adapt, applying the skills I had learned to the tasks at hand: to teaching, doing research, and writing about recreation and leisure.

Then began a decades-long discourse with students majoring in my department and with scholars from a range of disciplines working in and doing research about my adopted field. Most of the fruits of these efforts have been fortuitous. I could never have foreseen writing this book, for example. Whatever insights that might be found here are not mine alone but are the results of exchanges with my students and colleagues through the years.

Ironically, perhaps, from the beginning this still-ongoing discourse had to do with jobs, on several levels. My own search for work and move to leisure studies placed me in an academic department mainly concerned with preparing students for careers in leisure services: public parks and recreation and community centers; YMCAs, the Red Cross, and a host of other not-for-profit organizations; retirement and group homes; rehabilitation, nursing, and other health care facilities; sport businesses (professional and club sports) and fitness centers; and the gigantic travel and tourism industry. I found this to be a delight, and still do, because in contrast to students in so many of the departments on campus—history, for example—most of our students find jobs in the fields for which they prepared; ours is a very popular major.

However, concerned to learn about the practical business of designing activities and experiences, organizing and leading recreation programs, and managing and promoting leisure services, my students, particularly my graduate students, were puzzled by required courses taught by a historian dealing with theoretical matters. My first response was to try to adapt my dissertation to my students' needs and expectations. At Chapel Hill I had written about leisure as a public, controversial issue in the United States during the 1920s and 1930s under the tutelage of some of this nation's finest historians, including George Mowry, who suggested during one of his seminars that I look at the history of work and leisure. I proceeded with the assumption that by showing how important shorter working hours has been in American history, I might inspire students with a vision of a free, active, and engaged life that was an alternative to the passive consumerism and worthless leisure around them—a traditional vision of leisure's potential that I have come to call the "forgotten American dream."[1]

In addition, in the general education classes (for nonmajors) I taught, I included a critique of what Hannah Arendt called the "modern glorification of labor,"[2] challenging expectations that jobs might eventually become the most important way for most people to realize their potential as human beings and assumptions that college was all about preparing for those jobs. Those who had written foundational texts in leisure studies—scholars such as Sebastian de Grazia, Johan Huizinga, Joseph Pieper, and Robert Hutchins—had already begun these projects, showing that higher education, and a good deal of Western civilization, was founded on the leisure ideal of the Greeks. I still begin my classes by explaining why many modern words for school and scholarship originated with the Greek word for leisure (scholé) and then arguing along with Pieper that leisure rather than work had been, until the modern age, the basis of democratic culture and society and the hope for the future in the West—and it might (or must) be again.

Building on my graduate work, I tried to show how this old vision was democratized and made real, at least in part, by organized labor's modern struggles for shorter working hours in the United States—how work hours being cut nearly in half before 1930 gave life to what would have otherwise been a utopian, elitist fantasy. Showing how this "forgotten American dream," in turn, supported and justified labor's century-long shorter-hours cause, I pointed out that both have largely been abandoned—that with the ending of the shorter-hours process some eighty years ago, the dream that so many saw as the better half of human progress was gradually cast aside as well, replaced by truly fantastic hopes for the eternal creation of new work, wealth, and jobs.

Along the way, I found much needed support and encouragement from other historians interested in what I termed the end of shorter hours, notably David Montgomery at Yale, who encouraged me during a critical time in my life; Gary Cross at Penn State, who supported my efforts; and later Carmen Sirianni, who was instrumental in the publication of my first book, *Work without End*.³ Even though I had chosen leisure study as a profession, validation of my craft as a historian meant a great deal to me.

In classes and in my writings, I argued that this strange turn of events, what has amounted to a reversal in the definition of progress, might be best explained by a new, primarily twentieth-century view of work, what might be called, *pace* Max Weber, "the spirit of capitalism."⁴ This new belief elevated work, for the first time in history, to be an end in itself rather than the means to other, better things, and to be the primary arena in which to realize the full potential of human beings. Two historical corollaries followed the advent of this new belief: the perpetual need to replace the work continually lost to technology and the need for perpetual economic growth to support eternal work creation. This novel dream and its corollaries, together resembling, more and more, a new modern faith or religion (what Robert Hutchins once called "Salvation by Work") eclipsed both the forgotten American dream and the shorter-working-hours process that sustained it for so long.⁵ As a shorthand, I called this new, thriving faith Full-Time, Full Employment.

I traced the origin of the new belief to Franklin Delano Roosevelt's years as president and outlined its subsequent pervasive political, economic, and cultural ramifications, pointing to the politician's mantra "Jobs, jobs, jobs," the corporate apologist's job-creation defense of obscene corporate salaries and practices, and to the growing maldistribution of wealth as examples.

I then offered critiques of the belief in Full-Time, Full Employment, maintaining that eternal economic growth and everlasting job creation are not sustainable and that the new belief or expectation of "good jobs" for all is a "failing faith"⁶—a hopelessly utopian dream. In addition to gradually destroying the environment, ceaseless economic growth has become cancerous, destroying healthy culture, destabilizing the vital functioning of civil society and undermining the foundations of trust essential for economic stability, resulting in the colonization of the lifeworld and destruction of meaning. Full-Time, Full Employment has produced what Herbert Marcuse called "one-dimensional man,"⁷ someone nearly incapable of imagining anything better than work for more work or recognizing when he has enough—piling up ever more wealth, "security," reputation, and consumer goods. Yet salvation by work thrives. In the midst of our continuing job distress, we regularly recommit to the faith and with the biblical Job declare, "Though He slay me, yet will I trust Him."[8]

All the same, I argued, Full-Time, Full Employment is a failing faith, a dying god, because at heart it harbors a fatal contradiction. Capitalism's need to glorify work to ensure adequate labor supply is contradicted by the market's drive to eliminate jobs to maximize profit. Given the job-killing capacity of technology, capitalism's imperative to reduce labor costs as much as possible, and governments' flagging ability to create enough work to replace that being steadily lost to machines, computerization, robots, and the global marketplace, free time, as Henry Ford observed some time ago, is inevitable. As he put it, our only choice is "unemployment or leisure."[9] Out of necessity, the nations of the world will eventually have to either endure chronic unemployment for increasing numbers of their people or accept the possibility of leisure.[10]

Thus, I conclude my case to my students and readers by offering progressively shorter working hours and the forgotten American dream as sustainable progress. Economists since John Stuart Mill have repeatedly suggested shorter working hours as one of the few available solutions to the problems caused by capitalism and technology's steady destruction of jobs. I suggest that leisure studies and the professions it serves have the unique potential to help reform and redirect modern cultures by working to make leisure a more rewarding experience that might eventually encourage a revival of the shorter-hour process. I claim that our leisure professions, reclaiming our heritage, could lead the way, re-presenting the forgotten American dream, providing facilities, and designing experiences and programs that foster autonomy, community, and civility, helping restore active and engaged leisure activities: activities freely chosen and based in the human potential to create local culture and value beyond the marketplace and courthouse, in what was once widely recognized as the opening realm of freedom.

One of the primary purposes of my teaching, research, and writing is to show that there is a reasonable, moral, historical, and inspiring alternative to work and wealth without end. I write and teach hoping that, in some small way, I might contribute to the rekindling of that forgotten dream.

However, my best attempts to inspire continue to be met by practical-minded students wanting to know how to prepare for jobs currently available. My critique of the modern glorification of work is still met with "Yes, but I still need a job." From my students' perspective, the tasks of re-presenting the old dream and reigniting interest in active and engaged leisure seem daunting in the real world of fragmented communities, TV, consumerism, and overworked Americans and in view of the professions open to them that are all too often uninspired and uninspiring. They frequently let me know that they have far too few practical means to accomplish such lofty ends.

The chronic problem of bridging the gap between vision and professional practice has been compounded over the last two decades by contractions in leisure and recreation studies at universities and in services in the cities and towns across the nation. As the economy and governments struggle, less and less able to maintain Full-Time, Full Employment, funds for public facilities, most often beginning with leisure and recreation services, are cut back, and jobs in the public and the not-for-profit sectors are increasingly hard to find.

Moreover, far from the old dream's being reignited, "leisure" continues to be misunderstood and maligned, much more so today than when I first began my career. To the extent that work is glorified, as Hannah Arendt noted, leisure tends to be trivialized. This point was driven home for me in 2014 when I wrote an article for *Politico* about President Barack Obama's Affordable Care Act.[11] I simply noted in the piece that one of the act's provisions would give employees some flexibility to work less than full time and still be eligible for health insurance. The same story was being widely reported and commented on, and I suggested that this discussion was a good thing—perhaps signaling a renewal of debates about working hours that has been muted for years but that had been vitally important for nearly a century in the United States. I chose my words in as bipartisan a way as I could (the editors at *Politico* added the headline), giving prominent place to conservative businesspeople who once supported work reductions as reasonable, healthy outcomes of industrial progress and the free market—as natural a result as higher wages.

The response to the article was breathtaking, and a bit frightening. I faced weeks of personal attacks in the media. Sean Hannity, Herman Cain, Bill O'Reilly, and others poured contempt not on the points I made in the article but on my being a professor of leisure studies—it is clear from what they said and wrote that they never got beyond my name and position to read the *Politico* article. For months afterward, I received hate mail and phone calls from Fox News viewers, many using the very same language that Hannity, Cain, and others had used, some containing death threats, simply because I have chosen to teach and write about leisure.

With continuing cutbacks in traditional public and not-for-profit sectors, and with Iowa legislators and regents contacting deans in my college, cross-examining them about having a department of leisure studies on campus, my department changed its name and turned more to the world of private businesses—to "sports and recreation management" (our current department name) and the travel and tourism industry.[12] With the failure of university administration to replace faculty who left our department over the years, I found that I was needed in this new initiative and that new classes in travel and tourism now had priority over the history and theory classes that I have taught for decades.

The task was daunting but the prospects promising. Travel and tourism is one of the largest industries in the world (some claim it is the largest) and among the most important providers of jobs. Other leisure studies departments around the nation have shifted their emphasis to travel and tourism with great success. Today, some of the best research about leisure is being done in this area.

I began by offering a short, pilot travel and tourism section in one of my graduate classes. My hope was that I could continue to teach what leisure studies has long promoted as healthy forms of recreation to counter the more popular, unhealthy forms. The only change would be that these healthy experiences might be provided by private businesses.

I began by arguing that, historically, leisure studies and services have stressed the importance of community building. Leisure's healthy forms have most often derived from their community function: healthy leisure has traditionally (from the days of classical Greece) been defined as autonomous (free, self-directed, and intrinsically motived) and understood as active and engaged, expressing and teaching the skills of freedom (traditionally known as the *liberal* arts) and virtues necessary for community. Commercial recreation, beginning with Coney Island at the start of the twentieth century and continuing today with TV, spectator sports, and computer games, has been public leisure services' traditional whipping boy because it encourages passivity and keeps people isolated and dependent, teaching habits of helplessness and idleness rather than the skills of freedom and the virtues of active civic engagement.

I took issue with such a blanket condemnation, however, and had always taught that commercial recreation, to the extent that it offered healthy forms of leisure experiences, has been, and still could be, just as valuable as public parks and recreation, serving the authentic needs of customers. Roy Rosenzweig's account of late nineteenth-century saloons in Worcester, Massachusetts, is still one of my favorite examples:

> The saloon was actually a "democracy" of sorts—an internal democracy where all who could safely enter received equal treatment and respect. An ethic of mutuality and reciprocity that differed from the market exchange mentality of the dominant society prevailed within the barroom. . . . [The saloon provided] a space in which immigrants could preserve an alternative, reciprocal value system.[13]

Turning to travel and tourism, my students and I began to identify healthy commercial possibilities existing today. Students brought numerous examples to class: bed-and-breakfast establishments throughout the Midwest, wine tours in Wisconsin, Wilson's Apple Orchard just outside Iowa City, Buffalo Bill Days and the Rhubarb Festival in Lanesboro, Minnesota, and further afield, the slow-cities movement in Europe, all of which had healthy community-building components, all of which stressed customer interaction and encouraged visitors to be actively involved in whatever was going on. We also had exciting debates about the uses of new information technologies when some students suggested that social media offered prime examples of community-building experiences.

We began to discuss ways to build on these existing possibilities: ways to design new experiences, organize programs, lead groups in new activities, and market these as experience products, bringing to bear the skills students had learned in their experience-design, marketing, and business management classes. Budding student entrepreneurs in class were excited by the possibility of such green opportunities to enliven local economies and promote healthy forms of active, engaged recreation that were eco-friendly. We deemed these to be win-win possibilities: practical job opportunities that implemented the long-standing reform agenda of public recreation and leisure services.

As my class and I were reading the travel and tourism literature, we stumbled on Joseph Pine and James Gilmore's work. Their book, *The Experience Economy*, which some have called one of the most influential business books of the last few years, galvanized our class.[14] We found that people from various fields shared our enthusiasm. Professions as diverse as nursing, architecture, and city planning were finding opportunities to grow in the new, fertile ground of the experience economy.

We set about in class building bridges, connecting leisure studies' traditional curriculum and research to the experience economy, and discovering new, exciting possibilities for experience design—for what leisure studies had called programming and leadership for decades. Adding to the excitement, we found ourselves virtually alone, exploring possibilities only a few had recognized before.[15]

For years, I had included sections in my graduate classes devoted to reviewing theories and research from allied fields such as psychology and economics that related to our study of work and leisure. My class immediately saw the potential connections between new developments in positive psychology and the experience economy, which we began to investigate, finding ourselves again on a largely unexplored frontier.

I also pointed out the larger, economic implications of the experience economy, using the same readings I had relied on for decades. Works such as Staffan Linder's *The Harried Leisure Class*[16] and John Owen's analysis of the price of leisure[17] came alive as never before as the class found them newly relevant to the emerging experience economy. We also discovered the new research about happiness and well-being being done in neurobiology and began to read some of its literature designed for professions outside neurobiology. We immediately saw the relevance to our concerns with experience design and the potential applications in the experience economy. We discovered what some are calling a new science of happiness just beginning; a broadly based research initiative that includes positive psychology, interpersonal neurobiology, the economics of happiness, and several other fields that taken together might herald the birth of a new experience-design technology. Again, we discovered that few others had made these connections and that we were in uncharted waters for the most part.

Our class ended much too soon for me. Students turned their attention to final exams, other classes, and to looking for jobs, leaving me excited but with only a start of what was obviously a much larger project. This book is the continuation of our initial forays, a working out of the class's insights. It follows the story of one of my most memorable graduate classes: its discoveries, which became the book's organization, and its energy, which was the book's impetus.[18]

THE AGE OF EXPERIENCES

Introduction

In the early 1970s, Alvin Toffler predicted that soon "we shall become the first culture in history to employ high technology to manufacture that most transient, yet lasting of products: the human experience."[1] This new experience technology has been a long time coming. Even though heralded for decades, it has yet to make its hoped-for grand appearance; its promise to surpass the industrial and information ages and usher in a new age of experiences has yet to be realized. With this book, I provide an update on the progress of the new technology and the coming of the new age, suggest theoretical and practical ways to hasten their arrival, and reveal some of the hazards as well as promises already apparent.

The reason for the long delay has been the absence of some vital pre-conditions, prerequisites that have been met by three remarkable twenty-first-century developments: the dawn of the experience and transformation economies (discussed in Chapters 2 and 3), the advent of the new sciences of happiness (discussed in Chapters 5 and 6), and the coming of postmaterialist culture (discussed later in the Introduction). However, these three develop-ments have been slow coming together.

What I do in this book is help speed their convergence by showing how the free marketplace may support a new eudaimonic technology by more deliberate application of the findings of the new sciences of happiness to the design of experience products—products that will support the growth of the new experience and transformation economies and find ready markets in a growing postmaterialist culture.

This project entails a lengthy cataloging of the empirical findings of the positive psychologists and neurobiologists (Chapters 5 and 6) that may be applicable to the design of new experiences (Chapter 7) as well as an analysis of the economic consequences of the turn from consumption of tangible goods to experiences (Chapter 8).

Faith in and reliance on the market have their critics (Chapter 4). Some see the new economies strengthening the worst tendencies of capitalism, further alienating and enslaving workers and consumers. Because I share these concerns, I review these critiques in some detail. However, I maintain that the free market offers the potential for liberation that should be recognized, encouraged, and given a chance (Chapter 9).

Thus, in addition to the lengthy catalog of scientific findings, this project entails a careful analysis of the pitfalls of consumerism (Chapter 4) and warnings about the dangers of the "value capturers" and "branders," those who would the block the liberating potential of the eudaimonic technology (Chapter 3).

I also provide historical contexts for these developments (Chapters 1, 4, and 9), arguing that, in addition to the findings of the new sciences of happiness, history provides valuable examples that may guide the design and creation of experience products that will support and give direction to the experience and transformation economies.

Visionaries and economic theorists such as John Maynard Keynes outlined the specifics of what "liberation capitalism" looks like.[2] Their vision provides a guide for the coming of the age of experiences (Chapter 9). Salient in such guides is the realization that, increasingly, free time will be more in demand. As Keynes noted (and as I argue in Chapter 8), the migration of value, moving as time rather than capital from older economic sectors to the experience and transformation economies, offers the potential for liberation through shorter working hours as well as greater equality and sustainability.

Convergence

Considered separately, the coming of experience and transformation economies, the arrival of the new sciences of happiness, and the development of postmaterialist culture are remarkable enough, exciting large numbers of futurists, economists, businesspeople, and journalists and representing fundamental changes in society and the economy as well as significant advances in the sciences. However, seen together as converging, they are quite possibly epochal, propelling the experience technology onto the world stage and signaling the renaissance of a categorically different, postmaterialist progress.

Over a century ago Walt Whitman foresaw this possibility, calling it "higher progress," his term for what was once a widely held hope for "humane and moral progress" beyond the marketplace and politics.[3] This centuries-long hope has been largely obscured for most of the twentieth century by consumerism and the information age but now is reawakening in a new age of experiences.

Quite simply, over the last two decades, the new sciences of happiness have identified fundamental elements and principles of human well-being, discoveries essential for the development of the experience technology. This new technology is being given impetus by the experience economy that is already serving an emerging postmaterialist culture's growing demand for new kinds of intangible experience products. Thus, the conditions necessary for the advance of any new technology have been met: the laying of a scientific-knowledge foundation, an emergent social demand base for its products, and a responsive economy.

The result will be the coming of a long-awaited age of experiences in which how to live becomes a more important concern than how to make a living or even what to buy or how much to own—a possibility that the free marketplace, with its promise of liberation capitalism, is capable of realizing.

"Welcome to the Experience Economy"

In the nearly two decades since it was first identified, the experience economy has been expanding. As growth in the traditional sectors of the economy slows, businesspeople and economists have been turning their attention and hopes for the future to the creation and marketing of experiences. Some now predict that the future of modern economies depends on the success of the experience economy—the next economic wave surging ahead, building on and surpassing cell phones, computers, and the Internet.[4] Jon Sundbo and Flemming Sørensen, prominent Danish researchers, describe "a fundamental shift in the very fabric of the global economy" with the coming of the experience economy, an assessment they continue to reiterate and that many now share.[5]

Among the first to discern the coming of the new economy were Joseph Pine and James Gilmore with the 1998 publication of their article "Welcome to the Experience Economy" in the *Harvard Business Review*. Publication of their book *The Experience Economy*[6] followed the next year, and James Harkin welcomed it as one of the most important business publications in decades.[7] Later, Tom Kelley, general manager of IDEO, agreed that it is "one of the best business books of the twentieth century."[8]

Futurist Brian Solis observes that "the future of business is experiences" and that "experience is everything."[9] In the *Forbes* list of the top business books of 2015, Shep Hyken concluded the list with his "all-time favorite business book," *The Experience Economy*: It is "one of the most powerful books ever written about customer service and customer experience."[10] The senior vice president of marketing and communications for Four Seasons Hotels and Resorts, Elizabeth Pizzinato, observes, "The experience economy is what's driving everything."[11]

The Columbia University professor of marketing Bernd Schmitt's comments expressed some of the excitement of the time: "We are in the middle of a revolution . . . that will render the principles and models of traditional marketing obsolete. A revolution that will change the face of marketing forever."[12] Pine and Gilmore argue that, just as the manufacturing sector of the economy superseded agriculture and the service economy has outpaced manufacturing, the experience economy is now gaining ascendancy as the last, best hope for continued economic growth.

For an illustration, they began their book with the story of a friend who visited Venice, found an outdoor café in Saint Mark's Square, and ordered coffee. While he drank his coffee, he enjoyed the city and the people coming and going for a good while. When the check arrived, he found that he owed three to four times the regular price, but he reported that he did not feel overcharged at all because the experience was worth it—the café's business was booming.

Pine and Gilmore offer numerous examples of thriving businesses that have discovered the possibility, and profitability, of designing and selling experiences: Walt Disney World, Starbucks, Hard Rock Café, Chuck E. Cheese, Gameworks, Build-a-Bear Workshops. More recent examples include Airbnb, Comic-Con, the host of amusement parks following Disney World's model, escape rooms, Pilates and hot yoga classes, and Secret Cinema. Other examples are easy to find:[13] struggling malls throughout the nation are rebranding themselves as lifestyle centers; bookstores are upgrading their spaces to hold community events and promote customer interaction; professional sports teams are building fan experiences on the tradition of family nights; Arthur Murray studios and a myriad of local dance studios are finding new markets for their experience products; vending machines are offering various interactive features; and Best Buy and other retailers are improving and even selling the experience of shopping. Following the lead of other retail chains such as Home Depot, the nationwide outdoor and sporting goods cooperative REI offers hands-on classes in cycling, hiking, camping, snow sports, and rock climbing to build customer skills and interest and thus the demand for their more traditional, tangible products—their Seattle and Columbus,

Ohio, affiliates erected climbing walls at their stores for customers to try out products.

Architects, city planners, and hoteliers are among the professions most interested in the design of, and provision for, experiences. For example, early in 2016, Hilton Worldwide introduced its "revolutionary" brand, Tru by Hilton, redesigning some of its hotels to include a large central lobby, with spaces for eating, working, meeting, playing, and lounging. Explicitly catering to the millennial generation's preferences for simplicity and experiences, Tru by Hilton advertises that it is "embracing travelers' desire for human connection, creating an experience that is playful, energetic, and engaging—a sense of place unlike anything in our space."[14]

Museums and other exhibition venues are turning from inert displays to hands-on, interactive exhibits. Architects and planners designed the 9/11 Memorial Museum in New York City so that visitors might reexperience the images and drama of that fateful day. Distressed farms in the Midwest, with the help of the Leopold Center for Sustainable Agriculture in Ames, Iowa, are transforming themselves into tourist destinations, offering a sanitized experience of farm life to city folks, from planting to harvest, animal care to petting zoos, hayrides to cider making. Nurses and other therapists and counselors have discovered the value of active and enjoyable experiences and are prescribing them for their health-restoring and health-promoting benefits that help develop interpersonal skills and healthy lifestyles.

The travel and tourism industry, however, makes Pine and Gilmore's best case. Not only is travel and tourism already one of the world's largest industries (many argue that it is by far the largest); it is also the fastest growing, creating an array of hyphenated experience products such as cultural/ heritage-, film-, culinary-, volunteer-, medical-, disaster-, climate-change-, and eco-tourism. Scholars in the new, thriving discipline of travel and tourism now lead the way in research and theory. Hoping to revitalize dying local economies, cities around the world, particularly in Scandinavia and China, are redesigning their public spaces, prohibiting motor traffic to attract visitors who want to experience their unique cultures and places in more personal, customized ways, off the beaten tourist paths. Cities in the United States' Rustbelt, such as Cincinnati, Saint Louis, Pittsburgh, and Baltimore, rely on tourism to shore up their sagging economies.[15] Cittaslow, a slow-cities movement, begun in Italy, is now well underway in Europe, following on the heels of the popular slow-food movement that transformed restaurants around the Continent—proponents of both movements claim to have improved the experience of places and foods by slowing the pace; adding cultural and personal, interactive components; and most importantly, increasing the amount of time used to enjoy them.[16]

TABLE I.1 COMPOUND ANNUAL GROWTH RATE, 1959–2009

Economic sector	Employment growth (%)	GDP growth (%)
Commodities	−0.80	5.20
Goods	−0.10	5.40
Services	2.00	7.20
Experience economy	5.90	16.75

Source: B. Joseph Pine II and James H. Gilmore, The Experience Economy, rev. ed. (Boston: Harvard Business Press, 2011).
Note: These numbers underrepresent growth in the experience economy because they do not include opportunity costs.

TABLE I.2 AVERAGE ANNUAL PERSONAL-CONSUMPTION-EXPENDITURE GROWTH, 2014–2016

Economic sector	Growth (%)
Total expenditure growth	3.70
Total goods	1.60
Total services	4.70
Experience-related services	6.30

Source: Dan Goldman, Sophie Marchessou, and Warren Teichner, "Cashing In on the US Experience Economy," McKinsey and Company, December 2017, available at https://www.mckinsey.com/industries/private-equity-and-principal -investors/our-insights/cashing-in-on-the-us-experience-economy.

In the revised edition of their book, published in 2011, Pine and Gilmore report the rapid growth of the experience economy compared to other sectors of the economy (see Table I.1). Pine and Gilmore conclude that the experience economy has accounted for the lion's share of economic growth and nearly three-quarters of new jobs in the United States for years.[17] Research confirms their prediction that the experience economy will continue to grow—McKinsey and Company reported in 2017 that spending on experiences had grown nearly four times as much as spending on goods between 2014 and 2016 (see Table I.2).[18]

Around the world, management and marketing experts and researchers, together with the travel and tourism industry, now recognize the importance and potential of the experience economy.[19] According to Hélder Ferreira and Aurora Teixeira at the Research Center in Economics and Finance at the University of Porto (Portugal), there is widespread agreement among such experts worldwide that the experience economy is the essential next step, without which prospects for the future of modern economies are dim indeed.[20] Gary Ellis and J. Robert Rossman see in such developments the beginnings of a new technology.[21]

The New Sciences of Happiness: Positive Psychology

The same year (1998) that the *Harvard Business Review* published Pine and Gilmore's article, Martin Seligman began his term as president of the American Psychological Association. For his presidential theme, he challenged his profession to begin "exploring what makes life worth living and building the enabling conditions of a life worth living." With this challenge, he helped initiate what is now widely seen as a "tectonic upheaval in psychology"—what has come to be known as "positive psychology."[22]

Seligman pointed out that, up until his presidency, "[his] profession was half-baked." From their beginnings, psychologists had focused most of their attention and research on human ills: neuroses, depression, delusions, and the like. The best they had hoped for was therapeutic—restoring some function, some normalcy. However, Seligman argued, "It wasn't enough for us to nullify disabling conditions and get to zero."[23] A life cured of psychological miseries is no guarantee of happiness: "We needed to ask, What are the enabling conditions that make human beings flourish? How do we get from zero to plus five?"[24]

Time magazine reported that what followed was "an explosion of research on happiness, optimism, positive emotions and healthy character traits. Seldom has an academic field been brought so quickly and deliberately to life."[25] Stephen Joseph concludes, "It is beyond doubt that positive psychology [has become] a major force in contemporary psychology."[26] Reviewing research published in peer-reviewed journals, Stewart Donaldson, Maren Dollwet, and Meghana Rao agreed in 2015 with *Time*'s earlier appraisal: "There has been an explosion of activity in, acclaim for, and criticism of positive psychology" over the last fifteen years.[27]

For millennia, humans have been pursuing happiness, trying to unlock the riddle of human felicity. The Declaration of Independence lists such a pursuit as one of the fundamental, "self-evident" truths about human beings. Many and various solutions have been offered through the millennia. Now, at last, as leading researchers are quick to point out, empirical science has been brought directly to bear on this age-old question.[28]

"Several thousand people around the world" investigating what makes life worth living for well over a decade have produced remarkable results.[29] A broad consensus about the elements, the fundamental components, of human well-being has been reached. As a consequence of their discoveries and agreement about fundamentals, psychologists claim to be having considerable success developing *experiences* that deliver happiness, helping individuals flourish, as Seligman claims. Looking back in 2011, Seligman concluded, "Positive psychology makes people happier."[30] The Harvard psychologist

Daniel Gilbert agrees: "There is no doubt that the research has helped and will continue to help us increase our happiness."[31]

Throughout the history of science, few comparable advances have been made so rapidly—it took scientists well over a century to identify and agree about the elements of the physical world described by the periodic table.

For the growing industry built around experiences, the findings of a new science dedicated to identifying factors that improve the human experience present a veritable gold mine of insight. Catalogs of the most useful of those insights (Chapters 5 and 6) provide guides to the ways the experience economy can and should evolve in the near future.

The New Sciences of Happiness: The Neurobiology of Well-Being

Early in 1999, the year after Seligman's seminal presidency and Pine and Gilmore's groundbreaking publication "welcoming" the experience economy, Daniel Siegel published *The Developing Mind: Toward a Neurobiology of Interpersonal Experience.*[32] Emerging out of the beehive of neurobiological research in the 1990s (what some have called the "Decade of the Brain"[33]), his book was the culmination of his and others' attempts to define and initiate an interdisciplinary approach to understanding the mind and its *healthy* functioning.

Numerous writers, including Stefan Klein and Richard Layard, see positive psychology and advances in the neurosciences converging in a new science of happiness.[34] The *Harvard Business Review* spotlighted the new sciences with its January–February 2012 issue, titled "The Value of Happiness," noting that economists had joined psychologists and neurobiologists on this frontier, beginning to develop an "economics of well-being."[35] The journal quoted the well-known Harvard psychologist Daniel Gilbert as saying, "Having three separate disciplines all interested in a single topic has put that topic on the scientific map."[36] The *Economist*, quoting the Princeton psychologist Daniel Kahneman, winner of the 2002 Nobel Prize for Economics, reported that economists such as Robert Frank had joined psychologists in *asking* people what made them happy rather than relying exclusively on marketplace data. Economists had also begun to offer sumptuary advice to consumers about how to spend their money and time—advice based on their empirical findings.[37]

Looking back in 2010, Siegel reported the convergence of several scientific disciplines in the first decades of the twenty-first century, including psychopathology, emotions research, neurobiology, psychology, physics, systems theory, and mathematics. He called special attention to the convergence of the neurosciences and positive psychology, noting that "positive psychology has offered an important corrective to the disease model by identifying the characteristics of happy people, such as gratitude, compassion, openmindedness, and curiosity."[38]

Moreover, Siegel explained that neuroscience and systems theory had exposed a deeper reality that "underlies all of these individual strengths [discovered by positive psychology]": a "key mechanism" at the heart of human happiness that has become the focus of the recent convergence, or "consilience," of scientific evidence from various fields of research: "I've come to believe that integration is the key mechanism beneath . . . the presence of well-being. Integration—the linkage of differentiated elements of a system—illuminates a direct pathway towards health."[39] Thus have the neuroscientists and systems theorists progressed beyond positive psychology's identification of the elements of human happiness, revealing "a relational and *embodied process*"[40] governed by basic laws of differentiation and integration common to all complex, open, and adaptive systems, including a healthy functioning mind, which determine human happiness and well-being at the most fundamental operational level: a scientific breakthrough with profound implications.

A Eudaimonic Technology

The new sciences of happiness have made few efforts, however, to reach beyond traditional professional delivery systems based on the old therapeutic and clinical models and out to the private sector.[41] Few attempts have been made to guide the free market, assisting the entrepreneur and individual firms, helping them design and deliver profitable experiences. Similarly, those in the experience economy have made surprisingly little *deliberate* use of these new sciences. This is the gap this book intends to bridge. To this end I have cataloged the most relevant findings of these convergent lines of inquiry to show how our economy can harness the research to the benefit of consumers and providers alike. Such a bridge is critical and, for the most part, missing. To this point, the marketplace has been able to move in the correct direction only by fits and starts.

There are important exceptions, individuals and groups that have made attempts to apply the sciences of happiness to the marketplace.[42] Building on these initial efforts, I offer a more systematic approach in the pages of this book: identifying the advent of a new, eudaimonic technology, founded in the sciences of happiness; cataloging and analyzing its recent findings; and encouraging additional applications in the marketplace. In addition, I identify and analyze clinical, counseling, public, and pedagogical models and applications already existing within the new sciences of happiness professions that may be adapted to the free market by entrepreneurs and existing businesses.

By cataloging examples of the emergent, so far inchoate eudaimonic technology forming within the experience economy[43] and building on these examples, I offer a more explicit guide to experience design; a guide grounded in the new principles of well-being advanced by positive psychology and the systems approach to human flourishing discovered by neuroscientists.[44] By identifying and articulating the incipient new technology and outlining the scientific principles that might guide experience-product design in the future, I hope to promote a more deliberate development and dissemination of the new technology, looking ahead to the growth of a new range of experience industries.[45]

It is not surprising that the marketplace has anticipated what scientists have been finding out about happiness. In theory, the market is the primary arena in which happiness is determined and sought. Economists have used the word "utility" for over a century and a half, struggling with an elusive concept in ways strikingly similar to the scientific discussions about happiness and well-being.[46] In theory, as free-market advocates such as Milton Friedman would have it, the market resembles an enormous testing laboratory in which each dollar spent represents a data point. Social scientists' data sets gathered from tens or hundreds of test cases, occasionally even millions, pale in comparison with the tens of billions of votes that take place in the marketplace every day when consumers chose to spend their dollars on this experience over that service or over this product.[47] Economists have long argued that exchanges in the free market are the ultimate test of utility, more democratic and indicating far better than any other method what makes people happy.

Moreover, the history of technology offers numerous examples of science's theoretical discoveries being applied to the marketplace ahead of scientific advances, often serendipitously, by men and women more active in the marketplace as inventors and entrepreneurs, or even as mechanics and tinkerers, than as researchers or clinicians. Historically, practical and intuitive invention anticipates the deliberate application of scientific principles by experts—the first practical use of steam power, the Newcomen engine, designed to pump water from mines and built by a British ironmonger and Baptist lay preacher, is a case in point. Such practical-minded folk may not be fully awake to the genius of their discoveries or conversant with the scientific principles behind it. Moreover, it is the response of the free market that legitimizes their inventions, not the disciplined research and peer-review procedures of the sciences and academia. Cultural changes, creating new kinds of demand in the marketplace, are the seedbed for new technologies.

Certainly, scientists and engineers have found a home in research and development departments of modern companies and corporations. However, the research and development professions are not yet reaching out to new sciences of happiness. Similarly, even though management experts and marketing researchers have been following the development of the experience economy, agreeing about its importance, one searches their journals, along with the research and development literature, in vain for mention of the new happiness research coming out of neurobiology and positive psychology.

This book is designed to help remedy these oversights, building bridges to the worlds of marketing and management by outlining ways that the research done by the new sciences of happiness may be applied to the design of experience products.

The Coming of Postmaterialist Culture

The third development, emerging since the 1990s and converging with the experience economy and the new sciences of happiness that is helping to spawn a eudaimonic technology, is the growth of postmaterialist culture—a development that is providing new demand for experience products.

In his February 14, 2011, article, "The Experience Economy," David Brooks noted that "a shift in values" was well underway in the United States, signaling the advent of a "postmaterialist mind-set."[48] For the generations that grew up in the middle decades of the twentieth century, "income and living standards were synonymous." Increasingly, however, "rich and meaningful experiences" are beginning to replace jobs and consumer goods as the definitions of success and well-being. This postmaterialist "shift in values" has profound economic consequences, according to Brooks, redirecting consumption patterns from material goods and toward experiences.

Research identifying the coming of a postmaterialist culture dates to the early 1970s, when Ronald Inglehart, a political scientist at the University of Michigan, documented a change in values from one generation to the next in the United States[49]—a shift from concerns about wealth, safety, and consumerism to new aspirations: autonomy, quality of life, creativity, experiences, and self-expression.[50] Since then, a generation of sociologists and political scientists have confirmed that postmaterialist values continue to spread across the industrial world and grow with the coming of age of the millennial generation (born between the mid-1980s and early 2000s).

Following Brooks's lead, I suggest that this growth of postmaterialist values is indeed relevant to the experience economy. What the relation is, or should be, however, is debatable. On the surface, it appears that postmaterialism is expanding demand for experience products—just the fortuitous cultural shift needed. The business press has stressed this possibility, empha-sizing the wealth- and job-producing potential of the experience economy energized by the influx of new consumers.

However, David Brooks cautions that the "postmaterialist mind-set" raises the possibility that individuals and nations might "improve the quality of life without actually producing more wealth. . . . Many of this era's tech-nological breakthroughs produce enormous happiness gains, but surprisingly little additional economy activity." As people devote "more of their energies to postmaterial arenas and less and less . . . to the sheer production of wealth," the downside might be soaring unemployment numbers and anemic eco-nomic growth.[51]

It may be, as Brooks suspects, that the new postmaterialist values are in-imical to economic growth, leading people away from the marketplace, and all told, bad for business. While expanding the desire for experiences, such values may discourage economic activity in general.

Critiques of the Experience Economy: Practical and Ideological

Others, with different ideological perspectives, are also disturbed by the com-ing of the experience economy and doubtless will be dismayed by the prospect of a eudaimonic technology and an age of experiences. But instead of worry-ing with Brooks about the impact on jobs and wealth creation, writers such as Jacques Ellul, Andre Gorz, and Jürgen Habermas have long questioned the experience economy's basic principles, arguing that the extension of the mar-ketplace into previously free realms of human experience (commodification) represents a quantum leap in the colonization of the "lifeworld"[52] and the beginning of a brave new world where human community and personalities are made into products that are bought and sold—a world in which human beings are increasing helpless and manipulated by corporations interested primarily in converting human lives into profit. Dozens of dystopian films and books based on such fears, such as *Blade Runner* and *Brave New World*—even *Wall-e*—have raised such concerns over the last century.

In the United States, Jeremy Rifkin published *The Age of Access: The New Culture of Hypercapitalism, Where All of Life Is a Paid-For Experience* in 2000, objecting to the alienation and exploitation that he believes are the inevitable consequences of the experience economy and predicting that it will soon enslave us all, rendering us helpless pawns in a dystopia of conformity, growing inequality, false consciousness, and social chaos. Rather than freeing humans by offering more choices, the experience economy is creating an era of "hypercapitalism."[53]

Because of the obvious appeal of such arguments, and because I share many of these concerns, I present the critics' case sympathetically and in some depth in Chapter 4.

The Promise: A Renaissance of the Forgotten American Dream

Answering the critics and my own fears, I maintain that, while the experience economy may very well have tragic consequences, its expansion may just as easily address both the practical objections about anemic economic growth and unemployment made by people such as David Brooks and the ideological criticisms and ethical concerns presented by writers such as Gorz, Habermas, and Rifkin.

Whereas Brooks is disturbed by more people in the industrial nations devoting "more of their energies to postmaterial arenas and less and less . . . to the sheer production of wealth,"[54] some welcome the coming of postmaterialism as representing a *healthy* turn from consumerism and the marketplace: a rejection of the commodification of life. I propose that the eudaimonic technology has the potential to free humans from corporations and the marketplace rather than re-enslave them to more work and in more alienated consumption.

Moreover, rather than driving unemployment as Brooks fears, the experience economy may instead provide a time-honored solution, work sharing, employed for decades by the industrialized nations—long championed by organized labor and supported by prominent economists for over a century. In Chapter 8, I discuss the broader economic implications of the age of experiences, explaining that consumers will need time as much as, or perhaps more than, money. Following the reasoning of economists such as Frank Knight, Staffan Linder, and John Owen, I maintain that value should transfer from the older economic sectors (commodities, goods, and services) to the newer ones *as the spending of time* as much as the spending of money. In the coming age of experiences, value will be determined more by how time is spent and less by how money is spent.

More than in any of the other sectors of the economy, the currency that supports the experience economy is the coin of time. It is reasonable to predict that the demand for free time will grow with the demand for experiences; total work time should naturally decline and unemployment pressure lessen as labor supply is drawn down. A kind of free-market-generated work sharing should then take place as more and more people make the rational choice to maximize utility by spending more of their time on experiences and less on making money—making choices similar to those made by generations of employees in industrial nations who cut their working time virtually in half during the one hundred or so years after the Industrial Revolution.

This process should also address Rifkin's and other critics' concerns about corporate tyranny and consumer helplessness. As entrepreneurs develop new experience products that build autonomy and promote competency and control (two of the prime determinants of happiness according to the new sciences of happiness and the logical culmination of customer empowerment), consumers are gradually finding their way beyond the marketplace, creating together and freely sharing experiences in what was once known as "the realm of freedom"[55] (now popularly known as the sharing economy), no longer helpless or passive, and avoiding the corporate traps Rifkin and others see lurking ahead.[56] Credence to such claims is added by a growing, robust scholarship stream that some have labeled "consumer culture theory." This theory has confirmed the market's healthy culture-creating ability and liberating potential and has identified the experience economy as a prime example of consumer agency and free expression in diverse democratic cultures (see Chapter 4).

As David Brooks explained, with the coming of postmaterialism, "wealth and living standards have diverged." In the new competition for time, "rich and meaningful experiences"[57] are likely to be increasingly preferred and time spent doing them understood more and more as the definition of success and seen as an alternative to traditional consumerism and the mere accumulation of material wealth. Consumers should begin to prefer experiences and the time required to enjoy them over possible work or income, finding in experiences better ways to maximize utility, or as the new happiness scientists say, to flourish.

Free time should then reemerge from its historical dormancy as a normal good and be in greater demand in the marketplace, as it was during what I have called "the century of shorter working hours."[58]

A Promise Long Foretold

Long before the coming of modern consumer culture, a host of Americans assumed that, as the economy grew and technology improved, people's time and free experiences would become more valuable to them than new goods and services they had never needed or even seen before. Proof of that assumption was ready to hand, in the steady reduction of working hours and in organized labor's consistent, century-long commitment to the "progressive shortening of the hours of labor."[59] Americans were welcoming of, and seemed determined to continue to welcome, the opportunity to live more of their lives beyond the marketplace. Observers hoped that such progress would lead to a host of fortunate outcomes, anticipating today's discoveries of the new sciences of happiness.

Outside the marketplace, beyond getting, spending, and continually building material wealth, human beings, with the time of their lives liberated, might be expected to make more important kinds of progress: developing their potential to live together peacefully and agreeably; spending more of their lives and energy forming healthy families, neighborhoods, and cities; increasing their knowledge and appreciation of nature, history, and other peoples; creating their own beautiful things; freely investigating and delighting in the mysteries of the human spirit, exploring their beliefs and values together; finding common ground for agreement and conviviality; observing traditions and practicing their faiths; expanding their awareness of God; and wondering in creation.[60]

The flowering of Yiddish culture on the Lower East Side of New York City during the first decades of the twentieth century produced some of the most beautiful expressions of this forgotten dream. Writers such as Elizabeth Hasanovitz recognized the potential of America's prosperity in the forms of her union's demands for better wages and shorter work hours—the potential to free the human spirit and re-enliven her culture, in imminent danger of assimilation. Other prominent men and women such as Jonathan Edwards, Walt Whitman, John Maynard Keynes, Dorothy Canfield Fisher, Fannia Cohn, Frank Lloyd Wright, and Robert Maynard Hutchins and a host of ordinary people (from the Lowell "mill girls" in the 1840s to the determined women at Kellogg's cereal plant in Battle Creek who fought to keep their six-hour day in the 1970s and 1980s) envisioned progress as increased freedom to pursue happiness—what David Brooks called "high quality-of-life gains"[61] and what Jonathan Edwards, so long ago, foresaw as the realization of the kingdom of God in America.

Liberation Capitalism

Such sentiments were echoed by influential businesspeople who believed they were leading the way: W. K. Kellogg and his CEO, Lewis Brown, when they introduced the six-hour day to the cereal plants in Battle Creek, Michigan; Lord Leverhulme (founder of Lever Brothers) as he planned the future of his city, Port Sunlight, in England; Paul Litchfield at Goodyear Tire when he introduced and defended a six-hour day at his factory in Akron, Ohio; Henry Ford when he established the five-day week in his automobile plants. Ford reasoned that consumers would need more time as well as more money to be reliable consumers of his cars. Ford, with other businesspeople, also claimed that shorter hours were essential to ward off chronic unemployment.[62]

Walter Gifford, president of AT&T for most of the second quarter of the twentieth century, the corporation's heyday, believed that "industry . . . has gained a new and astonishing vision." The final, best achievement of business and the free market would be "a new type of civilization," in which "how to make a living becomes less important than how to live." Gifford predicted:

> Machinery will increasingly take the load off men's shoulders. . . . Every one of us will have more chance to do what he wills, which means greater opportunity, both materially and spiritually. . . . [Steadily decreasing work hours] will give us time to cultivate the art of living, give us a better opportunity for . . . the arts, enlarge the comforts and satisfaction of the mind and spirit, as material well-being feeds the comforts of the body.[63]

According to Gifford, communism and socialism could not compete. Advocates of these systems promised liberation but delivered slavery and had recently embarked on a novel government project of make-work to provide everyone with a full-time job. True liberation from the shackles of material necessity and from the prison of perpetual economic worries was through the free market, not authoritarian government more interested in keeping people at work full time. The free market provided individuals with opportunities to "buy" back their time to live freely and to enjoy more fully the fruits of their labors. Even as the Great Depression struck the United States, his faith and vision remained firm:

> We can . . . face the future with a confidence that not only will our standard of living become higher and higher so far as material needs and comforts are concerned, but that upon the foundation of this higher standard of material conditions will arise a spiritual and cultural development which will give our children and our children's children the priceless heritage of a finer civilization.[64]

For more than a century before 1930, working hours had declined—nearly cut in half. Labor unions played a vital part in these reductions to be sure, as did businesspeople such as Kellogg and Gifford and managers and researchers such as Frederick Taylor. However, shorter working hours were largely a product of the free market, reflecting individuals' choices to work less and live more.[65] With the resurgence of postmaterialist values, the economy may be expected to respond as it did before for so long. As Keynes and Gifford understood, the free market, delivering what really makes people happy, offers an exit. What I have called liberation capitalism can serve its customers by freeing them.[66] By delivering new, more valuable experiences, an expanding experience economy may be expected to provide consumers with ever-greater incentives to "buy" back more of their life to have time for all the new experiences.[67]

One of the possible outcomes of the experience economy, driven by a new eudaimonic technology, may be the renaissance of the forgotten American dream—a rebirth as postmaterialist progress out of the womb of capitalism. Liberation capitalism provides a conservative road leading to liberal values beyond the marketplace—to the cultivation of civic engagement and virtue and, as Gifford envisioned, a "finer civilization."

The Challenge of Continuing Alienation and Enslavement

No doubt, the threat of capitalism's increased exploitation and control still looms. Years ago, Herbert Marcuse warned:

> Automation threatens to render possible the reversal of the relation between free time and working time: the possibility of working time becoming marginal and free time becoming full time. The result would be a radical transvaluation of values [compare Brooks's "shift in values"], and a mode of existence incompatible with the traditional culture. Advanced industrial society is in permanent mobilization against this possibility.[68]

Thus mobilized and doing battle against the tide of postmaterialist culture and its "transvaluation of values," still struggling to maximize profits, corporations and the wealthy few may continue to promote helplessness and dependency, using the sciences of the mind to delude customers with commodified rather than liberating experiences. Time may continue to be trapped in an everlasting spiral of getting and spending, a process driven not by the customer's increasing free choice and utility but capitalism's insatiable need to convert human lives into profit.

The ultimate test of the experience economy is whether it grows more dependent on, versus liberated from, corporations and the marketplace. If experience products that deliver *authentic* well-being, in accord with the discoveries by the sciences of happiness about the importance of autonomy and competence, are brought to market and if the marketplace performs as it should, ceteris paribus,[69] with the better mousetrap outperforming inferior products, then the market might very well, on its own, provide the free time essential to usher in a new age of experiences.

We may expect to witness something of a historic experiment played out in the marketplace over the next few decades; an experiment in which scientists' objective research and empirical discoveries about human happiness test traditional, competing claims about the free market: the economists' long-standing claims that the marketplace best serves and delivers human happiness and utility in a democracy versus critics' protests that capitalism, by its nature, exploits, benights, and enslaves in service to the profit and power of the few, capturing and perverting the democracies in which it is parasitically embedded. We may witness the flowering of capitalism in the dawn of a new age of experiences and abundant free time, or Karl Marx and Herbert Marcuse may prove to have been right.

I have written this book to promote and encourage the former possibility.

Historical Context

Technology, Unemployment, and Progress

E udaimonic technology and the experience and transformation economies offer to resolve the long-standing ambiguity regarding the threat or promise of technology. Technology has long promised to deliver the good life with more and better products. But technology has also threatened to replace humans with machines at work. For over a century, shorter working hours was part of the solution—as machines replaced humans, shorter hours would set things right, guarding against unemployment.

The progressive shortening of the hours of labor, the signature cause of organized labor, was also a vital part of American history for over a century, during which working hours were cut virtually in half. This process was supported by a legion of observers in the United States, giving rise to what I have called "the forgotten American dream" of humane and moral progress beyond work and necessity.[1]

During the 1920s and the Great Depression, however, business and government, beginning to recognize the threat of leisure, turned to a new solution, Full-Time, Full Employment. Initiated by business's new gospel of consumption and strengthened by Franklin Delano Roosevelt's administrations, this solution proposed the eternal creation of work to replace work continually taken by machines, protecting against unemployment. Technology would be turned to the production of new consumer goods (TVs, air conditioners, etc.) that would require more rather than less work and would create consumer products eternally. Government's new role would be to back up technology and create jobs when the market failed, by any of the several ways

Roosevelt proposed during the 1930s and 1940s. Technology's role shifted from saving labor to embodying "science makes jobs."[2]

Labor's traditional solution to the technological dilemma, shorter hours, has been virtually obscured over the last fifty years. However, technology's ability to create jobs faster than machines replace humans is increasingly doubtful, as is government's ability to spend enough to ensure Full-Time, Full Employment. The eternal creation of work now seems to many a utopian fantasy.

However, the new eudaimonic technology promises to resurrect labor's old unemployment solution by increasing the demand for leisure. By employing the new sciences of happiness, the technology promises to create better experiences and transformations that will require more time for their consumption. Whereas technology once supported work reductions by the invention of laborsaving devices, eudaimonic technology will support shorter hours by increasing the demand for leisure necessary for consumption of its experience products, a process that may reawaken the forgotten American dream.

From Laborsaving Devices to "Science Makes Jobs"

Since the Enlightenment, people have been turning to science and reason to free them from the chains of tyranny, oppression, and brute necessity. Of all the definitions of progress, of all the myriad modern hopes about the future, the advance of freedom stands out clearly as one of the most prominent. Walt Whitman and others in the eighteenth and nineteenth centuries saw this advance as coming in stages. Reason, applied to government, produced constitutional democracies that promised to free all people from slavery, injustice, and oppression. Reason, embodied in a free marketplace (what Joseph Schumpeter was fond of calling a "matrix of logic"[3]), promised to enable all humans to advance materially toward abundance—to get enough. Finally, science and reason were creating increasingly powerful machines and efficient technologies, speeding that day when, as Benjamin Franklin foresaw, all the reasonable "necessaries" of life would be provided by a person's working six hours a day and then less and less as technology improved.[4]

Thus would science and reason release humans, increasingly, into a "realm of freedom,"[5] allowing them to pursue happiness as they chose, beyond the constraints of politics and the selfish strivings of the marketplace—making it possible for them to experience the world and other people freely, loosed from the chains of necessity, illusion, and want. For the most part, the "Luddite fallacy"[6] was a European phenomenon. Whereas workers in Europe occasionally revolted against the coming of new machines, complaining that they were taking their jobs, the advance of technology in the United States was more often acclaimed as liberating—as providing more and more people with the material necessities of life and more opportunities, more time, to enjoy them.[7]

Instead of massing to destroy new machines, workers in the United States more often embraced them, turning their hands to things mechanical and, in their unions, fighting for their fair share of the increased productivity, the new wealth, that technology was making possible. While some carped about technology's destruction of craftsmanship, most tended to accept technology simply because it improved their standard of living and eased their work burdens. Laborsaving machines were science's great contribution to humanity. Even though jobs were becoming less rewarding in and of themselves, higher wages and progressively shorter work hours compensated for the losses for many, providing ample opportunities outside work for them to recover the craftsmanship, creativity, and community being lost at their regular jobs.[8]

Bourgeois myths about happy workers—fulfilled and enjoying their jobs, singing their spirituals as they slaved in the cotton fields, sharing good fellowship around their machine presses and lathes, or finding their passion at work—were most often discounted by employees whose jobs were less and less engaging, creative, and satisfying and who sought work's bourgeois-imagined intrinsic rewards in their new, expanding leisure.[9]

Optimism about technological progress, based on the prospects of higher wages and the gradual reduction of working hours, continued through the first half of the twentieth century. Such optimism was bolstered by some of the most important scientific discoveries of the day. Frederick Taylor and the first scientific managers applied rigorous research methods to the workplace and discovered basic principles of organization, applicable to both production and personnel management. Their findings improved productivity dramatically and laid the foundations for the modern profession of business management. They helped make "efficiency" (producing more with less) a watchword of the Progressive Era.[10]

Aside from a few intriguing examples (e.g., Helen and Scott Nearing),[11] the dominant response to technological advances in the United States continued until the early 1930s to be optimistic, on the basis of the expectation that new jobs, higher wages, and shorter hours would continue to absorb industry's new productive capacity. However, with the coming of the Great Depression, concerns began to grow about chronic technological (structural) unemployment. Laborites such as William Green, businessmen such as Henry Ford and Walter Gifford, and economists such as John Maynard Keynes agreed that while jobs would be created as technology improved, workers would also have to be paid enough to buy the new consumer goods they were helping produce and would need increasingly more free time to use them. Steadily increasing productivity demanded these three solutions (the creation of jobs, higher wages, and shorter hours), otherwise chronic economic instability and growing unemployment would be the inevitable result of technology's advance.

Responding to what some called the threat of chronic unemployment during the early days of the Great Depression, Keynes, arguably the most influential economist of the twentieth century, answered that "the standard of life in progressive countries one hundred years hence will be between four and eight times as high as it is to-day." Some jobs would have to be created simply because "everybody will need to do some work if he is to be contented."[12]

Nevertheless, the ever-increasing productive capacity of the American economy would mean that the amount of work per capita would decrease to a minimum eventually. The dream of an economy that facilitates a better way of life for its workers began to solidify around not an increasingly unrealistic vision of good jobs but rather a more fruitful leisure facilitated by new technologies.

The Ideology of Full-Time, Full Employment: Origins and Questions of Sustainability

As the Great Depression wore on, technological unemployment became the center of public concern, however, prompting a novel government response. From the beginning of the labor movement, supporters had argued that shorter hours helped reduce unemployment, a view summed up by a popular saying attributed to Samuel Gompers: "So long as there is one man who seeks employment and cannot find it, the hours of labor are too long."[13] In the midst of the Great Depression, unemployment emerged as salient, the primary concern of labor and the primary defense of shorter hours.[14] During the battle against unemployment in the early 1930s, the first and only viable political solution was work sharing. Introduced as a conservative, Republican initiative founded on business volunteerism during Herbert Hoover's term in office, the share-the-work movement grew, dominating the politics of the Great Depression—both parties endorsed work sharing during the political campaigns of 1932. Outstanding examples of conservative, voluntary responses include Kellogg's and Goodyear Tire's six-hour workday initiatives.[15] The Democratic version of work sharing then emerged as a proposal to reduce work hours by law in 1932. Just before FDR took office, the Black-Connery bill was introduced in Congress. It mandated a thirty-hour week, to be enforced by stiff overtime penalties ranging from time and a half to three times payment for work done exceeding thirty hours. Because the bill was initially supported by clear majorities in both houses and by Roosevelt's administration (there was still no other politically viable unemployment solution around) and because it did in fact pass the Senate, most journalists reported the legislation was a done deal—the bill seemed sure to pass the House of Representatives and become law with Roosevelt's signature early in 1933.

Roosevelt balked, however, holding the Black-Connery bill at bay, buying time to come up with his own programs. Prompted by business opposition to the thirty-hour legislation (Republicans were still pressing for their volunteer approach to work sharing), key figures in FDR's administration, including Rexford Tugwell, Mariner Eccles, and Harry Hopkins, cast about for alternatives. They began to adapt some of the European unemployment strategies and new economic theories, such as countercyclical government spending, floating around academia to the massive unemployment problem in the United States.

Roosevelt's administration then cobbled together a series of initiatives, designed to counter work sharing, based on the theory that government could, and to avoid chronic unemployment must, *act to create work* to replace work lost to technological advances. With the introduction of this monumental new government commitment, a watershed moment in American history was reached.

I have argued that this work-creation initiative accounts for most of Roosevelt's Second New Deal—the years after 1935—including Eccles's (Keynesian) monetary policy intended to stimulate the economy with new government spending, growing debt, and liberal treasury policy; massive public works programs, especially those headed by Hopkins (the Works Progress Administration that he oversaw became one of the largest employers in the nation); and the growth of government and the military (especially with the coming of World War II and subsequent institution of a permanent standing army). All these served Roosevelt's fundamental purpose to combat what his administration believed to be the very real threat of chronic unemployment, a danger that could only be met by government's promoting enough economic activity to ensure all who were looking for work a full-time job—defined politically during the Depression, for the first time in history, as at least forty hours a week.

Before FDR's first administration, "full time" had been understood by labor and most other observers as a changing, ever-shorter workday and week. Working full time had meant different things at different times as the average workweek shortened. The idea that working hours would stabilize at forty hours, or any other set level, was no more common than the idea that wages would, or should, eventually stop increasing. However, Roosevelt branded anything less than forty hours as part-time—as sharing the poverty or sharing the unemployment.

Government-supported Full-Time, Full Employment, launched by Roosevelt, remains the center of American (and most industrial nations') domestic politics.[16]

Science and Technology Make Jobs

The history of science and technology in the United States mirrors these developments. Those who were most responsible for technological progress often felt most besieged by critics during the early years of the Great Depression. Having been lauded for decades for their new machines that had produced so much new wealth and free time, engineers and scientists faced accusations that the new technologies were destroying people's jobs and livelihoods. Laborsaving devices, long the primary reason for the popularity and public support of science and technology, became a public relations liability. See Figure 1.1.[17]

Traditionalists in the science communities, such as the technocrats, held their ground, continuing to defend their accustomed role as providers of laborsaving machines. Those active in the technocracy movement, taking their cue from economists such as Keynes and Thorstein Veblen and from the politics of the share-the-work movement, pointed out that the industrial nations were lagging behind the advance of science—working longer than necessary was irrational and ultimately the cause of the Depression. They

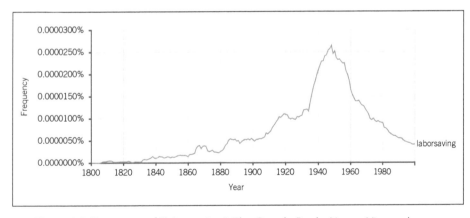

Figure 1.1 Frequency of "laborsaving": The Google Books Ngram Viewer shows the occurrence of the word over the decades

suggested that working hours be reduced to 660 per year by law to cure unemployment.[18] Subsequently, as people were able to find work, rational progress, expressed through the marketplace as progressively higher wages and shorter hours, *together*, would resume.

Most scientists and engineers followed Roosevelt and the nation, however, embarking on the bold, intrepid new venture to create enough work, then and for evermore, to replace jobs that technology and the free market constantly made redundant—a project that traditionalists in the scientific community continued to believe fantastic. Led by Vannevar Bush, most scientists and engineers abandoned labor saving as their primary social obligation and, reversing direction, turned overnight to the ideology of science makes jobs. Bush, as director of the Office of Scientific Research and Development and reporting only to Roosevelt, was one of the most important voices, along with Harry Hopkins, in Roosevelt's administration, preaching the gospel of work creation and leading the scientific community toward its new destiny—to an eternity of science makes jobs.[19]

Since World War II, the American scientific community has been among the truest believers in Roosevelt's vision of Full-Time, Full Employment, followed closely by other professional groups that owe substantial parts of their existence to government funding, certification, and regulation. During the war, federal and state governments and American colleges initiated a system of funding of the sciences that still endures. Much of higher education has been recruited to the service of the politically defined social goals of job preparation and work creation, following the traces Rexford Tugwell and Leon Keyserling laid down in the 1930s—Tugwell envisioned an army of "workers on work" in government and in America's colleges whose jobs would be to create work.[20]

Since World War II, the modern industrial nations, led by the United States, have struggled to maintain Full-Time, Full Employment. The project has dominated modern politics and government domestic policy.[21] However, over the years the project has become increasingly problematic. With unemployment in double digits, some of the nations in the European Union, including France, Norway, and Sweden, have returned to work sharing. Late in 2015 and into 2016, reports out of Sweden indicated that the nation was moving toward a six-hour workday, led by prominent international firms such as Toyota and by public employees in Stockholm and other major cities. In the fall of 2017, Germany's largest trade union, IG Metall, began pushing for a twenty-eight-hour workweek.[22] By contrast, the United States and some other industrial nations such as the United Kingdom have redoubled their efforts to maintain Full-Time, Full Employment even in the face of technology's increasingly rapid advances: the coming of cybernetics, robotics, and a global economy. Some economists and politicians are even pressing for the end of government regulation of working hours.[23]

How Sustainable Is Full-Time, Full Employment?

Since the advent of Full-Time, Full Employment, critics have branded the project unrealistic. At its inception, some in the scientific community thought such an eternal quest was absurd. On its face, the idea that human needs were entirely plastic and that new necessities could be created ad infinitum by the market, even with the help of science, defied reason.[24]

Moreover, critics continue to object to the project and its sustainability, for several reasons. Since the mid-nineteenth century when John Stuart Mill predicted that continuous economic growth, beyond the provision of basic human needs for all (a stationary state), would eventually destroy the natural world, economists and critics have pointed to what should be obvious to all, that unlimited economic growth in a finite world is simply impossible—for all peoples of the world to enjoy a material standard of living comparable to the United States, several Earths will be required.[25]

Political concerns worry others. Many now claim that governments' efforts to sustain Full-Time, Full Employment have reached and passed the point of diminishing returns as progressively slower economic recoveries and mounting public debt complicate governments' attempts to stimulate and revive their economies.[26] Moreover, as governments' efforts fail, chronic unemployment mounts and more severe boom-and-bust cycles occur. Boom periods obscure the long-term problem—job-killing machines continue to outpace the job-creating abilities of modern economies over the long term. Globalization, immigration, and the Internet now compound the problem of worldwide, chronic unemployment.[27]

Still others fear that growing inequality and the maldistribution of wealth will lead to increased exploitation of peoples around the world and to disruptive levels of immigration.[28] Such fears are exacerbated as conservatives' arguments that wealth must be increasingly concentrated (by tax reductions) to generate jobs become politically persuasive—the results of which are the further eroding of the civil and political orders.

What Robert Hutchins called "Salvation by Work" is a failing faith, less and less able to live up to its promise of good jobs for all—not only are too few jobs created, more and more of the new jobs have less and less to do with fulfilling human potential and aspirations.[29] In the spring of 2013, the Gallup organization found that "70 percent of American workers are 'not engaged' or 'actively disengaged' and are emotionally disconnected from their workplaces."[30]

Sustaining Full-Time, Full Employment has become an increasingly desperate undertaking, with supporters casting about to find sustainable, workable solutions. With few new possibilities discovered, old remedies are recycled. The conservatives' faith that new jobs will automatically appear if only government would reduce taxes and all the lazy layabouts would get to work has been renewed and is flourishing. As popular as these sentiments have become, given the long-standing inability of the marketplace, on its own, to hold unemployment in check, they have yet to stand test of time. For unemployment to be brought under control in the European Union and then for Full-Time, Full Employment to be maintained, national economies there will have to grow at record levels, far above historical averages, for decades into the future. Moreover, if governments around the world cut spending, substantially reducing the size of government, the military, and entitlements, the growth of unemployment, by all accounts, will be catastrophic. Of course, wars have always offered another kind of full employment.

Liberals continue to press their case for more government spending to maintain Full-Time, Full Employment. However, government job creation and stimulus-spending interventions are increasingly less effective and more costly, driving deficits and entitlement payments to what some see as alarming, unsustainable levels. The strategy of cutting interest rates, at record low levels and in some cases approaching zero, is less and less of an option. People across the political spectrum fret that government spending and debt cannot continue its open-ended growth as it has over the last fifty years.

The experience economy emerged in the midst of these increasingly desperate attempts to sustain Full-Time, Full Employment. The timing is remarkable. Joseph Pine and James Gilmore claim that the experience economy has arrived at just the right time, appearing as the last, best hope for sustainable economic growth adequate to ensure that full-time jobs are available for future generations.[31]

The Experience Economy

Customer-Added Value

Those on its frontier offer the experience economy as an answer to the continuing threat of chronic unemployment. Because technological advances continue to replace humans with machines and techniques at an accelerating rate, a new economic frontier beyond goods and services has emerged as a critical need. This chapter explores what may be part of a new answer to the old problem of unemployment, the new frontier of the experience economy. The new economy is defined and its distinguishing characteristic (customer-added value) identified—its spread and influence explored. The use of experiences to sell goods and services, experience marketing, is also discussed. Examples of experience products and experience marketing are provided as illustrations. This chapter also explores the kinds of jobs being created by the new economy. Initial commonsense approaches to experience-product design are reviewed, including an introduction to the critical concept of cocreation.

Pine and Gilmore begin the 2011 edition of *The Experience Economy* by calling attention to a phrase prominent on the 1999 edition's front cover: "Goods and services are no longer enough." They feared that even though hundreds of thousands of their book's first edition had been sold worldwide, this phrase, the "book's thesis," had not yet "sufficiently penetrated the minds of enough business leaders to give full bloom to a truly new— and desperately needed—economic order."[1] They attributed the economic downturn and faltering recovery that followed the 2008 financial crisis to the "failure to experientially innovate."[2] Accordingly, they took special care to reiterate, at least five times, their central claim: "Goods and services are no longer enough to foster economic growth, create new jobs, and maintain economic prosperity."[3]

They agreed, in part, with Jeremy Rifkin's (and others') gloomy analysis: "Rifkin is right to suggest that businesses will need fewer workers to deliver services in the future."[4] Predicting the end of work, Rifkin, echoing forecasters' perennial claims,[5] explains that computers, the Internet, globalization, and the coming of mass merchandizing are doing to the service industries, once the last, best hope for new jobs, what automation did and continues to do to manufacturing.[6] In a resurgence of interest about the topic, in the summer of 2015 Derek Thompson predicted the coming of "a world without work" in a cover story for the *Atlantic*.[7] His article followed publications such as Erik Brynjolfsson and Andrew McAfee's *The Second Machine Age: Work, Progress and Prosperity in a Time of Brilliant Technologies*[8] and Tyler Cowen's *Average Is Over: Powering America beyond the Age of the Great Stagnation*[9] that add advances in robotics to the traditional job threats posed by automation, offering as examples self-driving cars, trucks, and drones that are destined to replace hundreds of thousands of human jobs.

Those welcoming the experience economy agree that goods and services are becoming increasingly commoditized and mass produced and are losing all differentiation except price. Big-box stores are replacing local service providers and brick-and-mortar retailers while automation makes further inroads into manufacturing and transportation. Pine and Gilmore observe that "the Internet is the greatest known force of commoditization for goods as well as services, [providing for] friction-free transactions." They conclude, "The Service Economy, too, has justifiably faltered."[10]

Branding Rifkin a "professional pessimist," however, they see a bright future largely independent of government involvement—a new economic frontier opening beyond goods and services, signaling "a fundamental shift in the very fabric of the economy."[11] Growth in the new experience economy has the potential to generate wealth and create jobs in the private sector sufficient to sustain full employment. Pine and Gilmore predict, "Indeed, the masses will be employed by those businesses that recognize and create experiential output as a distinct economic offering."[12]

Indeed, much of the surge in job creation over the last decade seems to be jobs in the experience and transformation economies.[13]

Pine and Gilmore's work, and that of others who have followed their lead, represents the more conservative, free-market approach to Full-Time, Full Employment, an approach that keeps the faith that the marketplace, led by innovators and entrepreneurs, will create enough products and jobs—and do so in ways that are reliable and sustainable. They insist:

> Future waves of economic activity based on new [experience] economic offerings will provide ample opportunities to generate more wealth and create new jobs—if only businesses remain free to compete, unencumbered by government's view of what constitutes appropriate economic offerings to promote or protect.[14]

Capital as well as jobs will follow the experience economy. The money saved by the commoditization of goods and services will become increasingly available for new investments in, and greater spending on, experiences.

With Walt Whitman Rostow and others, Pine and Gilmore see a natural evolution occurring in modern economies. Whereas Rostow claims that economies naturally evolved in *stages*, from traditional societies, through an industrial takeoff phase, and on to an age of high mass consumption,[15] Pine and Gilmore suggest *an evolution of economic values added* to the otherwise valueless materials of the world, from agriculture and extraction (commodities) to manufacturing, to service, and on to experiences (see Box 2.1).[16]

This progression of economic values is often illustrated by the familiar example of spending on birthdays.[17] Years ago, birthdays were celebrated at home and largely beyond the reach of the marketplace. At most, spending was limited to the ingredients (commodities) needed to bake a cake (at a cost of less than one dollar). Gradually, store-bought presents, cake mixes, and candles were added to the celebration. Then the cake was ordered from the supermarket already made, adding up to ten times the cost of making it at home (tens of dollars). Parties were added to the event, which were then gradually expanded and catered. Then the whole celebration was relocated to Chuck E. Cheese's, Jeepers!, Dave and Busters, or a myriad of local family-oriented experience providers, increasing the cost of the birthday by a factor of ten once again (hundreds of dollars). Entrepreneurs are now offering the

---

BOX 2.1 PROGRESSION OF ECONOMIC VALUES

                                        Experiences
                                Services
                        Manufactured goods
                Commodities
    Time line ─────────────────────────────────────▶

services of professional planners and the option of having the party at exotic locations: Six Flags Over Georgia, Disney World, and elsewhere (thousands of dollars).

Each step in the progression of value added, from raw materials to manufactured goods, to services, to experiences, creates employment and generates new economic activity. Some now claim that spending on the experience economy accounts for the lion's share of new jobs and economic growth in nations throughout the industrial world. Jeremy Rifkin concludes, "The top fifth of the world's population now spends almost as much of its income accessing cultural experiences as on buying manufactured goods and basic services."[18]

Influence and Spread

The experience economy's appeal has spread widely during the last two decades, interesting more professional groups and researchers as well as businesspeople and investors. As early as 2009, Jon Sundbo noted, "The growing experience economy has now begun to receive much attention, especially in Scandinavia. . . . [T]he focus is both practical and scientific."[19] He reported that "the experience economy is . . . gaining an increasing part of global competition"[20] More recently, Hélder Ferreira and Aurora Teixeira found that "the experience topic is starting to draw more attention from academics seeking to solidify it."[21] They also found scholarly publications about "customer experience" increasing, most rapidly from 2009 to the date of their publication in 2012. They concluded that the experience economy "has achieved a broad geographical influence . . . solidifying its importance in terms of research, receiving increasing attention from marketing academics." They also found a convergence of disciplines "ranging from tourism, sport and leisure to hospitality, albeit with prominence in the areas of management and business," representing a multidisciplinary approach to "customer experience."[22]

Travel and tourism has emerged as the leader of the new economy. Jon Sundbo and Flemming Sørensen agree that the study of experiences not only "[has] become an independent field" but has become "a core phenomenon in tourism studies."[23] Following the lead of travel and tourism, architects and city planners have begun to redesign buildings and cities to facilitate experiences—what some are calling "Experiencescapes."[24] Museums and other exhibition venues are turning from inert displays to hands-on exhibits. J. Robert Rossman and Gary Ellis point out that park and recreation professionals and other providers of public leisure services were in the experience business long before Pine and Gilmore came along, but they admit that the spread of interest in the experience economy has enlivened their fields, stimulating the design and delivery of experiences—what their fields have been calling recreation programing for decades.[25]

Marketing experts have also recognized the importance of experiences, beginning to use them increasingly to sell traditional products. Since the beginning of marketplaces, sellers have catered to customers—improving the customer's experience continues a very long tradition. Indeed, just as the definition of the experience economy remains murky, it is not yet entirely clear how what is being touted as new experience marketing differs from what generations of shopkeepers have been trying to do.

Nevertheless, those who promote the experience economy maintain that the shopping experience is one of the few ways left for retailers to compete with the big-box stores, such as Walmart, and the Internet. They point out that increasingly more time and money is spent on lighting, decor, and fragrances; on lounge chairs, sample treats, and human store clerks to help, advise, and compliment customers; and on interactive opportunities to try out (experience) products. Because shopping has been the most popular recreational activity for substantial parts of the population for decades, it represents a vast, untapped potential, ripe for development of experience marketing, examples of which are easy to find today.[26] Pine and Gilmore predict, "In the full-fledged experience economy, retail stores and even entire shopping malls will charge admission before they let a customer even set foot in them."[27]

Experience Marketing: Land Rover "Branded Experiences"

Jaguar's Land Rover is one of the leaders in experience marketing today. The carmaker hired Mark Cameron in 2011 as its brand-experience director, responsible for global marketing. During the Profiting from Experiences marketing conference held in London on October 17, 2013, Cameron announced plans to involve 2 million existing customers and potential buyers in Land Rover's "branded experience" events by 2020.[28] During his presentation, titled "Creating Lasting Memories in the World's Most Capable Cars," he outlined the kinds of marketing experiences his company had begun to offer and the reasoning behind its turn to experience marketing.

He explained that most people who bought Land Rovers were sedate city folk who rarely, if ever, used the machine's capabilities—capabilities that make the Land Rover a special product worth the luxury price tag. Cameron maintained that providing customers with firsthand knowledge of what the vehicle can do, a knowledge best gained by actual experience, would help sell the car better than any other method. Even though most customers would never use the Land Rover for anything other than ordinary city and highway driving, the *memory* of its abilities to ford rivers, climb mountains, and go where few other ordinary vehicles would dare try was a vital part of its value to the customer.

Led by Cameron, the company has made the venerable test drive an experience that customers are willing to pay for. Renaming test drives as "experience drives" or "adventure drives," Land Rover also offers driving lessons, ranging from an hour ($275) to a whole day ($1,500).[29] The company provides instructors to demonstrate what the vehicle is capable of and to teach customers how to handle it and themselves while "navigating steep inclines, descents, side slopes and water crossing."[30] It invites customers to "push [the Land Rover] to the limits and realise the extent of your own capabilities. . . . Behind the wheel with a qualified instructor at your side, you will be able to develop your off-road driving skills on climbs and descents, through deep water, sand and mud."[31] The company also offers "Owner's Day" events as an opportunity for buyers to "spend the day with other Land Rover owners," driving their personal vehicles over obstacle courses—developing camaraderie and a kind of community based on their common "Land Rover experience."[32]

Arguably, the most impressive of the company's new experience offerings is its "Land Rover Adventure Travel" (or holidays)—an initiative that might well be called marketing-tourism, in keeping with the long list of hyphenated tourism offerings that have proliferated over the last decade. The company suggests "a 5-day adventure in the stunning Moab desert[;] this is your chance to experience some of the world's most spectacular trails. Your off-roading skills will be put through their paces."[33]

Paul Simonet, creative strategy director at Imagination EMEA, attended the Profiting from Experiences marketing conference with Cameron in 2013. He concluded that experience marketing's budget share was growing in companies worldwide. Companies such as Red Bull and Nike are transforming "the way marketers think about experiences" and betting larger parts of their marketing budgets on experience marketing. Mark Cameron agreed, noting that the experience-projects budget at Land Rover had increased to about 20 percent of what the company spent on marketing.[34] As a promotional device, the sellers of the new all-electric car Smart ForTwo offer a real-life version of the computer game Pong, with their autos replacing the traditional virtual paddles.[35]

Experience Marketing: Best Buy to Vending Machines

The multinational electronics retailer Best Buy has embraced the experience economy. For years, Best Buy offered consultation and advice about its products for free, considering the service necessary to support the sale of computers and other electronics. Meanwhile, the upstart Geek Squad was busy competing with the retail giant, offering superior information, diagnostics, and service, making a profit by charging for the novel, geeky experience. Eventually, the two merged, and today the Geek Squad invites customers to experience the personal contact, banter, and practical advice available, but now on Best Buy's premises. The company touts its Geek Squad as one of its most successful brand offerings.

Samsung, following the Geek Squad into Best Buy stores, now offers Samsung Experience pods: an arcade-like collection of their products, complete with helpful experts, interactive demonstrations, and virtual experiences—free for the time being but with the potential to become a revenue source.[36]

Pioneers in the experience economy advise others to follow Best Buy's lead and improve the shopping experience so as to make charging for it a realistic option. Some envision retail stores becoming more spa-like and featuring more active and interactive opportunities. Stores with plush, peaceful surroundings and attentive employees will offer one set of relaxing experiences. Others, catering to more active clientele, will offer minimountains to scale, golf balls to drive on an indoor range, tennis courts to use, and the latest models of airplanes, helicopters, boomerangs, and Nerf-Ball shooters to try out.

Vending machine providers have begun experience marketing, redesigning their products to entertain, amuse, and interact with customers. Coca-Cola installed vending machines on college campuses that randomly deliver multiple free Cokes to surprised buyers, who are encouraged to hand them around. Coke has also offered machines that show various dance moves on a screen and challenged passersby to mimic the dance. The machine's computer is programed to "watch" the dance and award free Cokes according to how well the customer performs. Other machines, using similar technology, challenge patrons to sing for their Cokes. In some Asian countries, Coke installed a two-story-high vending machine with a coin slot at the regular height and a large red button ten to twelve feet above the floor that dispenses a free soda. The design encourages creative responses from customers, who oblige by hoisting friends on their shoulders, building human pyramids, and so on. Often the results of these novel machines have been crowds watching and cheering the dancers, singers, and climbers interacting with the machines—a marketers' dream come true.[37]

Defining the Experience Economy

Such broad appeal and optimism about the future notwithstanding, substantial problems with definitions have arisen as researchers try to make clear, quantifiable distinctions between services and experiences. Robert Johnston and Xiangyu Kong conclude, "There appears to be a good deal of confusion in the literature about the definition of an experience and its distinction from a service."[38] Anders Sørensen and Jon Sundbo observe that it is "well known" that "there are no clear or generally recognised definitions of experiences, experience economy, experience production or experience consumption" and that "no authorized definition exists."[39] Even so, "there seems to be a general agreement that the experience economy—whatever it is—is growing, and will continue to grow in the coming years."[40]

Amid the uncertainty about definitions, Pine and Gilmore's original characterization has proved to be among the most stable and widely used. In the absence of something more precise, it has remained useful as a working definition.[41] For Pine and Gilmore, experiences are

> as distinct from services as services are from goods. . . . When a person buys a service, he purchases a set of intangible activities carried out on his behalf. But when he buys an experience, he pays to spend time enjoying a series of memorable events that a company stages—as in a theatrical play—to engage him in an inherently personal way. . . . No two people can have the same experience—period.[42]

Early on, Pine and Gilmore identified five distinguishing characteristics of experience products: intangibility, subjectivity or interiority,[43] value added (time, interest, skill, attention, etc.) by the customer, similarities to the theater (Pine and Gilmore insist that theater is a "model" rather than a metaphor for the experience economy), and memories as the takeaways.[44]

Pine and Gilmore's working definition notwithstanding, some have continued to object to the lack of precision and to argue that services and experiences have yet to be adequately differentiated. A good meal in a restaurant, perhaps the epitome of the service economy, seems to meet Pine and Gilmore's criteria for experience. There is no doubt that this imprecision has become a major problem for the experience economy, slowing its reception by mainstream academia and publicly funded researchers.[45] Definitions have varied so much, evolving in complexity and becoming more rather than less inclusive, that comparisons have become increasingly difficult and empirical research has been impeded. There is yet to appear some distinctive metric to work with. The lack of precision has also resulted in the promiscuous use of the terms, further crowding and clouding the topic.

Trine Bille at the Copenhagen Business School, reporting that many local and regional governments in the Nordic countries have taken great interest in and "formulated a strategy for the experience economy," cautions, "The experience economy does not lend itself to any consistent definition." Thus, research has lagged behind public interest and government action in that part of the world. The result is that "investments . . . are being driven more by politics [and hype] than by knowledge."[46]

Pine and Gilmore have responded, explaining that experiences are qualitatively different *additions* to existing services and reemphasizing the theater-like qualities of experience products that gradually unfold. They point out that experiences are produced by a customer's "being engaged by what the company reveals over a duration of time,"[47] adding that "the greater the (positive) memory created and the longer it lasts, the more value is created."[48] They and others also stress the increasing *intangibility and interiority* of experiences.

Building on Pine and Gilmore's five foundational elements, other researchers have struggled to differentiate experiences from services, offering a variety of definitions that are as often confusing as clarifying.[49] Pieter Desmet and Paul Hekkert define "product experience as a change in core affect that is attributed to human-product interaction" and as "all possible affective experiences involved in human–product interaction."[50] Hekkert and Hendrik Schifferstein maintain that experience products are distinguished by customers' "awareness of the psychological effects elicited by the interaction with a product, including the degree to which all our senses are stimulated, the meanings and values we attach to the product, and the feelings and emotions that are elicited."[51] Sundbo and Sørensen reiterate, "Experience . . . could be defined as the mental impact felt and remembered by an individual caused by personal perception of external stimuli . . . something extraordinary . . . outside daily routine."[52]

Johnston and Kong explain:

While a service is the process or activity, the customer's experience is their personal interpretation of the service process and their interaction and involvement with it during their journey or flow through a series of touch points, and how those things make the customers feel. [The experience] is inherently personal, existing only in the customer's mind. Thus, no two people can have the same experience.[53]

Still, facing a tide of indiscriminate use of the term and struggling to define the experience economy as a distinct part of the economy, companies and researchers have turned to customers for help, asking them to identify and assess the value of experiences and have adapted traditional marketing and product-design tools, such as questionnaires, surveys, and focus groups.[54] Enrique Alcántara and colleagues have refined such efforts with "a procedure for identifying experiences and for assessing their customer value" using a "logbook technique" followed up with field surveys. They then analyze the collected data to determine the fit between what customers identify as valuable in experiences and the experience products that are available or that may be developed using what they term "environmental design."[55] However, such customer input has added little to researchers' understanding and for the most part has been analyzed and cataloged according to Pine and Gilmore's original five-part definition.

In addition to asking customers to help identify experiences, others rely on extensive catalogs of illustrations. Assuming that readers as well as customers will recognize an experience when they see it, they use what might be called a show-and-tell definitional method, presenting example after example and noting features of various experience products that appear similar or distinctive.

Such efforts rely largely on ordinary, accepted language usage and generic distinctions between experience, product, and service.[56] Thus, these are largely intuitive, commonsense approaches, serviceable to some extent in the marketplace but of limited use as the basis of research and design. Moreover, relying on existing successful experience products, or on giving customers what they already think they want, limits the entrepreneur, who has traditionally led the way, innovating and offering customers things they never dreamed they could buy.[57]

Lacking a precise and widely shared definition, writers and entrepreneurs have cast about for better ways to understand the experience economy and to establish guides for the design of new experience products. Beginning with a commonsense, inductive approach to definitions, and collecting examples of marketable experiences, several researchers have attempted to sort these experiences into categories, arranged according to subsets of characteristics common to most or all such experiences.

Taxonomies

Using a database of companies in the business of selling experiences maintained by the Centre for Experience Research at Denmark's Roskilde University, Jon Sundbo "inductively developed" a taxonomy according to three "dynamic drivers": market demand, "innovation effort (innovation-push)," and technology.[58] Morris Holbrook created a "Typology of Customer Value" along two axes: intrinsic versus extrinsic motivation and self versus others orientation.[59] However, Pine and Gilmore's taxonomy is one of the best known and by far the most influential.[60]

Noting that experiences can "engage guests on any number of dimensions," they content themselves with dividing experience types into two main groups: customer *participation* in the experience and customer *relationship* with or connection to the experience environment.[61] These two dimensions are set along a continuum, ranging from passive to active in the *x* dimension of participation and from absorption to immersion in the *y* dimension of connection and relationship. For example, skiers, more active in creating their experiences, would be located farther along the right end of the *x* axis, while people who attend a play would be located closer to the passive, left end of the *x* axis.

Pine and Gilmore explain the *y*-axis, *environmental relationship*, dimension as describing the "kind of relationship . . . that unites customers with the event or performance."

> People viewing the Kentucky Derby from the grandstand *absorb* [at the top of the *y* axis] the event taking place before them from a distance. Meanwhile, people in the infield are *immersed* [at the bottom of the *y* axis] in the sights, sounds, and smells of the race itself as well as the activities of the other revelers around them.[62]

The *x* and *y* axes and fields suggested by the two variables are shown in Figure 2.1.

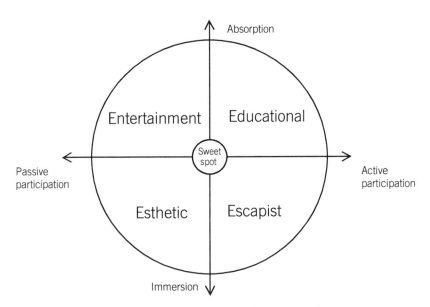

Figure 2.1 A model for experience design: The four realms of an experience. *Source:* B. Joseph Pine II and James H. Gilmore, *The Experience Economy* (Boston: Harvard Business Press, 1999). Used by permission of Harvard Business Publishing.

Four "realms of an experience"[63] are formed by the intersection of the x and y axes: entertainment, educational, esthetic, and escapist. Pine and Gilmore explain that customers seeking entertainment, one of the oldest experience products, "passively absorb the experience through their senses." Examples include such familiar activities as listening to music and reading for pleasure. In the other familiar experience realm, the educational, the customer also "absorbs the event unfolding before him." The educational realm, however, involves more active participation than does entertainment. Examples are also easy to come by: traditional course work, adult classes, retreats, workshops, conferences, symposia, and colloquia.[64]

Escapist experience products involve "greater immersion than entertainment or educational . . . guests . . . are completely immersed . . . as actively involved participants." Notable examples include gambling, computer-based games, theme park rides, and simulations such as Disney's Star Tours and Indiana Jones Adventures. Keying on Peter Guttman's *Adventures to Imagine,*[65] Pine and Gilmore suggest an intriguing possibility: "People [may] become actors able to affect the actual performances."[66] This is a possibility being explored by several innovative experience designers, including Comic-Con International.[67]

Last, in the esthetic realm, "individuals are immersed in the event or environment but have little or no effect on it."[68] Examples include enjoying the beauty of Saint Mark's Square in Venice over coffee, viewing a work of art, sitting in the grandstands at a sporting event, and watching the sunset in the Black Hills of South Dakota.

Pine and Gilmore summarize, "While guests partaking of an educational experience may want to *learn,* of an escapist experience want to *go* and *do,* of an entertainment experience want to *enjoy,* those partaking of an esthetic experience just want to *be.*"[69] Noting that the realms are not mutually exclusive, Pine and Gilmore recommend that experience products be designed to include as many of the four realms as possible. The more dimensions involved, the better the product. The entrepreneur and experience designer should aim for the sweet spot (the bull's-eye in the center of Figure 2.1), the optimal combination of all four of the experience dimensions that would, in theory, produce the most valuable experience.

Experience-Product Design: Commonsense Approaches

Nathan Shedroff observes that, like the experience economy, "Experience Design as a discipline is . . . so new that its very definition is in flux."[70] Such an impediment, however, has not deterred the proliferation of guides to experience-product design or the exuberance of those who promote them.

In addition to advising the entrepreneur to ask customers what they want and to aim for the sweet spot, Pine and Gilmore suggest that existing companies "ing" their products—that is, market new ways of using manufactured goods as an integral part of their value.[71] They insist that "manufacturers must focus on the experience customers have while using their goods"[72] and that "any good can be *inged*."[73] For example, instead of simply selling kitchen utensils, companies might sell the cook-ing experience; automakers, such as Land Rover, the motor-ing experience; comic book publishers, the enact-ing of comics on stage in a theater-like pageant.[74] They suggest that "*experientializing* the goods" has opened an entire metarange of opportunities to add value to existing products.[75]

One of most remarkable, convincing examples of "ing-ing the thing"[76] is duct tape; a product with a modest purpose and beginning that has become something of a pop icon after customers found new, amusing ways to use it. The manufacturer has capitalized on duct tape's celebrity, following the lead of their customers and making suggestions about how to use the product in, for example, making prom dresses, jeans, and Halloween costumes.[77]

Eataly, an upscale grocery store with locations in New York and Chicago, tries to replicate the experience of visiting an authentic Italian market without the bother of travel. With experts offering lectures about Italy's regional cuisines, demonstrating the preparation of meals and serving them to small groups, making wines available to taste along with the food, and informing customers what to look, smell, and taste for (experience) in the food and wines, Eataly has made going to the grocery store a theater-like experience, the next best thing to traveling to Italy.[78]

In 2006, Charmin opened elaborate restrooms on Times Square, promising the "best bathroom experience in [New York] city." Outside the facility an employee, costumed as a commode, attracted patrons to what might be best described as the theater of the toilet. Inside, themed music was played, "potty-dances" were staged by employees, and patrons were invited to take the stage and perform their versions. The stalls were stocked with an array of Charmin products to try and individually themed—decorated in familiar Americana motifs such as Route 66, the Wild West, and the like. The staff played their parts according to a script, attempting to make visiting the restroom seem as much of a big-city experience as a Broadway play. The company attributed part of the subsequent 14 percent increase in its sales to this bit of experience marketing.[79]

Pine and Gilmore contend that "this new [experience] economy demands models to work," emphasizing the theater as the quintessential model guide to experience design—the subtitle for the 1999 version of their book is "Work Is Theatre and Every Business a Stage." Theater is an important part of their definition. For them, an experience occurs in the marketplace "when a company intentionally uses services as the stage, and goods as props, to engage individual customers in a way that creates a memorable event."[80] Thus, the customer experience becomes part of the drama being enacted—generally the customer has a range of responses and opportunities to participate (freedom to cocreate) or watch from the sidelines.

By contrast, Nathan Shedroff lists six experience dimensions that he considers vital to experience design: time or duration, interactivity, intensity, breadth or consistency, sensorial and cognitive triggers, and significance or meaning. Together, these form a palette of possibilities for creating effective, meaningful, and successful experiences.[81]

Principles of Experience Design

Building on Pine and Gilmore's theater-model suggestions, Albert Boswijk, Thomas Thijssen, and Ed Peelen offer ten commonsense experience-design principles: Theme the experience, harmonize impressions, eliminate negative and intruding factors, pay attention to mood and atmosphere, add memories and memorabilia, involve all the senses, pay attention to authenticity (make the experience as realistic as possible), dramatize the structure (work toward a climax with an ending, resolution), deploy staff as actors (all employees play a role, staying in character), and customize it (work toward realizing the well-being of customers as individuals).[82]

One of the most common suggestions for designing a new experience product is to piggyback on existing technologies—to ride the cyberwaves of the Internet and social media. The computer world has responded, casually using the phrase "experience economy" to launch new digital gadgets, conflating "experience" with a miscellaneous array of uses in the cyberworld.[83]

Much of the casual use of the term "experience economy" has been by the media covering cyberspace—interactive games, chat rooms, and simulators and other kinds of virtual reality, from touring to sexting. Apple introduces cascading generations of iPhones, touting their new interactive and experience features. Google's Internet glasses, a lightweight, wearable computer, makes it possible for a person to be constantly wired, "experiencing" the virtual world. On the Internet, site designers, claiming to be at the cutting-edge of the experience economy, monitor the experience of the users of their sites, including such experience variables as length of wait time, amount of advertising, and the quality of links. In the hypercompetitive world of cyberspace, the quality of experience has become a major consideration.

Entrepreneurs with perhaps better claims to being part of the experience economy have opened brick-and-mortar parlors for gamers to play together and interact with each other, forming teams and alliances, thus adding value to a previously solitary Internet experience—allowing customers to create more of the experience product. In much the same vein, researchers and therapists at the State University of New York at Courtland have adapted popular video gaming technology to clinical settings, making it possible for people with physical difficulties to play some single-shooter (war) games. By dividing the virtual tasks—shooting the gun, moving the character, and so on—among two or more players, they transformed an otherwise solitary game into a team sport that all gamers could enjoy, overcoming physical limitations.

Cocreation, the Key to Experience Design, and the Definition of the Experience Economy

Boswijk and colleagues stress that the joint creation of experiences by customers and businesses is a necessary part of the experience economy, turning to the concept of cocreation to clarify the customers' contribution. They agree with C. K. Prahalad and Venkat Ramaswamy (and others) that the experience economy involves "a next practice," cocreation, in which the dialogue between an organization and an individual consumer provides the foundation for the joint creation of personalized value.[84] Nathan Shedroff points out that "humans are inherently creative creatures and when we have a chance to create we feel more satisfied and valuable." Therefore, he concludes, cocreation is an essential element of experience design. He outlines a process through which the experience designer and vendor encourage, promote, and enable customers to become increasingly engaged, able to create a sizable part of the experience product for themselves.[85] Pine and Gilmore agree, although they emphasize the importance of mass customization and "Adaptive Customization." They write, "All experiences are co-created, as we've always believed, because . . . they happen inside the individual."[86]

An excellent example of cocreation at its innovative best is San Diego's Comic-Con International, which holds a popular annual convention, attracting upward of 130,000 people. From its beginning, Comic-Con has been a leader in experience-product design, "experientializing" the lowly comic book. Charging fifty dollars a day (2015 prices), Comic-Con offers "the complete convention experience," including a 460,000-square-foot exhibit hall, nearly seven hundred themed programs, hands-on workshops, awards, art shows, and "portfolio reviews." One of its best-known experience products, featured in various episodes of the popular CBS sitcom *The Big Bang Theory*, is the masquerade costume competition, in which convention-goers become the entertainment. Comic-Con elaborates, using some interesting language:

Why is it called a Masquerade and not simply a costume contest or fashion show? Because it's more than just posing on stage, it's about portraying characters too, creating moods, sometimes a sense of story. It's an event of spectacle, drama, comedy, light-saber battles, even some song and dance, where you never know what's going to step onto the stage next. The Masquerade recognizes that the creative arts reside in all of us, the arts are not meant to be just a spectator sport, and that among our attendees there is plenty of their own amazing talents and creativity worth showcasing.[87]

Cocreation represents a significant advance in customization because experience products are differentiated by individual customers. Such customization points to what are arguably the most important characteristics of the experience economy, distinguishing it from services and manufactured goods: the customer contributes relatively more to the creation of the experience products' value.

Therefore, the following is offered as a working definition of the experience economy: The more value that is added by the customer, the more the product belongs to the experience economy and the less to goods or services. This continuum-based definition,[88] founded on the value added by consumers, avoids much of the complexity and lack of precision present in previous attempts at definition. Such a definition by continuum also anticipates a working definition of the transformation economy in which customers add value to the creation of products that are the customers themselves.

The Transformation Economy

The Customer Is the Product

The experience economy is not enough to ensure continued economic health. The transformation economy is the vital, next, and perhaps last stage of the progression of economic values. In this chapter, the transformation economy is defined, its role in the economy's growth and creation of jobs analyzed, and its hazards examined. I provide examples and an initial discussion of transformation-experience product design. The importance of the provision of a series of transforming experiences in which experiences improve as they build on previous experiences is emphasized as part of transformation-experience design. I discuss Hans Gelter's Total Experience Management as a guide to experience-product design. The topics of prosumer and the sharing economy are introduced. The formation of experience capital (skills) within individual customers is also analyzed as a radical shifting and redistribution of the ownership of the means of production in the new economies—customers will begin to own the means (skills) of production, a critical move toward equality. Finally, I examine the potential of the experience and transformation economies for ill or good. The potential of the transformation and experience economies for continued alienation or enslavement by the branders and value capturers versus autonomy or liberation by the catalyst-enablers is reviewed in preparation for Chapter 4's more thorough investigation of the hazards versus potential of the new economies and the eudaimonic technology.

The Transformation Economy

Many worry that experiences are as susceptible to commoditization as goods and services—that goods, services, *and* experiences are not enough to ensure continued economic health. Something more is needed to avoid rising unemployment levels and a sluggish economy. Indeed, experiences may represent a special case of declining utility. With repetition, experiences tend to get old fast—to lose their appeal even more rapidly than a surfeit of goods and services. Repeated experiences risk becoming boring, a disutility, and something to avoid. Moreover, compared to consumer durables (manufactured products that last three or more years), experiences appear ephemeral, insubstantial, the stuff of dreams.

To compete and grow their businesses, experience providers must offer more than memories as takeaways—something of the customer's own that increases and builds rather than fades, something to offer when customers repeat "been there, done that." What is needed are experience versions of consumer durables: experiences that last and become more valuable with use. What is needed are special kinds of experiences that build up a kind of *experience capital* in the consumer—that *change* consumers so that they become better at and more appreciative of the experiences they purchase. Joseph Pine and James Gilmore write, "With transformations, the economic offering of a company is the individual person or company changed as the result of what the company does. With transformations, the customer is the product!"[1] Hélder Ferreira and Aurora A. C. Teixeira agree: "In experience economy, customers become an essential part of the companies' offerings."[2]

The assumption that nearly everyone would like to *become* healthier, wiser, stronger, more skillful and accomplished, better looking, more interesting, better able to relate to other people, interested and involved in more things, better able to see and appreciate the beauty around them, better neighbors and family members—in short, better human beings—is fundamental for the transformation economy. Many agree with Pine and Gilmore's universal claim: "We want to transform ourselves."[3]

Flowing from this fundamental assumption, a new kind of specialized language specific to the transformation economy has gained wide acceptance.[4] In the transformation economy, businesses become "*transformation elicitors*,"[5] offering *effectual* experience products to customer *aspirants* and guiding development toward desirable goals through a gradual, unfolding *series of graded experiences*.[6] As these italicized words indicate, willing intent is generally required, on the part of both customer and vendor. Transformative experiences have purpose and direction.[7] Brian Solis, a principal digital marketing analyst at the Altimeter Group, explains that "aspiration and intention become the North Star," guiding "enablers in the delivery of magical experiences."[8]

Unlike simple experiences, residing only in a fading memory, transformative experiences change the "attitude, performance, characteristic, or some other fundamental dimension of the self" in ways that become habitual and are sustained over time.[9] Individual traits, habits, and perhaps even what generations of intelligent people, including the likes of Aristotle and Saint Thomas, called virtues, are the results.[10] For a price, the transformation economy promises to change the very *being* of the buyer. While the transformation economy's "products" are not tangible in the traditional sense of an actual physical object (a house, auto, or washing machine), nevertheless they are quite real, more enduring than experiences and often quite measurable.

Just as with the experience economy, those on the transformation-economy frontier have worried about definitions and ways to differentiate transformations from the earlier stages in the progression of economic values. Some lament, "Observers will surely argue that what we are calling transformations are really only a subclass of services."[11] Because the customer is the product, however, the transformation economy may lay more convincing claims to something new and distinct—to experience products that make clear differences *in* customers. Transformations are already being evaluated with metrics designed to gauge the extent to which customers are changed in their "attitude, performance, characteristic, or some other fundamental dimension of the self," ranging from weight loss to heart rates, to stamina and endurance. Other, less precise but nevertheless valid measures are more subjective: the mastery of dance steps, the acquisition of skills needed for around-the-home repairs and do-it-yourself projects, culinary skills and interest, the sensory skills necessary to enjoy complex wines, the growing fluency in a new language.

The Progression of Economic Values Extended

Stressing that the "natural progression"[12] of economic values is toward ever-greater economic differentiation, Pine and Gilmore conclude:

> There can be no greater differentiation than a transformation. . . . Just like the experience stagers before them, transformation elicitors are greatly increasing their share of the total economic pie. Today the only thing better than being in the business of staging experiences is being in the business of guiding transformations."[13]

Advocates argue that the transformation economy has emerged as the one remaining, reliable way to sustain economic growth and maintain acceptable

---

BOX 3.1 EVOLUTION OF PROGRESSION OF ECONOMIC VALUES

Transformations
Experiences
Services
Manufactured goods
Commodities
Time line ⟶

---

employment levels, appearing as the fifth and possibly the final stage in the progression of economic values (moving in time from left to right; see Box 3.1).[14]

On the basis of more than a decade of observation, researchers have concluded that a positive correlation may be shown to exist between the progression of economic values and at least five key variables. As an economy advances through the stages of value, the following occur:

- *Utility* increases.
- *Differentiation* grows: Products are increasingly customized and personalized.
- *Price or value*, or both, of products increases (for example, birthday celebrations become more expensive). Capital and time, both representatives of value, flow toward the higher economic levels.

As the economy advances beyond services into the experience and transformation economies, the following occur:

- Products become increasingly *intangible.*
- *Customers play an increasingly greater role* in the creation of the products they consume, to the point that the customer becomes the product, in possession of the means to produce new experiences.

These last two variables provide excellent ways to characterize and more accurately differentiate the experience economy and the transformation economy from manufacturing and service. Intangibility and consumer participation and transformation are the defining characteristics of the last two stages of economic advance.

A strong case may be made that together, the experience economy and the transformation economy have claimed the lion's share of economic growth, in both the nation's gross domestic product and the creation of jobs, for decades.

TABLE 3.1 COMPOUND ANNUAL GROWTH RATE, 1959–2009

Economic sector	Employment growth (%)	GDP growth (%)
Commodities	−0.80	5.20
Goods	−0.10	5.40
All offerings	1.60	6.90
Services	2.00	7.20
Experience economy	2.20	7.50
Transformation economy	3.70	9.20

Source: B. Joseph Pine II and James H. Gilmore, *The Experience Economy*, rev. ed. (Boston: Harvard Business Press, 2011), 272.
Note: In Table I.1, the experience and transformation numbers are combined in the experience economy. Again, because opportunity costs are not included, these numbers may be misleading and appear much lower than the real impact of the experience and transformation economies.

In the progression of economic values, each subsequent economic level has outpaced its predecessor, with the transformation economy surpassing them all.[15] See Table 3.1.

Examples

As with the experience economy, examples of the transformation economy abound and multiply daily.[16] The burgeoning health services fields, promising to transform sick people into well customers, are by far the largest group in the transformation economy so far. Included in this group, of course, are the medical, dental, psychological and counseling professions, and convalescent services, as well as countless alternative medical treatments and therapeutic offerings (recreation, music, aroma, etc.)—ours has been described as the "therapy culture."[17] Wellness centers and a host of other providers charge for keeping their clients healthy and fit (an increasingly measurable commodity). Other health-related groups offer to help customers transform bad habits and behaviors into better ones. Larger firms regularly offer wellness programs and training facilities to their employees. GlaxoSmithKline offers to help with giving up cigarettes, Jenny Craig to help with weight loss, fitness centers and personal trainers to help get you in shape, family and marriage counselors to improve relationships. Several medical-alert companies promise to deliver peace of mind, transforming customer fears and insecurity into confidence. Instructional offerings, in addition to traditional schools and colleges, proliferate: dance studios and clubs; meditation, yoga, kung fu, and tai chi instruction; and classes at Home Depot, hobby shops, musical instrument stores, and local grocers—together offering to transform customers into dancing, mellow and introspective, lithe and agile, slender, fearless, handy, creative, musical gourmet chefs.

Nordic walking (variously known as fitness walking, Viking hiking, or exerstriding) is a kind of vigorous speed walking. In 1997 the Finnish company Exel introduced this activity together with a new product, Nordic walking poles (two ski pole–like sticks—an excellent example of "ing-ing" a product), both of which became very popular. Subsequently, the company expanded its product line with Nordic blading poles and a new transformation product, its Nordic Fitness concept, designed to result in a changed customer living a complete, all-encompassing, healthy lifestyle aided by its products, instruction, information, and inspiration.[18]

The travel and tourism industry, already leading the experience economy, has made an impressive showing in the business of transformations as well. Introducing the term "transformative travel" in 1997, Jeffrey Kottler represented the aspirations of many in that industry when he wrote:

> Travel offers you more opportunities to change your life than almost any other human endeavor. People . . . report dramatic gains in self-esteem, confidence, poise, and self-sufficiency. They enjoy grater intimacy . . . become fearless risk takers, better problem solvers, and far more adaptable . . . [and] more knowledgeable about the world.[19]

The popular travel writer and TV host Rick Steves claims that travel can be a "political act." "Travel shapes who you are," he explains. Travel gives a person an "expanded global viewpoint," the ability to "connect with people" and to "empathize with the other 96 percent of humanity." It is among the best ways to "pry open your hometown blinders" and experience the world more fully, adding to the quality and meaningfulness of other experiences.[20]

One of the often cited but highly controversial examples of the transformation economy is CoreCivic (formerly the Corrections Corporation of America). Committed to delivering "proven and innovative practices in settings that help people obtain employment, successfully reintegrate into society and keep communities safe," the company promises *measurable* changes in their prisoners, keyed to recidivist rates—to some an attractive possibility given the problems the nation's prisons have experienced for years.[21] Insurance companies, such as Progressive Insurance, sell "assurance"—feelings of trust, satisfaction, and confidence—a less easily measured commodity. Safeco Insurance of Seattle "ensures" teens by monitoring their curfews and driving behavior to help them *become* responsible motorists while delivering peace of mind to parents.[22]

Transformation-Experience Design

Just as in the experience economy, few of those designing transformative experiences have advanced far beyond commonsense and standard business methods. Most, still relying on surveys, focus groups, and questionnaires, continue to depend on their customers to tell them what to offer. Many follow Pine and Gilmore's intuitive, three-stage process and simply ask customers what they want to change or to become ("diagnose aspirations"), intuitively design or "stage" a series of experiences that might facilitate the change, and then guide customers through that series, monitoring and ensuring progress toward their goals.[23]

Theorists and experience providers have offered additional practical advice about how to improve each of these three steps, some mundane, some inspirational. For example, Pine and Gilmore advise that "holding attention, changing context, fostering appreciation, altering states, having presence, and creating catharsis . . . are at the heart of orchestrating compelling [experience products]."[24]

Even while relying on traditional methods and common sense, the transformation economy's practical-minded pioneers have nevertheless identified founding principles of transformation-experience design that have become the subjects of more careful empirical research and market testing. Their commonsense guidelines and observations are being confirmed by researchers and entrepreneurs, and no discoveries about experience design are more important than these two:

- Transformations involve a plan—a *conscious* purpose or goal freely shared by vendor and customer.[25]
- Most transformations are gradual, realized by a process made possible by a graduated series of experiences that build competencies and hence experiences' value.

Building Experience Capital: Shifting Ownership of the Means of Production

Advancing beyond commonsense and traditional business strategies, researchers are beginning to show empirically how a series of transforming experiences work—how experience builds on experiences in the transformation economy. They have described a process in which customers, having spent more and more of their time, effort, and money, become increasingly invested in an experience. As measurable skills, confidence, interest, and abilities increase, the value of subsequent experiences grows, building on the foundation of previous investments.

Capital, as the means of future-experience production, then resides and compounds more and more in the individual consumer—a revolutionary outcome if ever there was one.[26] The first stages of many desirable experiences are often only moderately rewarding, sometimes unpleasant. That buyers seek demanding activities such as a rigorous fitness regimen, a foreign-language course, or even hot yoga is an indication that something more than the pursuit of an ephemeral good time is going on in the transformation economy. Accordingly, the successful entrepreneur offers customers a graduated "series of experiences."[27]

Continued practice and skill building are often a mixture of the enjoyable and demanding. But they are essential to avoid the traps of boredom, loss of interest, and commoditization—"no pain, no gain." They are unavoidable paths to experiences that are increasingly engaging rather than just more of the same. Psychologists and educators have recognized this phenomenon for centuries; insightful people, such as Aristotle, for millennia. Advertisers and marketers are only now beginning to develop strategies that persuade customers to invest themselves in transformative experience. Pine and Gilmore promise, "Much greater profits will accrue to those businesses with the wisdom to shift beyond goods and services to the use of experiences, no matter how painful, to transform their customers."[28]

More than any other, the new scholarly discipline of travel and tourism has investigated experience-based transformations over the last decade or so and has done important empirical research. Scholars have also made important theoretical contributions to the understanding of how experience builds on experience and how best to design opportunities for tourists (and others) that accomplish their purposes. Jon Sundbo explains that the experience industries are just beginning to "train the public to appreciate" new experiences.[29] He agrees with J. R. Bryson[30] that in the new economies investments are flowing away from traditional, tangible forms of capitalization, such as machinery and buildings and the training of service workers, toward "softer" kinds of capital that take the form of "audience development."[31]

Attempting to analyze the commonsense understanding of terms such as "experience" and "audience development," Sundbo and Flemming Sørensen point to an important linguistic distinction, noting that the English word "experience" may convey two different meanings that German and several other European languages distinguish by using different words. In German, *Erfahrung* can mean an enriching experience that, leading beyond itself, builds skills and prepares for other, richer experiences—a usage comparable to the English phrase "learning experience." Sundbo and Sørensen want to rule *Erfahrung* out of the experience economy because it is too broad, including all forms of education. They allow *Erfahrung* only as a by-product of *Erlebnis*, which is a transitory experience, more complete in and for itself (intrinsically motived, or autotelic)—for example, attending a sporting event. They conclude, "*Erfahrung* (including education) is not part of . . . the experience economy per se. However, *Erlebnis*, or 'pure experience' (expressive, short-time consumed) may include an *Erfahrung*, or learning, aspect."[32]

On the basis of distinctions such as these, one may conclude that while *Erlebnis* is a distinguishing characteristic of the experience economy, *Erfahrung* rightly belongs to transformations. Christian Jantzen agrees: "*Erfahren* . . . is at the core of the 'transformation economy' . . . [the] final stage of economic value creation."[33]

Hans Gelter, agreeing with J.M.C. Snel,[34] and emphasizing their "interconnectedness," explains that *Erfahrung* follows *Erlebnis* in a "transformational learning process"—a process of "creating meaning" as well as building competences and appreciation. Describing a kind of positive feedback loop, familiar to systems analysts, Gelter writes:

> After a process of reflection and comprehension the events of the *Erlebnis* are transformed to *Erfahrung* where the meaning of the experience is formed . . . where the assimilative knowledge is transformed into convergent knowledge. This new *Erfahrung* can [create] . . . new concrete experiences, new *Erlebnisse*.[35]

Gelter concludes that "carefully designed and staged chains of *Erlebnisse* may thus result in more major transformations according to the goals of transformational offerings of Pine and Gilmore," establishing the foundations for what he terms a "transmodern tourism offering."[36] Jantzen summarizes such observations: "*Erfahrungen* are not only outcomes of *Erlebnisse*, they are also sources of *Erlebnisse*."[37]

Innovative companies such as Exel with its Nordic poles may have anticipated these insights. Finland's Technology Agency conducted a study of what it termed "the leisure business cluster" in 2005.[38] The purpose of the study was "to highlight the consumer perspective in the current debate on the experience economy"—the aim, "to identify core activities and services that are important for innovations in the leisure business." The agency's summary report concluded, "Successful innovations typically open up new challenges for consumers and enable them to pursue *increasingly* demanding and interesting hobbies." The agency hoped this finding would guide innovation and leisure experience designers and offered Nordic walking as an example. They also noted the importance of using "ethnographic methods following from anthropology" to determine consumer preferences and motivations, to better design experience and transformation products going forward.[39]

Along with Gelter,[40] several theorists, including Snel and Albert Boswijk, have adapted John Dewey's well-known educational theories about the importance of experiences ("learning by doing") and engagement with the subject matter to be mastered. They have also employed Jean Piaget's psychological theories about development in their analysis of *Erfahrung* and *Erlebnis*, creating models and guides for the design of transformative experiences.[41] Abraham Maslow's well-known hierarchy of needs, in addition to Piaget's and Dewey's ideas, has been an important source for theory and experience design, providing what Hans Gelter termed "an appealing dynamic model that has been applied within tourism."[42]

According to Maslow, human needs may be classified into five basic groups, usually arranged in a hierarchy: physiological, safety, belongingness and love, esteem, and self-actualization.[43] These constitute, theoretically, the essence of human motivation, the fundamental causes of behavior. As the first, more urgent survival needs are met, humans have the time and energy to devote to the higher needs. Once enough food to live is found and shelter against the elements provided, humans have more opportunities for family, friends, creativity, invention, introspection, charity, service, and worship. Maslow's point is not that these needs are not present in most people most of the time. Indeed, some individuals may neglect or even forgo the more fundamental needs to give expression to their higher needs (for example, martyrs and ascetics). Maslow simply recognizes a hierarchy in the economy of human time and energy—a practical dividing of effort that guides most of us.

Jon Sundbo makes uses of Maslow's model to explain the growth of the experience and transformation economies, observing, "There is an increasing demand for experiences determined by several factors: seeking social status, more meaning and less boredom in life, and psychological self-realisation. . . . It is rooted *in fundamental psychological needs and societal factors*." He goes on to show how theoretical frameworks, such as Maslow's, have been and can continue to serve as the basis for innovations.[44]

For example, Gelter proposes to design experiences that guide tourists along the levels of Maslow's hierarchy. He attempts to construct a "'blue print' for developing "Transformational Experience Production," working toward "transmodern tourism." He explains that the "essence" and the final destination of "transmodernity is being for something, *i.e.* taking action towards ethnic, racial and sexual equality, sustainability and interconnectedness."[45]

Gelter then introduces the concept of "Total Experience Management," employing Maslow's hierarchy in a normative, prescriptive way as the basis of experience design. Quoting from Rolf Jensen's *The Dream Society*, Gelter enriches Maslow's hierarchy with Jensen's "dreams" to create a "total experience" that includes aspiration as the vital ingredient.[46] Agreeing with Pine and Gilmore about the importance of freely chosen goals and the "aspirant's" deliberate efforts to reach them, Gelter suggests providing tourist experiences that reach beyond routine necessity and, in accord with his transmodernism, make it possible for the customer to become someone or something different.[47]

Gelter's brilliant contribution is the introduction of an element of freedom and choice into Maslow's descriptive model. Whereas, according to Maslow, need and necessity are the primary springs of human behavior (i.e., hierarchy of *needs*), Gelter turns to free choice and will as his metaphors. The customer and the experience provider are not just passive, psychologically or economically determined beings, responding robotically to higher needs after lower ones are met. They are free beings, aspirants, facing the uniquely human challenge of what to do in their freedom. The exercise of free choice, will, and determination then emerge as important, even essential elements for progress along Maslow's hierarchy and as essential components of well-being—an insight confirmed by recent findings in the new sciences of human happiness.[48]

Maslow's hierarchy is not an escalator, automatically lifting people to more humane and richer experiences. Willing intention—aspiration—is an essential ingredient in successful experience and transformation-product design.

The problem of inertia haunts the transformation economy—the very real possibility that people will fall into a trancelike focus on products related to their more basic needs when the opportunities to realize the higher needs become available or simply remain unaware that there are better things to do. In these all-too-common occurrences, education or, even more importantly, effective marketing, is required to acquaint customers or clients with superior experiences and the role of transformations in reaching them. Experience products, particularly some of the offerings in cultural tourism, are proving to be among the most effective teachers, *guiding* customers along Maslow's hierarchy. After a century of condemnation of modern marketing techniques by a host of critics, the transformation economy may reveal the moral and humane possibilities of advertising.

Leaders in recreation and leisure studies such as Gary Ellis and J. Robert Rossman have made important theoretical contributions to the experience economy on this point. Concerned with public parks and recreation and nonprofit groups, as well as with commercial provisions of leisure services, such leaders have pointed to the vital importance of intrinsic motivation and autonomy in leisure activities for decades. Searching for ways to operationalize Pine and Gilmore's theater model, Ellis and Rossman propose a model for staging experiences on the basis of years of practical experience. Citing prominent researchers and theorists in their fields, they conclude that proper experience staging includes cocreation strategies that

> facilitate the opportunity for guests to have experiences that are of value. This notion of facilitating rather than fully providing the experience preserves the autonomy of the participant to help create the leisure experience. . . . Leisure scholars and other behavioral scientists consistently point to the pivotal importance of intrinsic motivation in determining the quality of experiences.[49]

Summary

The consensus of those who have written about the transformation economy is that conscious choice, vision, and imagination play vital roles in this new economic arena. Thus, writers such as Gelter and Boswijk anticipate (or apply) one of positive psychology's most important discoveries: that, as Martin Seligman writes, "human beings are often, perhaps more often, drawn by the future than they are driven by the past."[50]

Researchers in the transformation economy have also come to understand that transformation is a cumulative process in which experiences improve as skill, appreciation, and understanding grows. Whereas Dewey and Piaget had traditional educational venues (classes, seminars, lectures) in mind when they wrote, those in the transformation economy have turned to the design of commercial experiences that might perform many of public education's traditional roles. Certainly, education's traditional venues may be considered as parts of the transformation economy even though largely government funded. However, now there is a widespread expectation that the entrepreneur might compete, conceivably doing a better job teaching and training people with new experiences, successfully competing with tradition-bound and bureaucratically paralyzed educational institutions. With the advents of the Internet and social media, the private sector is certainly in a better position to realize educators' long-standing mission of transmitting information. It is also possible that the market will provide more effective ways to train and transform customers, educating them in the arts of freedom and aspiration—what used to be the liberal arts tradition in higher education.

Conversions

There are important exceptions to the generalization that transformations involve a cumulative process. Those who have written about the experience economy have also investigated intense, life-altering experiences—watershed moments that transform a person's perspective. Often customers have no clear idea about how to change or what they would like to become but are happily surprised when new perspectives are opened by an experience. Peak experiences, religious conversions, what Jantzen calls "epiphanies," have been part of the human experience for millennia. Those discovering practical economic applications of such things, such as Pine and Gilmore and Jantzen, agree that such revelatory "transformative experiences" are important parts of the transformation economy.[51]

One of the vital functions of these intense experiences is to reveal the dimensions of experience and potential for transformations—to bring customers to the realization that their experiences may improve and become increasingly rewarding as skill, interest, and active involvement increase. The revelation that there is an active and engaging world of experiences much more satisfying than watching the average four daily hours of TV or wandering around the Internet, malls, or amusements parks is often life changing. Such experiences then become the basis of customer aspiration and then transformation.

Museum designers have shown interest in such conversion experiences, and their work may serve as illustration. Richard Toon describes the importance of redesigning museums and science centers so that visitors have opportunities for solitude and reflection—spaces in which to be still and absorb the wonder they are experiencing. He argues that by building "reflection into the exhibit experience" a kind of "enchanted looking" (what some are now describing as "mindfulness") might be elicited: "The experience I am arguing for is one of transformation. The goal is nothing less than to change people so that they see the world in a different way . . . transformation is, ultimately, the role of the museum."[52] Quoting Pine and Gilmore, Toon notes that together with such "strange bedfellows" as higher education, fitness centers, religious organizations, and mental health providers, the museums and science centers' "product is the changed person." Toon concludes, "If we truly transform our visitors, then we place them in a new position from which to experience us again, as it were, for the first time."[53]

Transformations for What?

Researchers and businesspeople have realized that once the customer buys and consumes the initial experience product a second, more subtle kind of opportunity frequently becomes available, one that promises to *transform* the buyer. New kinds of marketing and new kinds of experience design are necessary for such transformations to occur. However, transformations are problematic in ways that simple experiences are not. How to manage the relationship between customer and provider has become the source of divergent approaches, centering on the possibility of customer autonomy and the ultimate purpose of transformations. The transformation economy raises larger questions: To what end? and Cui bono?

The transformation economy promises to "affect the very being of the buyer."[54] Therefore, issues of seller control vis-à-vis buyer autonomy are involved. The direction of transformations and the locus of control are key normative issues, raising such questions as: Should transformations be in the direction of increased reliance and dependence on the experience provider to maximize profit or in the direction of increased customer autonomy? Two kinds of relationships have been suggested by recent debates about the new economies that may be categorized as catalyst-enabler versus value capturer or brander.

Catalyst-Enabler

A number of theorists and experience providers, particularly those in travel and tourism and leisure services, attempt to guide customers to richer, more valuable experiences by encouraging them to become more active, engaged, and *invested* in the production of the experience product. For them, the cocreation relationship is primarily about building customer experience capital and therefore about increasing customer autonomy.

Catalyst is a useful metaphor to describe this kind of transformative-experience provider. Such vendors elicit customer change by furnishing the essential conditions, the environment, tools, information, expertise, encouragement, and programs in and through which transformations can occur and experience capital builds in their customers.

J.M.C. Snel maintains, "It is my strong conviction that experiences cannot be produced, managed, sold or directed either. You can however do your best to support, facilitate, and help people in having their experiences."[55] Christian Jantzen agrees:

> Users or consumers are the producers of the experiential quality and value of products. Designers, manufacturers, marketers, entertainers or retailers are at best merely providers of the frames and elements of specific experiences. Many personally valuable experiences actually occur without commercial intermediaries partaking in the process.[56]

Some of the most influential researchers and writers, noting the importance of cocreation in the experience and transformation economies, agree about the need for customer empowerment—for "end users [leading the way to] value creation."[57]

The catalyst-enabler, at his or her best, provides transformative experiences that promote customer autonomy. For decades, businesses have proclaimed the importance of empowering customers—the phrase has become something of a cliché. The transformation economy is taking the concept to a new, qualitatively different level. For the catalyst-enabler, increasingly autonomous customers are the natural outcome of customer empowerment. Liberated by transformative experiences, invested with their own experience capital and capable of producing and sharing experiences for themselves, customers *become* ever less dependent on the marketplace. Here is the liberation potential of the experience economy and the transformation economy. Here is capitalism's escape hatch. Here is liberation capitalism.

Britta Timm Knudsen, Dorthe Refslund Christensen, and Per Blenke describe the blurring of boundaries between consumer and producer. With the emergence of the "prosumer"—the empowered customer who is increasingly responsible for producing and freely sharing more and more of his or her experiences[58]—the balance of control and power shifts from traditional vendors and marketers to customers who are seeking extramarket, often nonpecuniary ways of trading goods, services, and experience. Using the Internet, renting from and sharing with neighbors and strangers, forming clubs and nonprofit organizations, holding fairs and trade shows, and making use of a variety of ephemeral marketing opportunities, consumers are busy creating a "sharing economy"—what the *Economist* variously terms the collaborative, peer, or access economy, which taken together are forming an "asset-light lifestyle."[59]

Integrating "entrepreneurship and empowerment into one central theme," Knudsen, Christensen, and Blenker suggest that with the advent of the prosumer, the entrepreneur's primary role has become the empowerment and liberation of customers.[60] George Ritzer and Nathan Jurgenson agree and, with Jeremy Rifkin, raise "the possibility of a new, prosumer capitalism" emerging as consumer and producer become one, producing on their own and sharing freely, beyond the reach of older, more exploitative, and expensive, forms of capitalism and traditional marketplaces—even beyond the confines of traditional educational institutions.[61]

Brander or Value Capturer

Even while endorsing cocreation as an equal partnership and emphasizing the importance of customer empowerment, others (arguably most) who claim membership in the experience and the transformation economies display a strong tendency to emphasize and expand the control of experience providers at the expense of customers.[62] Those who use the term "customer experience" casually and "the experience economy" as the latest buzzword usually ignore the liberation and empowerment possibilities emphasized by the catalyst-enabler.

There is a clear tendency in the transformation economy to understand transformations as changing consumers to have ever-greater dependency on the seller, capitalism, and traditional marketplaces.

In subtle ways, an asymmetrical bias is revealed in writers' syntax. The experience designer or provider is more frequently the subject of sentences and the customer is the direct or indirect object of transitive verbs, leaving no doubt who is in charge. For example, "By staging a series of experiences, companies are better able to achieve a lasting effect on the buyer."[63]

Less subtly, Selda Basaran Alagöza and Nezahat Ekici observe that as a group "marketing theorists and implementers are in search of unique and entertaining experiences to create customer dependence [and] . . . experiential marketing . . . aims to make consumers respond, act actively to purchase."[64]

Still, defending the transformation economy, Pine and Gilmore insist, "Transformations in free societies are by their very nature fully co-created, with the company only guiding what customers . . . must themselves undergo; to treat transformation otherwise is tyranny."[65]

Nevertheless, prosumers, customer autonomy, and the emergence of the sharing economy are seldom discussed in most accounts of the transformation economy in the popular media. More typically, branding—the transformation of independent-minded comparison shoppers into loyal brand followers—features prominently in the literature. John Schouten, James McAlexander, and Harold F. Koenig, making use of psychological findings about the transformative power of intense experiences, conclude that

> transcendent customer experiences, which have aspects of flow and/ or peak experience, can generate lasting shifts in beliefs and attitudes, including subjective self-transformation . . . and can strengthen a person's ties to a brand community, delivering a particularly strong form of brand loyalty.[66]

Indeed, branding is the essence of transformation for many marketers who claim to be part of the transformation economy. Arguably, being branded is the epitome of customer dependency—long criticized as the manipulation and exploitation of customers. Newbery, echoing Pine and Gilmore and happily predicting that consumers will become ever more dependent on the marketplace as economies progress, stresses the importance of keeping customers looking "to you [the experience provider] rather than a competitor."[67] Hendrik Schifferstein and Paul Hekkert declare that "the ultimate goal of experiential marketing is to [enhance] the brand image."[68]

The exploitative potential of the transformation economy is realized nowhere more fully than in efforts to use experiences to sell to and brand children. Marshall Lager, the managing principal of Third Idea Consulting, explains that "modern-day CRMists [customer relations managers] have fully embraced the experience economy. . . . Increasingly, the value of a business is predicated not merely on its products and services, but also on how interacting with it makes us feel. The name for this is 'the experience economy.'" Complaining that examples such as Starbucks are less than compelling and that "nobody gives a clear case for transformative experiences the customer can't do without," he proposes to remedy the situation by turning attention to children. Saying that "children are the currency," he invites the entrepreneur to "look at the predatory, avaricious gleam in [children's] eyes" as they enter Build-a-Bear Workshops or an American Girl Store and any of the Disney attractions: "These companies have sussed out the experience economy and made a killing at it, dipping a vacuum hose into our wallets by targeting young and impressionable minds seeking wonder." These companies offer experiences that are "finely tuned to get kids drooling for more [such] that any parent with means or a mortgage would feel like a bastard for not indulging Timmy or Sarah's desires."[69]

Juliet Schor has documented, in thorough detail, the darker side of marketing to children, pointing to the advent of a generation of "commercialized children" who have been shaped by marketers. In a relentless process beginning shortly after they are born, our children are transformed into reliable consumers, attached to specific brands. Their very identity has been tied, frequently for life, to what they buy and own—the emotional, familial, and social costs of all this are staggering, including the predatory, avaricious, drooling kids that Lager describes.[70]

Moreover, grand promises of perpetually expanding sales and profits, what Pine and Gilmore call "ample waves of gain,"[71] as well as explicit plans for the commodification of parts of human life never before colonized by commerce, leave little doubt where the majority of advocates of the experience and the transformation economies want the economy to go. There is also no doubt that the consequence for consumers will be growing dependency and loss of autonomy. As much of the value that customers add to experience products as possible must be captured as profit. The transformations of customers must become reliable sources of new income streams.

One of the most common claims made about the new economies is that they are the "very engines of growth":[72] economic drivers opening up new,

boundless fields for commercial development and ensuring economic prosperity well into the future. For bullish writers such as Pine and Gilmore and
Marshall Lager, future profits and jobs will grow luxuriantly on these new
frontiers, unconstrained by the limits that commodities, goods, and services
are now facing.

Even while emphasizing cocreation, Pine and Gilmore offer a fine definition of what critics of capitalism, such as Jürgen Habermas, have for decades
branded as "commodification" when they explain:

> But as the world progresses further into the Experience Economy,
> much that was previously obtained through noneconomic activity
> will increasingly be found in the domain of commerce. This rep-
> resents a significant change. It means that to obtain what we once
> sought for free, we now pay a fee.[73]

Those who agree that human progress is defined by the growth of capital wealth and the creation of jobs accept, with few reservations, the steady
growth of the economy into areas of life previously done "for free"—what
Habermas and Edmund Husserl have called the lifeworld. Critics have long
viewed with alarm the extent to which consumers are increasingly enmeshed
in the market, ever more dependent on the cash nexus, the market's connec-
tor. The prospect that we all may have to pay one day to have a conversation
with a live person or enjoy a walk in nature, may delight bullish advocates of
the experience economy and the transformation economy but will continue
to alarm a sizable number of us.

Pine and Gilmore respond to such worries; they "recognize [the] noneconomic spheres of social and personal experience" and agree that as "more of
life becomes commodified, we should carefully examine our lives . . . in terms
of what we choose to buy." Nevertheless, for them and most others expecting
that handsome profits are to be made in the new economies, the need for
economic growth remains paramount. Most accept as a fact of life that, "for
developed economies to remain prosperous, a shift to [paid-for] experiences
must occur."[74] To avoid "economic austerity," it is inevitable that ever more
of life becomes a paid-for experience. This is simple reality, the result of the
"natural evolution of the economy."[75]

Entrepreneurs and businesses, in line with Pine and Gilmore's guidelines,
are finding new ways to charge customers for their time. "Time is the currency of experiences"[76] has become something of a slogan in the new economies as businesses begin to charge entry fees, per-event fees, per-period fees,
initiation fees, access fees, and membership fees. Having gained admission
to an event or begun to patronize an experience provider, customers find it

increasingly common to find a second and then a third tollgate where new fees have to be paid for additional events, experiences, and transformations—a graded series quite unlike Hans Gelter's. As experiences open up to new experiences and then to transformations, additional expenses open up as well—costs build as a natural function of the progression of economic values in which "each successive offering creates greater economic value."[77]

In the terms empirical researchers have been using, *Erfahrungen* are valuable not because they promote autonomy but because they allow the creation and sale of new, more expensive experiences. Goods-intensive experiences—skydiving, expensive vacations, driving around in one's Land Rover—are necessary, inevitably replacing more time-intensive pursuits: walking in the park, watching the sun set, singing in the choir.

In keeping with a tradition in economic thought that goes back to the nineteenth century, for the modern brander and value capturer, value is measured by income and profit rather than intangible changes in the customer.

Following Pine and Gilmore's lead, most people who have written about the new economies understand "value" primarily in economic rather than the individual or cultural terms. The business of leading customers to new, richer experiences involves, perforce, a pricing strategy "capturing the experiential value" that customers create. For businesses to survive and for the economy thrive, as experiences grow and improve, prices and profits must grow as well.[78]

The contrast between this strategy and the catalyst-enablers' plans could not be starker. The catalyst-enabler proposes to build customer skills and abilities so that the means of experience production reside more and more within the customer (prosumer) and pay off directly to him or her in the form of constantly improving experiences. For the brander, the means of production and the profit (the wealth) continue to belong to, and accrue to, the provider.

Indeed, for many in the experience economy and the transformation economy, commodification is inevitable—human experiences and individual transformations, now the frontiers of the economy, must eventually become the settled plantations of the marketplace, with regular cultivation and harvesting. The experience marketer Clifford Scott pointed to that ultimate destination, that blessed day to come when "you don't realize it's an experience until you pay for it."[79]

4

Consumerism and Its Critics

Warnings and a Novel Dialectic

For many observers, the experience and transformation economies have sinister implications—that more and more of the normal processes of life and enjoyment will be bought and sold in the market and subject to a price tag alarms many. Commodification, alienation, further enslavement, and the spread of false consciousness appear to threaten. Such tendencies of capitalism to colonize the lifeworld have often been identified as "consumerism."

A review of the origins and development of consumerism, however, reveals a more complex picture, views that are hopeful as well as alarming. The historical origin of "consumerism" corresponds to the virtual ending of the shorter-work-hours process in the United States and the rise of a new understanding of progress and the economy ("a new economic gospel of consumption"[1]), followed closely by the redirecting of technology in the 1920s and 1930s from the creation of laborsaving machines to the current focus on the creation of new work. The public debate about the evils of consumerism began (and the word was coined) when critics questioned these three developments. Condemnation of consumerism has continued since then, many of the same themes of alienation and enslavement reiterated with new language—for example, commodification—and now applied by critics to the experience and transformation economies.

Taking issue with such condemnations, a new and robust scholarship stream has emerged revealing the positive potential of consumerism. Consumer culture theory details the ways consumer goods contribute to liberation and the creation of healthy culture, community development, self-expression, and the representation and production of various identities: ethnic, gender, subcultural, and so on. Building on these new, more hopeful views, I end the chapter by outlining what E. P. Thompson called a "novel dialectic"[2] through which the free marketplace might become the place for liberation, a renaissance of the forgotten American dream, and a renewed demand for increasing free time. The eudaimonic technology might speed these possibilities as technology is again redirected, this time from the creation of work to the design of liberating experience and transformation products. To assist this redirection, Chapters 5 and 6 are devoted to providing a catalog of the discoveries of the new sciences of happiness that might form the knowledge base essential for the eudaimonic technology.

The debate about consumerism is modern, originating in the early twentieth century. The word with its modern connotations first appeared in the 1920s, a product of technological advances and the evolution of capitalism. Responding to the coming of abundance, to the increasing ability of technology and the market to meet traditional basic needs, business people, economists, and marketers began to look as never before to new goods and services to keep the economy growing. Immediately, critics bemoaned these developments and have continued to do so, for a variety of reasons, until the present. More recently, however, scholars and researchers in consumer culture theory, siding with traditional promoters, have come to the defense of consumerism, recognizing a growing economy's positive contributions to individual freedom, social engagement, and healthy cultural formation.

A historical account of this ninety-year debate about consumerism provides a perspective from which one may observe the development of a larger, "novel dialectic" growing from capitalism's contradictions, including consumerism, and the possible emergence of a "new synthesis" made possible by the experience and transformation economies as they begin to more fully realize the positive potential of consumerism revealed by consumer culture theory.[3]

Origins of Modern Consumerism and Its Critics: Herbert Hoover and the 1920s

The enshrinement of Full-Time, Full Employment in public policy and American politics during Roosevelt's second term (outlined in Chapter 1) followed the laying of its cultural foundation during the 1920s. Business's "new economic gospel of consumption" proclaimed then that the economy could and should grow eternally, founded on a new, "optional consumption"—on the promise that people would continue to work for and buy things they had never seen before, in perpetuity.[4] The new "gospel" was met by a chorus of doubters who inaugurated a critique of consumerism that has been repeated, with changes rung on its major themes, since then, the latest iteration being complaints about the coming of the experience and transformation economies.

Just after the stock market crash of November 1929, Herbert Hoover's administration tried to calm fears about chronic "technological unemployment."[5] Pessimists were claiming that overproduction was the bedrock cause of the nation's economic distress, arguing that in the new economy of abundance, when most basic human needs were being satisfied by industry as never before, the demand for additional products, and hence the supply of jobs, would continue to dry up. Unemployment, in a land of plenty, would grow as technology advanced, replacing more and more people with machines. Economic growth would slow down and perhaps even stall.[6]

Speculation about chronic overproduction had begun earlier in the 1920s, a product of the economic downturn that followed World War I. Hoover began his efforts to counter such pessimism as Warren G. Harding's secretary of commerce. His concerns about the importance of finding ways to increase consumption levels date back to that time. The historians Vincent H. Gaddis and Mary O. Furner write that for Hoover "the key to solving the depression of 1921, and later to restimulating growth in 1929–1933, was consumption."[7] As the Great Depression began, Hoover's Committee on Recent Economic Changes stressed the importance of the consumer: "The American people must be brought to realize that by restricting purchases to bare necessities at this time, they are further decreasing the volume of business and spreading the catastrophe they so attempt to avert."[8]

Hoover faced more than unreliable consumer spending, however. Hoover's catchphrase, "economic modernization," the hope that the economy could grow indefinitely after basic human needs were met, had also faced onslaught by respected economists. Economists had long theorized that capitalism's perpetual expansion was the result of something very like a law of nature (Jean-Baptiste Say's law); as soon as a new product was conceived and produced, it created its own demand upon entering the stream of commerce because it increased the total value of the marketplace (guaranteeing adequate demand) by the exact amount of its exchange price. A general glut (chronic overproduction) was impossible; eventually the market will find its bottom and clear.

Nevertheless, the centuries-old popular belief in a *finite* material necessity had raised the specter of diminishing utility and the likelihood of what John Stuart Mill called an economic "stationary state." Even while recognizing the possibility of the growth of luxuries beyond the limits of "reasonable" material needs, Mill condemned the prospect, hoping that humans would, by "abridging labour,"[9] turn instead to freely cultivating the arts of living in their growing leisure. Supposing that human material needs were set (or at least not infinite), many agreed with Mill that they could be gradually met as industry advanced.[10]

Toward the close of the nineteenth century, economists such as Carl Menger, William Stanley Jevons, and John Bates Clark reasoned that, behaving rationally, humans would naturally buy those products they most urgently needed first. As the economy grew and wages improved, they would then be able to buy things they did not need as much—things that provided them less and less utility. John Kenneth Galbraith observed that, according to such logic, "the effect of increasing affluence is to minimize the importance of economic goals."[11]

The importance of economic goals would decrease because, as productivity and wages increased, the utility gained by the purchase of new, less needed goods would naturally decline *in relation to* the effort, the disutility (work), needed to produce them. The prospect of diminishing marginal utility was a key marginalist concept, forcing the conclusion that the need and the desire to work long hours would naturally decline as the economy and technology advanced.[12]

A gradual reduction in working hours was occurring, and would inevitably continue, because time was becoming worth relatively more than the new, less needed products. Humans were naturally beginning to "buy" more of their lives back from their jobs in order to enjoy the new products they were able to purchase and to have more time for the best things of life that remained free. The human tendency to keep up with the Joneses, to buy things that others, better off, were buying, also applied to leisure; humans coveted the free time others had just as much as they did others' material belongings. The backward bending supply curve of labor, arguably the oldest predictive model in the history of economics, was given a new lease on life. Noting the "drastic" decline in the workweek from just under seventy hours in 1850 to forty hours in 1975, Galbraith explained, "This decline reflects a tacit but unmistakable acceptance of the declining marginal urgency of goods. There is no other explanation."[13]

Such predictions appeared to be coming true during the 1920s. The "threat of leisure" moved from the halls of academia into the arena of public debate.[14] The *New York Times* and other popular media reported that labor unions were intensifying their already successful campaign for the "progressive shortening of the hours of labor."[15] The predictions of people such as George Bernard Shaw, Julian Huxley, and John Maynard Keynes that by the end of the twentieth century the average person would be working only two or three hours a day were often heard. Few (or no one) doubted that the century-long reductions that cut working hours almost in half (a process that had speeded up during the first two decades of the century), would stop with the forty-hour week. During the first part of the 1920s, businesspeople conceded that increasing leisure was not just a theoretical threat but a reality they would have to live with, a realization that was responsible for part of the pessimism that plagued the business world during that time.[16]

By contrast, optimists' vision of progress had more to do with the advance of leisure than the multiplication of luxuries. At the heart of the American labor movement, from its beginnings, was the call for shorter working hours. Supporting that call was a vision of humane and moral progress, counter-weights to the unchecked growth of capitalism and its tendencies to exploit people and cheapen their dealings with each other. From the labor movement's formative years, articulate laborites, such as the mill girls at Lowell, Massachusetts, defended their increasing leisure as one way to counter capitalism's selfish system, lessen their exploitation, expand their collective power, and best of all, increase their own time, in which they might claim their full humanity: spending more of their lives forming healthy families and communities, increasing their knowledge of the world and each other, investigating and reveling in the wonders of the human imagination and spirit, negotiating their values and beliefs, forging agreement and conviviality, observing traditional practices and faiths, and widening their awareness and appreciation of God and his creation.[17]

This vision, issuing from working classes of this nation, was endorsed and elaborated by some of American's visionary elites. Walt Whitman called the vision "higher progress,"[18] and thought it the crown of America's political freedoms and economic success, without which neither accomplishment was complete. Through the decades, labor's supporters expanded on the notion of humane and moral progress, adding their own hopes for freedom beyond political strife and economic worries—Whitman's words were frequently recalled. By the 1920s, higher progress approached its apogee in American history. The popular press and business, trade, and professional journals were rife with predictions of the coming age of leisure, practically within reach because of labor's successes and technology's advance.

The Birth of Consumerism: From Luxury to Optional Consumption

In the face of declining utility and the threat, or promise, of steadily increasing leisure, modern consumerism was born; Hoover and his committees began their economic modernization project that would culminate in

Roosevelt's Full-Time, Full Employment policy initiatives.[19] Recognizing that faith in the centrality of work remained strong and that there were many who were appalled by predictions of a coming age of leisure, Hoover, business leaders, and economists, rejecting labor's "progressive shortening of the hours of labor," set out to redefine, justify, and promote "luxuries."[20]

The condemnation of luxuries, however, was centuries old—much older than the Protestant ethic's condemnation of leisure and idleness. By the nineteenth century, luxury had become a metaphor for all the other sins of the flesh.[21] Such condemnations were based on the belief that God, or Reason, established limits to what Max Weber called "the striving for worldly goods"[22]—boundaries that enclosed the economy's rightful place in the lives of humans. Beyond these boundaries lay a nonpecuniary existence, a "realm of freedom,"[23] in which humans might legitimately flourish. The marketplace was founded by and for individuals seeking their own advantage. Outside, lay the promise of mutuality, civility, virtue, and salvation—of free, humane, moral, and spiritual exchange and progress. As Max Weber explained, the "striving for worldly goods, as an *end in itself*, as an *ethical value*," separate from larger, more inclusive rational, religious, civic, and moral purposes, has been widely accepted only during the modern age in the industrial nations, coincident with, and arguably a primary cause of, the rise of modern capitalism.[24]

Luxury continued its negative association with wanton display well into the twentieth century. Laborites continued to identify luxuries with the wealthy and their exploitation of working people. Some early welfare economists agreed, reasoning that an economy that produced luxuries for a few before producing the necessities of life for all was patently immoral.[25] For many, luxuries remained the visible sign of the unjust expropriation of workers' honest toil. Thorstein Veblen's leisure class flaunted their greed, consuming luxuries conspicuously without having to work for them.

Certainly ordinary middle- and working-class people had begun to find the consumption of un-necessaries enjoyable enough, continuing to put in the work hours needed to buy new products such as coffee, tobacco, and the items that filled the Sears Roebuck catalog. However, what Hoover, business leaders, and economists of the 1920s would endeavor was not simply to make luxuries more morally palatable; they would found the future of their businesses and the American economy on this unlikely, long-rejected cornerstone.

The conversion of luxury into an economic virtue entailed a new understanding of necessity. Traditionally understood, "necessity" was something unavoidable, beyond choice and without which a person cannot exist—for example, breath, water, sleep. During the early years of the twentieth century, the limited, traditional view of "necessity" that led to predictions of declining utility and fears about overproduction gradually gave way to the *novel* concept of a relativized necessity[26]—of a new "necessity" that was the protean product of the market and social pressure rather than a dictate of nature. The belief that something that is unnecessary today (the standard for the traditional measure of luxury), might, or must, become a necessity tomorrow is modern. Relativized necessity undermined the traditional understanding of luxury. What was lost during the 1920s was the centuries-old yardstick, a stable necessity by which to measure luxury.[27]

Certainly, Hoover and his committees were influential during the decade. In large part, however, they followed the lead and reported the progress of American business and economists and their spreading of the new economic gospel of consumption.[28] In its 1929 report, Hoover's Committee on Recent Economic Changes found,

> from study of the fact-finding survey on which this report is based, that as a people we have become steadily less concerned about the primary needs—food, clothing, and shelter . . . and we now demand a broad list of goods and services which come under the category of . . . "optional purchases." . . . [The committee's] survey has proved conclusively what has long been held theoretically to be true, that wants are almost insatiable; that one want satisfied makes way for another. The conclusion is that economically we have a boundless field before us; that there are new wants which will make way endlessly for newer wants, as fast as they are satisfied. . . . By advertising and other promotional devices, by scientific fact finding . . . a measurable pull on production has been created which . . . furthers the organic balance of economic forces . . . it would seem that we can go on with increasing activity. . . . Our situation is fortunate, our momentum is remarkable.[29]

Since then, historians have confirmed what the Committee on Recent Economic Changes reported. During the 1920s, economists first began to concentrate on the *problem* of sustaining consumption at levels high enough to ensure robust economic growth, the focus of business attention shifted from production to marketing, and "the consumer [became] the likely savior of private enterprise in America."[30] America's executive elites arrived at a "new concept of distribution" and a "new economy of consumption."[31] Advertising helped "to convert . . . the culture . . . [from] the producer's culture into the consumer's culture."[32] Frederick Lewis Allen, arguably the best-known chronicler of the 1920s concluded, "Business had learned as never before the importance of the ultimate consumer. Unless he could be persuaded to buy and buy lavishly, the whole stream of six-cylinder cars, super helerodynes, cigarettes, rouge compacts, and electric ice boxes would be dammed up at its outlets."[33] Joseph Dorfman found that a new subfield in economics ("consumption economics") developed, an indication of the "general interest" in and "wide-spread discussion" of the "new aspects of consumer spending" among economists during the 1920s and the "almost complete . . . acceptance of the doctrine formerly considered radical, of the economy of high wages."[34]

Hoover and other boosters of the new economic gospel of consumption generally avoided using the word "luxury," preferring words with fewer negative connotations. Hoover's committee chose "optional consumption."[35] Some, such as the economist Constance Southworth, not only avoided using the word but also skirted the problems of declining utility and shortening work hours, musing uncritically instead (as would generations of economists that followed) about covetous human nature and "the limitless capacity of the common man to want things"—except more free time.[36]

Critics pointed out that Hoover and the economists on his committee were not simply reaffirming Say's law; they and the business world were taking a normative stance and recommending action. Struggling with what many were calling the problems of overproduction, technological unemployment, and the threat of leisure, American business, along with Hoover's committee, discovered the practical need to create needs (and demand) in order to sustain economic growth—to deliberately change the culture rather than rely on some law to automatically do it for them.[37] Say's law that a "product is no sooner created, than it, from that instant, affords a market for other products to the full extent of its own value" gave way before a century of determined advertisers working diligently, and spending countless billions of dollars, to ensure that the products they represented would be sold and before politicians promising "jobs, jobs, jobs."[38] Neither government nor business could sit idly by, but had to, and did, take action to achieve what Hoover called an "organic balance of economic forces" to ensure the economic demand necessary to support Roosevelt's Full-Time, Full Employment. Efforts to promote consumerism became the hallmark of the twentieth-century economy.[39]

The establishment of luxuries as the foundation of progress triggered a flurry of critical responses.[40] Two kinds of criticisms may be identified: the traditional, which held that luxuries obscured the truly valuable and virtuous parts of life and that a new kind of spurious progress was aborning, diverting individuals from their true happiness and the nation from its authentic destiny, and the newer, more radical, which held that the individuals and corporations that owned the means of production were using luxuries, advertising, and science (psychology and behavioral engineering) to control and manipulate consumers, creating unhealthy dependencies that enslaved the people—a cancer-like process that gradually replaced free, healthy human culture and experiences, which had joined people together in communities for millennia, with a cash nexus.

Origins of Consumerism's Critics: Traditionalists

Traditionalists repeated condemnations that had been heard for generations: luxuries were distractions, silly baubles that wasted life, effort, and attention. One of the most common accusatory words was "materialism." Many agreed with William Wordsworth that "getting and spending" was "lay[ing] waste our powers,"[41] powers that might be devoted to the things of the mind and spirit, and leading people away from virtuous living—from duty, civility, and conviviality. Suspicious of capitalism's new moral imperative that identified work and wealth as ends and values in and for themselves, such critics held other rational and traditional purposes constant. Assuming that work and wealth remained the means to more important and enduring ends, they promoted several such ends, often associating them with shorter working hours and believing that they were in a battle against modern, psychologically based marketing methods. Throughout the twentieth century, other verities, such as the natural environment, continued to challenge the modern work and wealth absolute, providing renewed bases for criticism of luxury and consumerism.

At the beginning of the process, in the 1920s and 1930s, people such as James Truslow Adams complained that science and technology had been redeployed, turned aside from freeing humans for better things and distracting the nation from its authentic destiny—from what Adams called, coining the phrase, the "American dream."[42] According to Adams, until the twentieth century that dream had a spiritual core focused on "a genuine individual search and striving for the abiding values of life": the "communal spiritual and intellectual life."[43] Stephen Leacock, anticipating critiques that would grow throughout the century, agreed that consumerism was perverting American and Canadian cultures to focus exclusively on "material values" and leading the nations in a vain pursuit of the "phantom of insatiable desires."[44] Edward Sapir noted that "genuine culture" that provided a "harmonious, balanced, and self-satisfactory" life and recognized the "spiritual primacy of the individual soul," was being sacrificed to commercialism, since "part of the time we are dray horses: the rest of the time we are listless consumers of goods which receive not the least impression of our personalities. . . . Our spiritual selves go hungry."[45]

One of the most prominent opponents of the new gospel of consumption was Monsignor John A. Ryan. Criticizing the Hoover Committee and its report, Ryan brought together various strands of the traditional resistance to the modern embrace of luxury. He recognized that at the heart of the committee's report was the "absurd tenet of capitalism that production for its own sake is the end of industrial society." He noted, "By suggestion and implication they [the committee] convey the idea that national prosperity and national welfare are dependent upon the indefinite expansion of human wants and the indefinite multiplication of luxuries." He rejected their claims that "wants are insatiable and one want satisfied makes room for another" and "that material prosperity is largely based on the limitless desire of humanity for pleasure and luxury, that no great prosperity can be based merely upon the satisfaction of the primary needs of food, clothing and shelter." Their gospel of consumption belied "industrial sanity, social well-being, and desirable human life." Ryan branded the committee's conclusions about "optional consumption" "loose" and its hopes for "boundless fields" for economic growth opened by "extravagant luxuries" wrongheaded. What Hoover and his committee were proposing was "not a moral foundation for progress." He concluded, "The members of the Committee are in line with our baneful tradition of Puritan industrial ethics . . . in their preoccupation with the conception of prosperity which logically implies a belief in production for its own sake . . . the urge for production and even greater production [is a] squirrel-cage." Humane and moral "ends" and transcendent purposes had been forgotten.[46]

For these traditionalists, Walt Whitman's higher progress was being sacrificed to Mammon, a modern incarnate demon embodying the spirit of capitalism: "The single-minded concern with striving for worldly goods, as an end in itself."[47] This was the traditional critique of the modern consumerism.

Origins of Consumerism's Critics, Part 2: The New Slavery

Together with the traditional, a new critique of capitalism emerged during the 1920s. As James Truslow Adams noted, from the colonial days hopes for progress in America centered on the advance of freedom from the chains of slavery and necessity. However, with the coming of the gospel of consumption, he and other critics recognized a retrograde development—new kinds of enslavement and manipulation were emerging and beginning to grow in the marketplace. Before "consumerism" became part of the language, Samuel Strauss, editor of the New York Globe, used (probably coined) the term "consumptionism." "What is happening today is without precedent," he wrote. No one predicted that there would arise a new "science of compelling men to use more and more things. Consumptionism is bringing it about that the American citizen's first importance to his country is . . . that of consumer."

This "new force" had gained "dominion over men."[48] Others, such as George Alger agreed with Ryan that the economy was becoming a "squirrel-cage" as advertisers created "needs" and, with them, "a new slavery."[49]

As Strauss reported, use of rudimentary psychological principles to sell goods and services began in the 1920s.[50] In response, Thorstein Veblen[51] updated his conspicuous consumption thesis, noting the advent of "technicians . . . experts and experimenters in applied psychology, with a workmanlike bent in the direction of what may be called creative psychiatry."[52] These technicians were no longer content to rely on humanity's basic instincts ["ubiquitous traits of the race"] to want new things and to mimic the wealthy. They had turned instead to using emotions such as fear and shame to sell products, in the process initiating a new science, "consumption engineering." Veblen observed, "Human credulity appears to be peculiarly tractable under the pressure of a well concealed appeal to fear and shame."[53]

Critics of Consumerism: The Continuing Tradition

Strauss and Veblen set the tone for critics through the twentieth century who believed that science had been corrupted to manipulate and control consumers.[54] Numerous writers have elaborated such claims, as have TV programs such as Public Broadcasting Service's *Affluenza* (1977), *The Merchants of Cool* (2001), and *The Persuaders* (2003). Likewise, Veblen's accusations that consumers' preferences are manipulated have been echoed and expanded by writers such as Pierre Bourdieu.[55] Arguably, the most influential examples are Vance Packard's *The Hidden Persuaders* and *The Waste Makers*—his books were best sellers in the 1950s and 1960s and were certainly a factor in the dramatic rise in the pejorative use of the word "consumerism."[56]

In the first paragraph of *The Hidden Persuaders*, Packard describes modern advertising's "large-scale efforts" and "impressive success." "Unthinking," we, the public, had been "manipulated . . . beneath our level of awareness." Using "insights gleaned from psychiatry and the other social sciences," corporations and Madison Avenue were "channeling . . . our thought processes."[57] Surreptitiously, advertising was altering American culture; "materialism" was now in "an overdeveloped stage" and "acquisition" had grown into a "hazard of major proportions."[58]

To back up his arguments, Packard quoted the well-known theologian Reinhold Niebuhr: "The productive power of our industry threatens to make our culture subordinate to our economy." Most Americans had "become so intermeshed with . . . consumption" that "they tend to gain their feelings of significance in life" from what they buy rather than from "their meditations, achievements, inquiries, personal worth, and service to others." The "merchants of discontent" were creating a "psychologically sick . . . society," spiritually and culturally "impoverished."⁵⁹

In his introduction to Packard's first book, Mark Crispin Miller summed up Packard's claims: advertising was no longer content to "persuade"; its minions were intent on replacing the consumer's will "with their own imperatives."⁶⁰

Agreeing with these condemnations of consumerism, some in the humanities and social sciences have described a broad-based change in the cultures of the industrial nations in response to capitalism's need to sell products—a change in values and beliefs that is enslaving rather than liberating citizens. At the change's inception during the 1920s and 1930s, such views were hardly radical. Indeed, people such as Ryan reflected widespread, traditional suspicions about luxury and mainstream reservations about the expansion of the economy into previously free realms of existence. Throughout the twentieth century and up until the present, however, such views have appeared as increasingly radical, a function, at least in part, of what Hannah Arendt called the "modern . . . glorification of labor" and the ideology of Full-Time, Full Employment.⁶¹

Critical theorists such as Theodor Adorno and Max Horkheimer argue, with Karl Marx, that capitalism's growth imperative (an integral part of the economic base) predetermines the host culture's response (superstructure). Faced with the never-ending need to find new markets and ensure a stable and tractable labor supply, capitalism produces beliefs and values, traditions and institutions—cultural products designed to nourish and reproduce the exploitative economic system. The results are cultural industries and passive citizens, responding with false consciousness to appeals to buy and continue to work full-time, meekly allowing the time and energy of their lives to be converted into wealth and power for the few and perpetuating the conditions in which their work is alienated. Workers had even begun to love the chains that were their jobs, having been persuaded by bourgeoisie propaganda. Worker spending had been scripted as part of fetish-driven rituals and their leisure reduced to passive entertainment and mindless consumerism.⁶²

Jürgen Habermas presents one of the most valuable modern critiques because he provides a historical context. With that context he keeps a cultural-narrative alternative alive that has been obscured, forgotten even by consumerism's critics. Habermas points to a fundamental historical change that he describes in various ways but in no terms more compelling than "the collapse of the public sphere."⁶³ Before the modern era, culture was most often homemade, the product of "communities of discourse" that produced language and sign, understanding and meaning on their own in active public exchanges.⁶⁴

Writing about classical cultures, he describes a time when along the Mediterranean "civility," "communicative discourse," "critical-rational discussions," "discursive space," and face-to-face critical reflection and interaction with others, with language, with public rituals, were common. He sees that heritage reviving more recently in the fledgling culture building that took place in bourgeois communities of eighteenth- and nineteenth-century Europe—in coffee-houses, salons, and *Tischgesellschaften*.[65] Jacques Rancière adds that even the working classes, in the little time they had off from work, began to create and participate in their own local subcultures.[66] During "those nights snatched from the normal round of work and repose," they formed their own communities of discourse in the midst of capitalism's rise, creating in the process a working-class identity, as well as a new national language of class in France during the nineteenth century.[67]

Habermas maintains that these "communities of discourse" have collapsed, however, replaced in the twentieth century by a superculture that is passively consumed by most of us, being produced or performed by an increasingly small elite. Writing about the transformation of "a public that made culture an object of critical debate into one that consumes it," he concludes, "No longer cultivation [*Bildung*] but rather consumption opens access to culture goods."[68]

Instead of publicly doing and performing, transmitting and transforming their culture autonomously, citizens of industrial societies have become passive and private consumers in what was once the place for the discovery of common purpose and meaning. Citizens who once, contending with each other in public about the good and just life, helped create a commons of symbols and interchange have given up and adopted a "general attitude of demand." The commodification and commercialization of culture systematically displaces "critical-rational discourse."[69]

Instrumental rationality overgrows other ways that humans know and experience the world and each other, deforming communicative, moral, and dramaturgical action.[70] Commercial agents, institutions, and corporations co-opt fundamental culture-creating experiences and roles. No healthy public emerges from these commodified venues, however. A phantom public has replaced active cultural performance, exchange, and production. The result is private alienation in a narcissistic society that demands that its needs be met, even cultural needs for meaning and communicative interaction—an impossible, contradictory expectation.

Habermas characterizes this change as the colonization of noneconomic aspirations, a conclusion that Andre Gorz reiterates. In *Critique of Economic Reason* (translation of *Metamorphoses du Travail*), Gorz explains that capitalism's claim that all human values may be represented in the marketplace and its resulting imperative to expand the "economic sphere" indefinitely into previously free realms of human experience is fundamentally exploitative. One of Gorz's central metaphors is prostitution, standing for the commercializing and thus deformation of free human associations, exchanges, and experiences. Many, perhaps most, authentic cultural goods cannot be drawn into the commercial arena without distorting them beyond recognition. The market- and workplace are epitomes of individual self-seeking, precluding all but the most rudimentary, convivial human exchanges. Quoting Habermas extensively, Gorz observes that unrestrained capitalism is always imperialistic. But even more dangerous than its traditional colonization of peoples and nations is the market's recent, tumorous spread over traditional culture, nature, and nonpecuniary human experiences.[71]

Whereas writers such as Ryan, Strauss, and Abba Silver[72] in the first part of the twentieth century feared that consumerism would prevent the advance of higher progress, as the century wore on critics such as Habermas and Gorz began to fear that progress was retrograding as more and more of free human experience, previously beyond the reach of the marketplace, was being commodified. Progress was no longer understood as the expansion of the lifeworld, as it was at the beginning of the twentieth century. Consumerism now threatened to engulf all of free humanity.

Consumerism and the Experience Economy: The Commodification of Culture

Jeremy Rifkin extends these kinds of critiques to the experience and transformation economies. Adapting parts of Adorno and Horkheimer's critical theory and Gorz's language, Rifkin describes Joseph Pine and James Gilmore's "progression of economic values"[73] as "the metamorphosis from industrial production to cultural capitalism." He argues that the experience economy and "the age of access" are "about, above all else, . . . the marketing of cultural resources including rituals, the arts, festivals, social movements, spiritual and fraternal activity, and civic engagement."[74]

Rifkin agrees with Pine and Gilmore about the growing importance of the experience economy:

> We are making the transition into what economists call an "experience" economy—a world in which each person's own life becomes, in effect, a commercial market. In business circles, the new operative term is the "lifetime value" (LTV) of the customer, the theoretical measure of how much a human being is worth if every moment of his or her life were to be commodified in one form or another in the

commercial sphere. In the new era, people purchase their very existence in small commercial segments.[75]

Rifkin claims, however, that the experience economy represents the unfortunate culmination of capitalism; its final victory in which the entire culture is captured and all human experiences and relations become part of commerce. Moreover, as traditional occupations succumb to technology, jobs are created to "service cultural needs and desires" of the wealthy, an antidemocratic retrogression comparable to the world of servants and lords of nineteenth-century Britain.[76] The experience economy exacerbates class divisions, allowing a few entry while denying most access to most cultural and experience products. He invites his reader to

> imagine a world where virtually every activity . . . is a paid-for experience, a world in which traditional reciprocal obligations and expectations—mediated by feelings of faith, empathy, and solidarity—are replaced by contractual relations in the form of paid memberships, subscriptions, admission charges, retainers, and fees.[77]

He continues, "In a hypercapitalist economy, . . . all time is commercial time. Cultural time wanes, leaving humanity only with commercial bonds to hold civilization together. This is the crisis of postmodernity.[78]

A new slavery emerges in which fewer and fewer people own more and more of human wealth (including the time of others). Value becomes one-dimensional, economic value with the cash nexus crowding out all other possibilities. Transnational corporations and media's control of human life becomes total; "instrumental rationality" reigns—no alternative is "reasonable" or even imaginable.[79] By controlling experiences and information, "marketers come to play the role that schools, churches, fraternal organizations, and neighborhood and civic institutions used to in interpreting, reproducing, and creating cultural expression."[80]

The natural environment is put in increasing jeopardy. As the motley cultural bonds that have connected humans to nature and to each another for millennia are replaced by commercial experiences and the ties of profit, "the very social foundations that give rise to commercial relations" are eroded.[81] The environmental and social costs are too great. Hypercapitalism is parasitic and hence not sustainable. Eventually, it will collapse with the exhaustion of the host environments, natural and cultural, on which it feeds; the logical result of one of the several contradictions harbored by capitalism.

Arguing that consumerism has hindered the development of the public sector and the formation of public goods and common values, Rifkin sees the remedy in visionary public policy. Stressing with Galbraith the importance of spending on education, Rifkin contends that governments must act to promote healthy, participatory kinds of cultural formation, using the new technologies to create free public spaces, cybernetworks, and common experiences to counter the worsening commodification of the lifeworld.[82] He concludes:

> Finding a sustainable way to preserve and enhance the rich cultural diversity that is the lifeblood of civilization in a global network economy increasingly based on paid access to commodified cultural experiences is one of the primary political tasks of the new century.[83]

Consumerism: Its Modern Defenders

Over the last thirty-five years or so, critiques of consumerism, such as Rifkin's, have been brought into question by the ascendancy of a new, robust scholarship focused on the culture-creating and individual-expressive function and potential of the free marketplace.[84] Questioning what they characterize as the overly broad, "totalizing" claims of the critics of consumerism, researchers have focused instead on the complexity—the "gray, meticulous, and patiently documentary" detail and "everydayness" of the subject.[85] Eric J. Arnould, for example, sees criticism of consumerism as having becoming "ritualized," observing that something very like a "cottage industry" developed in the late twentieth century "devoted to the proposition that consumers as consumers cannot escape their degraded condition as pawns in a marketing power game."[86] He concludes, however, that in light of recent scholarship, "anticonsumption ideology is anachronistic, class-based, and confused by the question of materiality."[87]

With Craig J. Thompson, Arnould describes the recent rise of an alternative body of research that has been variously labeled as relativist, postpositivist, interpretivist, humanistic, naturalistic, and postmodern.[88] The pair, attempting to find a more "appropriate and compelling brand," offer the term "consumer culture theory" (CCT) as a better representative of the "core theoretical interests and questions that define this research tradition."[89] Arguably, the salient characteristic of the new research stream, aside from its diversity, is an emphasis on consumer *agency*. Whereas the older, critical accounts assumed that consumers were straws in the winds of advertising, CCT and its "research tradition" has found active players with their own agendas, able to work their wills and purposes out in the marketplace, often to the chagrin of those who hoped to control and manipulate them—consumers' reclaiming of Classic Coke has become a favorite example. Postmodern writers have also pointed to a marketplace wherein individuals are able to re-create selves and shift identities. CCT updates and empirically validates the traditional case for the agentic consumer who, as Milton Friedman famously claimed, is enfranchised with the spending of each dollar.[90]

Accusing critics of consumerism of devaluing popular culture, preferring their own elite cultural agenda for the hapless masses, those in the CCT tradition argue that the modern consumer operates in a much more fragmented and egalitarian world in which choice, control, and freedom expand. The more products, the more choice. The more choice, the more freedom. Opportunities for self-expression and civic engagement grow with the economy, as do occasions to challenge the status quo. A diverse, democratic culture, distinguishable from both high and popular culture, emerges within the multiple consumer worlds wherein individuals find like-minded people. Communities and identities form and re-form. Self-expression, sharing, and cocreation are facilitated. Jürgen Habermas's lifeworld appears to stir within the marketplace—Arnould and others see the need to escape the market as obviated by such enfranchising of consumers.

Historians offer some of the best examples of the liberating possibilities of consumer markets and products, illustrating "the emancipatory potential" of expanding consumer choices.[91] They have reported in detail how communities of discourse have regularly formed as people interacted through the medium of commercial products—products that came to serve as symbolic vehicles for communicative action and shared meaning. Historians such as Kathy Peiss, Vicki Ruiz, Lizabeth Cohen, Randy McBee, and George Sanchez demonstrate that ethnic subcultures and racial identities have been maintained, expressed, and enhanced over the years by consumer products and commercial offerings: stock car racing, motorcycles, dance halls, saloons, and amusement parks.[92] Working-class identities have formed around such products and services as well; challenges to gender roles have been facilitated—indeed, modern concepts of freedom and equality have often become enmeshed with the purchase of consumer goods.[93]

Arnould, with others, claims that not only do "successful, progressive practices of citizenship" take place regularly "through market mediated forms in our culture"; they "should" continue and expand in a democracy "because these are the templates for action and understanding available to most people."[94] Market-mediated forms also offer the possibility of building what Robert Putnam calls "social capital" and facilitating political action.[95] Arnould offers the example of the recent rise of the fair trade movement. Michael Schudson agrees: "Not only are peoples' individual needs defined socially, but their individual needs include a need for social connection which is some-times expressed materially."[96] Pointing to an "emergent theory of consumers' co-creative competence," Eric Arnould, Linda Price, and Avinash Malshe conclude, "The dominant logic of marketing is shifting from a firm-centric view of value creation to one that examines how customers engage themselves in the value-creation process."[97] Such words are strongly reminiscent of those currently in use in the experience and transformation economies—words such as the catalyst-enablers' "prosumer" and "cocreation."[98]

A Novel Dialectic and a New Synthesis

My leisure studies classes at the University of Iowa have debated consumer-ism for years. Students who have been persuaded by CCT often point out to their classmates (and, I will admit, their instructor) who are critical of consumerism that if Pine and Gilmore are correct, the experience economy is inevitable and we had better learn how to compete if we want a better out-come. They often accuse critics in class of having nothing better to offer than the other academics on campus who are content to carp about alienation and exploitation from the secure sidelines of academia, in mostly incomprehen-sible language, but never offer a reasonable, real-world alternative.

The CCTists in class have demanded that we ground our criticism and, looking beyond the ivory tower, find effective ways to counter the coloni-zation of the lifeworld we fear. During in-class debates, a synthesis began to emerge first in the form of questions: Why not participate in the expe-rience economy, designing experiences that leisure studies has claimed for decades were superior and, aggressively marketing them, compete with the "unhealthy" forms offered by the "evil" corporations? As CCT suggests, if we do have a better product, we should have as good a chance as any in the free market. Leaving aside pecuniary incentives, if liberated, intrinsically moti-vated, active, engaged, and skillful leisure activities are healthier, sustainable, and more virtuous, do we not have a moral obligation to design and provide such superior products and try our best to find markets for them?

Indeed, Pine and Gilmore issue this very challenge: "We would hope that concern about the possible deleterious impact of certain [commercial] experi-ences . . . would prompt critics to enter the economic arena and offer more virtuous forms of these economic offerings."[99]

For decades I have had my classes read the British historian E. P. Thomp-son's brilliant essay "Time, Work-Discipline and Industrial Capitalism"; it is one of the classic leisure studies texts. I noticed that a quote from the essay seemed to fit the class debates perfectly:

If we are to have enlarged leisure, in an automated future, the problem is not "how are men going to be able to consume all these additional time-units of leisure?" but "what will be the *capacity for experience* of the men who have this undirected time to live?" If we maintain . . . a commodity-valuation, then it is a question of . . . how this time . . . is exploited by the leisure industries. But if the purposive notation of time-use becomes less compulsive, then men might have to re-learn some of the arts of living lost in the industrial revolution: how to fill the interstices of their days with enriched, more leisurely, personal and social relations. . . . And hence would stem *a novel dialectic* in which . . . the old industrialized nations seek to *rediscover [forgotten] modes of experience.*[100]

I had often speculated about Thompson's "novel dialectic" with my students. However, in the context of the class debates about the experience economy, a new understanding of his text emerged, growing from his use of "experience" and the possibilities opened by CCT. Thompson seemed to be summarizing our debate. What, indeed, will be our "capacity for experience" in our new "undirected time to live?" Thompson seemed to identify the two possibilities we were debating: exploitation by "the leisure industry" versus the relearning of "some of the arts of living lost in the industrial revolution."

In light of both Thompson's and Hannah Arendt's theoretical writings, my students and I began to interpret *novel dialectic* in this way: As Arendt (and many others, including Max Weber) observed, capitalism contains inherent contradictions. For example, the imperative to economize (for the owner class to maximize profit) by reducing labor costs inevitably results in the reduction in demand for labor and the growth of free time either as unemployment or shorter working hours (for the working classes). Through time, as machines and new production methods save labor costs, reductions in paid work time are juxtaposed against capitalism's need to propagandize work as life's center—necessary in order to maintain work discipline and ensure a cheap and tractable labor supply and consumer base. This class-founded contradiction, the inevitable freeing of time set against the "glorification of labor," suggests three possible outcomes: growing unemployment and alienation in a world where only work is meaningful and the maldistribution of wealth worsens (an unsustainable situation, which might resolve itself in the collapse of capitalism); ever more severe forms of "work discipline" and re-enslavement to new artificial forms of make-work and meaningless and unsatisfying consumerism, perpetually re-created by industry and government, and re-enslavement to the alienation and false consciousness that results from the leisure industry's thoroughgoing exploitation of existing free time; or Thompson's "novel dialectic" that preserves the liberation offered by *growing* free time and in new, "enriched" uses of leisure that transcend industrial capitalism's meaningless consumerism—a "new synthesis" that might include the recovery of preindustrial, convivial "modes of experience" that challenge what Arendt called the modern "glorification of labor."[101] This "new synthesis" might include the renaissance of the forgotten American dream: what James Truslow Adams called "a genuine individual search and striving for the abiding values of life . . . the communal spiritual and intellectual life."[102] We began calling these last possibilities liberation capitalism.

Some in my classes were quick to add that liberation capitalism cannot be a simple nostalgia-driven project, limited to possibilities from the past. They maintained that Thompson apparently agreed:

> Of course, no culture re-appears in the same form. If men are to meet both the demands of a highly-synchronized automated industry, and of greatly enlarged areas of "free time," they must somehow combine in *a new synthesis* elements of the old and of the new.[103]

With this theoretical ground established, we set about to find ways to realize Thompson's "new synthesis." Since Thompson was short on practical suggestions, we embarked on the project on our own, turning to the experience and transformation economies as possibilities. We began to explore ways to develop the new economies' potential to create autonomous, engaged, convivial, active, and skilled activities and experiences—thus grounding Thompson's hope that humans might "re-learn some of the arts of living lost in the industrial revolution."

Looking for ways to recruit the market's beneficial, liberating potential (suggested by CCT) in service to this "new synthesis," we also turned to the recent rise of the sciences of happiness. Together with the leisure services professions, scientific fields such as positive psychology and neurobiology have developed an array of new, healthy experiences that promote happiness and well-being but so far have offered them mainly through professional, clinical, academic, and therapeutic venues.

CCT suggests that businesses and entrepreneurs are in a position to adapt the scientific discoveries about healthy experiences to the marketplace, designing healthy experience products and offering them in competition with the leisure industries' passive, impersonal, and alienating experience products. Whereas throughout most of the twentieth century, critics accused psychologists of abetting consumerism, manipulating individuals, and debasing cultures, the new sciences of happiness may offer beneficial guidance: practical methods and models. We decided that the new sciences of happiness may be seen as preparing the way for Thompson's "new synthesis" achieved through the marketplace with the emergence of the experience and transformation economies.

Liberation capitalism became our answer to Pine and Gilmore's challenge "to enter the economic arena and offer more virtuous forms" of experience products.

The New Sciences of Happiness

A Catalog of Positive Psychology's Elements of Well-Being

Chapters 5 and 6 catalog the discoveries of the new sciences of happiness (positive psychology and positive neurobiology) that may be applied in a eudaimonic technology to the creation of experience and transformation products. Theoretical and historical topics are addressed as they support and clarify scientific discoveries about human flourishing. The Easterlin paradox is discussed. Inventories of positive subjective experiences (PSE) and positive individual traits (PIT) that are most closely correlated with well-being are presented. Such inventories are vital to guide practical design of experience and transformation products and advance eudaimonic technology.

Positive Psychology: "Drawn by the Future"

Martin Seligman writes that "a basic and implicit premise of positive psychology," setting it apart from "the heritage of social science and the history of psychology," is that "we are drawn by the future rather than just driven by the past."[1] Whereas this foundational premise may be, as Seligman observes, "directly contrary" to twentieth-century developments in the social sciences and psychology,[2] Mihaly Csikszentmihalyi and others recognize that it is in keeping with the long-standing belief in human progress that has characterized much of the Western world since the Enlightenment.[3]

During the nineteenth century and until World War I, progress seemed certain in the industrializing nations: scores of utopian novels were published;

public education expanded and with it the hope for reason's victory over superstition and ignorance; technology advanced, promising release from the chains of material necessity; constitutional democracies spread, promising the rule of law and protection of individuals against tyranny and exploitation. Reason seemed ascendant, and with reason would come liberty and the pursuit of happiness.

The succession of wars, the rise of totalitarian governments with their toxic ideologies, the growth of corporate power, and the rising threat to the environment during the twentieth century, however, shook faith in progress. Instead of the utopias of a happier age, dystopias became best sellers. The perfection of the machine gun during World War I signaled a reassessment of the promise of technology—reason seemed to have been turned from liberation to the creation of instruments of mass destruction and techniques of mass subjugation. The powerful seemed more likely to be corrupted by the power given them by technology; the masses impervious to the education that once promised to protect them against tyranny.

The discoveries of Darwin, Freud, and Marx cast additional shadows on optimistic claims about human mastery and freedom. Reason, agency, and autonomy were brought into question by new claims that the unconscious mind and libidinal drives controlled choice and action (Freud), and that the liberty promised by constitutional democracies were illusions fostered by the owner classes intent on enslaving the proletariat (Marx). Progress under the direction of human beings seemed an illusion as well in light of an overarching evolution determined by random natural selection without a final purpose or plan and certainly without regard for humans as exceptional creatures (Darwin). Psychology's twentieth-century focus on the things that go wrong with the human condition and its lack of concern with how humans might do better than simply cope were parts of what Csikszentmihalyi calls a larger, "dismal" twentieth-century worldview and its "discounting of human nature."[4]

Woody Allen might be selected the patron saint of that melancholy time; his remarks in his 1977 film *Annie Hall* captured something of the mood.[5] In a bookstore, he selects *The Denial of Death* for Annie to read. Written by Ernest Becker, the book was widely influential among social psychologists, explaining away human qualities such as self-esteem, creativity, and spirituality as the defensive products of a universal death anxiety. Allen (as Alvy Singer) remarks:

> I feel that life is divided into the horrible and the miserable. That's the two categories. The horrible are like, I don't know, terminal cases. . . . I don't know how they get through life. It's amazing to me. And the miserable is everyone else. So you should be thankful that you're miserable, because that's very lucky, to be miserable.[6]

Csikszentmihalyi argues that psychology, continuing to discount human agency and in search of pristine objectivity, neglected what he and others now see as the key to understanding human beings: "reflective consciousness"— the "awareness of oneself as a thinking and feeling entity separate from, yet connected to, other human beings" that is the origin of the interior, subjective world of aspirations, choice, values, beliefs, and virtues.[7]

It is the subjective world that draws humans to the future, imagines what is good and worth striving for, gives direction to individual lives and meaning to history, and thus defines progress. Hopes, fears, longings, and dreams emerge as strong a set of motives as basic biological drives. They become salient in the human experience.[8] Yet, as Csikszentmihalyi notes, psychologists held such "value issues" at arm's length, often "bann[ing them] because they could be open to mystification," discounting them because they are hard to measure and seemed entirely culturally relative ephemera.

Csikszentmihalyi concludes:

> Positive psychology was started, in part, as an attempt to redress this reigning [dismal] image of what it is to be human, by focusing attention on ideas and kinds of behavior that people had found desirable and valuable in most cultures. . . . We are about to change . . . our vision of the human condition from one of dismal pessimism to a vision that foregrounds what is good about women and men and provides ideas and processes that will nurture, cultivate, and increase what is good about us and our actions. And this change is likely to pay dividends in many areas of life, from the economy to the arts, and from politics to religion.[9]

After Virtue

Instead of a cacophony of unrelated, relative cultural values drawing humans to a multitude of futures predicted by cultural relativists, positive psychologists claim to have found harmony and agreement, recording them in a handbook, *Character Strengths and Virtues*.[10] This handbook is Christopher Peterson and Seligman's answer to the catalog of human ills in the standard *Diagnostic and Statistical Manual of Mental Disorders*.[11] While hinting at the possibility of universals or absolutes in the traditional sense,[12] the handbook does make an explicit claim to averages, what "most cultures" agree is "desirable and valuable" and what goods, goals, and traditions have best stood the test of time. Historically, the strengths and virtues listed in the handbook have most often given direction to the idea of progress and the pursuit of happiness, are most strongly predictive of the survival of a specific culture, and according to research over the last two decades, remain the variables most strongly correlated with human well-being.

Cultural consensus about what is good and worth striving for has a rational basis: it may be explained in scientific, evolutionary terms. Csikszentmihalyi argues that with the emergence of "reflective consciousness," perhaps an evolutionary product of adaptive changes in human brain anatomy but certainly a continuing function of ontogenetic development, the awareness of self as both separate from and connected to others begins a developmental process—a process in which a person, first aware of his or her individuality, recognizes, values, and pursues private identity and goals.

Freedom as autonomy is the first, arguably the quintessential, human value and project, ontogenetically and phylogenetically. Early in their development, becoming self-aware, individuals struggle to differentiate themselves from parents and others, pursuing their own identities and agendas. Circumstances, natural and cultural, conspire, preventing free action and differentiation, producing conflict and requiring negotiation. In healthy development, the struggle for autonomy leads to the recognition of and respect for other individuals and to the realization of how much individual self-interests depend on other people.[13]

Adapting a term Richard Dawkins coined,[14] Csikszentmihalyi calls "the idea of 'freedom'" and similar constructs "memes": human inventions similar to genes in that they guide behavior and are passed from generation to generation. He notes, "With reflective consciousness the meme of freedom was abstracted from experience, and so it became a powerful goal—a source of well-being when present but a source of psychological pain when absent." Whatever its larger ontological status, most assuredly freedom "exists psychologically" as a powerful individual motive and driver of history, nearly as powerful as coded genetic instructions.[15]

Like genes, memes are susceptible to environmental factors. Some are passed down through generations (are selected) because they enable their human carriers to survive, others do not and are discarded. Unlike genes, memes are the products of human history, culture, and choice. Humans have the unique ability among living things to guide their evolution toward an imagined, more desirable future: to progress. With the natural selection of genes, animals may survive. With the cultural selection of memes, humans may thrive. Csikszentmihalyi notes, "And human behavior, much as it owes to the instructions coded in genes, is also constantly following the instructions of memes such as freedom, love, honesty, and democracy, just to mention a few."[16] "Reflective consciousness" also entails the recognition of other humans who "have the same capacity to think and feel."[17] A cultural dynamic naturally emerges as individuals attempt to reconcile their freedom and self-interests with those of others, recognizing interdependencies and negotiating and integrating needs, identities, dependencies, values, and beliefs.

The individual goods of freedom, autonomy, competency, and recognition or distinction, contrasted with the social, integrative virtues of living convivially with others (such as love and honesty) constitute the warp and woof of historical and personal narratives, interweaving and inseparable. Explaining "why human beings *need* the virtues," the moral philosopher Alasdair MacIntyre concludes that all "dependent, rational animals" must live in accord with a set of "virtues of dependency" to "flourish." He explains:

> It is most often to others that we owe our survival, let alone our *flourishing.* . . . The virtues that we need, if we are to develop . . . into that of independent rational agents, and the virtues that we need, if we are to confront and respond to vulnerability and disability both in ourselves and in others, *belong to one and the same set of virtues,* the distinctive virtues of dependent rational animals.[18]

The interweaving of private values with collective goods shows human culture as a complex, open system. Like all such functioning systems, responding effectively to challenges and adapting to change, components (individuals) must be *differentiated* but at the same time cooperate together, *integrated* and interacting as separate parts of the larger system. The human community as a system is unique because part of its successful functioning is a responsiveness to the challenges of an imagined future (the ideas of freedom and progress) and an openness to the changes that result from being "drawn" by that future.[19]

Long before the appearance of positive psychology, Robert Hutchins offered a historian's explanation for why democratic cultures have in the past failed, and will always fail, without the practice of "social virtues" such as "justice, prudence, temperance and fortitude."[20] Without such virtues, and without character strengths such as tolerance, veracity, openness, attentiveness, responsibility, and mutuality, citizens have never been able to agree about the good and true and cooperate with each other in ways sufficient to build a democracy, sustain a free culture, and progress. Thus, given the universal desire for and the project toward freedom, the social virtues must be universal as well; it is not possible for them to be culturally relative because without them no free culture survives.[21]

Elements of Positive Subjective Experiences: Freedom

Freedom, autonomy, agency, and choice characterize the PSE that help define human flourishing—without them, few people report that they are happy.[22] Csikszentmihalyi speculates that freedom may have been the original meme, growing as an idea that unfolds through time, exhibiting new facets while continuing to perform the elementary function of individual differentiation. Over the last two decades, scientists have investigated one of those facets: intrinsic motivation.

Freedom as Intrinsic Motivation

One of leisure studies' main contributions to positive psychology was its early recognition of the importance of intrinsic motivation, what some in the field also have called "autotelic" or autonomous motivation.[23] Social psychologists researching and writing about leisure in the 1970s and 1980s, such as John Neulinger and Seppo Iso-Ahola, found strong correlations between well-being, enjoyment, health, and happiness and activities that were done more for their own sakes and less for a future reward.[24] The fun individuals experience in play has often been proposed as one of the best ways to describe the subjective experience of happiness.[25]

Social psychologists have also discovered that not having a choice and not being able to control, at least in part, what is happening to and around a person is a sure source of unhappiness. They have found strong correlations between, on the one hand, well-being, happiness, and enjoyment and, on the other, the perception of freedom, lack of constraints, and availability of choice. Assuming that "leisure is a state of being marked by [individual] freedom,"[26] they operationalize freedom—make it something they can measure—by simply asking people if they feel they are free and then looking for correlates to that perceived freedom. They found that one of the strongest predictors of perceived freedom was intrinsically rewarding experiences. They also discovered that adding extrinsic rewards to intrinsically valued experiences could transform them into something more like work—into activity done increasingly for some future reward rather than "for its own sake."[27] Their work anticipated Seligman's claim: "Positive psychology, as I intend it, is about what we choose for its own sake."[28]

Freedom as Self-Determination: Autonomy, Competence, and Relatedness

The work on intrinsic motivation also anticipated the development of self-determination theory, also a key feeder of the positive psychology stream. Leading theorists and researchers Richard Ryan and Edward Deci conclude, "Perhaps no single phenomena reflects the positive potential of human nature as much as intrinsic motivation, [or] the inherent tendency to seek out novelty and challenges, to extend and exercise one's capacities, to explore, and to learn."[29]

Building on the findings about intrinsic motivation,[30] Ryan and Deci focus on the importance of self-determination in general, an initiative that, for them and others, represents a "Copernican turn in empirical approaches to human motivation and behavior change":

> Our interest was not how motivation can be controlled from without [the previous emphasis among psychologists], but instead in how human motivation is functionally designed and experienced from within, as well as what forces facilitate, divert, or undermine that natural energy and direction.[31]

Reviewing the existing empirical research and inventorying the factors that enhance well-being and promote "healthy psychological development," they concluded that there are three "innate psychological needs": competence, autonomy, and relatedness.[32] Some claim these needs are universal and that human thriving fundamentally depends on satisfying them. We languish if they are unmet or thwarted.[33]

Noting that "competence is one of the most researched issues in psychology," and a core element in intrinsically motivated behavior, Ryan and Deci explain that the experience of mastery and the feeling of being in control—of being an active, skilled agent rather than a passive observer—energize the individual, promoting a sense of autonomy. Autonomy and relatedness are essential for the functioning of all complex systems and are basic principles of psychological health and individual well-being.[34]

Ryan and Deci agree with Csikszentmihalyi that the "innate psychological needs" for competence, autonomy, and relatedness are the result of human evolution that has selected qualities of curiosity, proactivity, and social engagement. Individual development, therefore, prefers "proactive," integrative experiences.[35] Being the spontaneous expressions of innate needs, such experiences are autonomously motivated and enjoyable—producing positive emotions similar to the satisfaction of primary physical needs (food, drink, sex).

Experiences that give expression to these three innate needs, however, have outcomes other than the enjoyment of the experience itself. While autotelic experiences are not primarily motived by extrinsic purposes, nevertheless they often build competency, yielding "enhanced self-motivation and mental health." In the absence of such experiences, "diminished motivation and well-being" frequently result. Moreover, autotelic experiences create memories that provide future pleasurable reflection.[36] However, such extrinsic results are fortuitous additions, improving the value of the autotelic experience while preserving its intrinsic core. As Neulinger and Iso-Ahola found early on, emphasizing the extrinsic by-products of an experience risks diminishing the crucial intrinsic motive.

Edward Deci and Maarten Vansteenkiste maintain that "the critical starting point for a true positive psychology is an active-organism meta-theory," consisting of three "*elements*" or assumptions: that (1) "human beings are inherently proactive" and (2) that they are "self-organizing *systems*" with (3) "an inherent tendency toward growth, development, and integrated functioning." However, these things "do not happen automatically." Wisdom, will, imagination, and competence are necessary to actualize these tendencies.[37] These claims also support Seligman's assertion that humans are drawn by the future.[38]

Humanistic Psychology

Humanistic psychology is arguably the earliest of the modern sources of positive psychology. Associated with the works of Carl Rogers and Abraham Maslow, humanistic psychology broke with the pessimism and reductionism of Sigmund Freud and the behaviorists early on, emphasizing the importance of subjective experiences, purpose, and freedom. Focusing on positive human *potential* and the role of choice in realizing that potential, humanistic psychology sounded several of what would become central themes in positive psychology.

Offering "a therapist's view of the good life" as a "fully functioning person," Carl Rogers pointed to the therapeutic benefits of an "actualizing tendency" he had observed in his patients. He reasoned that the *movement* toward potential (self-development) was key:

> It seems to me that the good life is not any fixed state. It is not, in my estimation, a state of virtue, or contentment, or nirvana, or happiness. It is not a condition in which the individual is adjusted, or fulfilled, or actualized. To use psychological terms, it is not a state of drive-reduction, or tension-reduction, or homeostasis.[39]

The good life is an ongoing process of coping with what life brings—responding to setbacks, welcoming change, celebrating positive events. With intention and experience, a person can expand the ability to cope, building the skills necessary to respond appropriately and adjust to challenges and difficulties. Rogers summed up such claims with one of his best-known quotes: "The good life is a process, not a state of being. It is a direction, not a destination."[40]

Understanding that "the good life . . . is the process of movement," Rogers offered several "characteristics" of that movement, the first of which was an "increasing openness to experience," "the polar opposite of defensiveness."[41] Rogers provided a guide to those wanting to understand what character traits may promote "the good life":

> The individual is becoming more able to listen to himself, to experience what is going on within himself. He is more open to his feelings of fear and discouragement and pain. He is also more open to his feelings of courage, and tenderness, and awe. He is free to live his feelings subjectively, as they exist in him, and also free to be aware of these feelings. He is more able fully to live the experiences of his organism rather than shutting them out of awareness.[42]

Broaden and Build

In a somewhat similar vein, Barbara Fredrickson offered her "broaden and build" theory of positive emotions from a social psychologist's perspective. She explains that autotelic experiences (particularly play) lead to the discovery of richer kinds of experiences. She explains that a positive emotion such as

> joy sparks the urge to play, interest sparks the urge to explore, contentment sparks the urge to savour and integrate, and love sparks a recurring cycle of each of these urges within safe, close relationships. . . . [P]ositive emotions promote discovery of novel and creative actions, ideas and social bonds, which in turn build that individual's personal resources . . . optimizing health and well-being.[43]

The Elements of Positive Subjective Experiences: PERMA

Refining his "authentic happiness theory,"[44] originally designed as a "theory of what humans choose," Seligman offered the "construct" of "well-being."[45] "Well-being . . . is essentially a theory of un-coerced choice, and its five elements comprise what free people will choose for their own sake."[46] Well-being's five "measurable elements" are positive emotions, engagement, relationships, meaning and purpose, and accomplishment. Seligman gives the list the acronym PERMA. These elements have been empirically tested and confirmed to correlate with life satisfaction and well-being, while their absence is predictive of low levels of these things.[47]

Positive Emotion

For decades, following the work of Paul Ekman, researchers included happiness as one of the six basic emotions: anger, disgust, fear, joy or happiness, sadness, and surprise. William Compton and Edward Hoffman concluded that "research concurs that enjoyment, or happiness, or joy is a basic emotion."[48] Following the procedure of Robert Plutchik, researchers have tended to divide the primary emotions, including joy or happiness, into either positive or negative categories (happiness and sadness forming one of four opposing pairs).[49] Daniel Schacter and colleagues observe that since the term "conveniently carries the notion of an affective state . . . , emotion can be defined as *a positive or negative experience that is associated with a particular pattern of physiological activity.*"[50] They add, "Any definition of emotion must include . . . the fact that emotional experiences are always good or bad."[51] Michel Cabanac agrees: "Emotion is any mental experience with high intensity and high hedonic content (pleasure/displeasure)."[52] Paul Wong and others question the duality, however, insisting that "positives and negatives often coexist" and that circumstances often determine whether a given emotion is experienced as positive or negative.[53]

In a similar vein, Seligman insists that intrinsic motivation (expressed in an activity "done for its own sake") rather than positive emotion is the one criterion that each of his five PERMA elements of PSE meets. Positive emotion is simply one of five *intrinsically motivated* elements of human well-being, not necessarily a characteristic of all. He explains that the "primary problem . . . with 'happiness' is . . . that it underexplains what we choose" for its own sake. Historically, "happiness . . . is not closely tied to . . . hedonics—feeling cheerful or merry."[54]

These sorts of considerations, common among other psychologists, prompted Stephen Joseph to conclude in 2015, "One of the key developments [in positive psychology] over the past 10 years has been the shift in emphasis from hedonistic well-being [individual gratification and positive emotion] to eudaimonic well-being" that includes a wider range of collective experiences and social virtues.[55] The hedonic concerns "me" and the fleeting present; the eudaimonic is about the social, enduring things that concern "us."[56]

Engagement

Seligman points out that engagement, the second element of PSE, is distinct from positive emotion, even its "opposite," and suggests that "flow" is the best way to understand engagement. "Flow," a term coined by Csikszentmihalyi, is the essence of the autotelic, often described by athletes as "being in the zone"—at one with an intense activity that concentrates attention and effort. Time seems to stop; feelings and mood are suspended. A sense of being taken beyond the self (ec-stacy) is often reported. Arguably, flow concentrates attention more than any other kind of experience.[57] However, memory performs a vital role as well, allowing one to assess, understand, and enjoy the experience after it is over. Seligman writes, "The [positive] subjective state for engagement is only retrospective."[58]

According to Csikszentmihalyi, humans approach the pinnacle of happiness in flow: for Seligman, they flourish. In flow, a person is *engaged* by a positive, challenging experience that calls forth the best of his or her abilities, making optimal use of their "signature strengths."[59] Such experiences naturally draw one to the future.

> The experience of flow can provide the impetus to growth. An activity is initially absorbing because its challenges match an individual's ability. With practice, skills improve; unless one then takes on new challenges, the activity becomes boring. To recover the state of flow . . . the individual must seek greater challenges.[60]

In addition to enjoyable memories, flow's other *unintended*, but nevertheless valuable result is the development of "an ever more complex relationship with the environment," a precondition for future flow experiences, protecting against the boredom of inadequate challenge—avoiding the trap of "been there, done that."[61] Moreover, the experience of flow as a positive state is widespread, maybe even universal, showing cross-cultural stable features.[62]

Positive Relationships

For decades, researchers have been validating the commonsense claim that the most enjoyable experiences are shared with other people.[63] Agreeing with Csikszentmihalyi, Seligman argues that something in our evolutionary makeup profoundly resonates with the experiences we share with others—such experiences are deeply satisfying and worthwhile in and for themselves.

Seligman explains that the human ability to live and cooperate in social groups most likely provided the evolutionary advantage needed for our species to survive and dominate the planet; other social animals, such as ants and dolphins, tend to dominate their environmental niches as well. He takes issue with the assumption that humans evolved primarily as individual toolmakers to better control and manipulate the natural environment.

Rather than evolving as selfish individual workers, Seligman suggests that humans have a "social brain"; we evolved as intelligent creatures of the hive rather than *Homo faber*. Social problem-solving, not the mastery of the natural environment and advances in technology, best explains human success. Citing prominent social and neuroscientists, Seligman makes the case for group evolution as contrasted with the evolution of individuals—the survival of the fittest. Rather than the selfish gene proposed by Richard Dawkins,[64] Seligman points to evolutionary advantages of cultural traits ("hive values," or virtues), such as love, compassion, teamwork, self-sacrifice, generosity— memes that facilitate conviviality.[65]

For Seligman such findings are compelling, leading to the conclusion, "The pursuit of relationships is a rock-bottom fundamental to human well-being," satisfying something as essential in our makeup as pleasure seeking, and therefore an element of our flourishing—a conclusion consistent with self-determination theory's claim that the expressions of innate social needs are intrinsically motivated and enjoyable.[66]

Meaning

Seligman defines meaning as the subjective experience of "belonging to and serving something that you believe is bigger than the self."[67] Michael Steger observes, "There is the greatest consensus around defining meaning in life as 'the extent to which people comprehend, make sense of, or see significance in their lives, accompanied by the degree to which they perceive themselves to have a purpose, mission, or overarching aim in life'" and that what they do might "transcend the ephemeral present."[68]

Just as with the other elements of PERMA, research has demonstrated that having a sense of meaning is strongly predictive of "higher subjective well-being"[69] and "more frequent and intense experiences of positive emotions and vitality."[70] People who tell researchers that their lives are more meaningful tend to say that they are more satisfied with their lives as well.[71] In short, "people living a meaningful life are very likely to be happier."[72]

Moreover, reporting the presence of meaning, people also tend to report fewer negative emotions—less "negative affect." Those with "high levels of meaning" experience less "negative depression and anxiety"; report fewer problems with suicidal thoughts, drugs, and workaholism; and have less need for therapy. Steger concludes, "Life without meaning would be merely a string of events."[73]

Researchers such as Steger have distinguished between having and seeking meaning.[74] Whereas there is little doubt that being secure and confident about the purpose of one's life correlates with well-being,[75] seeking meaning is more complex. There is some evidence that seeking meaning may have to do with insecurity, a sign of a troubled, unhappy soul looking for some way to make sense of his or her existence (e.g., Woody Allen). Such dysfunctional searches are related to "negative perceptions of self and circumstances," "lower well-being," and maladaptive behaviors (drugs, etc.).[76]

By contrast, other seekers display healthy signs of curiosity, openness to experiences, and engagement.[77] Whether the search for meaning is healthy or unhealthy varies from person to person and depends several factors. For some the search is "marked by a thoughtful openness to ideas about life."[78] For example, curiosity often leads to exploration of the world and thus is related to well-being.[79] One of the original and most influential positive psychology theorists, the Austrian neurologist and psychiatrist Victor Frankl, believed that the search for meaning most often has healthy outcomes; it builds on itself, developing skills and insights for individuals that lead to greater horizons of meaning, satisfaction, positive experiences and relationships, and hope. His "logotherapy" is founded on the therapeutic benefits of a continuing search for meaning.[80]

As with the other PERMA elements, psychologists come close to making a universal claim about human nature when they write about the search for meaning. Frankl wrote that the search for meaning (or the "will to meaning") is "the primary motivational force" in humans.[81] Citing various sources, Steger and colleagues agree: "Human beings have a strong desire to understand themselves and the world around them."[82] The Canadian clinical psychologist Paul P. T. Wong writes, "The human quest for meaning . . . has always been here, springing from the deepest yearnings of the human—a never ending quest."[83] Individuals vary, however, in the willingness or ability to respond to the urge—as with other elements of PERMA, will, imagination, competence, and purpose are important variables. Meaning is a lifelong challenge.

For Wong, meaning rather than "what free people will choose for their own sake," is "central" to the good life. Whereas Seligman and others count meaning as one of several intrinsically motivated elements of well-being, Wong sees happiness, achievement, relationship, and self-acceptance important primarily as sources of meaning. Understanding the will to meaning to be at the center of human motivation, Wong also questions the privileging of positive over negative emotions. Finding that "positives and negatives often coexist" and that the valence of emotions frequently depends on circumstances and outcomes, Wong maintains that, since negative emotions and states are inevitable, "our ability to achieve the good life depends on our efficacy in coping with stresses, misfortunes, and negative emotions." Accepting and coping with negative parts of living builds vital skill sets, what Wong calls "resilience"—one of what he maintains are the four pillars of positive psychology (along with virtue, meaning, and well-being).[84]

Psychologists' claims about the universality of meaning seeking have been supported by other disciplines. The well-known anthropologist Clifford Geertz concluded:

> The view of man as a symbolizing, conceptualizing, meaning-seeking animal . . . has become increasingly popular both in the social sciences and in philosophy. . . . The drive to make sense out of experience, to give it form and order, is evidently as real and as pressing as the more familiar biological needs.[85]

The will to meaning springs from something as elemental in our makeup as the desire for pleasure. It is autotelic and cannot be subsumed as a means in the service of other more fundament purposes.[86] Moreover, it is egalitarian, a challenge to all. Steger notes that "meaning is not a commodity, something to be selfishly hoarded or flaunted. Meaning is supposed to be shared." Whereas hedonia "is marked by self-centered interest in immediate gratification," eudaimonia "is marked by more collectively-oriented interest in enduring effort and contribution . . . hedonia and eudaimonia are distinguished by their emphasis on Me versus Us, and the fleeting versus the durable."[87]

Accomplishments

Responding to a critic of his authentic happiness theory, Seligman admitted that he had overlooked an element of well-being in his original formulation. The critic pointed out that "success and mastery"—winning, accomplishments, and achievement—were clearly among those things "people chose for their own sakes" and hence should be included as a fundamental autotelic motive.[88] Seligman agreed, remembering people who had devoted their lives to piling up fortunes only to give large chunks of them away when they were old. Such people are representative of countless others who demonstrate that it is not the wealth, success, or fame that drives them, but an autotelic "winning for winning's sake."[89] Like meaning, accomplishments appear to be valued apart from the other PERMA elements, such as positive relationships. Indeed, some, the accumulators, build their lives around winning and mastery of their worlds, sacrificing things that generally make people happy. However, accomplishments are not necessarily felt to be in conflict with other elements of PERMA. Accomplishment may even promote elements such as positive emotions (pride).

Empirical evidence supports Seligman's claims about accomplishments.[90] There are also similarities between Seligman's accomplishments and competence and one of self-determination theory's three innate psychological needs (the basic need to feel effectance and mastery). The relationship between competence and enhanced subjective well-being has strong empirical support.[91] Seligman acknowledges his debt to the concept of competence proposed by researchers such as Byron Campbell in the 1960s.

Before Campbell's proposal, one of the original competence theorists, Robert W. White, coined the term "effectance" in the late 1950s to describe what he recognized as a nearly universal drive to "explore and influence" the external world. The feeling of competence that comes from "the ability to interact effectively with the environment" is the "master reinforcer," differing from the satisfaction of biological needs (food, sex) in that it draws a person to the future—competence is "conducive to an exploratory and experimental attitude."[92]

Carol Ryff and Self-Acceptance

In the late 1980s and 1990s, Carol Ryff, noting "points of convergence" in the psychological literature around the "defining features of well-being," proposed a "synthetic model," the "key dimensions" of which were self-acceptance, positive relationships, autonomy, environmental mastery, purpose in life, and personal growth.[93] This model of the "dimensions," or "defining features" of well-being has been widely influential; Wong insists that her model, rather than Seligman's PERMA, "is the gold standard for measuring well-being."[94] Some may also prefer her enumeration of the "defining features" over Seligman's listing of the "elements" of PSE.

There is significant overlap between Ryff's and Seligman's models, however, including "positive relations" and "meaning/purpose." Ryff's model and self-determination theory agree about autonomy, relatedness, and competency. Some also see a similarity between Seligman's "accomplishments" and Ryff's "environmental mastery."[95] Ryff and Corey Keyes see this "defining feature" of well-being in a person who "has a sense of mastery and competence in managing the environment; controls complex array of external activities; makes effective use of surrounding opportunities; is able to choose or create contexts suitable to personal needs."[96]

Positive Subjective Experiences versus Positive Individual Traits

According to the *Character Strengths and Virtues* handbook, "Positive psychology focuses on three related topics: the study of positive subjective experiences, the study of positive individual traits, and the study of institutions that enable positive experiences and positive traits."[97] The findings and models described so far in this chapter, including self-determination theory and PERMA, are mostly concerned with the elements or defining features of PSE. However, there is some overlap with PIT. The research about PSE has clear applications to the experience economy in which the customer adds value to experiences. Similarly, PIT may be more applicable to the transformation economy in which the customer is the product. See Table 5.1.

Character Strengths and Virtues

Certainly, PSE and PIT are related. PSE depend on the development of the social integrative virtues (individual traits such as veracity and attentiveness). As Alasdair MacIntyre explains, "Dependent, rational animals," must cultivate the Thomistic "virtues of dependency" to flourish. For example, to be better able to incorporate a PERMA element such as positive relationship into an experience, individuals need to develop positive, convivial traits such as honesty.[98] Seligman explains that PIT "underpin all five elements [of PERMA]. . . . Deploying your highest [signature] strengths leads to more positive emotion, to more meaning, to more accomplishment, and to better relationships."[99] The handbook describes the relationship between PSE and PIT: Peterson and Seligman's "classification project addresses [PIT] and in so doing hopes to shed light on [PSE]."[100]

The handbook promises to be an invaluable resource for the experience and transformation economies. So far, those designing experience products have relied primarily on asking customers what they would like to experience or be. By contrast, Peterson and Seligman envision the development of an empirically based "science of human strengths" that would be a sure guide to the development of experience products. They make a start toward that science with the *Character Strengths and Virtues* handbook, positing a set of virtues and strengths "susceptible" to theoretical and observational correction; the "proof" of the list "will be in the science that develops around it," the eventual benefit, "the identification or even the deliberate creation of institutions that enable good character."[101]

Peterson and Seligman try to avoid traditional deontological, rule-based prescriptions in favor of an "aspirational classification," preferring a hypothetical "drawn by the future" approach that emphasizes "the why and how of good character." Instead of moral laws, they emphasize choice and responsibility, making the hypothetical case that if you want to experience the good life, the best evidence shows you should do (or be) x rather than y.[102]

Their tentative list is "grounded" in the perennial virtues most commonly endorsed by moral philosophers, religious thinkers, and traditional cultures around the world and include six "core categories" that emerge "consistently

TABLE 5.1 ELEMENTS OF POSITIVE SUBJECTIVE EXPERIENCES AND POSITIVE INDIVIDUAL TRAITS APPLICABLE TO THE EXPERIENCE ECONOMY (TEE) AND THE TRANSFORMATION ECONOMY (TTE)

Researcher	Elements of positive subjective experiences—value added (TEE)					Elements of positive subjective experiences and positive individual traits—value added: competence	Positive individual traits—value added: virtues (TTE)
	Hedonism	Engagement	Relationships	Meaning	Autonomy		
Seligman (PERMA)	Positive emotion	Engagement	Positive relationship	Meaning/purpose	Motivation/autonomy	Accomplishment/competence	Strengths and virtues; imagination
Ryan and Deci (self-determine theory)			Relatedness		Autonomy	Competence	
Ryff			Positive relationship	Purpose in life	Autonomy	Environmental mastery	Personal growth; self-acceptance
Rogers (humanistic psychology)				Movement toward potential	Autonomy		Increasing openness to experience
Maslow				Belonging		Esteem	Self-actualization; love/belonging
Fredrickson (broaden and build)	Positive emotion				Autonomy		
Schwartz	Stimulation/hedonism		Benevolence/conformity	Self-transcendence	Self-direction	Achievement/power/recognition	
Wong				Meaning			Resilience; social virtues
Peterson and Seligman (character strengths and virtues)							Core moral virtues: courage, justice, humanity, temperance, transcendence, and wisdom

Note: This is a tentative list. As Seligman and others note, such findings are preliminary; subject to empirical tests and verification. For the experience economy and the transformation economy, the test will be the free marketplace.

from historical surveys": *wisdom and knowledge, courage, humanity, justice, temperance,* and *transcendence.*[103]

These six form the more general, "upper level of abstraction," better suited, perhaps, to theory and philosophy. By contrast, the twenty-four second-order character strengths are more concrete, better suited for practical applications and research. Character strengths are the "psychological ingredients" of the six overarching virtues—the more familiar, pragmatic ways the virtues are displayed "in action." They are the available "routes to displaying one or another of the virtues."[104]

Peterson and Seligman associate each of the six virtues with its own set of character strengths. Character strengths that employ or build wisdom and knowledge are creativity, curiosity and open-mindedness, love of learning, and perspective. Strengths that require courage to realize worthwhile objectives in the face of obstacles, external or internal, are bravery, perseverance, integrity, and vitality. Strengths that represent convivial skills important for the practice of our shared humanity are love, kindness and generosity, and social intelligence. Civic strengths vital for a healthy community and state (justice) are teamwork, fairness, and leadership. Strengths important in the practice of moderation (temperance) are forgiveness and mercy, humility, prudence, and self-regulation. Strengths that engage with and grow connections to a larger reality and that provide a sense of belonging, meaning, and transcendence are appreciation of beauty, gratitude, hope, humor, and spirituality.

Trying to winnow the large number of character strengths received from various traditions and influential thinkers around the world, Peterson and Seligman establish ten criteria. To be included in their list, a "positive characteristic" must satisfy "most" of the ten. They employ what may be understood as a simple qualitative analysis of their data—the "many dozens of character strengths" they had collected. They searched for central tendencies in this data set—for features most often shared by the "candidate strengths." The resultant ten criteria, taken together, form a kind of "family resemblance" that is sufficient to recognize the twenty-four character strengths that most favor each other.[105]

Their criteria are revealing. The first three promise to be as valuable a guide for experience product design as the actual list of character strengths.

Criterion 1: "A strength contributes to various fulfillments that constitute the good life, for oneself and for others."[106] With this criterion, Peterson and Seligman suggest that the most important of all transformations is the building of what has traditionally been called character. Just as an athlete builds an excellent physique with proper exercise, virtuous character is formed by the habitual practice of one's signature strengths.[107] The more opportunities for their expression provided by schools, therapists, professionals, or the marketplace, the better. Repetition predisposes a person to exercise his or her strengths and become increasingly prone to choosing those experiences in which most humans flourish. Both the possession (the pride of ownership and sense of identity) and the habitual exercise of signature character strengths are invigorating and intrinsically enjoyable, producing fulfillment in what the Greeks called *Eudaimonia* and providing a superior way to understand happiness and define the well-being.

The opposite is also true. One may become increasingly vicious by allowing defective, selfish kinds of action to become habitual, paying the price of having a predilection to make poor choices about what values to express in action.

Criterion 2: "Although strengths can and do produce desirable outcomes, each strength is morally valued in its own right."[108] Whereas Peterson and Seligman recognize that the character strengths often produce valuable social and economic outcomes, these results are not the primary reason for putting values into action. Just as with intrinsically motivated experiences, character strengths are worthwhile in and for themselves, both in their possession and in their employment. Virtue is its own reward. The many positive extrinsic results may be fulfilling but do not subordinate the exercise of character strengths as a means to other ends. The "sense of ownership and authenticity" are a delight, invigorating in themselves.

Criterion 3: "The display of a strength by one person does not diminish other people in the vicinity."[109] Peterson and Seligman suggest that character strengths are democratic and egalitarian. They are not only the epitome of free individual choice and practice; they are available to everyone. In the political and economic realms, freedom and equality often collide. A free economy is likely to produce economic inequality. Regulating an economy to better ensure a level playing field often constricts the freedom of some to seek their own economic advantage. However, in the civic arena formed by the exercise of character strengths, freedom and equality more often agree. Instead of coveting another's experience, "onlookers are elevated by their observation of virtuous action. Admiration is created more than jealousy because character strengths are the sorts of characteristics to which most can—and do—aspire." Similar to the playing of non-zero-sum games, "all are winners when someone acts in accordance with his or her strengths and virtue." Peterson and Seligman recognize that this criterion might be controversial but look ahead to empirical research to validate this claim.[110]

Sources of Unhappiness: Competence and Comparisons

Notable for its absence in the *Character Strengths and Virtues* handbook's list of character strengths is competence and achievement—among the most prominent of the individual motives and values and sources of PSE recognized by other researchers. (See Table 7.1 in Chapter 7.)

Ryan and Deci write:

> Competence is one of the most researched issues in psychology and is widely seen as a core element in motivated actions. In SDT [self-determination theory], competence refers to our basic need to feel effectance and mastery. . . . The need for competence is evident as an inherent striving, manifested in curiosity, manipulation, and a wide range of epistemic motives.[111]

Arguably, competence and achievement meet most of the handbook's criteria. It certainly satisfies criteria one and two—that the strength leads to fulfilling results and is also satisfying "in its own right." Moreover, throughout the handbook, competence in individual character strengths is often stressed as important. However, research has shown that this "core element" of human motivation[112] presents problems for Peterson and Seligman's criterion three. Ryan and Deci note:

> Competence is . . . readily thwarted. It wanes in contexts in which challenges are too difficult, negative feedback is pervasive, or feelings of mastery and effectiveness are diminished or undermined by interpersonal factors such as person focused criticism and *social comparisons*.[113]

The impulse to competence and accomplishments, in the intrinsic form that Seligman describes as "winning for winning's sake,"[114] has a downside, the agony of defeat—the opposite of a win-win situation.

Achievements versus Power

Shalom H. Schwartz has explored the ways that basic personal values and motives produce unhappy results (depressive affects)[115] as well as satisfactions (or subjective well-being). Claiming that "there is a universal organization of human motivations,"[116] he proposes "ten basic personal values that are recognized across cultures." Making an evolutionary argument similar to Seligman and Csikszentmihalyi's, Schwartz writes:

> These values are likely to be universal because they are grounded in one or more of three universal requirements of human existence with which they help to cope. These requirements are needs of individuals

as biological organisms, requisites of coordinated social interaction, and survival and welfare needs of groups.[117]

Entailing necessary goals, these universal values are "linked inextricably to affect . . . [and] infused with feeling," ranging from despair to euphoria.[118]

Two of the most interesting and researched of Schwartz's ten values are *achievement* ("personal success through demonstrating competence according to social standards") and *power* ("social status and prestige, control or dominance over people and resources"). Whereas both values spring from a more fundamental desire for positive social regard and recognition (what the Greeks called *thymos*), the desire for achievement is satisfied by convivial interpersonal dealings, but power aims toward "the attainment or preservation of a dominant position."[119]

A good deal of research from the "healthy values perspective"[120] has shown that achievement as the expression of the intrinsic, relational values promotes subjective well-being, while power as the expression of extrinsic values such as the esteem, admiration, and praise of other people often works in the opposite direction: focusing attention on extrinsic rewards, emphasizing social comparisons, and eliciting negative reactions from others.[121]

The Easterlin Paradox

One of the best-known and most controversial findings shedding light on how social comparisons affect well-being and life satisfaction is the Easterlin paradox. In 1974, Richard Easterlin claimed to show that, even though most people in some countries tended to be happier when their incomes increased, that was not true over time and across the nations of the world.[122] Whereas increases in annual gross domestic product were associated with increased happiness measures in developing countries, the same was not true for the wealthier nations—hence the paradox. For example, in the United States, income and GDP increased from 1946 to 1970, but measures of the nation's happiness did not, actually declining from 1960 to 1970.

Ed Diener and Seligman wrote in 2004 that even though "economic output has risen steeply over the past decades" there had been little or no improvement in "life satisfaction" in the industrial nations. Instead, depression and distrust had increased.[123] Economists such as John Kenneth Galbraith have explained for over a century and a half that utility (happiness) declines with the increasing consumption of specific products (Gossen's first law of diminishing marginal utility).[124] More recently, Diener, Seligman, and others have offered a similar, psychological explanation for the Easterlin paradox. When basic necessities are scarce during a nation's early development, increasing incomes are more likely to mean increasing happiness. However, when basic necessities are readily available, additional purchases and income provide less satisfaction (their utility declines, as economists have repeatedly claimed), and people are more likely to turn from concerns about money to "social relationships" and other extraeconomic sources of subjective well-being. Diener and Seligman propose, "As societies grow wealthy . . . differences in well-being are less frequently due to income, and are more frequently due to factors such as social relationships and enjoyment at work."[125]

Writing for the *Financial Times*, Andrew Oswald confirms that research by psychologists and economists continues to show that "the hippies were right all along"—that "once a country has filled its larders there is no point . . . becoming richer."[126] Politicians still assume that economic growth automatically means a happier populace. However, this conventional wisdom is belied by the industrial nations of the world like the United States having seen little or no increase in the overall happiness of their citizens over recent periods (since the late 1940s) of sustained economic growth.[127] Thomas Gilovich and Amit Kumar conclude that we still "live in a consumerist society in which large increases in wealth have not brought corresponding increases in well-being."[128]

One of the main reasons offered for this seeming anomaly is social comparisons. Psychologists have shown that the improvements in subjective well-being associated with our increasing incomes may be offset by the people around us being better off financially as well.[129] Moreover, rising incomes prompt rising expectations. We find ourselves on what psychologists have called a "hedonic treadmill,"[130] on which we have to keep running in place just to stay even with others and our own expectations, never getting ahead. Research continues to show "that having rich neighbors is associated with *reduced levels of subjective well-being, an effect that is likely due to social comparison*," particularly in nations with greater levels of income inequality.[131] F. Cheung and R. E. Lucas find that,

> although the association between income and life satisfaction is robust, the . . . evidence also suggests that absolute levels of income may not always drive the association. Instead, *relative income*—whether a person has more or less income than others—may be at least as important as, if not more important than, absolute income when predicting life satisfaction.[132]

While generating a good deal of press and public interest, the Easterlin paradox remains controversial. For example, Betsey Stevenson and Justin Wolfers have found for both individuals and countries "a clear positive link between average levels of subjective well-being and GDP per capita across countries, and find no evidence of a satiation point beyond which wealthier countries have no further increases in subjective well-being."[133] Stevenson and Wolfers conclude that their findings "indicate a clear role for absolute income and a more limited role for relative income comparisons in determining happiness."[134] On the other hand, Edsel Beja found that "income growth has very little impact in terms of increasing happiness over the long term."[135]

Even though the Easterlin paradox remains controversial, the search for reasons other than social comparisons that higher incomes may or may not be associated with higher levels of subjective well-being has spawned valuable research about spending patterns, intrinsic values, and beliefs as they relate to subjective well-being—research that may prove valuable in understanding the growing new markets for experience products.[136]

Extrinsic Goals and Materialistic Values

Yannis Georgellis, Nicholas Tsitsianis, and Ya Ping Yin also examine the "weak correlation between income and happiness."[137] They find that in addition to social comparisons, extrinsic goals and materialistic values often act "as mitigating factors."[138] "Being materialistic," having an orientation toward extrinsic goals such as recognition, wealth, and power, can offset gains in well-being usually associated with increasing incomes. On the other hand, being less materialistic improves well-being. They find:

> Being materialistic exerts a negative effect on life satisfaction. Materialistic individuals, valuing extrinsic more than intrinsic rewards, are generally less satisfied with their lives than those who believe that it is important to obtain respect from others or to be creative.[139]

Tim Kasser and colleagues confirm such claims. They report that whereas "intrinsic aims in life are . . . associated with higher levels of personal need satisfaction and well-being," materialistic values and goals, depending more on extrinsic satisfactions, are associated with "decreases in well-being."[140] Thomas C. Mann and Thomas Gilovich noted that a "vast literature" has confirmed that "approaching things from an extrinsic perspective tends to diminish the satisfaction they provide."[141]

Researching materialistic goals and orientations, Andrea Gaggioli and colleagues conclude, "Research findings have highlighted that people's well-being improves as they place relatively less importance on materialistic goals and values . . . over time."[142] Helga Dittmar and colleagues concur that materialism, defined as the "prioritizing of money and associated aims," is negatively associated with individuals' well-being.[143] Moreover, this "negative association is robust over a number of demographic, participant, and cultural factors." They suggest that there is something "inherent" in materialism that interferes with individuals' health and happiness and note that a "variety of spiritual and religious traditions . . . have questioned the value of materialism since the beginning of recorded history." In accord with these traditions, and in line with the recommendations of other psychologists, they recommend the enactment of public policies that reduce the cultural "endorsement of materialistic values."[144]

Todd Kashdan and William Breen attempt to explain the inverse relation between materialism and well-being. Their research confirms that people with stronger materialistic values are more susceptible to psychopathology, less concerned with the welfare of others, and report "more negative emotions." They also exhibit fewer dimensions of emotional well-being: relatedness, autonomy, competence, gratitude, and meaning in life. Kashdan and Breen hypothesize that "experiential avoidance" might be a reason for this phenomenon. Defining experiential avoidance as the reluctance to experience negative thoughts, feelings, and physical discomfort, they found that such reluctance inhibits the "movement toward intrinsically valued directions in life." Experiential avoidance also encourages the pursuit of extrinsic values and rewards, the hallmarks of materialism and recipe for reduced well-being, relatedness, autonomy, and so on.[145]

Alternatives to Social Comparisons and Materialistic Values

Experiential Purchases Tend to Make People Happier than Material Purchases

Exploring why "materialism leads to diminished well-being"[146] and adding to the "extensive literature" showing that prioritizing "the pursuit of money" (having "a monetizing mindset") is inimical to life satisfaction,[147] researchers have investigated whether the purchase of experiences is a better option.[148] The result has been an impressive and growing body of research showing that people find "more satisfaction,"[149] "greater well-being,"[150] and more "happiness"[151] from money spent on experiences than they do from the purchase of material goods, and the feelings last longer.[152] While satisfaction with material purchases tends to decrease over time, satisfaction with experiential purchases tends to *increase.*[153] Gilovich and Kumar offer "robust evidence" that spending money on experiences provide greater and longer lasting "hedonic benefits" than spending money on material purchases.[154]

Searching for reasons why experiential purchases make people happier, researchers have agreed that three fundamental psychological processes are salient: social comparisons, positive social connections, and personal identity.[155] Arguably the most important reason found so far is social comparisons. Whereas comparisons are often a source of unhappiness when people amass wealth or purchase material goods, they have less negative influence when experiences are bought.[156] Experiences "spark less intense social comparisons,"[157] tend to be enjoyed more "on their own terms,"[158] lead to "increased vitality,"[159] and "are less prone to hedonic adaptation."[160]

Supporting these claims, psychologists have done exemplary research showing that when offered the choice between a world in which they earned $50,000 while others made $25,000 and a world in which they made $100,000 while others made $200,000, most people chose the former. By contrast, offered a world in which they had two weeks' vacation while others had only one, and a world in which they had only four weeks' vacation but others had eight, most chose the latter.[161]

Moreover, in game-theory terms, buying material goods more often produces a win-lose situation; buying experiences, more often a win-win.[162] Experiential purchases also tend to promote positive social interactions and connections. In contrast to when they purchase material goods, people report that they feel *more* connected to others who made a similar experiential purchase, even though the purchase others made was better or more expensive than their own.[163] Experiential purchases are also more often an occasion to share in conversation. Mann and Gilovich write:

> When people learn that they and another person have had the same experience, they feel more kinship toward that person than when they learn that they have purchased the same material good. . . . [Their] interactions tend to be experienced by both parties as more rewarding.[164]

A preference for purchasing experiences is also associated with "higher extraversion, openness, [and] empathic concern."[165] Guided by self-development theory, Jia Wei Zhang, Ryan Howell, and Peter Caprariello find that spending on experiences for intrinsic reasons is associated with greater autonomy, competence, relatedness, flourishing, and vitality.[166] Gilovich and Kumar conclude:

> It appears, then, that the enhanced sense of social connection that experiential purchases provide is both broad and deep. . . . The feelings of social connectedness prompted by experiential consumption

appear to make it easier to get in touch with the better angels of our nature.[167]

Finally, "experiences tend to be more closely associated with the self than possessions."[168] Even though people may identify with and be "heavily invested psychologically" in the things they own, nevertheless, material purchases are "out there," separate from the self. By contrast, experiential purchases are "in here," becoming "quite literally" part of the essential self. "To a notable degree, people are defined, by themselves and by others, by what they have done."[169] Life experiences become part of the very fabric of our being; "they are woven into our memories and shape our identity."[170] Carter and Gilovich observe, "Because our experiences become our memories, they are more truly a part of the self than are possessions. . . . Satisfaction with material purchases tends to decrease over time, whereas satisfaction with experiential purchases tends to increase."[171]

By contrast, Kashdan and Breen point out that experience avoidance, discussed earlier, is "conceptually related to Roy Baumeister's . . . escape from self theory."[172]

Certainly, materialistic individuals tend to evaluate their own worth and the worth of others in terms of the acquisition of wealth and possessions. For some, the thought of buying and having more and better things may be fused with the self. Such individuals pay a price for their materialism, living their lives "amidst continuous evaluative judgments," constantly aware of what they do not have, alienated from the experiences that would truly satisfy them—having no time for, interest in, or ability to enjoy the present, intrinsic joys of life.[173]

Given psychologists' numerous claims about universal needs and values (human essence), it is reasonable to conclude that to be materialistic and money minded is to be alienated from the authentic self and its authentic, experiential needs.

Buying Time

Building on their findings about material versus experiential purchases, psychologists have joined economists in trying to understand how the two scarcest of human resources, time and money, are (or should be) economized. They have investigated the different ways people think about and experience the two, how subjective well-being is influenced by the ways that people spend one or the other, the trade-offs they make between them, and the results of people focusing attention on one or the other.[174]

In general they have concluded that, whereas "people who value having more time over having more money report greater happiness,"[175] those who put money and the accumulation of material goods first typically report lower subjective well-being. Researchers also provide evidence that "prioritizing time versus money" as a habitual or stable preference is related to greater subjective well-being over time.[176]

Researchers explain that people think about time and money in vastly different ways. Unlike money, time cannot be borrowed or saved. Whereas each moment is unique, money is interchangeable (fungible). Accordingly, people are "more averse to the risk of losing or wasting their time than their money." However, money is easier to count and keep track of—more tangible. Time is more ambiguous. Consequently, people have difficulty, and less interest, in keeping track of how time is spent or how much of it is invested in any particular activity.[177]

The little and inconclusive but suggestive research that has been done on the subject suggests that people prefer to spend their time rather than their money on experiences: "Consumers show a relative preference to pay in money for utilitarian purchases and in time for hedonic purchases."[178] This finding provides an important new insight into the economics of the leisure-time versus work-time choice.

The reasons psychologists have found to explain why valuing time over money is associated with greater subjective well-being are similar to those discovered about material versus experiential purchases. Expenditures of time have more to do with personal identity—people more often report that how they spend their time reflects who they are more than how they spend their money.[179] Life stories are more often about how a person spent time. As the author Annie Dillard observes, "How we spend our days is, of course, how we spend our lives."[180] Moreover, spending time rather than money more often produces more positive social interactions and connections: "The time spent connecting with others tends to be the happiest part of most people's day."[181] Furthermore, social comparisons are less troubling. If our neighbor takes more time off work or retires earlier than we do, most of us will offer congratulations (see the above research example comparing incomes and vacations).

To analyze how people think about time versus money, researchers have employed a creative strategy. Theorizing that by "activating time (vs. money)"—that is, by "merely mentioning time vs. money" to subjects—changes might be observed in their happiness and even how they viewed products. Once they were "thinking about time (vs. money)," individuals reported "increase[d] feelings of personal connection [to a product]," which led to general approval. Quite simply, "People . . . like products more when they think about the time they have spent with that product vs. the money they have spent."[182]

Moreover, when thinking about money, people value personal connections less. By contrast, thinking about time predisposes a person to prioritize social connections[183] and to "socialize more and to work less,"[184] a finding consistent with the claim that consumers prefer to pay for experiences with time.

What Consumers Should Buy: Experiences, Leisure, Relationships, Savoring, Meaning

Extrapolating from their findings, researchers have made sumptuary judgments, giving suggestions about how consumers *should* spend their time and money in ways that will make them happier—suggestions that should prove to be a gold mine for advertisers responsible for marketing in the experience and transformation economies.[185]

Reviewing the research up to 2017 to determine how best to "advise people how they *should* spend their time to maximize subjective well-being," Cassie Mogilner, Ashley Whillans, and Michael Norton recommend, perhaps facetiously, that people "*should* consider spending more time engaging in activities that elicit positive versus negative moods."[186] They also point out some other rather obvious facts: leisure activities are more liable to promote positive emotions than work or commuting. But they go on to note that the kind of leisure is important; active leisure (volunteering, socializing) is more strongly associated with positive emotions than passive leisure (watching TV, relaxing).

Expanding their advice about "happier ways to spend time," Mogilner, Whillans, and Norton suggest cultivating social connections, helping others, increasing the variety of activities and experiences, paying attention to and savoring the present, and "extracting meaning from time." Their advice about how to spend money includes spending on others, buying experiences, and buying time.[187] As is true for the buying of experiences, there is a wealth of research showing that altruism is not only a universal value but also one of the surest paths to happiness.[188] The link between well-being and charitable giving and prosocial behavior is well established and stable worldwide.[189]

Psychologists also have investigated the frequency versus intensity of positive experiences, finding that regular, moderate feelings of subjective well-being produces greater overall well-being than occasional, more intense positive experiences. They conclude that "frequency is actually more important than intensity."[190]

Heeding psychologists' advice, marketers in the experience and transformation economies should be able to compete confidently in the marketplace, convincing customers to spend their time and money in ways they *should*— buying experience products that research proves really do make them happy. Such findings may be the harbinger of a new kind of legitimate, psychologically based advertising that might replace the empty and often misleading promises, the ballyhoo, of some of the older forms critics such as Vance Packard condemned.

Motivating Consumers to Buy What They Should

Researchers' findings about ways to "motivate consumers to choose to spend their money on experiences over material goods—thus bringing them greater happiness" will also be of obvious interest to marketers in the experience and transformation economies.[191] Mogilner and Jennifer Aaker recommend that simply prompting consumers to think about time (versus money) motivates them "to choose to spend their money on experiences over material goods," adding that *in general*, it "may be better" to think more about time rather than money. They call the application of such research findings to the marketplace an "important next step."[192]

Researchers have used interventions in their research that marketers interested in taking this next step might adopt. They have used verbal and visual cues about time; asked subjects to remember, talk, and write about things such as gratitude; and used activities and training programs to attempt some form of cognitive restructuring, a primary goal of advertisers for nearly a century. The following is a selective list of the most common interventions.

- Focusing attention on time (versus money)[193]
- Focusing attention on time spent on the experience product (savoring)
- Guided reflection on purchases (memory augmentation)
- Mindfulness interventions (the most researched topic) such as yoga
- Strength-based interventions (identification and application of signature strengths)
- Affect-based interventions
- Gratitude interventions[194]

What Consumers Should Buy: Time

With economists, psychologists realize that people often face a choice between time and money.[195] Over the last decade, they have taken note of an emerging body of research that has explored the trade-off and evaluated the relative happiness benefits of choosing the one over the other.[196] A. V. Whillans,

A. C. Weidman, and E. W. Dunn find that "valuing time over money" is strongly related to subjective well-being. Moreover, they find that students who prioritize time over money are more likely to favor occupations that provide more time off, while adults with similar preferences worked fewer hours. They explain that the preference for time may be associated with increased happiness because people who chose time are freer to experience intrinsically rewarding activities such as socializing and exercising.[197]

Whillans asks a question economists have been exploring for centuries: "When attempting to maximize well-being, what should people do: give up money to have more time or give up time to have more money?" As an economist would, she presents the choice as mutually exclusive, assuming that "taking more time for oneself . . . often comes at the expense of having less money and earning more money often cuts into free time." But whereas economists assume that the choices people make in the marketplace to sell their time (by working) are mostly rational and reveal the relative utility (the happiness) experienced by the consumer from having more time versus more money, Whillans examined "whether and how trading discretionary income to have more free time promotes happiness."[198]

Theorizing that the "trade-offs people make between time and money shapes happiness," she proposes that by paying others to do routine or unpleasant chores for them during their time off work, people with discretionary incomes will be happier—a hypothesis that she answers in the affirmative with some solid research.[199] She also confirms that "people who report valuing time over money are more likely to buy time."[200] Extrapolating from her findings, she hints at broader applications: "The question of whether using money to buy time can promote happiness is therefore likely to be relevant for a broad range of the population."[201]

Relevant indeed. For over a century, academics, labor unions, and businesspeople have been concerned with the trade-off between work and leisure. However, they have focused their attention on the length of workday, workweek, work year, and work life, assuming that more leisure means less work and money.[202] So far, psychologists have not followed economists or historians in more thoroughly exploring the work-time versus leisure-time choice. Psychological research has, however, provided important ways to enrich the broader study. Whillans's narrow sumptuary advice to people with discretionary incomes that they would be happier "transform[ing] their cents into more enjoyable seconds," hiring others to do unpleasant weekend work ("scrubbing . . . toilets") for them, may apply to the broader economy when employees with discretionary income but with unrewarding and unpleasant jobs, perhaps even a few janitors and maids, heed the solid, research-based advice about how best to spend their money and lives and choose to work less.[203]

6

The New Sciences of Happiness

Positive Neuroscience—More Catalogs and Models

This chapter continues Chapter 5's cataloging of the findings of the new sciences of happiness that may be applied by the eudaimonic technology in the marketplace. Focusing on positive neuroscience, this chapter investigates what Daniel Siegel calls a "key mechanism" underlying the elements of positive subjective experiences and positive individual traits at the heart of human happiness.[1] Systems theory is discussed because it reveals the critical function of this key mechanism: differentiation and integration. Various strategies are reviewed that allow individuals to more effectively differentiate and integrate the elements of their world and more successfully respond and adapt to changes, avoiding the dysfunctions of chaos and rigidity. Neuroplasticity and the ability of the human mind to change the brain, envisioning and choosing to progress toward well-being, are also discussed. Ways to construct a technology that goes beyond simple happiness (positive emotion) to include richer kinds of experiences that realize the eudaimonic potential of the new sciences of happiness are reviewed. A play model or method is proposed that will help realize this potential, from the bottom up, by guiding the design of experience and transformation products that provide the positive emotion of play (making them, therefore, more successful in the marketplace) but also build toward the elements outlined by the *Character Strengths and Virtues* handbook.[2] Other models that may be used for experience design are reviewed.

Positive Neuroscience—the Neuroscience of Happiness

Positive psychologists pioneered the study of well-being and emphasized the importance of time, experience, memory, and meaning. Their work is reinforced by the findings of researchers in other disciplines. The sciences of happiness have made "parallel findings"[3] about human well-being, displaying what Gardiner Morse called "intersecting interests."[4] Daniel Siegel suggests that such findings and interests represent a consilience, a significant convergence of theories and research results.[5] He describes a broad interdisciplinary field of inquiry that gathers and synthesizes these parallel findings in the sciences of happiness that are open to a variety of ways of knowing about the world: the arts, humanities, contemplative and spiritual practices, and the wisdom of received traditions. Such an open forum would be the place to reveal more general, synthetic "principles" that represent a deeper understanding of "reality, the human mind, and well-being."[6] With the founding of interpersonal neurobiology, Siegel has continued this ongoing open process.[7]

Positive psychology and neurobiology lead the way in this consilience, this "jumping together" of theories and research about well-being.[8] Whereas psychologists have had significant success identifying the elements (the empirical features) composing positive subjective experiences and positive individual traits, "positive neuroscience"[9] has made advances in the investigation of the "neuroanatomy of pleasure"[10] and the "neural mechanisms of human flourishing."[11] From the different perspectives of their disciplines, psychologists and neuroscientists have identified correlates of positive emotions (hedonics) and well-being (eudaimonics) and their sources.

Daniel Siegel provides a solid foundation for a neurobiological approach to well-being with his careful definition of mind and description of a "healthy mind." He defines the mind as "a relational and embodied process that regulates the flow of energy and information."[12] Taking a systems approach to understanding the mind, he explains that mind has components that form an open and complex system. The embodied part of mind is a complex system in itself, including the three-tiered brain of the spinal column, cranial nerves, and clusters of neurons around the heart and the gut. But mind is also an *open* system, processing and regulating the energy and information received by the embodied brain as sensory data from outside (the relational component).

Whereas positive psychology has been able to determine many "empirical features"[13] of well-being such as gratitude, compassion, open-mindedness, and curiosity, Siegel claims that "integration is the key mechanism beneath both the absence of illness and the presence of well-being. Integration—the linkage of differentiated elements of a system—illuminates a direct pathway toward health."[14] He concludes, "Eudaimonic well-being is perhaps closest to how interpersonal neurobiology views integration as health."[15]

Integration requites differentiation—each component of the system knowing its place and doing its job and performing its unique function. In a healthy system, the differentiated parts relate, integrating and functioning harmoniously. Siegel illustrates the harmony metaphor this way: Imagine a group of singers, undifferentiated, singing the same note. Rigidity—no music, no harmony. Imagine the singers, differentiated (soprano, alto, etc.) but not integrated, singing whatever comes to mind. Chaos, dissonance. Imagine the singers, differentiated, singing the parts of the same music together, integrated. Harmony, health.

In addition to harmonious internal coherence, the mind's health is also a function of its ability to respond and adapt. Since the mind is an open system (having a relational component), it must deal with external input that it cannot control or predict with certainty. Having to respond to unpredictable input, open systems are particularly susceptible to chaos and rigidity—irrational or random reaction and the shutting down of function. An open system's well-being depends on resilience: the ability to respond appropriately and reliably to external and internal changes. The danger lies in reaction: the reflexive, inappropriate, or destructive response to new challenges. Well-being also depends on adaptability: the ability to learn skills that help a person adjust more efficiently to an open environment and to become resilient.

To avoid dysfunction (chaos and rigidity), the mind, like all complex and open systems, must be *flexible*, able to *adapt* to change and outside challenges, yet remain *coherent*. A healthy mind is also *energized* and *stable* as it processes and regulates energy and information. Like Martin Seligman, Siegel is a lover of acronyms, and he suggests FACES (flexible, adaptive, coherent, energized, stable) as a way to remember his recipe for well-being.

Like other very complex systems, the mind is also self-regulating. It not only has the capacity to monitor itself but can regulate and modify how it responds and adapts. In contrast to the determinism of a previous gloomy age, one of the most important discoveries of the sciences of happiness is that humans have the capacity to control how they respond, not only to external challenges but also to what is going on inside them.

Siegel suggests the term "mindsight" for a strategy to achieve and maintain well-being by monitoring and modifying. He uses the image of a "wheel of awareness" to illustrate mindsight.[16] Well-being depends first on being aware, able to effectively *monitor* what is happening inside and outside. Agreeing with psychologists, neurobiologists emphasize how much well-being depends on attention, of being awake and present, of being mindful. Well-being also depends on the ability to respond, being able to *modify* impulsive, counterproductive reactions. Unlike other animals, humans have a well-developed prefrontal cortex with a midregion executive perfectly positioned in proximity to the two lower parts of the brain, designed to monitor what is happening inside and out and to modify how the system responds.[17]

Neuroplasticity

Not only are humans able to choose how they respond to immediate stimuli. They are also able to modify how they are likely to respond in the future. Arguably, neuroplasticity and self-regulation are among the main reasons for saying the new findings of neurobiology are positive and for identifying a neurobiology of happiness. Before the 1960s, most researchers agreed that the brain grew and changed as it developed in childhood but afterward remained static, unchanging except for deterioration during later stages of life.[18] The discovery of neuroplasticity, that the mind and brain continue to develop and grow (as well as decline) throughout a lifetime, has sparked hope and optimism.

Siegel defines neuroplasticity as the "capacity for creating new neural connections and growing new neurons in response to experience."[19] He expands his original definition of mind to include this claim: Mind is an embodied and relational *emergent* process that regulates the flow of energy and information.[20] Rick Hanson explains that the brain "takes its shape from what the mind rests upon."[21] What scientists term "experience-dependent neuroplasticity" has recently been a "hot area of research" among neuroscientists.[22] Hanson concludes that "rewiring"[23] the brain, "hardwiring happiness," is now widely recognized as realistic.[24]

Claiming that the mind can change the brain, Siegel explains that by focusing awareness we are able to regulate the mind's flow of energy and information.[25] As we focus on the things we are experiencing, consciously managing our response and remaining levelheaded, neural pathways are activated—our brains are alive with energy and information. The better we become in our ability manage our responses to people and events around us, the better our mental health: "Interpersonal integration stimulates internal integration."[26] Just as muscles of the body are strengthened by exercise, neural pathways are strengthened with use and by positive experiences.[27]

Siegel offers another acronym, SNAG, for this phenomenon: attention to experience "*s*timulates *n*euronal *a*ctivation and *g*rowth" in interconnected neurons.[28] "Neurons that fire together, wire together" is a widely used aphorism for this process.[29] In addition to creating cells (neurogenesis) and building new "neural pathways" (synaptogenesis), neuroplasticity also involves myelinogenesis (the formation of insulating sheaths along neural circuits that greatly improve their function) and epigenesis, a "process by which experiences impact the regulation of gene expression."[30]

With some notable exceptions, all the cells in a human being have the same DNA sequences. Why muscle cells and brain cells are different is due to epigenesis (changes to the genome that involve function but not changes in the nucleotide sequence). Differentiating, cells turn on (express, or activate) or off (inhibit) genes by using chemical markers such as histones along the chromosomes. Siegel suggests that experience and the focus of attention can control how cells are expressed in the brain. Since "experiences alter the way genes are expressed" they have the potential to integrate all the various components of the mind/physical brain.[31]

Metaregulation: The Emerging Mind

The discovery that over time people are able to reprogram how they habitually respond and adapt to experience suggests that the human mind may be unique as an *emerging* system. Unlike other complex systems, mind has the capacity to metaregulate—to regulate how it regulates itself. Recognizing that coherence, controlled response, and adaptation are related to well-being (and survival), and recognizing that chaos and rigidity inhibit function (are maladaptive) and are unpleasant in and of themselves, individuals have the capacity to choose not only to modify (regulate) their immediate behavior but to change the underlying neuromechanisms responsible for behavior they would like to avoid.

As Mihaly Csikszentmihalyi suggests, the mind can even go beyond the desire to become a smooth-running, efficient machine, concerned with mere adaptation and survival. Humans are free to initiate change for better things—to flourish. They can and have dreamed, imagining what might be, fixing in mind an ideal that draws them and others toward the future, giving themselves and others good reasons to regulate what they do—motives that may become as strong as instinctual drives. Csikszentmihalyi suggests freedom as one such metaregulating meme. Peterson and Seligman's list of character strengths and traditional virtues in their *Character Strengths and Virtues* handbook is an encyclopedia of metaregulation possibilities.

Experience: Application and Design

Even though "experience-dependent neuroplasticity"[32] is an important neurobiological construct, a careful definition of "experience" is hard to find in the literature. Siegel comes close with the "flow of energy and information" part of his definition of mind. However, this definition is much too broad to be of practical use. Siegel offers some examples of positive experiences: the subjective experiences of awareness, knowing, and memory and educational and sensory experiences. He also provides a more useful list of specifics, suggesting that a "healthy mind platter" consists of "seven daily essential mental activities to optimize brain matter and create well-being," including such experiences as play, aerobic exercise, restful sleep, positive relationships, self-reflection, novelty, and humor.[33] Along with positive psychologists, both Siegel and Hanson emphasize the importance of paying attention: being present in the moment, savoring it, and remembering the good things that happen.[34]

Discussing "ways to create good experiences," Hanson also offers useful advice: being aware of the physical self, "softening" (opening up to new experiences), having positive thoughts, being kind to oneself, caring about and wishing for good things to happen to other people, "finding good facts" in your life, and having pleasant memories.[35]

So far, however, the new sciences of happiness have focused largely on word-based, top-down applications of their findings, delivered in clinical settings, counseling offices, and classrooms. Self-help, do-it-yourself happiness handbooks have proliferated. Even conservative, empirical-minded scientists such as Seligman and Siegel have published books designed for nonscientists, written as practical guides for individuals to use and for professionals in other fields, even the humanities and social sciences.

At the beginnings of the new science of happiness, Martin Seligman and Mihaly Csikszentmihalyi summed up its purpose as the "scientific understanding and effective interventions to build thriving individuals, families, and communities," purposes now shared by neuroscientists.[36] The new sciences have broadened their scope somewhat, emphasizing the importance of public policy initiatives, government programs, and public facilities; establishing new institutes; and finding funding from public grants and private donors. But so far they have not advanced far beyond the delivery forms used for older, therapeutic purposes.

With important exceptions, the new sciences have largely avoided the free marketplace. They have yet to thoroughly explore non-word-based interventions and have yet to imagine ways to design experiences that rely more on bottom-up processes and are more suitable for commercial purposes. Certainly, many of the ways that the new sciences of happiness have intervened in people's lives over the first two decades of the twenty-first century may be included as important parts of the experience economy and the transformation economy. Counseling sessions, seminars, online curricula, and self-help books have commercial dimensions.

However, critics see books about mindfulness such as *Buddha's Brain*[37] as appealing too much to the lotus-eaters among us: a narrow segment of the population, upscale and educated. To appeal to a broader, more diverse customer base, it is necessary to design experiences that depend less on words and more on enjoyable experiences. As Seligman suggests with his PERMA list (recall from Chapter 5: positive emotions, engagement, relationships, meaning and purpose, and accomplishment), it is also vital that the experience product is as intrinsically motivated as possible. A barrier to the marketplace also exists because word-based and directed experiences tend to emphasize extrinsic payoffs, still following the old therapeutic model: "You ought to have (or buy) these kinds of experiences for your own good and well-being." The brain's executive is still very much in control of things. Often, such experiences look a good deal like work.

Mark Twain remarked that for some "wildcat religions" heaven was a place to "pro-gress, pro-gress, pro-gress—study, study, study, all the time— and if this isn't hell I don't know what is."[38] Many of us, weary of self-improvement, interested primarily in diversion and a good time, might agree about the hellishness of perpetual self-improvement and positive thinking.

For the sciences of happiness to found a new experience technology, capable of producing abundant and cheap experience products competitive in the marketplace, some way must be found to bypass the traditional top-down methods of delivery. Experiences that depend less on the guidance of professionals and the discipline and direction of the executive brain and that are more spontaneous and immediately enjoyable in and for themselves must be developed.

To compete, experience designers must find ways to emphasize and amplify both the positive emotions (hedonics) and the intrinsic motivation associated with an experience. In a competitive marketplace, the promises of immediate enjoyment have generally been more successful than assurances about long-term gains. Enlarging the immediate enjoyment of an experience product, however, cannot be done at the expense of its eudaimonic potential. A new eudaimonic technology will succeed only if the hedonics of new experience products are somehow tied to eudaimonic development. Otherwise, the experience and transformation economies increase the risks of exploiting consumers and commodifying human life even further.

Sugarcoating important but difficult learning experiences has a venerable tradition. Plato advised that all lessons for children be as play-like as possible. The same advice applied to adults when it came to teaching them the liberal arts and philosophy—Socrates advised the strategy of "luring the soul" to the Good and True with playful experiences (e.g., the *Symposium* banquet and Socrates's word games).[39] Experiential education is a more recent example of using enjoyable experiences to teach.[40] Today, researchers and practitioners in travel and tourism are again leading the way, designing enjoyable commercial experiences that include the building of skills and competencies—that transform individuals. Some maintain that *"Erfahrung* . . . is at the core of the 'transformation economy.'"[41] Their theoretical formulations and research demonstrate how *Erlebnis*, a simple enjoyable experience, may be improved by adding an *Erfahrung* component (a learning experience), beginning an important "transformational learning process,"[42] a chain in which subsequent *Erlebnisse* are enriched, providing access to even finer *Erfahrungen*.[43]

Play: "Liberat[ion] . . . from Top-Down Processing"

Neurobiologists' findings about play offer some of the most exciting possibilities for commercial experience-product design, providing a valuable theoretical foundation for the *Erlebnis-Erfahrung*, bottom-up chain. Siegel observes, "Play can be seen to liberate us from top-down processing."[44]

Play is a fundamental human experience, an experience atom. A number of prominent twentieth-century writers agree with Eugen Fink that play neither is "derived from any other manifestation of life" nor has "necessary antecedents or results."[45] With Fink, Johan Huizinga and others understand that not only is play worthwhile in itself; it creates its own meaning—it is meaningful on its own terms. Play is experienced more as the source than the object of meaning.[46] Meaning is created within the context of play—the playground.[47]

Neurobiologists have arrived at similar conclusions. For Jaak Panksepp, play is "a core, genetically established system that . . . has to be engaged, not something built from experience." It is "a primal social-engagement process . . . fundamental for the emergence of social cooperation and friendships."[48] Siegel writes, "Play is an innate, primary emotional drive . . . it is a fundamental part of life for us as mammals."[49]

The subcortical origin of play is key to neurobiologists' definition and understanding. Panksepp and Siegel define play as "an innate, primary emotional drive," one of seven "primal emotional systems" (seeking, rage, fear, lust, care, panic, and play) that "correlate to activity in the subcortical region." Moreover, play is "an experience expectant process," overlapping with and reinforced by seeking, the most primitive of drives common to most life forms. Play is also exceptional because of its uniquely "joyous" affect.[50] Theresa Kestly observes that play is one of the "major brain sources of joy."[51] Philosophers have long understood play to be the epitome of human felicity. For Eugen Fink, play is the "color of joy."[52]

Play is also exceptional because it regularly enframes other emotions, representing them in modified, play forms, thereby regulating and transforming them.[53] Animals and humans regularly play with emotions such as lust (flirting) and rage, practicing safe, protected ways to express and regulate these emotions, in the process rehearsing and learning socially valuable, adaptive behaviors. Play-fear, play-rage, and the like are manageable, transformed by "the color of joy." Because of this ability to re-present the other emotions, play strengthens "the body's system for regulating arousal,"[54] allowing the emergence and practice of "social cooperation and friendships" from the bottom up.[55]

Stephen Porges explains this phenomenon physiologically in terms of the operation of two divisions of the autonomic nervous system. Play simultaneously involves the sympathetic nervous system (including the dorsal branch of the vagal system), stimulating breathing and heart functions and exciting primitive fight and flight reactions, and involves the parasympathetic system (the ventral branch of the vagal system), promoting a receptive state, calming and soothing, appropriate for positive social interactions.[56] Play involves both the "social engagement system and the sympathetic system," mobilizing the individual in the absence of threats.[57] Play, energized by primordial reactions (e.g., fight), tames them, redirecting (regulating) their energy into positive and enjoyable social interactions and encouraging the regular rehearsal of such regulatory skills.

For example, competitive games, simulating conflict, excite rage and aggression. The rage is tamed, however, by the game, its rules, and the fun. In the heat of competition, accidental collisions occur. If the ventral vagal tone is strong and the player is enjoying the game, all is immediately forgotten and the game continues. If the ventral vagal is too weak to counter the dorsal branch's excitement, players may begin to fight, even though they know better, and the playing is brought to a halt.

Regulating subcortical systems, play presents the conscious mind with patterns of regulated behavior, reinforced by positive emotion and all the pleasurable brain chemicals released by "the color of joy." Such patterns engage the conscious mind, which recognizes them as meaningful and even useful.[58] The executive brain responds and joins in the fun, and playing along, reinforces neural play pathways. As Kestly points out, "Play promotes neural integration."[59] Thus, hedonic play initiates the construction of eudaimonic social patterns from the bottom up, beginning and strengthening the *Erlebnis-Erfahrung* chains Hans Gelter describes.[60]

Siegel suggests that the interactions among play, the awareness of being at play, and "managing the emotion of play" are among the best ways to SNAG the brain, offering "the regulatory aspect of the [conscious] mind an opportunity to create higher degrees of integration with new levels of complexity to be achieved."[61] Along with the new neural play pathways, "new forms of awareness emerge."[62]

Play is the rehearsal of this regulation, the mind's "key mechanism beneath both the absence of illness and the presence of well-being."[63]

One of the notorious drawbacks of top-down learning is that its benefits fade rapidly. Without repetition—refresher courses—interventions are soon forgotten, and individuals return to their "set point," to business as usual.[64] One of the most convincing arguments against optimistic attempts to improve well-being and happiness is that most of us have a set point. However, as a primary emotional system, reinforced by "the color of joy," play provides a powerful incentive to repeat positive kinds of behaviors, not because they are good for the person but because they are enjoyable in and for themselves, increasing the likelihood of SNAGing the brain and changing the happiness set point.

As the play pathways strengthen and improve with use, remembered as "schema," they become available for other kinds of "useful," socially adaptive behaviors: building empathy,[65] language, manners, and virtues—what Seligman calls the values of "the hive" and enumerates in the *Character Strengths and Virtues* handbook. From his perspective as a historian, Huizinga claimed that "civilization arises and unfolds as play" and that "culture itself bears the character of play"—the components of cultures, such as language, religion, and law, emerging and evolving from the bottom up as play over time.[66]

Some time ago, Gregory Bateson offered a germane insight into how play not only regulates subcortical impulses but is a bottom-up source of meaning, abstract communication, and empathy.[67] Bateson pointed out that the communication of all emotions except play is relatively straightforward. Through the workings of the autonomic nervous system, responding to stimuli, various physiological signs appear, such as facial expression, which are recognizable as emotions[68]—for example, this dog is mad. Play is different.

Play is more than a simple sign because of its characteristic ability to re-present, or "enframe" other emotions, animals (playmates), and things (playthings). This re-presentation involves abstract communication (communication about things that are not "real") that is also paradoxical. Bateson uses the example of play fighting.

Bateson and his dog meet, the dog puts his elbows on the ground, his rear in the air, tail wagging, signaling, "I'm playing." Bateson signals, "I'm playing," as well with facial expressions, vocalizations, body posture, and so on. This communication is unique because it not only communicates the emotion of play; it becomes an abstract symbol, referring to the signs that follow the "I'm playing" signals. In playing, the dog's fierce growl and biting behavior, the man's grabbing and aggressive posture no longer mean what they ordinarily do. They have become symbols of ordinary signs: play growls, play bites, play grabs. Each player understands that the other's play bites are not real and, even more remarkably, understands that the other player understands the same thing. Thus, arguably, play may be as much a source of empathy as the controversial mirror neurons.[69]

Such metacommunication is the hallmark of the complex language of humans. Deficiencies in this kind of communication are often devastating.[70] However, as Bateson points out, acquiring the ability to metacommunicate—to recognize and use signs and symbols to refer to and change other signs and symbols—cannot be done with words (from the top down). Using words to teach a person metacommunication requires that the person have a preexisting ability to metacommunicate. Initial metacommunication is possible only as a bottom-up process, achieved by subcortical processes such as the experience of play—for Bateson, play is "the crucial step" in the "evolution of communication."[71]

In some of the same ways that play may be related to language and empathy, it may also be an origin of the imagination. Unlike animal play, as far as we know, human play is "uniquely characterized by imagination."[72] Certainly, all mammals share the evolutionary advantage of play's seeking and experimenting. Generating what-if kinds of *behavior*, play, in league with the seeking impulse, is crucial for the exploration of environments and for trying out new behaviors important for survival.[73] However, adding imagination to play, humans further distinguish themselves as *Homo ludens*, the master player among the animals. As play reinforces and builds imagination, humans, alone, may be "drawn by the future," guiding their own evolution, advancing beyond survival to thriving.

Victor Turner, Play, and *Communitas*

Victor Turner traced modern leisure back to what he saw as a more fundamental reality—to a phenomenon at the evolutionary foundation of cultural change and transmission. Leisure is a modern manifestation, or an analogue, of tribal and simple agrarian societies' antistructures. Certain rituals and celebrations, particularly rites of passage such as the coming of age, allow participants in archaic cultures to stand outside the static social order and, in the ritualistic passage (antistructures, often lasting for days) between well-defined social roles (child to adult, for example), objectify and play with established norms, rites, and duties.[74]

Citing the Belgian folklorist Arnold van Gennep as his authority, Turner called these experiences "liminal"—"literally 'threshold' movements betwixt and between the formerly familiar and stable and the not-yet familiar and stable."[75] He noted in particular the liminal's playful quality—that these "new forms of symbolic action" are "particularly conducive to play . . . and to experimental behavior . . . undertaken to discover something not yet known. . . . In liminality new ways of acting, new combinations of symbols, are tried. . . . [I]n liminality people 'play' with the elements of the familiar and defamiliarize them."[76] In rites of passage, for example, gender identities are often played with; in pilgrimages, festivals, masques, and carnivals, normal social roles are suspended in favor of new kinds of convivial, playful identities and associations (e.g., the medieval Feast of Fools).

This fundamental playful or "flowing" aspect of culture has been expressed throughout history. Tracing the liminal over time—from ritual in tribal societies; through the fiestas, carnivals, and charivaris of feudal peoples; to the mass amusements, tourism, and celebrations of today—Turner detected a general evolution as the liminal becomes more private and free, less public, formalized, and obligatory (with both positive and negative results).

Leisure and vacations have emerged in modern times as an enlarged private "freedom to transcend social structural limitations," with the *potential* to establish "an independent domain of creative activity, not simply a distorted mirror-image, mask, or cloak for structural activities in the 'centers' or 'mainstreams' of 'productive social labor.'"[77]

The evolution is so striking that Turner coined a new word, the "liminoid," which he closely identifies with modern forms of free time.[78] Turner argued that modern leisure and work are unique historical products and that modern free time provides playful openings for new discourse, new ways of talking about existing social forms and roles and, consequently, a unique opportunity for cultural transformation (see Csikszentmihalyi's guided evolution and Seligman's "drawn by the future"). Certainly most of leisure is wasted in meaningless consumption and mass media, often the object of manipulation and exploitation by the powerful. Modern leisure, however, much more than archaic liminality, has the potential to promote autonomy, social experimentation, stimulating creativity and providing the "seedbed for cultural creativity."[79]

> [But] leisure is freedom to enter, even for some to help generate, the symbolic worlds. . . . It is freedom to transcend social-structural normative limitations, the freedom to play—with ideas, with fantasies, with words . . . , and with social relationships (new forms of community). . . . [I]n this modern "leisure," far more even than in tribal and agrarian rituals, the experimental and the ludic are stressed. There are many more options in complex, industrial societies. . . . [Leisure activities,] being optional, . . . remain part of the individual's

freedom, of his growing self-mastery, even self-transcendence, [and in] . . . "flow." . . . Leisure is thus potentially capable of releasing creative powers, individual and communal. . . . It is . . . possible to conceive of leisure as a betwixt-and-between, neither-this-nor-that domain between two lodgements . . . [the] occupational and familial and civic [arenas].[80]

Communitas—Apart Together

Turner's descriptions of the cultural role of the liminal are similar to Johan Huizinga's claim that culture changes (or "emerges") through the medium of play.[81] Turner describes the liminal as a "the seedbed of cultural creativity [from which] new symbols and constructions [feed back]" into the existing social and economic orders.[82] Huizinga speaks of the "play circle" as being set apart from ordinary life and of people in play "being apart together" in ways strikingly similar to Turner's discussions of *communitas.*"[83]

On the basis of his anthropological research, particularly his and Edith Turner's research of pilgrimages,[84] Turner concluded that during liminality people experience "being apart together," outside the normal realms of commerce and convention, as unusually intense and absorbing—flow-like. Quoting Turner about the similarity between flow and liminal situations, Csikszentmihalyi agreed that experiences of *communitas* "provide . . . an emotionally rewarding closeness comparatively free from the constraints of social roles, class, and responsibilities. This feeling of participation in turn helps to cement the bonds of social solidarity after the episode ends."[85]

New kinds of freely chosen, intentional, and positive social connections are possible in *communitas.* Such an "unmediated relationship between person and person" is inherently free and equal, playful, and based on sharing and mutuality.[86] In modern times, leisure and vacations have become opportunities to stand outside one's own culture, and "try on" other ways of life, other customs, values, foods, celebrations.[87] The anthropologist Edith Turner called attention to this, noting that it was "interesting . . . that anthropologists studying tourism have seen the vacation tour as a quest for antistructure."[88] *Communitas* is community forming from below, open, exploratory, dynamic, unpredictable, creative, and playful. Edith Turner wrote:

> Communitas [is] . . . the deep, rich substance of the thing it is . . . the gifts of each [to each] . . . a spring of pure possibility. . . . [Communitas] has agency, and seems to be searching. It has something magical about it. There appear to be innumerable threads of crisscrossing lines

of meaning, *flows* of meaning. . . . [Communitas] resides in the poor and those considered inferior . . . a gift coming up from below. . . . In communitas there is a loss of ego.[89]

Play: A Model

Whether or not play was an evolutionary factor in the development of self-awareness, communication, empathy, and imagination, as Bateson, Turner, and Huizinga suggest, it is clear that in the development of children, play is important for each of these things. An extensive amount of research has been done about the importance of play in the development of children, employed for decades in schools and clinical settings, that is relevant to adult play and experience product design.[90]

Just as play contributes to child development, because of neuroplasticity it has the potential to promote adult development as well, even through retirement years.[91] Quoting Stuart Brown and Christopher Vaughan, Bonnie Badenoch and Theresa Kestly point out that play is as important for adult well-being as it is for the flourishing of the child.[92] Siegel concludes that, for adults, "being playful . . . supports healthy neuroplastic growth," releasing "chemicals that support brain growth." Play offers the chance for "our brains [to] carry out new combinations of firing patterns" and for "new ways of knowing" to emerge through the life span.[93]

Playing frees us even as adults,[94] energizing us, promoting spontaneity and positive social interactions and engendering exploration, creativity, and imagination.[95] Play focuses attention, often the prelude to the all-absorbing experience of flow.[96] The play space, created by rules, allows exploration of new kinds of social interactions at the same time that it teaches fairness and mutual regard. Play is the essence of positive emotion, its fun a common-sense definition of intrinsic motivation. All these key elements of human well-being, confirmed in the consilience of the recent discoveries of the new sciences of happiness, are rehearsed and strengthened by play.

Traditional psychological insights about the importance of play for the cognitive development and socialization of children should contribute to a model for the design of a series of *Erfahrungen* experience products for adults.[97] Jean Piaget's developmental stage theory includes play as a primary way that children assimilate new experiences and accommodate to them, *integrating* them into recognized patterns of thought and behavior.[98] Mildred Parten suggested that for children differentiation and integration occur through play in six graded stages.[99] Even though these play stages were observed in the development of children, adult social development through play may be expected to follow the same sequence. (See Box 6.1.)

BOX 6.1 SIX STAGES OF PLAY DEVELOPMENT
(Mildred Parten and Jean Piaget)

- **Unoccupied** play (infants)
  - Random seeking
- **Solitary play** (2–3-year-olds)
  - Solitary play with toys
- **Onlooker play** (2½–3½-year-olds)
  - Differentiation
  - Mostly watching others play
  - Some exchanges—communication about the others' play, not participation
- **Parallel play** (2½–3½-year-olds)
  - Differentiation
  - Side-by-side playing with similar toys
  - Some mimicking, some individual exchanges
- **Associative play** (3–4-year-olds)
  - Beginning of integration
  - Individuals play together
  - Spontaneous, rule-governed play is infrequent
  - Some cooperation, language use, and problem-solving, and the beginning of symbolic play (make-believe play governed by rules)
- **Cooperative play** (3–6-year-olds)
  - Increasing integration
  - Groups play together (teams form)
  - Self-aware playing
  - More rule-governed, set games (e.g., red rover)
  - Symbolic play (and symbol use) become more complex, with rules changing, negotiated by the players

---

While recognizing that play is an irreducible atom of human experience, theorists have identified its several facets and tried to catalog them. The resulting catalogs, such as Roger Caillois's, may be useful in experience design (see Box 6.2).[100] Play may thus be recommended as a model of experience design that includes but broadens Joseph Pine and James Gilmore's theater model (see Box 6.3).[101]

The Problem in Applying Play Theory

The challenge remains to apply the new insights about the importance of adult play more efficiently. Notwithstanding the abundant evidence

BOX 6.2 ROGER CAILLOIS'S CATEGORIES OF PLAY

Six characteristics define the nature of play:

1. Free
2. Separate (from ordinary life, both as a playtime and a playground)
3. Uncertain (with unpredictable outcomes that depend on player choices)
4. Unproductive (not governed by "outside" purposes)
5. Regulated (by rules alternative to ordinary life)
6. Fictive (based in a transient and imagined reality separate from ordinary life, for "the time being")

There are four play forms:

1. Agon: competitive games in which skill is more important (e.g., chess and tennis)
2. Alea: games of chance (e.g., poker)
3. Mimicry: games based on imitation and enframing of ordinary reality (e.g., the theater, Comic-Con, cosplay)
4. Ilinx: "a state of dizziness or disorder" (e.g., riding roller coasters, spinning until you fall down)

Caillois also suggests the cataloging of play forms using a continuum, ranging from paidia (free play, more spontaneous and inventive, with flexible rules that may change, such as festivals and concerts) to ludus (more disciplined, with set rules, specific skills involved, often with a tradition—for example, golf).

BOX 6.3 MODEL OF PLAY

- Play, the essence of freedom and autonomy (you cannot be forced to play)
- Play, the essence of intrinsic motivation (fun, the "color of joy")
- Play, a way to express and develop positive subjective experiences (e.g., PERMA)
- Play, a way to express and develop positive individual traits (e.g., character strengths and values)
- Play, a way to express and develop attention, imagination, empathy, communication, identity
- Play, a way to enframe other emotions (as well as people, events, etc.) and allow monitoring (recognizing) and modifying (controlling) behavior
- Play, a way to express and develop bottom-up integration skills

supporting their case, proponents such as Kestly have noticed "a bias against the importance of play"[102] and have felt the "need to justify our play practices"[103] in clinical settings. Researchers remain reluctant as well, paying "insufficient attention to play."[104] Instead of recognizing the evidence supporting the value of play, schools have been eliminating playgrounds and recess, preparing students exclusively for exams and jobs. Such an extrinsic, results orientation has effectively obscured the value of intrinsically motivated play experiences as well as the value of spontaneous, from-below creativity, exploration, and reorganization.

The devaluing of play and leisure has been going on for years—Huizinga noticed and bemoaned this fact, maintaining:

> Real civilization cannot exist in the absence of a certain play-element, for civilization presupposes limitation and mastery of the self, the ability not to confuse [the self's] own tendencies with the ultimate and highest goal, but to understand that it is enclosed within certain bounds freely accepted.[105]

Teaching leisure studies for decades, I have experienced similar difficulties. I regularly find that many of my students are profoundly confused when I explain that the origin of "school" and "scholarship" are found in an ancient language's word for leisure and that higher education's liberal arts were originally, and up until about a century ago, designed for doing things that are worthwhile in and for themselves—for the universe of intrinsic experiences that adults as well as children enjoy. Thus, the liberal arts are poorly suited for what Joseph Pieper called "the world of total work."[106] Nevertheless, leisure studies as an academic discipline languishes in American colleges— consider your own response my being a professor of leisure studies.

With Kestly, I continue to hope that the professions and educators will begin to recognize once again the importance of play and leisure and begin to find more practical applications for the research findings of the new sciences of happiness. However, such hopes may be unrealistic given the dominance in schools of education for jobs.

Public Policy

Many of the leaders of recent attempts to provide additional free time, such as the Take Back Your Time organization, have relied on public policy. I have been a strong advocate of this approach for years.[107] However, the politics of job creation and the economics of Full-Time, Full Employment, entrenched in American politics since Roosevelt's administrations and still supported by both major political parties, have prevented public policy enabling work reductions. With the turn to the right in American politics, the dominant morality of work and wealth for themselves has been reaffirmed and is now, arguably, more powerful than at any time since the Germany of pre–World War II. Whereas public policy may play a role eventually, removing barriers that prevent people from choosing the hours they would like to work, the free marketplace presents itself as a much more promising alternative.[108]

Experience Design

Applying the Catalogs and Models

How can the principles and processes discovered by the happiness sciences reach their liberating and virtue-producing potential? It will take business leaders and entrepreneurs stepping up and incorporating these findings into the ways they design and offer products for the market. This chapter offers practical guidance in the application of the principles and processes outlined in Chapters 5 and 6 to the design of experience and transformation products by analyzing numerous successful products and businesses already existing. It also uses the models and methods outlined in Chapter 6, with the addition of a table of consiliences, and suggests new ways that successful applications may be achieved. A convenient summary checklist of the principles of experience design is provided. Warnings about branders and value capturers and other hazards are reiterated. The potential of the free market to re-present liberation and the virtues and to empower individuals who own, increasingly, the means (needed skills and virtues) of production, is reaffirmed by the potential of prosumer capitalism.

The characteristics of the eudaimonic technology are discussed. Producing intangible products, eudaimonic technology differs from previous technologies (e.g., manufacturing and transportation), which made tangible, material products. The eudaimonic technology is less dependent on mass-scale production, intensive capitalization, and centralized ownership. It depends instead on freely shared, open, and decentralized resources (e.g., the Internet). In the new economies, leisure is as basic a resource as money capital.

Moreover, a primary function of eudaimonic technology is the creation of inexpensive, readily available, intangible experiences and transformations that enrich the leisure that previous technologies have made possible. Comparisons with appropriate technology (e.g., small is beautiful) are made. Equality and other benefits of the eudaimonic technology are discussed.

Designing Experiences

According to the *Character Strengths and Virtues* handbook, "Positive psychology focuses on three related topics: the study of positive subjective experiences, the study of positive individual traits, and the study of institutions that enable positive experiences and positive traits."[1] In the turn to practical applications of research, in the down-to-earth meeting of theory and practice, experiences have become central concerns of the new sciences of happiness. Leaders such as Christopher Peterson, Martin Seligman, and Daniel Sigel have focused on directing and creating experiences that promote happiness and well-being and that lead to a person's flourishing on the basis of sound psychological principles. Such experiences repeated often enough become habitual and thus change (or as Joseph Pine and James Gilmore, in the context of the marketplace, put it, "transform") the individual.[2] Whereas positive psychology's leaders have been interested in influencing public policy, helping businesses to improve working environments, and assisting other institutions (educational, the military, and the media), relatively little has been done investigating the potential of the marketplace and facilitating its potential to "enable positive experiences and positive traits."[3]

A strong case can be made, however, that the new sciences of happiness validate several of the developments underway in the experience and transformation economies. Such developments suggest new theoretical and practical approaches to the future design and marketing of new experience products—additions to the models already in use based on Abraham Maslow, Jean Piaget, and John Dewey's theories.[4] However, other developments in the new economies are brought into question by the new sciences.

Overall, positive psychology's "basic and implicit premise" that "we are drawn by the future rather than just driven by the past"[5] confirms the fundamental assumption of the experience and transformation economies that we all want to improve ourselves and strengthens Pine and Gilmore's hope that experience products will help change the "attitude, performance, characteristic, or some other fundamental dimension of the self" in positive ways.[6] The nomenclature used in the experience and transformation economies is the language of positive psychology: businesses are *"transformation elicitors,"* providing *effectual* experience products to customer *aspirants*.[7] Experience designers in the new economies have recognized that the customer's conscious intent, expectations, and will are vital.

Martin Seligman's goal to build "a science that measures and builds expectations, planning and conscious choice"[8] promises to provide one of the necessary underpinnings of a new eudaimonic technology driving the experience and transformation economies.

For centuries economists have maintained that the marketplace produces the greatest good and the greatest happiness for the greatest number partly because it expands consumer choices and in so doing promotes freedom. According to the new sciences of happiness, freedom and choice are most characteristic of those subjective experiences associated with human flourishing. Such findings seem to validate the experience and transformation economies' expansion into the marketplace—more experiences and more transformation equal greater freedom and happiness.

In addition, the empirical findings that buying experiences is generally a more positive experience than buying material goods[9] support the claim that the experience and transformation economies, by "enabling positive experiences," lead the way in the progression of economic values, as does the more general finding that "spending time makes you happier than spending money."[10] Thomas Gilovich and Amit Kumar's conclusion that "overall well-being of society might be advanced by shifting from an overwhelmingly material economy to one that facilitates experiential consumption,"[11] is surely an endorsement of the direction some parts of the new economies have taken.

However, distinctions (proposed in Chapter 3) between entrepreneurs and businesses that seek to be catalyst-enablers and those seeking primarily to brand customers and capture the new customer-added value must be kept in mind before applying the new sciences' seal of approval to the experience and transformation economies. Since the transformation economy is founded on the possibility of changing customers, to "affect the very being of the buyer,"[12] the kind and direction of such transformations remain vital issues.

Catalyst-enablers are certainly interested in providing an experience product that will sell. They tend to understand, however, that the customer's active participation and autonomy are keys to their success. Hence they tend to be more interested in providing experiences that promote customers' active involvement, vision, choice, and coproduction of value. Through transformative experiences (*Erfahrungen*) offered by experience providers, the customer as prosumer emerges, increasingly skillful, *owning* the ability to create ever finer and enjoyable experiences (*Erlebnisse*). Customers become increasingly autonomous, building their own experiences and creating their own exchange venues in a sharing economy. The end user eventually leads the way to "value creation."[13] Britta Timm Knudsen, Dorthe Christensen, and Per Blenker see entrepreneurs empowering and liberating customers.[14] George Ritzer and Nathan Jurgenson anticipate "the possibility of a new, prosumer capitalism,"[15] Albert Boswijk, Ed Peelen, and Steven Olthof look forward to the "creative city."[16]

The research findings from the new sciences of happiness validate the catalyst-enablers' agenda: increasing autonomy, competency, and agency in the promotion of customer well-being. If entrepreneurs continue to design and offer experience products in accord with this agenda, the economy performs as it should, and marketers do their job of informing and educating, the catalyst-enabler should succeed and a new prosumer capitalism develop, ceteris paribus.

By the same reasoning, branders and value capturers in the experience and transformation economies should be at a disadvantage. Attempts to transform customers into loyal brand followers, increasing their dependence on vendors and the marketplace, should create dissatisfaction or at least relatively less happiness, if the new sciences' findings about autonomy and choice are true. The essence of the colonization of the lifeworld is the contraction of freedom and choice—the overgrowth of those parts of human experiences traditionally done for free beyond the marketplace. More and more of human life must become a paid-for experience for ordinary kinds of capital formation and economic growth to continue as usual.

For value capturers, the value added by the customer in the experience economy must be captured by continually finding new ways to charge customers for that value and for their own time—leisure must be commodified. Transformations in the transformation economy do not liberate but bind the customer ever closer to the marketplace. If the findings of the new sciences of happiness are true, customer satisfaction in the world of branders and value capturers must be sustained as an illusion, supported by the building of false consciousness.

The cover of Albert Boswijk, Ed Peelen, and Steve Olthof's book, *Economy of Experiences*, depicts the sword of Arthurian legend. The authors hoped the image would remind readers of the quest for the Holy Grail. For them, the Grail quest is to find "the essential connection with what people need, with what makes their lives more enjoyable, fuller or . . . 'more meaningful'"—the "essential connection" between the market and authentic well-being.[17]

Traditionally, seeking that connection, designers and marketers have asked people what they thought would make their lives "more enjoyable, fuller, or . . . 'more meaningful,'" testing products with focus groups or doing demographic research. These are tried-and-true methods based on a democratic understanding of the market. Let the people (or a group of representatives) determine what should be produced, then let them vote with their dollars to confirm the market research and the designers' creations.

It is the innovator, Joseph Schumpeter's creative destroyer, with vision, however, who goes beyond what people think they want. The entrepreneur is able to find or invent new things to bring to market—things beyond the imagination of most of us. The entrepreneur is the very engine of economic growth and value creation without whom economies reach a stationary state and stagnate.

Certainly much of the entrepreneur's innovation is purely intuitive. However, the alternative to giving people what they say what they want or relying solely on the entrepreneur's imagination is to turn to existing scientific research about human needs and the findings about the sources of genuine happiness. For the experience and transformation economies, the Holy Grail, the "essential connection" between the market and authentic human well-being, is the new sciences of happiness.

Much good work has been done finding ways to apply the theories and models of John Dewey, Abraham Maslow, and Jean Piaget (see Chapter 3) to experience-product design and innovation. But relatively little has been done to use the findings of the new sciences of happiness. There are important exceptions. The most important include the European Centre for the Experience and Transformation Economy, headed by Albert Boswijk. Boswijk and the center suggest that the experience economy may be in the process of delivering what the new sciences of happiness have been discovering about the importance of autonomy and community, albeit fortuitously.[18] A few researchers and theorists, such as Gary Ellis and J. Robert Rossman, writing about public parks and recreation and the travel and tourism industry, have also explored links between the experience economy and the new sciences.[19] Danish researchers at the Center for Food Science, Design, and Experience at Aalborg University, notably Christian Jantzen, have also suggested links with positive psychology and neurobiology.[20] Bernd Schmitt has recognized the relevance of positive psychology and Martin Seligman's work to experience marketing,[21] and educators and researchers at Roskilde University in Denmark are doing groundbreaking research on experience design.[22]

These initial efforts provide a foundation for a more systematic approach to making that "essential connection" between the market and the new discoveries about happiness Boswijk and his group seek. Daniel Siegel describes a consilience of sciences researching human well-being: a convergence of research findings that I summarize in a table of consiliences (see Table 7.1). Such findings, as Seligman notes, are preliminary, subject to review and correction by future research and by the test of the marketplace. Supplementing Table 7.1 are checklists of the principles of experience design (see Box 7.1). The stages of play development, Roger Caillois's categories of play, and the play model discussed in Chapter 6 (see Boxes 6.1–6.3) should also be useful as guidelines for experience designers.

Analytics

So far, the sciences of happiness discoveries have mostly found their way into the marketplace fortuitously, by way of individual intuition. It is the entrepreneur's genius that delivers new experience products to the market that *really* make people happy, as proved by empirical science. Because of this, the products remain somewhat inchoate—the entrepreneur unaware of or uninterested in the science confirming his or her insights. To work toward a eudaimonic technology in which the new experience design principles are more systematically applied, however, it is essential to make these implicit insights explicit.

Analysis of how the new principles of happiness have already appeared and are working in successful experience products is a practical way to work toward this goal, creating a casebook of examples. In my classes, I use this strategy with my students, asking them to analyze a businesses or experience product in the experience or transformation economy by using Table 7.1, the checklists in Box 7.1, and the play analytics guidelines (stages, characteristics, and model) to find the keys to the business or product's success. The better their case that one or more of the consiliences is succeeding in the market (or if not, why not), for example, the better their grade. After they become somewhat familiar with what the new sciences' findings about happiness look like in existing experience products, I ask my students to design a new experience product for the company they are researching, applying a different one of the consiliences, checklist items, and so on. I argue that with enough of this practice, they should be able to approach a potential employer after graduation and offer their services as an experience-product designer or, better still, strike out on their own as entrepreneurs.

I employ a similar strategy here. I also supplement a top-down approach to experience design (table of consiliences, checklist, and play guidelines) with *a bottom-up design strategy*. Gathering and analyzing existing experience products, I attempt to identify meaningful and useful patterns already existing in the market, still below the level of general awareness and purposeful

TABLE 7.1 CONSILIENCES: ELEMENTS OF POSITIVE SUBJECTIVE EXPERIENCES AND POSITIVE INDIVIDUAL TRAITS THAT MAY BE EXPRESSED AND DEVELOPED BY EXPERIENCES IN THE EXPERIENCE ECONOMY (TEE) AND THE TRANSFORMATION ECONOMY (TTE)

Researcher	Elements of positive subjective experiences—value added (TEE)						Positive individual traits—value added: virtues (TTE)
	Hedonism	Engagement	Relationships	Meaning	Autonomy	Elements of positive subjective experiences and positive individual traits—value added: competence	
Seligman (PERMA)	Positive emotion	Engagement	Positive relationship	Meaning/purpose	Motivation/autonomy	Accomplishment/competence	Strengths and virtues; imagination
Ryan and Deci (self-determination theory)			Relatedness		Autonomy	Competence	
Ryff			Positive relationship	Purpose in life	Autonomy	Environmental mastery	Personal growth; self-acceptance
Rogers (humanistic psychology)				Movement toward potential	Autonomy		Increasing openness to experience
Maslow				Belonging		Esteem	Self-actualization; love/belonging

Fredrickson (broaden and build)	Positive emotion			Autonomy		Broaden and build
Schwartz	Stimulation/hedonism	Benevolence/conformity	Self-transcendence	Self-direction	Achievement/power/recognition	
Wong			Meaning			Resilience; social virtues
Peterson and Seligman (character strengths and virtues)						Core moral virtues: courage, justice, humanity, temperance, transcendence, and wisdom
Maslow	Self-awareness, openness to				Esteem	Self-actualization; love/belonging
Siegel	Play (the emotion)	Positive relations	Meaning*	Fun		Differentiation/integration (monitor and modify)
Hanson	Positive emotion					New experiences

Note: This is a tentative list. As Seligman and others note, such findings are preliminary, subject to empirical tests and verification. For the experience economy and the transformation economy, the test of these consiliences will be the free marketplace.

* See Daniel J. Siegel, *Mindsight: The New Science of Personal Transformation* (New York: Bantam Books, 2010), 281.

BOX 7.1 CHECKLISTS OF PRINCIPLES OF EXPERIENCE DESIGN

The experience economy threshold:

☐ Customers create value

The transformation economy threshold:

☐ Customers change (e.g., skills acquired)

General principles of experience of design (provided by the experience):

☐ Autonomy (vs. helplessness/no control)
☐ Participation (vs. passive watching)
☐ Growth (skills, interest, enthusiasm)
☐ Belonging (meaning)
☐ Others/relationships (positive interaction)
☐ Memory (reflection)

Elements of positive subjective experiences (provided by the experience):

☐ Intrinsic motivation
☐ Autonomy/choice/freedom
☐ Integration/positive relationships/empathy/communication
☐ Positive emotion
☐ Engagement (flow)/the experience of competence
☐ Meaning/purpose/belonging
☐ Accomplishments

Positive individual traits (expressed, practiced, and developed by the experience):

☐ Resilience
☐ Competency (Fredrickson's broaden and build theory)
☐ Self-esteem, self-acceptance
☐ Imagination
☐ Empathy (e.g., wisdom and knowledge, creativity, curiosity, open-mindedness, love of learning, perspective)
☐ Courage (e.g., bravery, perseverance, integrity, energized vitality)
☐ Humanity (e.g., love, kindness/generosity, social intelligence)

- Justice (e.g., teamwork, fairness, and leadership)
- Temperance (e.g., forgiveness and mercy, humility, prudence, self-regulation)
- Transcendence (e.g., appreciation of beauty, gratitude, hope, humor, spirituality)

Coping skills—FACES (expressed, practiced, and developed by the experience, especially play):

- Flexible
- Adaptive
- Coherent
- Energized
- Stable

Key mechanism beneath the presence of well-being (expressed as and developed by the experience):

- Differentiation
- Integration
- Measured response and adaptation

Strategies for experience design:

- Monitor and modify; SNAGing the brain
- Focus attention (mindfulness, savoring)
- Encourage imagination (purpose/meaning seeking—drawn to the future)
- Reinforce memory (reflection, thankfulness)

Research and findings relevant to experience design and correlations with well-being:

- Control of attention (savoring and mindfulness)
- Thankfulness/gratitude
- Forgiveness
- Signature strengths' use
- Generosity
- Memory (recall a positive experience)
- Thoughtful self-reflection
- Frequency of positive experiences rather than intensity
- Buying experiences (vs. buying material goods)
- Positive communities

Ten commonsense principles for experience analysis/design (Boswijk, Thijssen, and Peelen; Pine and Gilmore):

☐ Theme the experience
☐ Harmonize impressions
☐ Eliminate negative and intruding factors
☐ Pay attention to mood and atmosphere
☐ Add memories and memorabilia
☐ Involve all the senses
☐ Pay attention to authenticity (make as realistic as possible)
☐ Dramatize the structure (work toward a climax—ending, resolution)
☐ Deploy staff as actors (all employees play a role, staying in character)
☐ Customize (work toward realizing the well-being of customers as individuals—differentiation)[1]

Pine and Gilmore's strategy for transformations:

☐ Diagnose aspiration
☐ Stage experiences
☐ Follow through[2]

Hans Gelter's addition to Pine and Gilmore's strategy:

☐ "Carefully designed and staged chains of *Erlebnisse* may thus result in more major transformations according to the goals of transformational offerings of Pine and Gilmore"[3]

Maslow's hierarchy:

☐ Needs: physiological, safety, belonging/love
☐ Esteem
☐ Self-actualization[4]

Victor and **Edith Turner's insight:**

☐ *Communitas*[5]

[1] Albert Boswijk, Thomas Thijssen, and Ed Peelen, *The Experience Economy: A New Perspective* (Amsterdam: Pearson Education, 2007), 169–172; B. Joseph Pine II and James H. Gilmore, *The Experience Economy*, rev. ed. (Boston: Harvard Business Press, 2011), 91.
[2] Pine and Gilmore, *The Experience Economy*, 263.
[3] Hans Gelter, "Total Experience Management—a Conceptual Model for Transformational Experiences within Tourism," in *The Nordic Conference on Experience, 2008: Research, Education and Practice in Media*, ed. Sol-Britt Arnolds and Peter Bjork (Vaasa, Finland: Tritonia, 2010), 52.
[4] A. H. Maslow, "A Theory of Human Motivation," *Psychological Review* 50, no. 4 (1943): 370–396.
[5] Victor Turner, *Blazing the Trail: Way Marks in the Exploration of Symbols*, ed. Edith Turner (Tucson: University of Arizona Press, 1992).

intent[23]—practical patterns that might be employed in the future design of new experience products.

Examples and Analyses

Airbnb

In late January 2018 Brian Chesky sent an open letter to the Airbnb community (employees, hosts, and guests). The letter was remarkable on several levels: the success that he reported, his enthusiasm for the future, and his and the company's vision. Chesky wrote that he was "absurdly lucky" to be writing the letter, having begun the company only ten years earlier, more or less by chance when he and cofounder Joe Gebbia were virtually broke. Most people thought their original concept, that some people would want to share their homes with strangers and others would want to stay with them, a bit harebrained. Their idea, however, paid off: Chesky reported that "a decade later, people have checked into an Airbnb nearly 300 million times."[24] Hosts in over 190 countries around the world serve about 2 million guests per month.[25] According to Leslie Hook in the *Financial Times*, Airbnb's earnings for 2017 were $100 million, the company's total revenues for the year were $3.5 billion, and bookings worldwide had grown 150 percent from the previous year.[26]

A leader in the sharing economy, Airbnb provides an Internet booking service. People with space available for short-term rental list their accommodations on Airbnb's webpage. The company provides some oversight and assurances: hosts and guests must provide Airbnb with valid identifications, addresses, and payment information. The company provides an analysis of risk based on a database of several variables ("risk scoring") and offers safety workshops for hosts.[27] Both the guests and the hosts have opportunities to review their experiences that are then posted on the Internet along with the Airbnb listings. The company maintains that these reviews are important sources of quality control and reassurance—"superhosts" have a proven track record and are more closely monitored. In return for their brokerage services, Airbnb receives 0 to 20 percent of the transaction cost from the buyer and usually 3 percent from the seller.[28]

The company and its founder acknowledge their role as catalyst-enablers. In 2016 Nathan Blecharczyk observed, "We are only the facilitators."[29] Chesky agreed: "The truth is that we, Airbnb the company, did not do most of this. Our hosts, and the broader Airbnb community, created most of this."[30] Airbnb extends the democratization of travel and opens up the tourism industry to amateurs[31] providing inexpensive lodging for the traveler and a chance to make money for the hosts.

Surely, one of the factors that accounts for such an unlikely project's remarkable success is the optimism and vision of the founders, Chesky, Gebbia, and Blecharczyk. Even more than their brokerage services, they are selling the possibilities of community and belonging. For Chesky, "This is going to be about being an insider and immersing in a community, and that's a profound shift."[32] From its beginnings the company planned to serve a larger social good by bringing people together. In some remarkably purple prose for a business executive, Chesky writes:

> We should be able to offer more than people sleeping in one another's homes. We imagine a world where every one of us can belong anywhere. A world where you can go to any community and someone says, "Welcome home." Where home isn't just a house, but anywhere you belong. Where every city is a village, every block a community, and every kitchen table a conversation. In this world, we can be anything we want. This is the magical world of Airbnb. We will probably never fully realize this vision, but we will die trying.[33]

Chesky points to the loss of community and personal contact in the modern age. Industrialization and the growth of impersonal institutions and mass media have left a vacuum. "People stopped trusting each other."[34] The "universal human yearning to belong," he explains, represents a vast reservoir of unmet needs today that he and his company are trying to satisfy.[35] Airbnb intends to use technology to "bring people together."[36]

Trust, community, and belonging are central Airbnb themes,[37] selling points that the company reiterates in its promotions and presentations. Airbnb advises travelers to experience "a place like a local rather than as a tourist."[38] Charlie Aufmann, design manager at Airbnb, remembers what he saw during his first year with the company:

> Deep, cross-cultural connections being formed through Airbnb is the true beauty and innovation of what our product and community can do for the world. Staying with a stranger in a foreign place creates an opportunity for authentic understanding for someone completely different from you. With trust as the social glue to keep it all together, the relationships being formed on Airbnb provide us an opportunity and challenge way bigger than anything we could have imagined: making the world a more welcoming place.[39]

Hosts and guests report that they feel they are part of something good and larger than themselves and that they are helping build trust, civility, understanding, and community. The yearly meetings of hosts and guests with the company employees have had something of a Woodstock-like feel—full of the enthusiasm and joie de vivre of true believers.

Noting that the experience economy will be a "massive business," Chesky reported in 2018 that the company has expanded its offerings, listing "peer to peer experiences"[40] (originally "city hosts") on their webpage in addition to lodging.[41] "Curated and vetted" by Airbnb, locals design and offer their experience products on their own, which Chesky characterizes as "deep insider immersions into somebody's world."[42] Depending on their locality for the stories, traditions, crafts, music, and drama that express the character of the place, experience providers offer a world of possibilities: truffle hunting in Italy with a third-generation practitioner of the art, a traditional Irish music pub crawl, street dancing (plus lessons) in South Bronx, a samba party in Rio, plant identification hikes in the mountains of North Carolina, an olfactory tour of Paris perfumeries. Chesky reports that experiences are growing faster than accommodations on Airbnb and as of 2018 "doing a million and a half bookings on an annualized basis."[43]

Analysis

I ask my students to do a thorough analysis of the experience product they present to class, using as many of the principles, guidelines, and design models that may be relevant. I shorten the process here, presenting an analysis that focuses on the most important checklist elements, looking also for new, unexpected patterns and insights that appear from below, in the real world of Airbnb commerce.

Airbnb experiences meet the threshold condition for the experience economy; value is added by customers. Hosts join in, coproducing the experience product, often providing the conviviality and community Airbnb hopes for. Judging from the guest reviews on the Airbnb webpage, transformations also occur—guests report that they are less afraid, more willing to take chances, more trusting, and more interested in additional experiences that allow them to grow. Participants in Airbnb experiences often report in their reviews that they gained a new skill, awareness, insight, interest, or knowledge or new friends.

Elements of Positive Subjective Experiences

The promise of meaning and purpose—the *M* in PERMA (positive emotions, engagement, relationships, meaning and purpose, and accomplishment)—in the forms of belonging and community formation and positive relationships are the potential value-added elements of Airbnb experiences. Certainly, intrinsic motivation is a vital part of successful experience products; after all, many of the guests are on vacation. The sense of accomplishment (the *A* in PERMA), of overcoming fears and taking the plunge, is also part of the positive subjective experience.

Positive Individual Traits That May Be Expressed as and Developed by Airbnb Experiences

The company's promise to "bring people together" and its vision of community imply the recovery of some civic virtue and character strengths. However, scientific measurement of the acquisition of positive individual traits (e.g., loyalty) has yet to be done. Such a project might be of interest to researchers or something for the executives at Airbnb to consider. For now, the best that can be said is that many of the guests and hosts report personal transformations in their reviews and believe them to be part of the value received for the money spent. There are negative experiences reported, of course, which are duly posted on the Airbnb website. In theory, negative reviews discourage future buyers—positive subjective experiences and experiences that express or build character strengths and virtues should be even more likely to win out in this information-rich virtual world than in the traditional marketplace. The better mousetrap should have an even better chance.

Memory, Meaning, and Community

The reviews on the Airbnb website are in the millions, a ripe field for empirical research. So far the research results have been tentative.[44] One of the reliability issues that concerns researchers is that most of the reviews are positive, hence of questionable accuracy—other rating services have considerably more negative reviews of the company, often of the same accommodations. Arguably, one reason for positive reviews is that they are intended not simply to transmit accurate information but primarily to recollect, share, and extend the experiences. Not only do reviews offer guests and hosts a chance to reexperience the day in memory, itself pleasurable, but they are opportunities to tell their stories—to find and publish the meaning they found in the experiences they shared.[45]

Together with the experiences, the reviews function as a kind of *communitas*, a virtual gathering of like-minded people sharing their stories just as they had shared experiences. Both experiences and stories conform to Edith Turner's description of *communitas*, the playful and temporary suspension of ordinary conventions.[46] *Communitas* provides opportunities to leave behind, for the time being, one's culture and responsibilities and playfully explore other ways of life, foods, festivals, customs, and values. Mihaly Csikszentmihalyi's observation that such liminal experiences are often "emotionally rewarding"[47] is confirmed by the many times that guests describe their experiences as positive, often as fun. Having fun with their hosts, perhaps the guests do not notice or forget the mouse droppings in the corner.

Just as in play, the gathering in *communitas* suspends disbelief—to play the game, you must believe. To doubt the game is to be the spoilsport, the one who breaks the circle of "being apart together."[48] It is not surprising, then, that such a large percentage of Airbnb reviews are positive.

Determining the extent to which Airbnb's main purposes—trust, community, and belonging—are being realized will require an empirical study beyond the scope of this book. Determining the extent to which the multitude of Airbnb hosts provide experiences that put into practice one or more of the principles of experience design will require a case-by-case analysis and at least one additional book. The best that can be accomplished here is to offer examples (see "Nonna's Kitchen" later in the chapter).

Critique and Additions

After analysis, my class moves on to a critique of the company and to possible additions—new experiences that might improve the company's experience offerings. The strongest critique of Airbnb has been that the vision of bringing people together to form "deep, cross-cultural connections" and of building "a world where every one of us can belong anywhere" and actual Airbnb experiences are still miles apart. For learning experiences to last more than few weeks, they need to be reiterated in the classroom or in some other way—the more frequent the repetition, the better for lasting improvement. As Siegel maintains, to SNAG (stimulate neuronal activation and growth) the brain, repetition is vital. Pine and Gilmore agree, some plan (intent) and series of monitored follow-ups are needed after the initial transformation experience.

During class discussion, students have suggested that learning experiences, such as Airbnb cooking classes, be offered in a graded series, more advanced experiences following elementary ones. This strategy may offer more realistic opportunities for stable groups to meet more than once and deepen contacts, addressing the problem of transforming ephemeral *communitas* into more permanent community. Reunions of some the guests who stayed at a particular Airbnb were also suggested. Perhaps Airbnb could sponsor reunions as a rebate to guests and as a reward to some of the successful superhosts—the company paying for groups to get together again to broaden and build more lasting positive relationships.

Integration from Below

Simply analyzing and critiquing Airbnb, looking through the checklist of the principles of experience design for matches, is to fail to notice a meaningful pattern appearing from below. What is somewhat surprising to those who are not true believers is that Airbnb's dream of the restoration of convivial human relationships has had such resonance—that the desire to belong seems to be a potent driver in the marketplace. Of course, many, or even most of the over 300 million guests staying with Airbnb hosts do so because the price is cheaper than standard offerings. But there is also no doubt, judging from the myriad reviews, that a significant number of hosts and guests share the company's vision of renewed trust and belonging and believe that they are making the dream real. Positive psychology's essential claim, that humans are "drawn by the future,"[49] seems to have bubbled up through the marketplace that is Airbnb. The company may be a template for the new eudaimonic technology, modeling the importance of inspiration, vision, and belief as more important than the cool, rational, and straightforward application of technique and a checklist.

Travel and tourism researchers and scholars have noticed other instances of the commercial possibilities of experience products offering the chance to be part of a larger cause. Hans Gelter identifies a group of "Transmodern" tourism offerings: the essence of "Transmodernity is being for something, *i.e.* taking active action towards ethnic, racial and sexual equality, [environmental] sustainability and interconnectedness."[50]

Nonna's Kitchen

An Airbnb "lifestyle experience" takes place in Sabina, just outside Rome. The price for the four-and-a-half-hour experience includes train fare, wine, a cooking class, and a homemade meal around the table of one of the locals. The experience hosts begin things by giving guests a tour of the medieval hilltop city, its castle, and sights. Most importantly, guests "cook with one of the best chefs ever: Our grandma, Nonna Nerina." Nonna teaches guests traditional ways to make pasta from scratch and by hand—at least three kinds. The pasta making is hands on—guests doing with their dough the things Nonna does with hers (she speaks mainly Italian). During the pasta making, the hosts tell their stories, sharing their culture and traditions.[51]

The reviews have been virtually all positive and revealing as to what value guests say they received for the money they spent. One expects at least some robust cultural critiques: of Nonna's domestic enslavement, of the peddling of domestic bliss à la *Donna Reed* and *Leave It to Beaver*. Combing through reviews of Nonna's kitchen, however, one finds scant evidence of such sensibility. Instead there is a uniform openness to spending vacation time doing what were essentially domestic chores—a novel openness to experiences largely closed by modern norms.[52] In Nonna's kitchen, there is a suspension of ordinary social roles (housewife, servant, host, guest) that allows the convivial (and playful) framing of other (more traditional Italian) ways of life. Turner's *communitas* emerges. Such a suspension allows taking the time for, paying attention to, and savoring the ordinary: preparing and eating pasta. In their reviews, none of the guests reported wanting to quit their jobs and return to the kitchen. But both women and men wrote that they were eager to get back home and try out their new skills and insights about conviviality, but in their free time. Pasta making had acquired a new valence, as psychologists might say—a transformation into an intrinsically enjoyable, free activity. In economic terms, pasta making was transformed into intrinsically motivated productive consumption (IMPC),[53] an experience that guests were willing to pay over a hundred dollars for.

The sense of *communitas*, of "being apart together"[54] in a time set apart, during vacation, while playfully (note the frequency of the word "fun" in guest reviews below) exploring new activities, cultures, relationships, and "being different together,"[55] is pronounced in the reviews.

A count of word frequency is revealing as to the kinds of discourse and storytelling that take place in the reviews. In over 350 reviews, words used most frequently (articles, etc., have been omitted) are the following.

"We" appeared 492 times; "experience," 428; "pasta," 335; "with," 278; "family," 208; "us," 234; "our," 206; "amazing," 121; "home," 116; "making," 115; "fun," 88; "welcoming," welcomed," or welcome," 88; "authentic" or "real," 68; "loved" or "love," 63; "highlight," 44; "group," 41; "warm," 37; "learn," 32; "friendly," 27; "together," 26; "different," 26 (note the identical numbers of "together" and "different"); "met," 25; and "unique," 23.

Typical comments about Nonna's were the following:

- Oh my goodness! This was such a fantastic experience!!! We learned, we laughed, we dined, we visited. When the day ended and the food and wine were finished, we left with priceless memories of Giada, her mother, and her aunt. Their gift of hospitality is truly unparalleled, and they are, to us, Italy's finest treasures.
- What fun!! It was really hands on and relaxed. We ate sooo much pasta. . . . I love Nonna and wanted to bring her home. Thanks for a fabulous day.
- At the end, everyone sat around a large dining table and we all enjoyed wine and pasta like a big family. This was so much fun and we all returned home with a new skill! Thank you, Chiara and Nonna!
- Chiara and her Nonna have taught me things I will use for a lifetime.
- Chiara and her aunt were so warm and welcoming that the whole group felt like family by the time we left.

- [This] is an especially good experience for those looking to interact with other travelers—our group was very fun and made the experience that much more memorable.
- The group of people we were with were a lot of fun. It was great to connect with people from around the world.
- My mom (also a grandmother) and Nonna formed a great bond.
- The group size was small enough I felt like I was having a feast with my close family and friends.
- While the meal was beautiful the people we met that day were even more beautiful. We hope to stay in contact with them even.
- The whole family puts so much love and enthusiasm into this experience and are so eager to show you their picturesque region.
- We were treated more like honored family then tourists.
- Chiara and her family made us feel like we were family members as well.
- [We felt] like we hadn't just been tourists or even guests in the home, but that we had been welcomed as honorary members of the family in a uniquely Italian way!
- They made us feel like family in a country far from our own.
- [They] welcomed us like family.

Acknowledging the power of Airbnb's vision to motivate hosts and guests, it may not be overly cynical to suggest that the restoration of trust, belonging, and community will probably require more than one company. The company may even acknowledge the difficulty of building stable, long-lasting relationships using the services they now offer. Other companies in the experience and transformation economies offer experiences that depend on the patronage of local populations and offer greater possibilities for building community out of *communitas*.

Analysis
Nonna's kitchen meets these elements of the checklist of experience design: belonging (meaning/interconnectedness), positive relationships, *communitas*, memory, skill acquisition (broaden and build), and differentiation and integration ("being different together").

Ballroom Dancing: Rich Rowray

Several national franchises offer ballroom and social dance lessons and opportunities, such as Dance With Me, Arthur Murray Dance Centers, and Fred Astaire Dance Studios.[56] National organizations (notably USA Dance) and local clubs abound.[57] Most medium-sized cities support at least one commercial studio. When I announce the semester project to my classes, I present my own project as a model for theirs. My choice has always been the local ballroom dance teacher and his studio.

Rich Rowray has offered dance lessons (simplified recreational ballroom and social dancing) in Iowa City for decades. To give his graduates more opportunities, he organized two local dance clubs that continue to grow. In his promotional literature and during his classes, he explains that his vision is to bring back ballroom and social dancing. He points out that most of us have become passive in our leisure time, watching TV and getting fat. At best we are "bowling alone,"[58] having given up on most opportunities to interact freely and enjoyably with other people. Dancing is Rowray's solution, his way to restore community, reacquaint his students with their physical body, and have some fun. He invites students not only to learn to dance but to share his mission.

He offers a graded series of classes, from beginner to advanced, in several cultural traditions: polka, salsa, Charleston, tango, foxtrot, swing, the hustle, cha-cha-cha, and more. He offers to transform his students from fearful, standoffish wallflowers to confident, skillful dancers. He intends, and says explicitly, for his students to be set free by his classes and own the means of production—the ability to create their own experiences the rest of their lives. One couple is in their upper eighties, still dancing and still enjoying the music, the company, and movement. They are inspirational and my favorite couple.

Learning to dance requires learning new skills of differentiation and integration. Dance partners have to learn different roles and steps and coordinate them. Ballroom dancing requires one person to lead and the other to follow: always a challenging negotiation—my dentist and his wife went for days without speaking to each other after some of their early classes. The required negotiation of roles and interactions simulate some of the real challenges of marriages and close relationships, except they are done within the safe confines of the ballroom. The same strong emotions are present, the same challenge to regulate strong impulses (as a kind of playing, dancing stimulates both the sympathetic and the parasympathetic systems, allowing for regulation from below—unless the couple is my dentist and his wife). My wife, a couples therapist, maintains that learning how to dance rehearses skills necessary for a healthy marriage, building abilities to regulate emotional responses and to live together agreeably.

Belonging to the clubs Rowray founded, strangers in the community form bonds, sharing not only the dances but their stories during lulls in the music. These relationships grow and are nurtured by repetition (dances usually are held at least once a month), making it possible for a stable community to form from the initial *communitas* of the first few lessons. As the community grows, more people in town want to learn to dance, and new customers are created for Rowray's business.

Analysis

The experience economy threshold of customers creating value is met. The transformation economy threshold of customers changing—acquiring skills and so on—is met. Elements of positive subjective experiences include intrinsic motivation (the fun is obvious); autonomy/choice/freedom (the whole point of Rowray's classes is to encourage students to dance, on their own, the rest of their lives); integration/positive relationships/communication (met by clubs and regular dancing); positive emotion (fun); engagement/the experience of competence (skill-building classes); meaning/purpose/belonging (customers may be part of Rowray's vision if they wish); and accomplishments (increasing skills give many people a sense of accomplishment—particularly shy people who never thought they would be able to dance).

Positive individual traits (expressed as and developed by experiences) include competency (broaden and build); self-esteem and self-acceptance; empathy; courage (including bravery, perseverance, vitality); humanity (including social intelligence); transcendence (in perhaps an appreciation of beauty or humor); differentiation; integration; and measured response and adaptation.

Strategies employed include focused attention in that participants practice mindfulness and can savor their experiences.

Dancing meets several play criteria: It is intrinsically motivated, free, set apart from ordinary life and temporary (for the time being), and rule governed, and it frames and regulates other emotions and drives (sexual desire) and focuses attention. Mildred Parten's later play stages (see Box 6.1) are expressed in dancing: associative and cooperative play, developing differentiation, and integration. Dancing may be categorized (see Caillois's categories in Box 6.2) as a form of ilinx (letting go into an altered state or reality), approaching flow.

Other Community-Building Experience Products

Many others share Chesky's and Rowray's concern for the loss of community, what Morton Grodzins characterized as a modern, widespread "*gemeinschaft grouse.*"[59] Unlike the social commentators Grodzins criticized, however, entrepreneurs such Chesky and Rowray have experience products to sell that they believe will help meet an authentic but neglected human need and find a market.

Chesky's belief that there is reservoir of unmet needs for personal contact and interpersonal experiences seems to be borne out by the market in ways other than the success of Airbnb. Some of the more prominent experience-economy players are restaurants such as Rainforest Café and Medieval Times. By adding just a hint, a soupçon, of interpersonal experiences and play to their offerings, these chains have been successful in one of the most competitive of businesses. Rainforest Cafés have simply added animatronics and theatrical setting (sets, lights, and sounds) to simulate a jungle. Customers join the game, the fantasy, and play along with the sights and sounds that accompany the meals, being apart together in the make-believe world. Medieval Times restaurants offer a fantasy of medieval pageantry, jousts, horses, and wenches (waitresses), along with charred chickens. Apart from the joint pretending (what may be recognized as an adult version of "parallel play"; see Box 6.1 for the stages of play development), interpersonal contact is minimal or nonexistent—an opening for product innovation.

Hotels and movie theaters have tried to compete as well. Tru by Hilton offers space for people to get together (in "the Hive"),[60] dine-in theaters now offer tables for people to eat, socialize, and watch a movie together,[61] some providing leaders for groups to discuss the movie or play afterward. Other businesses add creative activities to the chance to socialize, offering the possibilities of accomplishment and competency.

For example, art classes have evolved. Artists throughout the United States now offer the experience of painting as a group activity (a party, a night out), complete with wine and occasional instruction.[62] Crafts are marketed in similar fashion. Decorate-it-yourself pottery design and decorating shops are found in cities throughout the nation. Fabric store classes have increasingly focused on socialization, spawning sewing and knitting clubs. Build-a-Bear Workshops add creativity (children combine options to make their own bear) to opportunities for parallel play for customers.

Adding exploration and seeking and a generous measure of game playing to positive interpersonal relations, escape rooms have enjoyed a recent fad-like success worldwide—over eight thousand were estimated to exist in 2017.[63] Groups of family or friends are locked together in a room and given a time limit to escape. Depending on their abilities to find and follow clues and solve puzzles together, the groups fail or succeed. After he and his daughter Malia were able to meet this challenge in Waikiki, Hawaii, with twelve seconds to go, a newspaper reported, "Former President Obama Joins the Global 'Escape Room' Craze."[64]

If people such as Milton Friedman, Joseph Schumpeter, and Deirdre McCloskey are right, the free market should promote adult development through play-like experiences—for example, parallel play functioning as the prelude to richer, more pleasurable associative play. Competition should force Rainforest Café and Medieval Times to add richer, deeper, and longer-lasting kinds of experiences to the simple *communitas* of a joint fantasy experience.

Individual Skills

With the loss of community, the loss of craftsmanship has long concerned social critics. During the push for the eight-hour day at the beginning of the twentieth century, laborites argued that increasing leisure would allow workers to recover the craftsmanship and control they had lost at work in freely chosen hobbies and self-selected projects. Frederick Taylor and his fellow "scientific managers" agreed: the assembly line and the ongoing advance of technology would continue to replace skilled, high-paying jobs with machines, leaving only repetitive, "deskilled" work.[65] Concerns that jobs are becoming ever more boring, straitjacketed, impersonal, and meaningless and ever less challenging and rewarding have grown for a century.

Today, innovative companies and entrepreneurs see the needs for creativity and pride of workmanship still going unmet and are offering experience products to fill those needs. Along with fabric stores nationwide, Home Depot is offering DIY workshops, teaching skills needed for projects ranging from bath to kitchen do-overs. The social experience of learning with other amateurs, with the personal guidance of an expert, is a part of the company's marketing strategy. People who learn to lay flooring at Home Depot may be more liable to buy what they need for their projects from the store.

For years, the Public Broadcasting Service has offered a series of DIY woodworking shows. One of the most popular has been the *Woodsmith Shop*.[66] Underwritten by Kreg Tool Company, Powermatic (makers of home shop equipment), and Old Masters (stains and finishes), each program guides viewers through a project recently featured in *Woodsmith* magazine. The program functions as experience marketing for both the underwriters and the magazine, but it also contributes to the experience and transformation economies, encouraging and teaching autonomous home craftsmanship.

The IKEA Effect

Another major player in the DIY market has only recently (since 2008) emerged to become the largest furniture retailer in the world. IKEA, a Swedish-based firm, offers quality, innovatively designed furniture at bargain prices. Part of the company's appeal is its proven ability to engage customers. Believing that a healthy slice of its demographic will enjoy the experience of designing their own interiors, the company offers the chance to personalize:

We don't believe in perfect homes. We believe in homes that are a perfect reflection of the people who live inside. Where everything looks the way you want it to, works the way you need it to, and just generally makes you feel good—without costing a fortune. That's why we've filled this section with tons of different home ideas, from home decoration ideas to organising tips to inspiration for making your home more green. So, you'll have all you need for creating a space that you love calling home.[67]

The company is best known, arguably, for customers having to put their furniture together. This do-it-yourself aspect of IKEA products may have initially been part of its effort to keep prices down, substituting the customers' labor for work they would otherwise have to pay for. It has become the company's distinguishing feature, however, even though now customers can have the company assemble their products, for a fee.

When a group of my students presented IKEA as their semester class project, I was initially reluctant to agree that the company was part of the experience economy. Others in class agreed. Those of us who had experienced the agony and humiliation of struggling to put together unassembled products, following unintelligible directions and missing vital parts, failed to see the appeal—where was the intrinsic motivation, where was the fun of assembling furniture? Was this not a kind of exploitation of customers who were being made to work for free for the company?

My students came through, however, meeting our objections and earning excellent marks. They did their homework and were able to point out that some good research had been done in 2011 about what is now widely known as the IKEA effect.[68] Researchers have found that people value the things that they have had a hand in building more than things they buy readymade, even though the effort is minimal and requires little skill.

My students argued that rather than intrinsic motivation, accomplishment and the feeling of competency were the key checklist subjective experience elements that account for IKEA's success. They also argued, on the basis of the research they had read, that self-assembly focuses attention, producing a more positive regard for and attachment to the object.

Branders and value capturers have also seen the IKEA effect's profit potential. Explaining "how to profit from the IKEA Effect," Tyler Tervooren suggests that businesses "can reap massive rewards by putting the Ikea Effect to work. . . . Whenever you can, let [customers] customize the products and services you offer to fit their needs. . . . Make them feel like their own creativity and effort went into getting what they need from you. They'll pay more for it."[69] Such a feeling, however, even though created by the company, is very likely to get out of control, ranging beyond the ability of companies and managers to capture its value.

Made to "feel like" they are creative and in control, customers will be prone to seek additional opportunities for autonomy and creativity, to broaden and build[70] on their own—if the sciences of happiness research findings are true. Such a broadening and building, and appetite for autonomy, will be hard for the market to contain, harder for companies to capture as profit. Such appetites have before, and may once again, be best satisfied beyond the reaches of the marketplace.

For instance, the cherishing and attachment that comes from focused attention makes consumers reluctant to replace the prized object they have helped create with a newer model, helping liberate consumers from the throw-away economy.[71] Consumer culture theorists agree—the same kind of attachment is often found to products that help establish and express cultural or gender identity.[72]

A good example of how customer-created-value additions are difficult for the market to contain is the expansion of DIY through the Internet. While the DIY markets for tools and supplies are expanding rapidly (growing at a rate that is projected to reach nearly $14 billion by 2021),[73] the value represented by customers' time and value-added contributions has largely escaped capture.

Hometalk

Billing itself as the world's largest DIY community, Hometalk, with 1.2 billion views on Facebook in 2016 and 12 million official members according to *Forbes*, began in 2011 as a home improvement website.[74] Yaron Ben Shaul (chief executive officer) and Miriam Illions (chief marketing officer) originally hoped to offer amateurs enough information for them to do projects on their own. Attempting to provide a forum in which do-it-yourselfers could ask contractors questions and contractors could provide model projects, the company reasoned that both the consumers and the providers of information would win—the companies and contractors by publicizing their services and by building goodwill and their consumer base.

However, as Ben Shaul explains,

what actually happened was that the contractors were not sharing content in any meaningful way, but there was genuine interest in

DIY content created by community members. When we saw that, we quickly spun off Hometalk into its own entity, a user-generated platform where users can share their projects and experiences with each other.[75]

Hometalk provides an excellent example of how entrepreneurs may recognize and capitalize on a from-below pattern they observe in the market. Shaul and Illions recognized that customers, sharing their stories and helping others, were finding value in the virtual, interactive community formed by their website (positive social relations, altruism, *communitas*). Arguably, something of the IKEA effect was happening as well; telling their stories, the craftspeople were paying additional attention to the items they had created and valuing them even more. Through this process Hometalk emerged as a catalyst-enabler of a largely autonomous sharing community and was handsomely rewarded for it.

A New Eudaimonic Technology

Judging from its implicit appearances so far in the marketplace, as the principles of design (suggested by the table of consiliences, checklists, and play development, characteristics, and model) are more purposefully applied to experience design, the eudaimonic technology will develop in markedly different ways than older technologies did. So far, the eudaimonic technology seems to be less dependent on mass-scale production, intensive capitalization, and centralized ownership. In contrast to what some call hard technologies (makers of tangible, material products that depend on copyrighting and patenting of engineering techniques), eudaimonic technology produces intangible values, depending more on "softer" resources: "social networks, human interactive processes, and motivation techniques"[76] and "softer" sources of information—the Internet, the social sciences and their probabilities, and even the humanities for the wealth of received wisdom.

In addition to producing intangible, subjective values, eudaimonic technology is coming to depend more on freely shared, open resources of the new commons: the Internet and the sharing economy. Moreover, capitalization is appearing to be softer as well, also mostly intangible and, most importantly, substantially owned by consumers in the form of individuals' time and skills. Certainly, larger capital-rich concerns are engaged and benefiting nationwide; Disney World, Hilton, upscale bourbon whiskey producers, and casinos. However, one may argue, as I have been, that the growth of the transformation economy entails the gradual evolution of eudaimonic technology toward softer, more widely dispersed resources—for example, Airbnb.

From the historian's point of view, the distinction between hard (older) and soft (newer) technologies depends on their historical purposes. Hard technologies have, since the Enlightenment, been primarily concerned with "solving the economic problem,"[77] freeing more and more human beings from the slavery of chronic material scarcity. Efficiency, producing more with less, has always been a primary concern, as have the "absolute" human needs: food, clothing, and shelter—the concept of declining utility depends on the assumption that some needs are more pressing than others. Science and hard technologies have allowed humans to master the physical world, freeing them for better things—expanding their choices of material goods, to be sure, but also allowing them to choose increased leisure to enjoy these goods and, just as importantly, to experience more of their lives freely, beyond the marketplace.

Soft technologies will be concerned with the uses of the free time that the hard technologies have made possible—serving the leisure needs of people in the form of new experience products.

The Purpose of Eudaimonic Technology: The Mass Creation of Intangible Experiences and Transformations That Serve and Prepare for Leisure

Reflecting on the "the accumulation of capital vs. shorter work time and the possibilities for freedom"[78] during the Great Depression, John Maynard Keynes anticipated some of the findings of the new sciences of happiness:

> Now it is true that the needs of human beings may seem to be insatiable. But they fall into two classes—those needs which are absolute . . . , and those which are relative in the sense that we feel them only if their satisfaction lifts us above, makes us feel superior to, our fellows. Needs of the second class, those which satisfy the desire for superiority, may indeed be insatiable. . . . But this is not so true of the absolute needs—a point may soon be reached, much sooner perhaps than we are all of us aware of, when these needs are satisfied in the sense that we prefer to devote our further energies to non-economic purposes.[79]

Sociologists' findings about the advent of postmaterialism confirms that some kind of turning point may have been reached and that a transition is underway from material values and economic concerns to more humane and moral possibilities.[80] But Keynes predicted that such a turning of energy would be problematic.

The economic problem is not—if we look into the future—the permanent problem of the human race. . . . If the economic problem is solved, mankind will be deprived of its traditional purpose. . . . I think with dread of the readjustment of the habits and instincts of the ordinary man . . . for the first time since his creation man will be faced with his real, his permanent problem—how to use his freedom from pressing economic cares, how to occupy the leisure, which science and compound interest will have won for him, to live wisely and agreeably and well. . . . It is a fearful problem for the ordinary person, with no special talents, to occupy himself.[81]

As Keynes explained, as technology developed and capitalism expanded, humans forgot most of the old arts of living—those preindustrial, convivial ways and skills that E. P. Thompson believed may yet be revived through a modern, "novel dialectic."[82] Thus, when the inevitable happens and significant amounts of leisure are at long last available, humans no longer have the imagination, skills, or traditions needed for the challenge.

Whereas the "science and technology" Keynes had in mind promise to "solve the economic problem" and to free humans to enjoy more of their lives, the eudaimonic technology promises to help solve the "leisure problem."[83] Thus, the eudaimonic technology may be characterized, historically, as a soft technology because it serves to guide and enrich the leisure made possible by the hard technologies.

The eudaimonic technology has the potential to use the new sciences of happiness to produce more and better goods, services, and experiences that enable humans "to live wisely and agreeably and well," as Keynes predicted, in freedom beyond the market. Compensating for capitalism's amnesia, the eudaimonic technology may make it possible to reacquaint humans with their humanity through the marketplace by means of the efficient production of positive subjective experiences and activities that express and promote positive individual traits (character strengths and virtues). Businesses and entrepreneurs will succeed by providing richer experiences of the self, community, the natural world, and for many, the mystery at the heart of all being.

Small Is Beautiful

Other distinctions between hard and soft technologies are also useful in describing the emerging eudaimonic technology. In many of its recent appearances, eudaimonic technology resembles what has come to be widely known as appropriate technology. Popularized by Ernst Friedrich Schumacher in the 1970s with his book *Small Is Beautiful: Economics as If People Mattered*, the concept of small-scale, decentralized, self-sufficient hard technologies became familiar: for example, human-powered water pumps, universal nut shellers, drip irrigation, and solar-powered lighting.[84] Such small-scale technologies were attractive to developing nations because the capital-intensive technology transfers from the richer nations were benefiting only small, richer segments of their populations. Small-scale machines and techniques were more democratic, available to all, with minimal capital investment, allowing communities to be more self-sufficient and individuals to be more self-reliant. Small-scale technology also helped reduce the labor surplus plaguing developing nations. Some attempts were made in the 1970s to apply these principles in the United States, and the ecological benefits of small-scale technology still have significant appeal.[85]

The nascent eudaimonic technology resembles these early efforts in the sense that its techniques are available to all for small-scale development of experience products. Capital requirements are minimal. For the entrepreneurial cousins who have made the experience of making pasta with Nonna a success on Airbnb, few resources are needed besides a grandmother and her kitchen. Moreover, since it is difficult to patent an idea, the barriers of copyright and patent present fewer problems for the dissemination of the technology.

Equality

Like appropriate technology, eudaimonic technology is opening the possibility that more of a nation's population will share, and share more equally, a nation's benefits and values, immediate and long term. Whereas, by replacing work with machines and techniques, traditional technologies built ever-greater maldistributions of wealth, eudaimonic technology opens the possibility that the new values it produces, because they are intangible and more easily possessed by individuals, will, perforce, be more equally distributed. Moreover, since those values depend for their expression on a human's lifetime, time may reemerge as the true measure of value, adding some credence to John Ruskin's' observation, "There is no wealth but life."[86]

Like appropriate technology, eudaimonic technology may also address the problem of labor surplus. Labor intensification characterized appropriate technology in the developing nations: jobs were created and some of the labor surplus used. The situation is different in the industrialized nations. There is no doubt that jobs are being created in the experience and transformation economies. However, the eudaimonic technology promises to absorb some of the labor surplus of the industrialized nations by encouraging the voluntary choice of working less, a choice that diverts the productive efforts of an individual from a job in the capitalist marketplace to intrinsically motivated productive consumption (IMPC) in leisure. Such a free-market transfer might realize the utopian socialist Charles Fourier's dream of "glorious" labor, valuable in and for itself, to which people will run "as to a festival."[87] Work (as free productive effort, or IMPC) and leisure may become indistinguishable.

Appropriate technology's early efforts were less than a great success. Largely dependent on government programs and nonprofit grants, these efforts have proved to be difficult to sustain, the technology too expensive to be widely distributed without continuing public support. However, over the last two decades, the movement has seen something of a resurgence. Turning to free-market solutions, and led by people such as Paul Polak and his International Development Enterprises, appropriate technology has harnessed the profit motive to small-scale development, turning to capital markets to produce reliable profit chains extending from international funds to local entrepreneurs.[88]

Something similar may be seen in the history of the United States. Originally, public and nonprofit institutions addressed the "leisure problem"[89] but with little success after the initial salad days of the early twentieth century were over. True believers in the potential of leisure time to humanize American culture such as Robert Hutchins and Frank Lloyd Wright then turned from altruism and public resources to the profit motive and the free market to realize what they believed was the authentic American dream in danger of being forgotten.

8

The Economics of Experiences

*The Liberating Potential of the
New Economies and Technology*

There is no wealth but life. Life, including all its powers of
love, of joy, and of admiration. That country is the richest
which nourishes the greatest numbers of noble and happy
human beings; that man is richest, who, having perfected
the functions of his own life to the utmost, has also the
widest helpful influence, both personal, and by means of his
possessions, over the lives of others.
—JOHN RUSKIN, *Unto This Last*

Having seen how some businesses are able to create experiences and
transformations that apply what the new sciences of happiness have
discovered about well-being, questions arise: How might the economy
accommodate these developments? How much can the new economies grow?
This chapter analyzes the economics of the experience and transformation
economies and the potential economic impact of the eudaimonic technology. Since the new economies include the question of the supply of free time
needed for new consumption, an analysis of the economics of leisure is undertaken. Staffan Linder's, John Owen's, and Gary Becker's theories about a consumption maximum, the price of leisure, opportunity costs, and productive
consumption are reviewed. I conclude that Becker's theories cannot explain
productive consumption and the price of leisure in the experience and transformation economies. A new formulation, intrinsically motivated productive
consumption (IMPC) is offered as a better way to understand the economics
of the new economies and technology. I review findings from consumer culture theory that support the IMPC interpretation. Older economic theories
about the demand for leisure, such as Frank Knight's, are offered as better
models. On the basis of these analyses, I predict that the demand for leisure
will increase with the growth of the experience and transformation economies
and the eudaimonic technology; that value will migrate from money capital to
individual time use beyond the marketplace; and that the historical shorter-
hours process will be reborn, giving life to the forgotten American dream.

Optimists predict that the advance of the experience and transformation economies will mean the creation of jobs, more business opportunities, and robust economic growth. These two new stages of "the progression of economic values" appear to some as the last, best hope for modern economies otherwise facing stagnant growth and a jobless future. Certainly, parts of the new economies are flourishing.[1] But the future is clouded by one, strictly limited resource. Time.

Staffan Linder: Time Limits and the Consumption Maximum

Basic economics texts often explain utility by using a two-good model, which assumes that utility is a measure of preferences for goods (things that give us satisfaction) determined by choices in the marketplace. The simplified model illustrates the complex choices most of us have to make by reducing choices to two: leisure or income. The more we work, the more income we have; and the less we work, the more leisure we have. "Your money or your life!" Income and leisure are the prototypical scarce things that we all have to economize. We try to "maximize" utility, the "aggregate level of satisfaction," by choosing between the two—in language popular today, we try to find a balance.[2]

Building on the simple insight that both time and income are necessary for us to be consumers, Staffan Burenstam Linder created something of a stir among economists and in the business world some years ago with his book *The Harried Leisure Class*.[3] Making the minimal assumptions that consumption takes time, that utility is a function of time needed for consumption (goods and services give us no satisfaction if we do not have time to use them), and that time is limited, Linder argued that as the economy grows and production (and incomes) increases, more goods and services will have to be consumed in the limited amount of time we all have. Those commodities whose consumption is time intensive (requiring relatively more time, such as reading a book) would have to be given up in favor of consumption of commodities that are goods intensive (requiring more spending and relatively less time; e.g., skydiving). Efficiency in production will have to be matched by efficiency in consumption.

The alternative, of course, is to relieve some of the pressure and maximize utility by taking additional leisure, turning to more time-intensive consumption.[4] However, Linder noted that working hours had been stable for decades, which had created a need for more consumption in the same amount of free time. Not fully satisfied with Gary Becker's explanations (see more on Becker later in the chapter), he was at something of a loss to explain why Americans had given up on work reductions, becoming more and more "harried." He concluded that a "growth mania" had inflicted the nation, resulting in irrational behavior in the marketplace that was unfortunate and ultimately unsustainable.[5]

The "growth mania" was unfortunate because the dreams about progress throughout the ages—dreams about a democratic culture where every person would have the time necessary to enrich his or her life in nonpecuniary ways outside the economy—were giving way to the harsh realities of the modern consumer imperative.[6] Even the "pleasures of the table and the bed" were diminishing in favor of an orgy of consuming.[7]

The "growth mania" was unsustainable because "economic growth [with stable or lengthening work hours] entailed a general increase in the scarcity of time" that would eventually lead to a "consumption maximum."[8] Before long, more and more people with relatively less time to use, consume, or experience new things would discover the utility (and marginal satisfaction) of additional purchases approaching zero. According to Linder, "Total affluence [unlimited production requiring unlimited consumption and thus unlimited time to consume] is a logical fallacy."[9]

The "consumption maximum" that is the compelling conclusion of Linder's economic calculus is in direct contradiction to optimistic predictions about the unlimited economic growth potential opened by the experience and transformation economies. Yet optimists such as Joseph Pine and James Gilmore agree with Linder's assumption about the importance of time in consumption, concluding, "Time is the currency of experiences."[10] Indeed, one of the ways that scholars distinguish the experience economy from the service economy is that consumption in the experience economy is more dependent on time use. In Pine and Gilmore's estimation, "What truly makes an experience a distinct economic offering, providing new sources of revenue growth, is requiring customers to explicitly pay for the time they spend in places or events."[11]

Where Will the Time Come From? The Price of Leisure

Economists have long assumed that the amount of time a person is willing to work is influenced by wages.[12] But the effect an increase in wages has on the choice between leisure and income is problematic.

For years economists assumed that leisure was a normal good[13] and that as wages improved most people, sacrificing some of their potential wage income for free time, would tend to "buy" more of it—they called this the income effect. This assumption seemed safe enough. As wages improved, working hours had decreased for nearly a century in Western nations by the mid-decades of the twentieth century. Some economists, the marginalists and later Frank Knight and Arthur Pigou, tried to explain the decline in working hours by pointing out that people's free time was becoming more valuable to them than all the new, less needed luxuries industry had been able to invent. John Kenneth Galbraith summed up their argument: "The doctrine of diminishing marginal utility . . . put economic ideas squarely on the side of the diminishing importance of production under the conditions of increasing affluence. . . . The effect of increasing affluence is to minimize the importance of economic goals."[14] In short, after basic material needs are taken care of, most humans will begin to prefer some additional opportunities to enjoy their lives.

Lionel Robbins[15] argued, however, that leisure was an exceptional good. Unlike other normal goods, the price of leisure increases when wages increase—after a raise, most people have to "pay" more (by giving up more potential income) to take an hour off work. For example, when wages increase from fifteen dollars to seventeen dollars an hour, the price of leisure increases by two dollars an hour. Just as with all other goods, when the price of leisure increases, people are prone to look for alternatives (the substitution effect). If the price of beef goes up, we are more likely to substitute chicken. Whereas Frank Knight and Arthur Pigou assumed that as people's incomes increased most would automatically work less and less, Robbins reasoned that the effect was *indeterminate*.[16] People could continue "to forgo"[17] some of their potential wages in favor of additional leisure. Even though it had become more expensive after the raise, leisure was still a valuable thing to have. Alternatively, they could change their minds and choose to work the same hours, or even longer, preferring additional income to buy other goods and services rather than (as a substitute for) more leisure. The best course for the economist was to concentrate on empirical descriptions.

As the economist John Owen[18] wrote, "All an economist could say" about the century-long reduction in working hours Knight and Pigou had observed was that "for the average worker the income effect of a rise in the wage rate [was] in fact stronger than the substation effect." Predicting the future according to that trend—in 1930 John Maynard Keynes predicted a three-hour workday by 1980—was hazardous.[19]

Obviously, as Staffan Linder noted in 1970, early predictions of fewer work hours proved to be far off the mark.[20] What has happened over the last half century or so has been the reverse of what Robbins and his colleagues were witnessing; the substitution effect appears to be swamping the income effect.

Those who remain bullish about the experience economy have yet to fully come to grips with Linder's simple point that time is a limited commodity and with his predictions about the advent of the harried leisure class appearing to be coming true. According to some more recent accounts, working hours have lengthened significantly, so much so that we are working upward of five weeks longer each year than we did in the 1970s.[21] These numbers are controversial, but no one disagrees that the great majority of us feel stressed and overworked. Over the last two decades, overwork has been a topic of national concern (search online for the term "overwork" for articles posted during the last twenty-four hours for examples).[22]

The retirement age is increasing. The *New York Times* reported a "steep turnaround" in workforce participation rates of males fifty-five to sixty-four years old, concluding that "retirement [is] turning into a brief rest stop."[23] Not only does the United States trail all industrial nations in vacation days taken per year (ten vs. twenty or more days on average); vacations may be contracting. Catherine Rampell reported in the *New York Times* that "Americans working in the private sector are less likely to have paid vacation days than was the case 20 years ago."[24] Nearly a third of all full-time employees in this country, failing to use all their vacation days, lose them each year—which prompted Hilton Hotels to assemble a Leisure Time Advocacy task force a few years ago.[25]

NBC News concluded that "the concept of the weekend is dying."[26] The salaried middle classes have seen their yearly working hours increase by 660 hours—20 percent more than twenty-five years ago. *U.S. News and World Report* found that nearly 40 percent of this group worked more than fifty hours a week.[27] Within a few years most in this group will likely be working sixty hours a week if things keep going the way they have since the 1980s.[28]

What are the chances of selling new and more experiences to fatigued white-, blue-, or pink-collar employees after they have worked an exhausting eight- to ten-hour day, or during the weekend when they are trying to catch up on chores, or during their shrinking vacations when simple rest is a priority?

Some economists have questioned these findings, carefully reviewing data that show some increase in free time at least through 1980.[29] Whether the substitution effect has entirely swamped the income effect for nearly eighty years or the substitution effect has simply strengthened, it is important to understand this long-lasting change. As Robbins demonstrated, since the relative strength of the income effect vis-à-vis the substitution effect is indeterminate, other independent variables (regressors) must be found to account for the change.

John Owen, with other economists, suggests that the increasing price of recreation,[30] the decline in fatigue, the availability of consumer credit, and more enjoyable work are all factors.[31] Staffan Linder suggested that an irrational "growth mania" was responsible. Historians have offered their explanations: the coming of modern advertising and consumerism, the beginning of government support of Full-Time, Full Employment, the weakening of labor unions, and cultural changes concerning the valuation of work vis-à-vis leisure.[32]

Gary Becker, Opportunity Costs, and More Time at Work

Gary Becker's analysis is particularly apropos. Becker influenced a generation of economists by pointing out that all time off work is not simply leisure. Some leisure is more like work because it is spent in productive effort.[33] Preparation of meals is a prime example of people, often together in a household, combining their free time with market goods to produce useful commodities. Assuming that "households are producers as well as consumers," Becker wrote, "a household is truly a 'small factory': it combines capital goods, raw materials and labour to clean, feed, procreate and otherwise produce useful commodities."[34] Becker reasoned that people with higher incomes, because their opportunity costs (the cost of forgone earnings) are greater, will choose to pay others to prepare their food, do chores for them, and so on.[35] They will want to substitute the cheaper time of others for their own more expensive leisure.[36] Thus, as wages increase, the ratio of goods used to consumption time will increase, and people will substitute purchased goods and services for free time spent in household production.[37]

Becker explained:

> A rise in earnings . . . would induce a decline in the amount of time used at consumption activities, because time would become more expensive . . . goods would be substituted for the more expensive time in the production of each commodity, and . . . goods-intensive commodities would be substituted for the more expensive time-intensive ones. Both substitutions require less time to be used at consumption, and *permit more to be used at work*.[38]

Agreeing with Becker, Stephen Hill concludes, "A rise in earnings leads to the substitution of time-intensive commodities by goods-intensive ones. A shift away from time-intensive commodities could result in a fall in the time spent in consumption *and therefore an increase in the time spent at work*."[39]

Becker observed that technology had not only increased productivity at work; it had improved the productivity of consumption time. Advances such as supermarkets and electric razors had made it possible to produce more efficiently during time spent away from paid work. Whereas the century-long "decline in hours worked appeared to be evidence that the income effect was sufficiently strong to swamp the substitution effect," because of recent improvements in the productivity of consumption time the reverse was predictable. He explained, "The higher real income resulting from an advance in the productivity of consumption time" would strengthen the substitution effect and "cause hours of work to increase."[40]

All the reasons, listed above, for why leisure has grown very little or declined since the mid-twentieth century do not foreclose the possibility of change—the choice between income and leisure remains, as Robbins stated, *indeterminate*. Indeed, some of those reasons, those explanatory variables, are changing while new relevant variables are emerging, signaling a stronger demand for leisure time with the coming of the experience and transformation economies.[41]

In the Experience and Transformation Economies, Productive Efforts Are Useful Commodities

Becker assumed that households "produce commodities by combining inputs of goods and time according to the cost-minimisation rules of the traditional theory of the firm."[42] In the experience and transformation economies, however, such rules do not apply. Unlike Becker's small factory, households and individuals in the experience and transformation economies do not "combine[] capital goods, raw materials and *labour*"[43] to produce useful commodities in the same ways. The useful commodities produced are fundamentally different because *the productive effort (the "labour" input) involved is itself the useful commodity*. Becker's original distinction[44] between leisure and "productive consumption" is lost.[45] This simple fact causes fundamental problems for Becker's analysis when applied to the experience and transformation economies and for his assumptions about the strengthening of the substitution effect and shift toward goods-intensive leisure.

In the experience economy, the value added to an experience product by the customer is identical with the production of the experience. Certainly, businesses that make experience products available in the market provide essential input to the productive consumption equation—they represent the same cost as those goods needed for household production in Becker's model. In the transformation economy, however, when customers, increasingly skillful, begin to own the means of production (are able to produce experiences on their own), they require fewer expenditures for experience providers, further decreasing the price of productive consumption.

For example, my wife and I love to cook. Over the years, as consumers in the experience economy, we have purchased books and tapes, taken classes and tours that provide experiences, instruction, and encouragement. We frequented good restaurants for inspiration. Gradually, we have acquired a few skills. Transformed with these skills, we enjoy nothing better than dinner parties at home for friends that we prepare together. The effort is intense, often sweaty. But we are happy to give up our work time, income, and night out for this productive activity and for sharing with our friends. Our productive consumption becomes our play, the physical product (the meal), and is a contribution to community, adding a eudaimonic dimension to the experience. The option of hiring caterers, even though often entertained while we are cleaning up, is not a serious one. Because of such IMPC, the time spent at our regular jobs becomes as much of an opportunity cost as our leisure time.[46]

The option of hiring others to do our IMPC for us is not reasonable in most of the experience and transformation economies. Certainly there are exceptions—in Japan busy people may hire an ersatz family to visit their elderly parents.[47] But the thought of hiring someone to travel, go dancing, gamble, engage in a hobby or spiritual practice, or in the ironic example Becker used and the best loved by my students, "to procreate" for them is attractive to few people.[48]

Consumer culture theory and empirical research supports this interpretation of IMPC. Adam Arvidsson notes that productive consumption has a long history as theory, including, but not limited to, the economists' uses.[49] He notes that over the last forty years there has been "a shift in the very nature of consumer culture." Consumers have moved from a passive identification with brands and products to a relatively more active, productive role, creating their own identities, cultural products, and collaborative venues to share them.[50] Clay Shirky agrees that a shift in leisure behavior from passive consumption to active creation and collaboration has been going on since the 1940s and promises a regeneration of community, social capital, and civic virtue.[51]

The advent of new technologies such as computers and social media helps explain this shift to more active involvement because they reduce the cost of cultural production (videos, text messaging, etc.), facilitate the "mediatization of consumer goods and social relations in general," and allow consumers to connect easily in communities or "publics." Moreover, higher levels of education have produced a "cognitive surplus"—an oversupply of people, particularly millennials, with redundant skills, underemployed and looking for creative outlets.[52]

The result is an "information" or "knowledge" virtual economy, existing beyond traditional markets, in which collaborative production is the norm and common resources are used and built. Collaborative production is organized by participant producers rather than bosses or the marketplace—a more democratic, bottom-up form or economic organization in which the values of the hive are more important. Ownership is subordinate to production because participants contribute to a tragedy-free commons[53]—to shared investments that grow, enriching the whole.[54]

In addition, civic and ethical purposes rather than personal financial gain provide stronger motives to produce in the virtual spaces. Arvidsson observes that in the information and knowledge economies intrinsic motives are salient: "Enjoyment of the consumer products . . . [is] enhanced by some form of productive consumption." Accordingly, "there is no discernable link between concrete productive participations and the perspective of monetary rewards."[55]

Some have seen this collaborative production as transcending traditional economic rationality and the assumption that monetary rewards are the main drivers of productive effort. In the new extramarket economies, productive effort is its own reward (that is, IMPC), providing a hedonic experience. The "mode"[56] of production is altruistic and convivial, taking place in voluntary, free venues that function more as communities than competitors, adding a eudaimonic dimension to production.

Time for the Experience and Transformation Economies: The Rebirth of Shorter Hours

The rise of productive consumption over the last two decades, reported by consumer culture theory research, is a new variable supporting the possibility that the demand for free time, necessary for such production, may also increase, accompanied by an increase in demand for time-intensive experiences. These two possibilities are supported by several other factors.

John Owen reasoned that because work had become more pleasant in the twentieth century employees had been taking less leisure time.[57] The same logic may be applied to IMPC. Replacing the labor-like, cost-incurred productive consumption of Becker's households, IMPC is not merely easier but enjoyable in itself (a satisfaction gained). In IMPC, work (productive effort) and leisure merge, an outcome that supports the possibility of an increase in the demand for leisure and a greater preference for time-intensive consumption experiences.

Moreover, the eudaimonic technology promises to produce experience products that provide greater satisfactions (a possibility supported by the new sciences of happiness) than those gained by the purchase of goods and services. These new, potentially more competitive experience products will require increasingly more time and fewer goods inputs (more so as the transformation economy grows), thus making leisure more attractive and further strengthening the income effect. As technology improves IMPC, one may expect that the cost of time-intensive commodities, which according to Becker "have been luxuries,"[58] will decline relative to the cost of goods-intensive commodities.

With the growth of IMPC, Silly Putty's old ad campaign touting "hours of fun" should find new appeal for savvy experience designers.

The claim that demand for time-intensive experiences and for leisure will increase is further supported by Pine and Gilmore's observation that the growth of the experience and transformation economies will require increasing consumption time.[59] Indeed, one of the best ways to distinguish experience products from services is the amount of value added by customers, which entails increasingly time-intensive experiences. The research findings of the new sciences of happiness support the possibility that time-intensive consumption will be in greater demand. Whereas some believe that goods-intensive experiences (e.g., skydiving) are still better bets, psychologists have found that "consistently feeling moderate subjective well-being has a more beneficial effect than an occasional experience of bliss" and that "frequency [of experiences] is actually more important than intensity."[60]

Goods-intensive consumption, consuming and doing more in less time, is foreign to the universe of things done for their own sake. The point of IMPC is not to get it over as soon as possible but to linger.[61] Research findings about the importance of attention (mindfulness) for enriching experiences emphasize the need for ample time.[62] Linder and Becker recognize the human price paid for increasingly goods-intensive leisure: that many of life's best things simply cannot be done going full speed, such as the "pleasures of the table and table" conversation and enjoyment of the natural world.[63]

James Gleick points to the downside, the disutility, of goods intensification. He observes that going "faster" has resulted in a truncated existence for most of us in which appreciation, joy, and wonder are shortchanged. In the whirl of goods-intensive consumption, we are less capable of sustained concentration, sorrow, and memory.[64] Memory, by most accounts the essential, durable part of the experience and transformation economies, requires increasing consumption time.[65] Gleick points out that much of our cultural heritage is unavailable to us; we do not have the time, patience, or attention necessary to appreciate the music of the likes of J. S. Bach.

The Slow Foods and Slow Cities movements in Europe demonstrate that time-intensive leisure and tourism are now competitive in the marketplace, meeting the widespread needs for human contact and leisurely enjoyment engendered by the enduring "time famine."[66] The time famine has created a world of deficits in basic human requirements—needs that will drive the demand for innovative experience products.

Moreover, by avoiding the costs of employment such as overhead and taxes, IMPC has competitive price advantages. Producing valuable experience products outside the marketplace, IMPC also avoids costs associated with corporate profits, marketing, distribution, and retail sales—there are few or no middlemen. Therefore, IMPC should be cheaper than, and more competitive with, goods and services that are provided directly by the market—by extension, time-intensive experiences also should be more economical than goods-intensive experiences.

In addition, the advent of postmaterialist values[67] should increase the income elasticity of leisure and the demand for time-intensive experiences.[68] Eventbright, a leading "event technology platform" in the experience economy, commissioned a Harris poll in April 2017 that found that a shift in values from tangible goods and property to experiences is increasingly evident across all age groups in the United States and is associated with an increasing desire (80 percent of the sample) for more person-to-person connections.[69] But the shift is most noticeable in the millennial generation (born between 1980 and 1996). Millennials, who will become the dominant economic cohort in the 2020s, are leading the way to experiences and are "key drivers of the experience economy." Eventbright's research has consistently shown that that three out of four millennials prefer to buy experiences rather than things, "from concerts and social events to athletic pursuits, to cultural experiences." For millennials, "experiences [are] the most valuable currency," providing access to such things as identity, belonging, personal growth and expression, meaning, and "deep human connections." Experiences also are a prime source of political expression, providing a way to "take action."[70] In contrast to earlier generations, today's millennials depend less and less on their jobs as the place to realize their dreams, leading a trend that seems to be spreading. According to a 2015 Gallop poll, nearly 70 percent of U.S. employees are not "involved in, enthusiastic about or committed to their work."[71]

Bullshit Jobs

Research has shown that millennials are frequently underemployed, working intermittently or part-time. They also have trouble finding jobs commensurate with their educations. Graduates with degrees in the arts and sciences, those areas of study at the heart of the liberal arts tradition, find it increasingly hard to find suitable jobs. A report from the Federal Reserve Bank of New York in 2014 showed that for college graduates, underemployment (working at a job for which a person is overqualified) rates held steady at about 33 percent for decades before the middle of the first decade of the 2000s, but rates have been increasing among graduates ages twenty-two to twenty-seven and rose to 44 percent by 2012.[72]

Finally, the possibility that the demand for time-intensive experiences and leisure will increase is supported by the new sciences of happiness general findings that spending money on experiences is associated with greater well-being than spending money on things and that, in general, "spending time makes you happier than spending money."[73] Some psychologists make the bolder claim that "subjective well-being is associated with time affluence across all income levels . . . having more time is more important than having more money."[74]

All these factors should strengthen the income effect and support the growth of time-intensive experiences. The experience and transformation economies make it possible to avoid Linder's consumption maximum, and economic growth take the form, at least in part, of increased leisure, returning to a pattern that characterized the century-long progressive shortening of the hours of labor, the pattern familiar to Knight and Pigou.

Economic Consequences of the Experience and Transformation Economies

For the experience and transformation economies to expand, value in the form of time will have to come from the manufacturing and service sectors. The historical migration of capital from the earlier stages of economic development to later stages is a commonplace observation. But these newest stages must compete more directly for time since both depend more heavily on time for their development. Because of the increased demand for IMPC, experience providers will have to compete with manufacturing and services not only for money capital but, more importantly, for the one uniquely limited human resource, time. Unlike the competition for capital, which can continue to form in the earlier stages of economic development, the competition for time is a win-lose game.

Wealth Redistribution and the Declining Importance of Economics

Historically, economists such as Paul Douglas and John Ryan maintained that progressively shorter hours act to redistribute wealth.[75] Ryan reasoned that, by reducing the supply of labor, shorter hours would increase its price, redirecting capital from profits and luxuries to wages. Something similar may occur with the experience and transformation economies. As wealth now in the form of capital migrates to the new economies in the form of individual time, a natural dispersal should occur—fewer people will be able to claim ownership of the time of others. Government intervention will not be necessary. It is also highly unlikely that legislation guaranteeing a minimum annual income or limiting work hours will be enacted in the United States in the foreseeable future. What is very possible, however, is that ordinary people, finding better things to do with their lives in the experience and transformation economies, will shorten their work hours on their own when they are able to afford it, gradually choosing to buy back their lives instead of continuing in thrall, sacrificing their lives for the profit of the ultrarich. The century-long shorter-hours process provides ample historical precedent for such a possibility.

This migration will undoubtedly be at the expense of the growth of work and wealth, as generally understood. Critics will be likely to reject this possibility, clinging to the belief that traditional forms of wealth and work in the marketplace are the only true measure of human value, progress, and flourishing.

As John de Graaf and David K. Batker put it, however, "What's the economy for, anyway?"[76] Increasing pecuniary wealth and expanding work in the marketplace are only two possibilities among many. Moreover, work and wealth as ends in themselves are recent historical products, not eternal truths. The new economics of happiness give different answers to de Graaf and Batker's question, providing new measures of a nation's well-being, an alternative to gross domestic product, that include personal happiness, leisure time, equality, and sustainability, all of which are more appropriate measures of value in the experience and transformation economies. The economics of happiness also confirms the findings of the other sciences of happiness that spending money on experiences is a more reliable path to well-being than spending on goods.[77]

With the coming of the transformation economy, IMPC will tend to disappear from the economists' radar, leaving little more than its "shadow price" (the amount of income people are willing to give up for leisure) as a measure. This book's tables (e.g., Tables I.1 and 3.1) showing the growth of the experience and transformation economies are thus somewhat misleading because the value of the time spent on experiences is not included.

Becker realized, "The only economically relevant features of any type of consumption or leisure activity are its associated foregone earnings and contributions to utility."[78] Since IMPC collapses the distinctions Becker made between leisure and productive consumption, Knight and Pigou's older reasoning about leisure's relation to the marketplace may be increasingly relevant, arguably, in the growing experience and transformation economies. Years ago Frank Knight observed:

In so far as men act rationally—i.e., from fixed motives subject to the law of diminishing utility—they will at a higher [income] rate divide their time between wage-earning and non-industrial uses in such a way as to earn *more money*, indeed, but to work *fewer hours*. Just where the balance will be struck depends upon the shape of the curve of comparison between money (representing the group of things purchasable with money) and leisure (representing all non-pecuniary, alternative uses of time).[79]

John Maynard Keynes agreed, predicting the coming of a three-hour workday and that "a point may soon be reached, much sooner perhaps than we are all of us aware of, when these [absolute human] needs are satisfied in the sense that we prefer to devote our further energies to non-economic purposes."[80]

Another pre-Becker economist, Graham Laing, professor at the California Institute of Technology wrote, "After all, there is no need for human beings to be obsessed with economics." He concluded that "the definite and final disposing of the whole problem of material wants should release most men from the terrific preoccupation which now obtains with this relatively boring and unfruitful aspect of life."[81] John Kenneth Galbraith summed up the older, perhaps newly relevant reasoning about work and leisure: "The effect of increasing affluence is to minimize the importance of economic goals."[82]

Equality and Sustainability

In the opening realm of freedom provided by progressively shorter work hours, equality might also be more within reach. Equality beyond the pecuniary realm has an objective measure to be sure—we all have the same amount of hours each day. As psychologists note, however, equality and inequality are also subjective. The research findings from the new sciences of happiness suggest that whereas inequality (and unhappiness) is deeply felt when people think about pecuniary matters, they are less likely to envy the experiences or abilities of others. Experiences "spark less intense social comparisons"[83] and tend to be enjoyed more "on their own terms."[84] The same is true for character strengths and virtues. One of the criteria for inclusion in Peterson and Seligman's lists is that "the display of a strength by one person does not diminish other people in the vicinity."[85] For example, generosity and thankfulness are more often the cause of admiration than a source of envy.

Beginning with John Stuart Mill, economists and others have warned that perpetual economic growth is not sustainable—limits have been suggested, including environmental limits and the finite amount of time available for consumption. Those who have warned about unsustainable, perilous growth, including Mill and the Club of Rome, have often recommended increasing leisure as one of the few remedies available, pointing out that if progress were to be understood more in terms of human life and experiences beyond the marketplace, growth would no longer be a problem.[86] The New Economics Foundation suggests that a standard twenty-one-hour workweek would reduce inequalities, unemployment, carbon emissions, and overwork and improve quality of life and strengthen families.[87] Others agree that shorter hours promise a range of benefits.[88] Researchers in leisure studies agree as well.[89]

Producing experiences and transforming individuals, the experience and transformation economies offer intangible products that are relatively eco-friendly, avoiding many of the hazards associated with the production of material goods.

Participating freely in the capitalist marketplace, humans may choose to gradually leave it for more valuable things. The experience and transformation economies are the gateways of liberation capitalism, preparing individuals to produce more experiences and value on their own and assisting them in investing more of their lives in acquiring skills, interests, and character strengths and virtues that become the means of production of increasingly richer and freer experiences. In the experience and transformation economies, the socialist dreams of equality and of the merger of work and play, as well as the communist vision of the proletariat's ownership of the means of production, may be within reach, available through the free marketplace rather than government controls or revolution.

9

Historical Guides to Experience Design and the Age of Experiences

This final chapter presents yet another catalog of possibilities for experience design but one based on historical examples rather than scientific research. The century-long shorter-hours process was supported by numerous individuals who recorded the ways ordinary people were flourishing and looked ahead to the ways increasing free time would allow humans to advance: a vision Walt Whitman called higher progress. A history of these things offers a wealth of practical examples that might serve as models, making a casebook of sorts for today's entrepreneurs and experience designers. Examples are offered and analyzed, such as Robert Hutchins's *Great Books of the Western World*. The problem of equality is revisited. The contours of liberation capitalism are explored: as they were predicted by John Maynard Keynes and as they have taken shape in the experience and transformation economies. E. P. Thompson's novel dialectic is interpreted as resulting in a new synthesis: the continuing liberation of time, made possible by the advent of the new economies and eudaimonic technology. Warnings about the threats posed by such developments are repeated yet again, and new obstacles and dangers are revealed in the emergence of an unconscious faith in the perpetual expansion of work and wealth for themselves. Such an unconscious faith, by refusing the given, turns a blind eye to what humans have believed for millennia were the primary sources of happiness: accepting, celebrating, and participating in the givenness of the world and human life. The book ends with the historical model of the Sabbath as a guide for the coming age of experiences.

Historical Models

Mihaly Csikszentmihalyi notes that positive psychology had its beginnings, in part, in an attempt to counter the negative image of human life that dominated much of the twentieth century (see Chapter 5). Developing a more positive "vision that foregrounds what is good about women and men,"[1] he examined other cultures, past and present, to find what most people valued and hoped for.[2]

Finding a more positive view of humankind has several methodological implications, one of which was to

> take seriously the wisdom our ancestors have drawn from their own life experiences. An evolutionary perspective suggests that if an organ of the body or a behavior of the organism persists over time and space, it is likely to be of enduring utility. . . . The reason why most animals keep being born with eyes is that seeing gives a huge survival advantage. The same argument can be made about memes: they endure over time because they provide some advantage. It would be hubris—the overweening pride that the gods send to those they wish to destroy— for a science of man to ignore the discoveries of past generations.[3]

Another implication of the search for a more positive image of humanity is to question the lofty neutrality some demand of science. Csikszentmihalyi argues that just as an engineer values sound bridges and physicians are partial to curing illnesses, it was reasonable for psychologists to take sides and, turning from the pervading pessimism about humanity's chances, become advocates for positive change—to lead with a vision and purpose toward those things that allow humans not simply to survive but to flourish:

> Positive psychology can help provide an emergent image of . . . humankind . . . by realizing that the future will depend on the decisions we are making in the present . . . [and] by taking seriously the best of the past. . . [and] the experience of earlier generations codified in older sources of wisdom.[4]

Such reasoning informed the creation of the *Character Strengths and Virtues* handbook's lists.[5] Employing their own "empirically minded" brand of historical analysis, gathering and collating historical data, Christopher Peterson and Martin Seligman concluded that there is "a strong convergence across time, place, and intellectual tradition about certain core virtues."[6] Agreeing with Csikszentmihalyi, they "lean to" and hypothesize "a deep theory about moral excellence phrased in evolutionary terms"[7]—that the core virtues and character strengths

> are evolutionarily predisposed. These particular styles of behaving may have emerged, been selected for, and been sustained because each allows a crucial survival problem to be solved. Without biologically predisposed mechanisms that allowed our ancestors to generate, recognize, and celebrate corrective virtues, their social groups would have died out quickly. The ubiquitous virtues, we believe, are what allow the human animal to struggle against and to triumph over what is darkest within us.[8]

Drawing heavily from ancient European and Asian sources and religious traditions, the *Character Strengths and Virtues* handbook did not make full use of a rich, distinctively American tradition. U.S. history offers countless examples of the ways people in this country have pursued happiness, that most American of purposes, explicit in one of the nation's founding documents.

The Forgotten American Dream

Csikszentmihalyi's proposed "vision that foregrounds what is good about women and men"[9] has precedent in the United States. Such a vision may be understood, at least in part, as a renaissance of a forgotten American dream—a vision of the steady progress of freedom and a future increasingly rich in humane and moral possibilities.

I argue in *Free Time: The Forgotten American Dream* that an important way the pursuit of happiness found practical expression in the United States was through the century-long reduction of working hours, a process that cut working time virtually by half.[10] Led by organized labor, the process involved countless decisions by individuals about what they believed would make them happy, including the fundamental choice between free time and income.

Leisure's gradual increase and labor's struggles inspired generations of articulate supporters who noted, often in great detail, the variety of ways ordinary people were flourishing because of laborsaving devices and looked ahead to what the American Federation of Labor called, on several occasions, "the progressive shortening of the hours of labor."[11] A history of these things offers a rich historical data source for the *Character Strengths and Virtues* handbook as well as a wealth of practical examples that might serve as models, making up a casebook of sorts, for today's entrepreneurs and experience designers.

What Csikszentmihalyi calls the meme of freedom was at the heart of the shorter-hours movement. For many, shorter hours represented the culmination of history as the progress of liberation—the working out of what Fried-rich Hegel interpreted as the dialectic of history. Walt Whitman,[12] with many others of his day, maintained that American history was unfolding in three stages of freedom: political (the gradual spread of human rights in a consti-tutional democracy and the rule of law, freeing humans from oppression and tyranny), economic (material prosperity freeing humans from the slavery of material want), and the final, culminating stage of "higher progress."[13]

Higher progress was freedom's final challenge to uncover experiences and conditions that are their own reward, that are, as Whitman put it, "address'd to the loftiest, to itself alone."

> It may be claim'd, (and I admit the weight of the claim) that common and general worldly prosperity, and a populace well-to-do, and with all life's material comforts, is the main thing, and is enough. It may be argued that our republic is, in performance, really enacting to-day the grandest arts, poems, &c., by beating up the wilderness into fer-tile farms, and in her railroads, ships, machinery, &c. And it may be ask'd, Are these not better, indeed, for America, than any utterances even of greatest rhapsode, artist, or literatus?
>
> I too hail those achievements with pride and joy: then answer that the soul of man will not with such only—nay, not with such at all—be finally satisfied; but needs what, (standing on these and on all things, as the feet stand on the ground,) is address'd to the loftiest, to itself alone.[14]

The search for the autotelic, beyond obligation and reward, would be human-ity's "greater struggle"[15]—even more of a challenge than securing economic and political freedom (a sentiment echoed by John Maynard Keynes some sixty years later). How to meet the challenge of higher progress would re-quire the best of human imagination: of vision sufficient to open "democratic vistas."

Whitman's image of his standing on a high prominence, composed of the first two stages of freedom's advance, political and economic, and gazing to the future, glimpsing democratic vistas ahead,[16] is a poetic version of Selig-man's "drawn by the future."[17]

Leisure Models

Beginning in Colonial America and extending through the nineteenth and first half of the twentieth centuries, writers such as Whitman, Jonathan Edwards, and William Ellery Channing recorded what the people around them were finding to do with the new freedom offered by increasing lei-sure—including the bad with the good. Rather than remain neutral, with Csikszentmihalyi, they took sides, recommending some free activities they believed (often on the basis of the traditional sources, cited by Csikszentmi-halyi and the *Character Strengths and Virtues* handbook) produced genuine human felicity and discouraging others that made people miserable—few recommended idleness or the increased use of alcohol, for example.[18] "What is darkest within us"[19] needed to be guarded against. Drawn by the future, such writers also imagined how the new freedom would continue to engender humane and moral progress (again, often on the basis of traditional sources), envisioning the kinds of free experiences humans would gradually find that made them happiest.

Whitman's vista of free activities that would constitute higher progress included, above all, the experiences of what psychologists might recognize today as differentiation and integration. For Whitman, the autonomous (dif-ferentiated) individual was the epitome of the intrinsic—of the thing valued in and for itself. At the same time, what he called the "adhesiveness"[20] of individuals was the *free* experience of their joining together (of integration) and was the fulfillment of the promise of humane and moral progress.

Differentiating, individuals celebrate, sing, touch, play, loaf, and loiter. This is Whitman's inventory of positive experiences.

I celebrate myself, and sing myself,
And what I assume you shall assume,
For every atom belonging to me as good belongs to you.
I loafe and invite my soul,
I lean and loafe at my ease—
Observing a spear of summer grass[21]

Whitman's "adhesiveness," involving those integrative experiences that bind each of us to each, included comradeship, manly love, and intercourse of several kinds, real and metaphorical. But first on his list was poetry, the loving, binding experience of the erotic word. With his new poetry forms, Whitman deliberately broke from the rigidity of what he called the feudal past. But he also intended to leave behind the obsolete divisions of cultural classes: the elite culture producers versus the lower-class culture consumers. He envisioned, and sought to help further, a democratic culture in which everyone participated as creator, or at least coproducer—his poetry is often an invitation for the reader to join him as copoet, playing word games. He de-liberately demystified literature, trying to convince his readers that the world of culture creation did not have to be the domain of special genius but must become the functioning reality of community integration in a democracy.[22] His insight about the value and function of democratic culture production has been echoed over a century later by consumer culture theory.

Democratic genius does exist, however, and Whitman offers himself as a specimen. Unlike the genius of feudal literature, the genius of democratic culture is the one who is best able to engender creativity in other people. The genius-democrat would be a catalyst, encouraging in others the active, engaged formation and sharing of their culture's multiple experience forms, from cooking dinner to composing music—experiences through which humans, adhering together, integrate, finding community and harmony.

Throughout the history of shorter hours in America, it was Whitman's vision of higher progress that was most often the source of inspiration for other visionaries.[23] However, his secular, often earthy leisure lists, contrasted with what others, more religious and spiritually minded, believed would make people truly happy and fulfill the promise of higher progress. Jonathan Edwards predicted that eventually science and technology would "so facilitate and expedite . . . necessary secular business that [humans] will have more time for more noble exercises, and . . . the whole earth may be as one community." Having witnessed the First Great Awakening, which swept New England in the 1730s and 1740s, he thought he had seen firsthand a sample of these "more noble exercises" in his local congregation. His list included experiencing the peace of God and his presence, enjoying community and fellowship, accepting God's gifts and giving thanks, doing charitable work, paying attention to and delighting in the natural world and ordinary experiences (finding the "comfort of our meat and drink"), Bible reading, giving praise, forgiving, and repenting (in awe of, and trembling before the Divine Majesty). Describing the kinds of activities he observed during the Great Awakening, experiences he thought would characterize the coming kingdom of God, Edwards was struck by the people singing together, quoting one woman who said she could imagine nothing better than to "set and sing this life away."[24]

Some of Edward's followers, including Samuel Hopkins, distilled Edwards's lists of occupations suitable for the coming kingdom (and the coming of plentiful leisure), advising others to hone the skill of "disinterested benevolence"—the regular habit of taking joy in the joy of others. This was life's supreme and "beautiful good in itself," what Edwards called its *bonum formosum*.[25] Disinterested benevolence, something of a nineteenth-century meme itself, showing up in unexpected places such as in the novels of Harriet Beecher Stowe, should have a place in the *Character Strengths and Virtues* handbook.[26]

One of the prominent nineteenth-century supporters of labor and its struggle for the ten-hour day, Edward Ellery Channing expected that increased leisure would open opportunities for authentic human happiness. It would take a while for people to sort out their new freedom—they would experiment and likely wander down numerous blind, unhappy alleys. Eventually, they would learn by experience. Like Edwards, and on the basis of his understanding of tradition, Channing recommended conviviality (simple everyday conversation, stories, pastimes), the enjoyment of nature, spiritual practices and religious observances ("developing the idea of God") and "and physical vigor . . . valuable for its own sake." Channing was remarkably fond of dancing. He recommended that, as leisure increased, dancing should become "*an every-day amusement*, and may mix with our common intercourse. . . . The body as well as the mind feel the gladdening influence. No amusement seems more to have a foundation in our nature. . . . [G]race in motion . . . is one of the higher faculties of our nature."[27]

Dozens of nineteenth-century observers, including Abraham Lincoln,[28] expected that technology (what was once called "laborsaving machines") would continue to free humans for better things—for humane and moral progress. I provide a short catalog of these visionaries, their observations and expectations, in *Free Time*, a catalog that I hope might serve as a casebook of models for the experience and transformation economies.

During the first decades of the twentieth century, the number of such visionaries swelled as the eight-hour day and the five-day workweek arrived, and the thirty-hour workweek of six-hour-days was initiated by companies such as Kellogg's in Battle Creek and Goodyear Tire in Akron. Discourse about shorter hours and higher progress continued through the 1970s, plans were made to meet "the challenge of leisure,"[29] public resources developed, and new experiences marketed designed explicitly for people with more leisure time.

Henry Ford and many other conservative businesspeople understood that without additional free time the market for consumer goods would be limited. Ford observed, "Leisure is a cold business fact . . . where people work less they buy more." Not only do consumers have to have additional free time to use all the new products they are able to buy but, he reasoned, "business is the exchange of goods. Goods are bought only as they meet needs. Needs are filled only as they are felt. They make themselves felt largely in the leisure hours."[30] Others agreed that shortening the workweek "promises more leisure to use up motors and golf balls and holiday clothes.[31]

Among the more prominent voices making practical preparations for increasing free time was the educator Robert Hutchins. Hutchins is an example of how the century-long discourse about the coming of an age of leisure may have direct relevance to the advent of the experience and transformation economies—as a metaphorical bridge between the forgotten dream of higher progress and those economies. Hutchins is an excellent representative of the forgotten dream. He was inspired by Whitman's higher progress and strove to become, with Whitman, a catalyst and an enabler through the design and sale of liberating and empowering experiences and products. Hutchins turned from public and nonprofit resources and venues to the free market, and he thus may be included in a casebook of examples useful for entrepreneurs and businesses looking for inspiration and direction today.

Robert Maynard Hutchins

One of the most publicized university presidents in American history, Robert Hutchins is best known for his stand for tradition. From the beginning of his tenure as president of the University of Chicago in 1929, Hutchins consistently opposed the vocational and careerist direction taken by the colleges, a direction taken early in the twentieth century by educators such as Charles William Eliot and furthered during the Great Depression by influential members of Franklin Delano Roosevelt's administration, including Rexford Tugwell and Leon Keyserling.[32] Hutchins believed that teaching the liberal arts as the preparation for work was a radical break from the past and was eroding freedom and collegiality at the university, replacing them with competition for grades and positions. He insisted that the liberal arts must continue to educate people to live together freely, not to work. Teaching the arts and skills of freedom had been the genius and special mission of the academy since Plato and Aristotle—no other institution had this specific, invaluable task. Without intelligent preparation and the acquisition of appropriate skills, the freedom of expanding leisure would be impossible, even unimaginable.[33]

With Whitman and Friedrich Hegel, Hutchins saw progress as the advance of freedom in stages:

> Freedom is not an end in itself. . . . We want to be free for the sake of doing [and being] something that we cannot be or do unless we are free. . . . We [first] want our private and individual good, our economic wellbeing. . . . Second we want the common good [which is the proper role of government]: peace, order, and justice. But most of all we want *a third order of good* [cf. Whitman's "higher progress"], our personal or human good. We want, that is, to achieve the limit of our moral, intellectual, and spiritual powers. This personal, human good is the highest of all goods we seek.[34]

Answering his critics who accused him of being an anachronism, Hutchins presented himself as thoroughly modern, addressing those challenges of his

day that his critics misunderstood or ignored. Contrary to what the followers of Freud and Marx were saying, freedom had not become passé. Freedom
continued to occupy the center stage of world history, more so in the twentieth century than ever before.[35]

In the introduction to *The University of Utopia*, he quoted John Maynard
Keynes's prediction that technology would replace more and more human
labor,[36] agreeing that "if we survive . . . the machines will do the work." The
challenge of leisure had grown exponentially. Whereas since the Classical Age
the liberal arts colleges had taught only a small elite class, modern technology
was freeing the masses. Instead of human slaves, freeing only the aristocracy,
moderns had at their disposal "machine slaves" with the potential to liberate
all. The ancient Greek educational mission to educate for the freedom of
leisure had become a national challenge that the modern university, led by
Chicago, was uniquely positioned to meet. Schools and scholarship, having
their historical and etymological origins in Greek *scholé* (leisure), faced a new
task of preparing everyone for the "third order of good."[37]

During the 1940s, Hutchins attempted to streamline undergraduate education. Refocusing on the liberal arts core and jettisoning parasitic growths
(the miscellaneous vocational, "professional," research, and elective offerings)
Hutchins designed an open curriculum. Class attendance was optional—
credit hours and grade point averages were done away with. At the end of two
years, or before if they thought they were ready, students sat for comprehensive exams. If they passed, they graduated.[38]

Learning by experience was the educational focus. Students were given
the freedom of the campus, its Midway Plaisance, and the city and challenged to manage that freedom—Hutchins frequently bragged that classes
were much better attended when they were made optional. The content of
classes was based on the traditional liberal arts core, the trivium and qua-
drivium, and focused on reading traditional texts, what came to be known as
the *Great Books of the Western World* at Chicago and nationally.[39]

Part of the content of the Great Books classes was the rehearsal of the
traditional virtues. These early classes (in the 1940s) and *Encyclopaedia Britannica*'s Great Books project have similarities to the *Character Strengths and
Virtues* handbook. All three attempted to provide a compendium of strengths
and virtues that, according to received wisdom, are more likely to afford a
person a greater measure of well-being and be a sure guide to how freedom
is best employed.[40]

As important as the contents of the texts were, the way they were taught
was most critical. For Hutchins and his close ally Mortimer Adler, it was not
enough for students to read and hear about the virtues. The experience of
putting them into practice was essential. Therefore, the original Great Books

classes followed Socrates's dialogic method. Adler and the other class and group leaders and tutors reviewed the assigned texts and then posed questions relevant to the readings and contemporary issues.[41] Students then wrestled with the questions together, putting into practice the traditional virtues such as veracity, openness, attentiveness, mutuality, responsibility, tolerance, prudence, and fortitude. It was this group experience and relationships that formed rather than the text itself, its retention or correct interpretation, that were of first importance.[42]

This was the practice of philosophy Socrates recommended: a group of friends chasing after an ever-elusive Truth—for Plato and Socrates, this was humanities' most enjoyable form of playing.[43] The ephemeral truths (common agreements) that were produced by such classes as they addressed contemporary issues were shadows of the unchanging, ever-out-of-reach Truth, but nourishing nonetheless—satisfying as answers to current issues, enhancing community building, and aiding individuals as they rehearsed the virtues.[44]

Such practice of the virtues formed habits, character traits predisposing individuals to right action and to flourishing (eudaimonia). Such habits were the foundations of civility and culture. Without them, mutual effort and agreement were impossible. The virtues were not culturally relative because in their absence no agreement about values and practices was possible—no *free* culture could endure.[45] Despotism, slavery, chaos, and misery were more likely.

The Great Books classes became popular on campus, so much so that nonstudents began to sign up. Hutchins cultivated this popularity. Part of his grand scheme was to direct more of the university's resources to adult education, gradually transforming it into a community center for the active, lifelong participation in the life of the mind for all—a kind of educational experience center.[46]

With such an agenda, Hutchins made enemies. He was swimming against the tide of twentieth-century pessimism, relativism, and determinism: those forces that led the sciences and humanities, including psychology, to focus on humanities' ills and lose hope for the progress of freedom—those forces against which the new sciences of happiness are contending. Aside from fundamentally different ideas about humans and their potential, Hutchins's opponents at Chicago saw adult education as a dead end for their careers and reputations. For careerists, the project of democratic culture, of opening the creation of culture and knowledge to everyone, was anathema. What Hutchins and his supporters saw in their opposition was a gnostic-like thrust in twentieth-century higher education to further mystify knowledge and culture creation, reserving access only to the anointed—a retrogression that Whitman, years before, had branded as the survival of feudalism.

Above all, Hutchins and Adler opposed the vocational direction taken by higher education. Attempts to create work to replace that taken by machines entailed a new understanding of work and wealth as valuable in themselves, what Hannah Arendt called the modern "glorification of labor."[47] This glorification involved a new understanding of progress as the eternal creation of new work and wealth.[48] Freedom was no longer the goal of history; new necessities, perpetually uncovered by economic growth, would be needed to support the eternal renewal of work. Replacing freedom with ever-expanding need, work, and wealth also involved the creation of a highly unlikely goal: jobs that were intrinsically rewarding and enjoyable in and for themselves. Hutchins and Adler explained that, although ideal and good jobs may still be possible for the elite (as leisure was once reserved for the aristocracy), for most of modern humanity, such jobs were a utopian dream, the product of muddled thinking:

> Work . . . can be considered as having two forms: subsistence-work and leisure-work. The first of these has its compensations outside of itself, in its product or reward . . . [and] is being eliminated by machinery. . . . [L]eisure work is intrinsically rewarding . . . it is the activity of our free time. . . . [There is] no justification for confusing these important parts of life as though they were not profoundly different from one another. . . . Subsistence-work is pursued for the sake of economic goods that it obtains. . . . Both wealth and work are sought as means to an end beyond themselves. That end, in the most general sense and also the most ultimate sense, is happiness, and happiness is achieved in and through leisure activity.[49]

Hutchins and Adler made distinctions between productive work done as a paid-for job, and productive "leisure-work," what I have called intrinsically motivated productive consumption (IMPC). Other observers of the century-long shorter-hours process made similar distinctions. As early as the first part of the nineteenth century, William Ellery Channing described the clear difference between productive work done to satisfy material needs, in accord with the "laws of nature" (that established finite human needs), and "intellectual and liberal [free] *occupations*"—activities done freely for their own sake rather than for a reward and outside the cash nexus, representing "another [free] state of being."[50]

Facing a faculty revolt at Chicago,[51] Hutchins turned first to the university's extension services and then to libraries, museums, educational television, and private, nonprofit organizations to meet his adult education objectives. His Great Books classes were increasingly popular, spreading throughout the

Midwest: by 1946 there were sixty-seven classes in the Chicago area, thirty in Detroit and Cleveland, and fifteen in Indianapolis, all together enrolling four thousand to five thousand students. Reporters and Hutchins predicted that in a few years, hundreds of thousands of students would be enrolled nationwide.[52]

Through his Great Books Foundation, Hutchins began publishing cheap editions of the books to facilitate the groups.[53] Gradually, the foundation ceded publication to the *Encyclopaedia Britannica*—Sears had donated the encyclopedia business to Chicago in 1943. Hutchins devoted more and more time to managing the company, moving his office to the Chicago Loop for a while during the late 1940s. In June of 1947, Britannica announced publication of a new fifty-four-volume set of 432 *Great Books of the Western World*, costing $200.[54]

With his move to Britannica, Hutchins may be counted as among the pioneers of the experience and transformation economies. With increasing book sales, Hutchins found the support he needed at Britannica to keep his adult education vision alive. Part of the Great Books sales campaign, which had a nationwide reach, was to sell the community aspect of the Great Books classes. The experience of reading the books with others was presented by salesmen as one of the most important values offered by Britannica—instruction was given about how to organize groups and who in the community might be willing to lead them. As part of their pitch, salesmen described a future, soon to come, when Great Books groups throughout the nation would help revitalize local neighborhoods, assisting in the advent of a democratic culture.[55] A true believer, the assistant national sales manager Kenneth M. Harden, maintained, "[Salesmen] are not just making money. They are carrying [Hutchins's] banner."[56] As he was leaving Chicago for the Ford Foundation, Hutchins challenged his former colleagues, and higher education in general, which he thought had degenerated in the United States into "a mess": "Why not do this: Why not sell the idea of a liberal education."[57]

Selling his books, Hutchins continued to emphasize increasing freedom. Selling the idea of a liberal education remained central—he would often remark that people could always get the books from the library for free. Uninterested in maximizing profit and sales, he was content with the slow growth of the Great Books project that followed its initial, fad-like popularity. The branders and value capturers at Britannica, however, focused increasingly on profits, beginning to market the book set as an object to own rather than a culture-creating resource (a marketing ploy followed by other publishers who formed book-of-the-month clubs with mass appeal in the 1950s). The value capturers at Britannica used hard-sell, door-to-door tactics, eventually running afoul of government regulators.

Nevertheless, the Great Books survived. During the 1960s Britannica offered an annual Great Books Today series, addressing current topics in the news and increasing sales. The annual publications included relevant excerpts from the Great Books, or new additions, and commentary, sometimes modeling a dialogue about the issue.[58] But the books became controversial in the 1970s and 1980s and never fulfilled Hutchins and Adler's dream of the books being a catalyst to help revive the liberal arts tradition and engender a more democratic, creative culture.

The Great Books project provides a model, one in a casebook of historical examples, that might guide entrepreneurs and business today. The realization, which galvanized Hutchins and Adler, that modern mass leisure is potentially the last, best incarnation of human freedom has virtually disappeared in the schools. Largely abandoned today by modern colleges that have turned to preparing students for work, the whole of the two-millennia-long tradition of teaching and practicing the liberal arts in and for freedom is fair game for the free marketplace.

In this educational vacuum it remains, then, for business and entrepreneurs to respond to Hutchins's challenge: "Why not sell the idea of a liberal education?"

In addition to Hutchins's main concerns, reading and writing, the liberal arts curriculum provides a menu of possibilities for the entrepreneur: music, history, science, the arts. Examples of businesses selling the free experience of these things abound today in the experience and transformation economies. Paint and Sip Studio #197 in Asheville, North Carolina, offers painting experiences for thirty-five dollars: BYOB, food, and friends and, they advertise, "We'll take care of the rest."[59] Genealogy, storytelling, and local history and historical sites offer rich possibilities for the entrepreneur to combine history with enjoyable social experiences (bus tours, organized by local historians, are frequent events at retirement homes across the nation). Airbnb experiences throughout the world are increasingly popular.

The challenge remains to grow the skills of freedom from these, for the most part, simple beginnings. Models are useful. Aldo Leopold offered an early model of an *Erlebnis-Erfahrung* chain, observing that outdoor recreation advanced in a series of experiential stages: the initial, spontaneous enjoyment is followed naturally by the desire for deeper engagement and interaction, followed by the desire to learn more about nature, followed by appreciation that nurtures a "sense of husbandry"—the assuming of moral responsibility for the natural world.[60]

Modern technology has the potential to revitalize Hutchins and Adler's projects. Today MOOCs, massive open online courses, are commonplace. One can only speculate what the pair might have done with this technology.

Prominent educators and scholars worldwide now offer their courses and lectures online for free—to receive course credit from an institution costs money, but it is a fraction of the going rate for brick-and-mortar and ivy offerings. But so far, few have followed Hutchins and Adler's lead and organized MOOC community groups.

One of the important research findings about MOOCs is that people who sign up for free are not likely to complete the class. The best way found so far to encourage students is by offering credits they have to pay for, promising a return for their effort—something to show on their résumé when looking for a job. Another possibility is to follow the Great Books classes' example and add to the intrinsic enjoyment of the class content by providing the experience of a live class: of people watching the lectures and reviewing topics together in discussion, interacting to form relationships that improve the subsequent lectures. There is precedent for this suggestion in the gaming rooms open throughout the United States, where people share the experience of playing video games together. An entrepreneur might imagine for MOOCs something similar to the Asheville paint-and-sip-wine art-experience shop—a suggestion offered by one of my students who also thought a glass or two of wine would improve my classes.

Liberation Capitalism

Writing in 1930, John Maynard Keynes outlined his vision of liberation capitalism. His essay "Economic Possibilities for Our Grandchildren" is, like Hutchins's great books, a bridge connecting the forgotten dream of higher progress to the experience and transformation economies.[61]

Keynes thought it reasonable to expect that within a century technological advances and the cumulative "power of compound interest" would solve the "*economic problem*," barring calamities such as wars and irrational human behavior that might postpone the solution a while longer.[62] Explaining what he meant by "solving [mankind's] economic problem," Keynes pointed out that human needs fall into two categories: absolute and relative. Absolute needs are determined by nature, and everyone has them—"We feel them whatever the situation of our fellow human beings may be." By contrast, the origin of relative needs is the "desire for superiority" and control. They are felt when we compare what we have with what others have. We feel unhappy when we have less, happier when we have more than others. Hence they are insatiable, "for the higher the general level, the higher still are they."[63]

He predicted, "A point may soon be reached, much sooner perhaps than we are all of us aware of, when these [absolute] needs are satisfied in the sense that we prefer to devote our further energies to non-economic purposes."[64]

The Problem of Equality

Writing about "bourgeois equality," Deirdre McCloskey has resurfaced the old debates about abundance and the claims of economists such as Keynes that, before long, people who have benefited from modern technology and a free economy would be able to meet their basic needs—to be ensured a life of what Monsignor John Ryan (the "Right Reverend New Dealer" economist) called "reasonable and frugal comfort"[65]—and then proceed to something better. Emphasizing the importance of ideas, she concludes that "the idea of equality and liberty and dignity for all humans caused and then protected a startling material and then spiritual progress."[66]

Throughout American history, economists and other observers looked forward to abundance as a time when everyone would have sure access to the basic necessities (what Benjamin Franklin called "necessaries"). Once these were met (Franklin thought that the nation was already at the point when a six-hour day would do the job), humans could turn their attention to "humane and moral progress"[67]—McCloskey's "spiritual progress." Centrally important in the history of economic liberalism has been the anticipation of access to the "realm of freedom."[68]

Walt Whitman is a fascinating example of this tradition. The Whitman scholar Ken Cmiel observed:

> Far from being a protosocialist, Whitman praised the "true gravita-
> tion hold of liberalism in the United States," which he described as
> "a more universal ownership of property, general homestead, gen-
> eral comfort—a vast intertwining reticulation of wealth." . . . Whit-
> man . . . "hailed with joy" the "business materialism of the current
> age." If it could only be spiritualized, all would be well.[69]

According to economic liberalism, true equality, as well as liberation, is found outside the economy. In the realm of necessity, the free market requires and produces inequalities. But it also produces the greatest good for the greatest number. One of the most important of these goods is access to the "realm of freedom."

In their free time, individuals have a much better chance at equality. All have twenty-four hours each day. But more importantly, all have access to the virtues, to beauty, creativity, and love. According to McCloskey, we are well past Ryan's reasonable and frugal comfort. Today virtually all of us have access to the "necessaries" and much more—even the less fortunate have access to material goods and services that would have amazed the kings and queens of old. Like Keynes and so many others in the economic liberalism tradition,

McCloskey understands equality as ability of all to access not only consumer goods but also nonmaterial goods; respect, liberty, and dignity.[70]

The Heart of Liberation Capitalism

Keynes's prediction that the time will soon come "when [basic material] needs are satisfied in the sense that we prefer to devote our further energies to non-economic purposes"[71] is the heart of liberation capitalism. This economic logic is the foundation for the continuing growth of the experience and transformation economies. Such growth will be determined by the free market and by the rational choices people will make to buy their time back from their jobs, choosing "to devote [their] further energies to non-economic purposes"[72]—to leisure and IMPC.

Liberation is the exact moment when an individual decides that he or she can afford more time off. Such liberation closely resembles what Karl Marx and writers such as Herbert Marcuse promised would be the best fruits of communism and socialism; the primary difference, of course, being that such liberation would be the fruit of liberation capitalism.

In *Capital*, Marx famously observed, "The realm of freedom actually begins only where labour, which is determined by necessity and mundane considerations, ceases. . . . Beyond begins that development of human energy which is an end in itself, the true realm of freedom. . . . The shortening of the working-day is its basic prerequisite."[73]

Herbert Marcuse observed:

> Since the length of the working day is itself one of the principle repressive factors imposed . . . , the reduction of the working day to a point where the mere quantum of labor time no longer arrests human development is the first prerequisite for freedom. . . . The argument that makes liberation conditional upon an ever higher standard of living (the perpetual expansion of work and wealth) all too easily serves to justify the perpetuation of repression.[74]

Now such visions of liberation are more within reach by capitalism than communism or socialism.

Transition

The transition will not be easy, however. Having solved the economic problem, Keynes's "grandchildren" will then face an even more daunting challenge: "the permanent problem of the human race."[75]

Thus for the first time since his creation man will be faced with his real, his permanent problem—how to use his freedom from pressing economic cares, how to occupy the leisure, which science and compound interest will have won for him, to live wisely and agreeably and well.[76]

The "problem of leisure"[77] is a product of history. Over the centuries, work came to be highly valued because it was largely devoted to meeting absolute needs. Work was also a vital part of human progress, allowing creation of capital wealth necessary to build toward abundance. By the twentieth century, work had become a primary source of meaning, identity, and purpose. Work became virtuous in itself (the most important way to be a socially responsible individual), evolving into a centrally important moral imperative—the Protestant-based work ethic evolved into "the spirit of capitalism." Thus, as the economic problem is gradually solved, according to Keynes, "mankind will be deprived of its traditional purpose. . . . There is no country and no people," Keynes wrote, "who can look forward to the age of leisure and of abundance without a dread."[78]

Not only will average people lose purpose and direction; they will be at a loss as to how to occupy themselves on a day-to-day basis—most of their creative talents and interests would be work-related. Most people would have no idea what to do, giving in to temptation, to what the *Character Strengths and Virtues* handbook calls "what is darkest within us,"[79] or wasting away in boredom. Judging from their current direction, the schools would be of little help. Thus, faced with the problem of leisure, Keynes's grandchildren might expect "a general 'nervous breakdown.'"[80]

The "dread of the readjustment of the habits and instincts"[81] might cause humans to resist the coming of the freedom proffered by abundance. Free to choose meant free to reject freedom. Some might behave irrationally, valuing work and wealth as ends in themselves rather than the means to solve the economic problem. It is against this danger that Keynes warns us, "chiefly," at the end of his essay, "Do not let us overestimate the importance of the economic problem, or sacrifice to its supposed necessities other matters of greater and more permanent significance."[82]

On the other hand, the grandchildren might manage the problem of leisure and over time adjust. In the first place, work might gradually taper off (as it had been doing for a century when Keynes wrote), allowing time for people to get used to being free. At first they could "spread the jam as thin as possible," working three-hour days and a fifteen-hour week. Keynes reasoned that "three hours a day is quite enough [work] to satisfy the old Adam in most of us."[83]

Some might relearn how to enjoy their leisure wisely and, like Walt Whitman, become models: "Those peoples, who can keep alive, and cultivate into a fuller perfection, the art of life itself and do not sell themselves for the means of life, who will be able to enjoy the abundance when it comes." Others (and why not entrepreneurs and businesses in the experience and transformation economies) might become guides and teachers: "We shall honour those who can teach us how to pluck the hour and the day virtuously and well, the delightful people who are capable of taking direct enjoyment in things, the lilies of the field who toil not, neither do they spin."[84]

Even though much of the wisdom and skills needed to adjust to and thrive in the coming age of leisure had been largely forgotten during the last few centuries, eclipsed by the modern work ethic, still Keynes saw his grandchildren "free . . . to return to some of the most sure and certain principles of religion and traditional virtue."

Keynes predicted:

There will be great changes in the code of morals. We shall be able to rid ourselves of many of the pseudo-moral principles which have hag-ridden us for two hundred years, by which we have exalted some of the most distasteful of human qualities into the position of the highest virtues. We shall be able to afford to dare to assess the money-motive at its true value. The love of money as a possession—as distinguished from the love of money as a means to the enjoyments and realities of life—will be recognised for what it is, a somewhat disgusting morbidity, one of those semi-criminal, semi-pathological propensities which one hands over with a shudder to the specialists in mental disease. All kinds of social customs and economic practices, affecting the distribution of wealth and of economic rewards and penalties, which we now maintain at all costs, however distasteful and unjust they may be in themselves, because they are tremendously useful in promoting the accumulation of capital, we shall then be free, at last, to discard.[85]

A Novel Dialectic

Keynes's prediction that his grandchildren would eventually be "free . . . to return to some of the most sure and certain principles of religion and traditional virtue,"[86] lends credence to E. P. Thompson's "novel dialectic." Speculating about what would happen "if we are to have enlarged leisure," Thompson shared Keynes's concerns that there would be problems; for Thompson, in addition to the challenge of readjusting work values, the danger would be consumerism and "exploitation by the leisure-industries." However, he also shared Keynes's hopes that humans would "re-learn some of the arts of living lost in the industrial revolution: how to fill the interstices of their days with enriched, more leisurely, personal and social relations. . . . And hence would stem *a novel dialectic* in which . . . the old industrialized nations seek to *rediscover [forgotten] modes of experience.*[87]

I interpret Thompson's "novel dialectic" (see Chapter 4) as being driven by one of capitalism's contradictions: its need to eliminate work to maximize profit versus its need to propagandize work to ensure a compliant labor force. The contradiction could be resolved either in ways that continue and exacerbate human exploitation or in a new synthesis that realizes the promise of the continuing liberation of time, made possible by the advent of a eudaimonic technology through the free market. Continuing to shorten the hours of labor, industrial nations might find ways to teach and retrain people in new, enriched uses of leisure—usages that include Thompson's preindustrial, feudal, and folklike "modes of experience" and Keynes's "sure and certain principles of religion and traditional virtue."[88]

In this "new synthesis," technology would be redeployed, at least in part, from freeing people from work to helping them "re-learn some of the [old] arts of living," providing new experiences and teaching new skills and virtues appropriate for their increasing leisure. A new eudaimonic technology would be needed.

Supported by the new eudaimonic technology, the experience and transformation economies may make it possible for humans to relearn character strengths and virtues found in the *Character Strengths and Virtues* handbook. The wealth of new insights about human flourishing discovered by the new sciences of happiness will also be available for the design of new experience products—Thompson saw the need to "combine . . . elements of the old and of the new."[89] Moreover, the history of the United States provides a wealth of examples of possibilities and models of what Walt Whitman called higher progress that may be consulted. Because they have been largely forgotten, their re-presentation through the market may appear as novel.

The experience and transformation economies also make it possible for the recovery of adult, culture-creating play through the marketplace—the lost, culture-creating play of adults that Socrates, Huizinga, Turner, and Habermas described and recommended. Such a recovery will help reestablish the foundation of democratic cultures where men and women actively share and create art, theater, conversations, stories, conviviality, traditions, meaning, and values, free from both corporations and governments. In such areas, greater equality is possible.

Finally, the synthesis would be novel because, unlike the Marxist dialectic, it would be realized through the free marketplace. The experience and transformation economies may be understood as harnessing the profit motive to the production and marketing of new liberated and liberating experiences, increasing the demand for free time. Thus, the profit motive is harnessed to the production of human freedom, fulfilling the original promise of liberation offered by technology and history.

Freedom Is Not Determined: Warnings Reiterated

Instead of liberating us, however, the experience and transformation economies may continue to serve primarily the interests of profits and the wealthy, further exacerbating wealth maldistribution. Thompson's novel dialect may yet be resolved in the direction of continuing exploitation and increased slavery. Unemployment may worsen while the morality of work and wealth as ends in themselves grows; social and class divisions that are based on work attitudes worsen; and new kinds of alienating, make-work, and servant jobs appear, disguised by false consciousness as important and meaningful. The leisure industries may further exploit the existing or even diminishing free time. The value capturers and branders may promote increasing dependence on the market and their experience products, as Jeremy Rifkin fears. The aggressive sale of expensive, goods-intensive experience products (e.g., pricy bourbon and suborbital airliner rides) may make it possible to maximize profits and continue the commodification of the lifeworld, at least for a while.

It also is reasonable to expect that modern governments will continue to expand, driven by their consistent, century-long project to create enough work to replace that taken by machines—enough to sustain Full-Time, Full Employment. Arguably, the single greatest government intervention into the marketplace has been the effort to create enough jobs to replace the work made redundant by economic growth and technology: to maintain perpetual Full-Time, Full Employment.

Work by government fiat has a long history, dating back to the corvées of the ancient Sumerians. Frank Lloyd Wright saw modern attempts to create jobs by government policy an updated version of ancient slavery, supported not by force but by the inculcation of work values that made men and women complicit in their own enslavement.[90] Government attempts to create jobs may continue to compete with leisure for a while.[91]

The Religion of Work

The greatest impediment to liberation is what E. P. Thompson and John Maynard Keynes identified as those beliefs and values about and habits of work, acquired through recent centuries—the modern work ethic. As

Max Weber and Hannah Arendt pointed out, the modern work ethic dates back only to the Reformation. Arendt wrote of the "modern glorification of labor,"[92] Joseph Pieper of the advent of the "world of total work,"[93] and Jacques Ellul of the new "ideology of work."[94] No other people in history has valued work as we moderns do, as an end in itself; no other civilization envisioned nothing better for future generations than enough work to fill the majority of people's lives.

Work occupies the center of the Modern Age: the enduring economic imperative, political mandate, center of morality, and source of social identity. The Protestant work ethic has ascended as the spirit of capitalism. Some have claimed that work has become the modern religion, what Paul Tillich called an "unconscious faith," answering what he maintained are the "existential questions" we all must answer (questions of identity, purpose, meaning, salvation, and social responsibility).[95] Robert Hutchins called the new faith "Salvation by Work."[96]

Among those who make such claims are theologians who ought to recognize a competing religion when they see one. The Swiss Protestant theologian Karl Barth, whom Pope Pius XII described as the most important theologian since Thomas Aquinas, working systematically,[97] concluded:

It is true: in human work . . . an apparently self-sufficient cosmos is constructed out of human ability, enterprise and achievement . . . this human edifice, like a canopy, obscures the true cosmos beyond . . . indeed screening out even God, leaving people with the deception that they behold God . . . in the culture which they have created and which has taken on an apparent life of its own."[98]

Barth maintained, "Human work cannot be done for its own sake. . . . No independent meaning of work, no intrinsic necessity, can be proved in the framework of Christian ethics. On the contrary, the idea of an independent value . . . of work for work's sake, can only be dismissed."[99]

The French theologian and philosopher Jacques Ellul, recognizing a modern "work ideology," concluded:

The great danger of work is that we become so immersed, seduced by our own work, that we bow down before it, and attribute to the works of our own hands all kinds of divine qualities. . . . Work [in and of] itself can become the source of idolatry, and the "work of our hands" may well create a false religion. . . . And the Church did not see it. On the contrary it confirmed the Ideology of Work, and supports this idolatry to this day.[100]

Keynes warned of something similar. He detected in those who "blindly pursue wealth" the quest for immortality. In both work and wealth without end, we "strive to secure . . . an immortality": a "spurious and delusive immortality." This irrational, "blind" pursuit for work that is its own reward and wealth for more wealth will likely continue "unless . . . some plausible substitute" is found.[101]

Threats to the Religion of Work

The coming of an age of experiences threatens the religion of work. The prospect of any religion's failure is an awful thing for its votaries. Unlike most human beings throughout history, most of us have no idea that there may be life beyond work. Ellul suggests that one of the punishments for our "work-idolatry" is the inability to imagine, much less believe in, an alternative.[102]

During the Great Depression, the prominent legal scholar Felix S. Cohen wrote, "Adam's children inherited the [curse of work] and soon learned to make a virtue of necessity. Idleness came to be regarded as a sin rather than the source of love, art, inspiration, and wisdom." When God relents and decides to lift the curse, he sends "messengers" to humans in the form of machines that will ease their work and restore their original freedom. Instead of embracing this freedom in the modern form of increased leisure, humans choose work, continuing to "sing new hymns in praise of the sweetness of chains" because they had so long "praised each other and themselves for their industriousness. . . . The message of the machine is that we will have work without end."[103]

Hannah Arendt observed:

> The advent of automation . . . in a few decades probably will . . . liberate mankind from . . . the burden of laboring and the bondage to necessity. . . . [Then] scientific progress and technical developments [will have achieved] something about which all former ages dreamed but which none had been able to realize.
>
> However . . . the modern age has carried with it a theoretical glorification of labor and has resulted in a factual transformation of the whole of society into a laboring society. The fulfilment of the wish, therefore, like the fulfilment of wishes in fairy tales, comes at a moment when it can only be self-defeating. It is a society of laborers which is about to be liberated from the fetters of labor, and this society does no longer know of those other higher and more meaningful activities for the sake of which this freedom would deserve to be won. . . . What we are confronted with is the prospect of a society of

laborers without labor, that is, without the only activity left to them. Surely, nothing could be worse."[104]

Thompson, Keynes, and Bertrand Russell,[105] among many others, agreed that the transition from work to leisure will be difficult, or perhaps impossible, because it had become nearly unthinkable. However, all these writers pointed out that a reliable guide is ready to hand, available to be recovered from the great traditions of the past. Keynes, for example, suggested a "plausible substitute" for the religion of work may be found in the "return to some of the most sure and certain principles of religion and traditional virtue."[106]

Additions to the *Character Strengths and Virtues* Handbook

The *Character Strengths and Virtues* handbook has made an impressive start, listing the traditional virtues and character strengths and recommending them as sure guides to human well-being and flourishing. One might suggest that other basic insights about the human condition, beliefs common to most of the received traditions in both the East and the West, might be useful additions to the *Character Strengths and Virtues* handbook, satisfying its criteria.

Among the most fundamental of these insights is that humans are creatures, part of a larger reality (history, nature, evolution, God) that they did not create. Aldous Huxley found nearly universal agreement about the existence of a "ground of all existence," separate from what humans have done or might control.[107] As the psalmist put it, "It is He that hath made us, and not we ourselves."[108] Part of a larger reality, all have a common humanity, "We are his people, the sheep of his pasture." In our essence, our creatureliness, we are fundamentally alike: we are essentially brothers and sisters.

Perhaps the earliest formulation of this principle is what Nurit Bird-David called "the giving environment." On the basis of her anthropological research, she found that many hunter-gatherer people share a worldview that recognizes the givenness of human life, a view that informs their economies and lives of giving and sharing.[109]

Such beliefs have frequently been endorsed by reason—certainly during the Enlightenment. A child of the Enlightenment, Thomas Jefferson, referring to "the Laws of Nature and of Nature's God," wrote, "We hold these truths to be self-evident, that all men are created equal, that they are endowed by their Creator with certain unalienable Rights, that among these are Life, Liberty and the pursuit of Happiness."

The received traditions also agree that these fundamental tenets are frequently, or even universally, ignored and willfully opposed. Humans have consistently denied their creatureliness, attempting to go it alone and become godlike, refusing to obey the Laws of Nature (a peculiar undertaking) and Nature's God, to become the authors of their own being: their own source of value, meaning, truth, and salvation. The results are always bad, including destruction of the natural world, alienation from that "ground of all existence," and enmity between people.

Traditional religions are full of stories of human beings who attempt to be gods or godlike and pay a heavy price for it. Greek mythology is replete with reminders that *Hubris* (pride) is inevitably pursued by *Nemesis*;[110] Adam and Eve's original sins of pride and disobedience in the Garden of Eden were punished by the loss of Eden and its freedom and by the "curse of work."

In modern times, the foundations for the modern religion of work were laid in the nineteenth century by philosophers such as Friedrich Nietzsche and Frederick Engels. Nietzsche's *Übermensch* is incapable of accepting anything as given. Instead he prides himself as the sole source of meaning and values, imposing his will, submitting to no authority, and attempting to remake the world and himself in his own image, a paradoxical project at best: one entailing superhuman effort and endless work and estrangement from human community.

Many of capitalism's modern defenders, agreeing with critics such as Karl Marx and Engels, have proposed that humans are essentially *Homo faber*, working animals who shape their environment with their labor and tools. Engels explained that as they shape their environment, humans then have to adapt to the world they have created, continuing in a never-ending cycle of work effort and readaptation that perpetually re-creates human needs and selves.[111] Such self-creating creatures will never have enough, will never be at peace, and will ever have to work to meet their ever-changing and ever-expanding needs.

Hannah Arendt wrote:

"[Modern man is in] rebellion against human existence as it has been given, a free gift from nowhere (secularly speaking), which he wishes to exchange, as it were, for something he has himself made. . . . [Marxists and capitalists share these beliefs,] which play such a great role in twentieth-century thought. . . . [They] pretend that man is his own producer and maker . . . even though it is clear that nobody has "made" himself or "produced" his existence; this, I think, is the last of the metaphysical fallacies, corresponding to the modern age's emphasis on willing as a substitute for thinking.[112]

Modern attempts to sustain work and wealth as ends in themselves, to save work from the threat of laborsaving machines, have entailed the perpetual creation and re-creation of human needs and values. There is universal agreement that Keynes's "absolute needs," dictated by nature, cannot sustain the economic growth essential for Full-Time, Full Employment. The open-ended creation of needs and values through the marketplace is nothing less than the godlike project of the eternal re-creation of human beings. The price paid, as Felix Cohen pointed out, is that we shall have "work without end."

Homo faber, the eternally self-seeking, self-re-creating working creature, has emerged as capitalism's image of humanity.

The insight, gleaned from the "certain principles" of religious traditions, that might be recommended as an addition to the *Character Strengths and Virtues* handbook is that playing god is a primary source of unhappiness, while accepting and living within the limits of nature and of nature's God offer surer ways to human felicity. Ecologists have argued for decades that living within limits is essential not only for progress but for human survival.

Indeed, such wisdom is implicit in the handbook and the table of consiliences offered in Chapter 7 (Table 7.1). The new sciences of happiness have found that some character strengths and virtues are most strongly associated with human well-being because they are built into the human experience by evolution (are given) and remain essential to the healthy functioning of humans as a group. For the neurobiologist, there are qualities that are essential for the healthy functioning of all complex, open systems (and thus are "given"), including the human mind/brain. Living within the boundaries established by such strengths, virtues, and qualities that are "given" produces well-being. Ignoring or contravening them is a recipe for misery.

Accepting the Given

One of the most salient of Keynes's "sure and certain principles of religion and traditional virtue" is that human felicity is found in the acceptance of the givenness of the world and of our being. The alternative is to struggle and rail against what Martin Heidegger called our being "thrown into existence" as finite creatures—into a world and a death we can never master or fully understand and experience only as tragedy.[113] Such despairing refusal of the given is the source of much of the twentieth century's dismal, tragic image of humans and their chances, and the pessimism that the new sciences of happiness have attempted to counter.

Walter Kerr, American playwright and critic of the mid-twentieth century, mounted his critique of "work without end" and his defense of leisure at roughly the time Hutchins and Arendt mounted theirs.[114] He began to question "happiness" (what he termed "pleasure") and ask why it seemed to be diminishing in an age of unprecedented prosperity. He concluded that the modern tendency to refuse what had been given had resulted in "the decline of pleasure." Moreover, coming to believe that "all value was extrinsic, and that no value was intrinsic," men and women had assumed a "private responsibility that might well be called intolerable."[115] Imagining themselves modern Atlases, they had assumed responsibility for upholding "all that was real, all that was worth-while, all that was valuable," and believed that

> the moment we stopped supplying [the universe] with fresh charges [of meaning] in the shape of formulas, it would drop. Each of us . . . had perforce to accept the responsibility not simply of knowing but of creating [meaning] . . . and of perpetually maintaining it in the sustained tensions of . . . thought. . . . We had got ourselves in the position of the man who does not trust airplanes and who therefore does one wholly unnecessary thing: he gets a grip under the armrests attached to his seat and helps hold the plane up.[116]

Such a project was insane, the prelude to depression, mania, and despair, and unsustainable. It was bound to collapse eventually, as did all human attempts to play god. Kerr recommended as a remedy that we "declare ourselves a bonus":

> We have achieved a high degree of skill in one kind of groping, the hard kind, the theoretical kind. Our futures now depend upon a most attractive activity: upon our developing a matching skill in the easy kind, the loving kind, the arm-in-arm kind . . . our freedom to grow in stature rests unconditionally upon our ability to play . . . [and] produce pleasure.[117]

Authentic happiness (and essential well-being) began with the acceptance of the fundamental givenness of life. A necessary precondition of this acceptance was the rejection of the illusion of *Homo mensura*—that humans are the sole source of meaning, value, and purpose. The natural world, human history, others, the body, birth and death, and God—that mystery at the heart of all being—would always be gifts: there for us from our beginnings; there to be our delights; not there to be constantly refashioned, fretted over, worked at, and modernized to suit our needs, for which we had begun to take responsibility with predictably dire consequences.

The wellspring of authentic pleasure would always be the acceptance and celebration of what is, of what Byrd-David saw in hunter-gatherers' veneration of "the giving environment." Pleasure (and authentic human happiness), Kerr wrote, is an interior experience of the rectitude of things, a seen certainty of the consonance of things. When I become aware that I am in harmony with my own being, I am pleased. When I become aware that I am in harmony with all other, or any other, being, I am pleased.[118]

Humanity's future "depended" on the restoration of pleasure. Such a restoration "depended" on "re-creation," on the free recovery of intrinsic enjoyment and celebration of the world, others, and the Other. Kerr concluded, "I am pleased in that instant that I discover that I am not alone. My joy, like the discovery, is profound."[119]

Alasdair MacIntyre argues that all "dependent, rational animals" must recognize and live in accord with a set of "virtues of dependency" in order to "flourish."[120] Josef Pieper agreed that the source of the twentieth-century malaise, its loss of hope and "spiritual crisis," was the unwillingness to accept the world and the self as given—direct results of the delusion that we are or should become the author of our own being. Modern men and women mistrust "everything that is effortless" and refuse "to have anything as a gift."[121] For Pieper, the tragic consequences of such pride are "alienation, distrust, loneliness, and ultimately despair."[122]

Pieper wrote his famous book *Leisure: The Basis of Culture* just after World War II for the express purpose of offering a better model for the rebuilding of Europe. The image of humans as supermen, in total charge of the world and themselves, had been a tragedy indeed for Europe and Germany and likely would be again if the work ideology that spawned "arbeit macht frei" (work sets you free) continued and spread worldwide.

The Sabbath as a Model for the Age of Experiences

Abba Silver, a leader in the struggle to save Shabbat in America in the 1920s, saw the Sabbath (revered by the three major Western faiths[123]) as the model for genuine human progress: "It is a sign and symbol of man's higher destiny."[124] The Sabbath had reminded the people for millennia of their creatureliness and that their work was not the main thing in life or an end in itself. The Sabbath gave meaning and purpose to work and the rest of the week; it was a time set apart. It offered human flourishing in community celebration and in communion with the eternal: the supreme joys and fulfillment of life.

With Keynes, Silver expected that as economic progress continued, working hours would get progressively shorter. Just as Shabbat gave purpose and meaning to the rest of the week, reduction in working hours might help fulfill the promise of history, expanding opportunities for learning, family, community, ritual, and tradition—for those free parts of life that were its crown. In the face of the ascetic demands of the new religion of work without end, Silver took his stand: "We must say to ourselves . . . so far shall I go in my pursuit of the things of life and no further. Beyond that I am a free man, a child of God. Beyond that I have a soul and I must give to it time, energy, and interest."[125]

In the play *Fiddler on the Roof,* Tevye, the milkman, imagines, "If I were a rich man . . ." He speculates in song about how wealth would change his life: a great house with three staircases, one going up, one down, and one "just for show"; his wife, Golde, with a "proper" double chin. But the hypothetical begins to puzzle him, what would he do all day long? He puts off answering for a while, singing nonsense syllables: "Daidle daidle deedle daidle dumb." Finally, and seriously, he decides that he could afford to spend his days in the synagogue, praying, sitting in his place by the Eastern wall, conversing with the rabbi and biblical scholars about the holy books. He concludes, "That would be the sweetest thing of all. Oy!"

The insights about human flourishing contained by the Sabbath and Tevye's song and their potential to inform progress and fulfill human happiness should act as beacons to those of us who expect great things from the experience and transformation economies and the eudaimonic technology—a new age of experiences.

Afterword

The simultaneous flowering of a postmaterialist culture, the development of a multidisciplinary science of well-being, and the shift of our economy toward experiences and transformations signal the advent of a eudaimonic technology. This new technology has the potential to free us, creating more, better, and cheaper experience and transformation products that bring increasing happiness and well-being but that also require more and more time to enjoy them. As consumers need increasing amounts of free time, value will shift in the marketplace from money capital to time. Individuals will begin to take back possession of more and more of their lives and take ownership of more of the means (the necessary skills acquired in the transformation economy) of production. Greater equality as well as liberation will ensue.

This book shows the ways that these changes are already underway in the marketplace in the forms of innovative companies and entrepreneurs meeting consumers' growing preferences for experiences and transformations. This book also provides practical guides (models, checklists, catalogs, and tables), showing how these processes may be accelerated by innovative experience designers who deliberately employ the research findings of the new sciences.

Whereas government policy may play a role in these developments, the marketplace has the potential to help realize the promises of the experience and transformation economies, especially if the lessons of history, happiness studies, and success stories of innovative companies are heeded.

The danger that the new economies might increase consumer dependence and alienation, however, must be admitted and addressed—warnings are posted throughout the book and ways are outlined that preserve the promise of liberation capitalism and protect against the threats of branders and value capturers.

I have cataloged the relevant findings from the new sciences of happiness (positive psychology and positive neuroscience) that may guide the design of liberation experiences and advance the eudaimonic technology while avoiding the pitfalls of commodification. Such a catalog has the potential to guide businesses and entrepreneurs in the design of experience products that liberate more than they alienate and enslave and that, just as importantly, are competitive in the free market.

Reviewing economic theory, I show how the traditional analysis of the demand for leisure applies in new ways in the new economies, showing how and why free time should increase (leisure becoming once again a normal good) and perhaps, after a half-century hiatus, return to previous, continually growing levels (what the American Federation of Labor once called the progressive shortening of the hours of labor).

This book also provides a historical context for the experience and transformation economies and the eudaimonic technology and re-presents the nearly forgotten vision of liberation capitalism as the practical, economic realization of what Walt Whitman called higher progress—of the forgotten American dream that was centrally important in American history before the mid-twentieth century. Even though the dream has remained dormant for decades, it may now reawaken in the experience and transformation economies with the help of the new eudaimonic technology, introducing the age of experiences.

Notes

FOREWORD

1. Benjamin Hunnicutt, *Free Time: The Forgotten American Dream* (Philadelphia: Temple University Press, 2013).
2. "Commoditize" should not be confused with "commodify." For an extensive discussion of "commodify," see Chapter 3.
3. Stanley Lebergott, *Pursuing Happiness: American Consumers in the Twentieth Century* (Princeton, NJ: Princeton University Press, 2014).

PREFACE

1. Benjamin Kline Hunnicutt, *Free Time: The Forgotten American Dream* (Philadelphia: Temple Press, 2013).
2. Hannah Arendt, *The Human Condition* (Chicago: University of Chicago Press, 1958), 129.
3. Benjamin Kline Hunnicutt, *Work without End: Abandoning Shorter Hours for the Right to Work* (Philadelphia: Temple University Press, 1987).
4. Unlike Weber, I argue that the "spirit of capitalism" (i.e., wealth and work as ends in themselves) was not widespread until the twentieth century—until then remaining primarily the domain of the bourgeoisie. Labor's struggle for shorter hours is evidence of a different agenda. Only in the last century has the need to sustain everlasting economic growth to ensure Full-Time, Full Employment become widely embraced. It is only recently that government policies have been designed to ensure, in perpetuity, that wealth would build on wealth and new work would be found so that everyone might work full time. Max Weber, *The Protestant Ethic and the "Spirit" of Capitalism, and Other Writings*, trans. Peter Baehr and Gordon C. Wells (New York: Penguin, 2002), 294–295.

5. Robert Hutchins, *The University of Utopia* (Chicago: University of Chicago Press, 1953), ix.

6. Benjamin Hunnicutt, "Work Is Our Religion, and It's Failing Us," *Huffington Post*, May 18, 2018, available at https://www.huffpost.com/entry/post-work-world_n_5afbe686e4b0779345d43a20.

7. Herbert Marcuse, *One-Dimensional Man: Studies in the Ideology of Advanced Industrial Society* (New York: Beacon Press, 1964).

8. Job 13:15 (King James Version).

9. Henry Ford and S. Crowther, "Unemployment or Leisure," *Saturday Evening Post*, August 2, 1930, p. 19. For shorter hours as an unemployment solution and as a centrally important political issue, see "Hoover Expected to Call a Parley on Five-Day Week," *New York Times*, August 2, 1932, p. 1. See also Associated Press, "Edsel Ford for Shorter Week to Absorb Labor Surplus," *New York Times*, March 3, 1931, p. 6. Even before the widespread interest in the new leisure, which surfaced in 1933–1934, the unemployment-or-leisure theme was sounded by prominent people such as Henry Ford. See H. Ford, *Moving Forward* (Garden City, NY: Doubleday, 1930), 16–88, esp. chap. 5; I. Craven, "Leisure," in *The Encyclopedia of Social Sciences*, ed. E. Seligman (New York: Macmillan, 1932), 9:402–406; "Hoover Outlines 9-Point Program to Spur Revival," *New York Times*, July 30, 1932; and "Hoover Approves 6-Hour Day to Spread Work," *New York Times*, October 2, 1931. For business interest in general, see "Spread-Work Plans Gain Ground on the Employment Front," *Business Week*, October 1932, pp. 14–15; "American Industry and the Five-Day Week," *Congressional Digest* 11 (1932): 225–247; and L. C. Walker, "The Share-the-Work Movement," *Annals of the American Academy*, January 1933, p. 13.

10. Ford and Crowther, "Unemployment or Leisure."

11. Benjamin Kline Hunnicutt, "Why Do Republicans Want Us to Work All the Time?" *Politico*, February 7, 2014, available at https://www.politico.com/magazine/story/2014/02/jobs-leisure-republicans-want-us-to-work-all-the-time-103282.

12. The change in the department name occurred before my *Politico* article appeared. Iowa state legislators and regents have contacted our deans, asking about leisure studies, for years.

13. Roy Rosenzweig, *Eight Hours for What We Will: Workers and Leisure in an Industrial City, 1870–1920* (New York: Cambridge University Press, 1983), 58.

14. B. Joseph Pine II and James H. Gilmore, *The Experience Economy* (Boston: Harvard Business Press, 1999). See also James Harkin, *Big Ideas: The Essential Guide to the Latest Thinking* (London: Atlantic Books, 2008), 57.

15. We were delighted to find that Robert Rossman and Barbara Schlatter, prominent scholars in parks and recreation, were leading the way. See J. Robert Rossman and Barbara Elwood Schlatter, *Recreation Programming: Designing and Staging Leisure Experiences*, 6th ed. (Urbana, IL: Sagamore, 2011). After completing the manuscript for *The Age of Experience*, I discovered J. Robert Rossman and Mathew D. Duerden, *Designing Experiences* (New York: Columbia University Press, 2019). I regret not having access to this splendid work as I was finishing up my book. For a more complete list of researchers exploring links between experience design and the new sciences, see Chapter 7.

16. Staffan Burenstam Linder, *The Harried Leisure Class* (New York: Columbia University Press, 1970).

17. John Owen, *The Price of Leisure: An Economic Analysis of the Demand for Leisure Time* (Rotterdam, Netherlands: Rotterdam University Press, 1969).

18. I thank these students in my class: Bryan Triplett, Austin Showalter, Kelvin Bell, Ryan Farnsworth, Joseph Glenn, Matt Ingram, Erin Mykleby, Kathryn Nasenbenny, Chris Polizzi, and Chris Yabut.

INTRODUCTION

1. Alvin Toffler, *Future Shock* (New York: Random House, 1970), 237. Toffler predicted that, at the coming of the new technology, "we shall also witness a revolutionary expansion of certain industries whose sole output consists not of manufactured goods, nor even of ordinary services, but of pre-programmed 'experiences.' . . . The experience industry could turn out to be one of the pillars of super-industrialism, the very foundation, in fact, of the post-service economy" (226). For others who foresee the coming of the new technology, see Manel Baucells and Rakesh Sarin, *Engineering Happiness: A New Approach for Building a Joyful Life* (Berkeley: University of California Press, 2012); Cristina Botella, Giuseppe Riva, Andrea Gaggioli, Brenda K. Wiederhold, Mariano Alcaniz, and Rosa M. Baños, "The Present and Future of Positive Technologies," *Cyberpsychology, Behavior and Social Networking* 15, no. 2 (2012): 78–84; and Brenda Wiederhold and Giuseppe Riva, "Positive Technology Supports Shift to Preventive, Integrative Health," *Cyberpsychology, Behavior and Social Networking* 15, no. 2 (2012): 67–68.

2. Benjamin Hunnicutt, *Kellogg's Six-Hour Day* (Philadelphia: Temple University Press, 1996), 13.

3. Walt Whitman, *Democratic Vistas*, in *Prose Works, 1892*, vol. 2, ed. Floyd Stovall (New York: New York University Press, 1964), 410; Benjamin Hunnicutt, *Free Time: The Forgotten American Dream* (Philadelphia: Temple University Press, 2013), 65.

4. Hélder Ferreira and Aurora Teixeira conclude that, "[on the basis of] the existing literature, it is consensual among scholars that, with the commoditisation of products and services, companies have to learn how to design, create, deliver and manage experiences that customers are ready to pay for." Hélder Ferreira and Aurora A. C. Teixeira, "'Welcome to the Experience Economy': Assessing the Influence of Customer Experience Literature through Bibliometric Analysis," FEP Working Papers no. 481, January 2013, p. 6, available at http://wps.fep.up.pt/wps/wp481.pdf.

5. Jon Sundbo and Flemming Sørensen, eds., *Handbook on the Experience Economy* (Cheltenham, UK: Edward Elgar, 2013), 22. See also the 2006 study prepared for the European Commission, "The Economy of Culture in Europe," which claims that cultural and creative industries have become important factors driving economic growth and job creation. KEA European Affairs, "The Economy of Culture in Europe," October 2006, available at http://ec.europa.eu/assets/eac/culture/library/studies/cultural -economy_en.pdf. In addition, see Flemming Sørensen and Jon Sundbo, "Experience Economy Brimming with Potential," *ScienceNordic*, March 3, 2014, pp. 6–14.

6. B. Joseph Pine II and James H. Gilmore, *The Experience Economy* (Boston: Harvard Business Press, 1999). See also B. Joseph Pine II and James H. Gilmore, *The Experience Economy*, 2nd ed. (Boston: Harvard Business Press, 2011). All references herein are to the 2011 edition.

7. James Harkin, *Big Ideas: The Essential Guide to the Latest Thinking* (London: Atlantic Books, 2008), 57.

210 / NOTES TO THE INTRODUCTION

8. See the editorial reviews for the book on Amazon, at https://www.amazon.com/ Experience-Economy-Updated-Joseph-Pine-ebook/dp/B0054KCGCG.

9. Brian Solis, "Stop Talking about Technology and Start Designing Experiences," *Brian Solis*, April 29, 2014, available at http://www.briansolis.com/2014/04/ experiences. See also Macala Wright, "Does Your Brand Have a Customer Service Strategy?" *PSFK*, August 13, 2015, available at http://www.psfk.com/2015/08/brain -solis-customer-experience-strategy-experience-architecture.html.

10. Shep Hyken, "Top Ten Business Books from 2015," *Forbes*, January 30, 2016, available at http://www.forbes.com/sites/shephyken/2016/01/30/top-ten-business -books-from-2015/#67ba5bbf44b0.

11. Forrest Cardamenis, "Consolidated, Focused Messaging Will Help Fight Disruption," *Luxury Daily*, January 21, 2016, available at http://www.luxurydaily.com/ consolidated-focused-messaging-will-help-fight-disruption.

12. B. Schmitt, *Experiential Marketing: How to Get Customers to Sense, Feel, Think, Act and Relate to Your Company and Brands* (New York: Free Press, 1999), 1.

13. Perform an Internet search for "experience economy" for the last week for new examples.

14. Indus Hotels, "Home2 Suites and TRU by Hilton," available at http://www .indushotels.com/tru.aspx (accessed September 2, 2019); Hilton, "Hilton Worldwide Changes the Game with a Revolutionary New Midscale Brand," January 25, 2016, available at https://newsroom.hilton.com/corporate/news/hilton-worldwide-changes -the-game-with-a-revolutionary-new-midscale-brand.

15. Aaron Cowan, *A Nice Place to Visit: Tourism and Urban Revitalization in the Postwar Rustbelt* (Philadelphia: Temple University Press, 2016).

16. See, for example, the website of *Slow: The Magazine of the Slow Food Movement* (edited by Carlo Petrini), at http://www.slowfood.it; and Lisa J. Servon and Sarah Pink, "Cittaslow: Going Glocal in Spain," *Journal of Urban Affairs* 37, no. 3 (2015): 327–340.

17. Citing government sources, Jon Sundbo observes, "Analyses show that the experience economy is growing and gaining an increasing part of global competition." J. Sundbo, "Innovation in the Experience Economy: A Taxonomy of Innovation Organisations," *Service Industries Journal* 29, no. 4 (2009): 435.

18. Dan Goldman, Sophie Marchessou, and Warren Teichner, "Cashing In on the US Experience Economy," McKinsey and Company, December 2017, available at https://www.mckinsey.com/industries/private-equity-and-principal-investors/our -insights/cashing-in-on-the-us-experience-economy. On the basis of a 2014 Harris national poll it commissioned, Eventbrite concluded, "Since 1987, the share of consumer spending on live experiences and events relative to total U.S. consumer spending increased 70 percent. People want to experience more, and businesses are evolving and entering the market to meet that demand." Eventbrite, "Millennials: Fueling the Experience Economy," 2014, p. 2, available at https://eventbrite-s3.s3.amazonaws.com/ marketing/Millennials_Research/Gen_PR_Final.pdf. For other analysis on spending on experiences, see Simon Usborne, "Just Do It: The Experience Economy and How We Turned Our Backs on 'Stuff,'" *The Guardian*, May 13, 2017, available at https:// www.theguardian.com/business/2017/may/13/just-do-it-the-experience-economy-and -how-we-turned-our-backs-on-stuff; and Mintel, "American Lifestyles 2015: The Connected Consumer," April 2015, available at https://store.mintel.com/american-lifestyles

-2015-the-connected-consumer-seeking-validation-from-the-online-collective-us-april -2015. See also Mintel, "America Is Back to Pre-recession Spending Habits of 'Save Less and Spend More,'" June 3, 2015, available at http://www.mintel.com/press-centre/ social-and-lifestyle/america-is-back-to-pre-recession-spending-habits-of-save-less-and -spend-more.

19. See, for example, Michael Jones, "The Hot New Thing That Consumers Are Buying," *Forbes*, February 23, 2016, available at http://www.forbes.com/sites/ michaeljones/2016/02/23/consumers-want-experiences; and Nick Cowling, "Millennials Want Experiences, Not 'Stuff,'" *Marketing*, December 17, 2015, available at http:// www.marketingmag.ca/consumer/millennials-want-experiences-not-stuff-column -164421.

20. Ferreira and Teixeira, "'Welcome to the Experience Economy.'" See also Caroline Tynan and Sally McKechnie, "Experience Marketing: A Review and Reassessment," *Journal of Marketing Management* 25, nos. 5–6 (2009): 501–517.

21. Gary Ellis and J. Robert Rossman observe, "The principles identified by Pine and Gilmore, when practically applied, can be thought of as a 'technology' that may be used successfully by many organizations within the experience industry. . . . The technology is robust and may be applied in commercial and noncommercial settings and successfully integrated with other techniques for programming and staging experiences." See Ellis and Rossman, "Creating Value for Participants through Experience Staging: Parks, Recreation, and Tourism in the Experience Industry," *Journal of Park and Recreation Administration* 26, no. 4 (2008): 9.

22. Martin Seligman, *Flourish: A Visionary New Understanding of Happiness and Well-Being* (New York: Free Press, 2011), 1.

23. Claudia Wallace, "The New Science of Happiness," *Time*, January 9, 2005, available at http://content.time.com/time/magazine/article/0,9171,1015832,00.html.

24. Ibid. Subsequently, Seligman and others have repeatedly acknowledged that humanistic psychologists such as Abraham Maslow, Carl Rogers, and Erich Fromm made earlier and significant contributions to the study of human well-being.

25. Ibid.

26. Stephen Joseph, "Applied Psychology 10 Years On," in *Positive Psychology in Practice: Promoting Human Flourishing in Work, Health, Education, and Everyday Life*, ed. Stephen Joseph, 2nd ed. (Somerset, NJ: Wiley, 2015), 2.

27. Stewart I. Donaldson, Maren Dollwet, and Meghana A. Rao, "Happiness, Excellence, and Optimal Human Functioning Revisited: Examining the Peer-Reviewed Literature Linked to Positive Psychology," *Journal of Positive Psychology* 10, no. 3 (2015): 185.

28. Pelin Kesebir and Ed Diener, "In Pursuit of Happiness: Empirical Answers to Philosophical Questions," *Perspectives on Psychological Science* 3, no. 2 (2008): 117.

29. Seligman, *Flourish*, 17.

30. Ibid., 2.

31. Gardiner Morse, "The Science behind the Smile, Interview with Daniel Gilbert," *Harvard Business Review* 90, nos. 1–2 (2012): 152.

32. Daniel J. Siegel, *The Developing Mind: Toward a Neurobiology of Interpersonal Experience* (New York: Guilford Press, 1999). See also Daniel J. Siegel, *Pocket Guide to Interpersonal Neurobiology: An Integrative Handbook of the Mind* (New York: W. W. Norton, 2012), introduction.

33. Edward G. Jones and Lorne M. Mendell, "Assessing the Decade of the Brain," *Science*, April 30, 1999, p. 739.

34. Stefan Klein, *The Science of Happiness*, trans. Stephen Lehmann (New York: Marlowe, 2002); Richard Layard, *Happiness: Lessons from a New Science* (New York: Penguin, 2005), 10. Dacher Keltner and Emiliana Simon-Thomas created one of the first massive open online courses dealing with the science of happiness, at https://www.edx.org/course/science-happiness-uc-berkeleyx-gg101x#.VKWDDSPF9c5.

35. Justin Fox, "The Economics of Well-Being," *Harvard Business Review* 90, nos. 1–2 (2012): 78–83.

36. Morse, "The Science behind the Smile," 85.

37. "Economics Discovers Its Feelings," Happiness and Economics: Special Report, *The Economist*, December 19, 2006, available at https://www.economist.com/special-report/2006/12/19/economics-discovers-its-feelings.

38. Daniel J. Siegel, *Mindsight: The New Science of Personal Transformation* (New York: Bantam Books, 2010), 86–87.

39. Ibid. See also Siegel, *Pocket Guide to Interpersonal Neurobiology*, 243.

40. Siegel, *Mindsight*, 52. Siegel's definition of mind is one of the best: "The human mind is a relational and embodied process that regulates the flow of energy and information" (74).

41. I have selected "eudaimonic" technology instead of "happiness" or "hedonic" technology because, as Stephen Joseph notes, "One of the key developments [in positive psychology] over the past 10 years has been the shift in emphasis from hedonistic well-being to eudaimonic well-being." Joseph, "Applied Psychology," 2.

42. See Chapter 7 for a partial list. Pine and Gilmore do cite a few psychologists' research but mainly to support their claims about the superiority of experiences over goods and services. Pine and Gilmore, *The Experience Economy*.

43. This book continues Pine and Gilmore's attempts to make clear that "experiences represent an existing but previously unarticulated genre of economic output. Decoupling experiences from services in accounting for what businesses create opens up possibilities for extraordinary economic expansion—just as recognizing services as a distinct and legitimate offering led to a vibrant economic foundation in the face of a declining industrial base . . . a new base is emerging." Pine and Gilmore, *The Experience Economy*, xxiii.

44. See Chapter 8 and Table 7.1.

45. Toffler, *Future Shock*, 221. Toffler also predicted the "psychologization" of the economy and the emerging of "experience engineers" and "experience designers" (229) who, through "experiential production" (234) create experience products in the coming "experience industries" (221). Toffler concluded, "For the satisfaction of man's elemental material needs opens the way for new, more sophisticated gratifications. We are moving from a 'gut' economy to a 'psyche' economy" (236).

46. In his popular introductory textbook, N. Gregory Mankiw writes, "The concept of *utility* . . . is a person's subjective measure of well-being or satisfaction." Mankiw, *Principles of Economics* (New York: Cengage Learning, 2014), 573. See also J. Dorfman, *The Economic Mind in American Civilization* (New York: Viking, 1949), 3:243.

47. Even though some of the new happiness economists have turned to social science research methods, most economists still rely on the market to determine value and utility. For economists' turn to social science, see "Economics Discovers Its Feelings."

48. David Brooks, "The Experience Economy," *New York Times*, February 14, 2011, available at https://www.nytimes.com/2011/02/15/opinion/15brooks.html.

49. Inglehart's initial efforts spawned the World Values Survey. Survey data are available at http://www.worldvaluessurvey.org/WVSContents.jsp.

50. P. R. Abramson and R. Inglehart, *Value Change in Global Perspective* (Ann Arbor: University of Michigan Press, 1995). See also R. Inglehart, *Cultural Shift in Advanced Industrial Society* (Princeton, NJ: Princeton University Press, 1990); and R. Inglehart, *Modernization and Postmodernization: Cultural, Economic and Political Change in 43 Societies* (Princeton, NJ: Princeton University Press, 1997).

51. Brooks, "The Experience Economy."

52. Jürgen Habermas, *Lifeworld and System: A Critique of Functionalist Reason* (New York: Beacon, 2005).

53. Jeremy Rifkin, *The Age of Access: The New Culture of Hypercapitalism, Where All of Life Is a Paid-For Experience* (New York: J. P. Tarcher/Putnam, 2000).

54. Brooks, "The Experience Economy."

55. Hunnicutt, *Free Time*, 14.

56. See Britta Timm Knudsen, Dorthe R. Christensen, and Per Blenker, eds., *Enterprising Initiatives in the Experience Economy: Transforming Social Worlds* (New York: Routledge, 2015), 12.

57. Brooks, "The Experience Economy."

58. Benjamin Kline Hunnicutt, *Work without End: Abandoning Shorter Hours for the Right to Work* (Philadelphia: Temple University Press, 1987), 9. For one of the best summaries of the history of working hours available, see Robert Whaples, "Hours of Work in U.S. History," *EH.net*, August 14, 2001, available at http://eh.net/encyclopedia/hours-of-work-in-u-s-history.

59. Hunnicutt, *Work without End*, 81.

60. A more complete catalog of such great expectations is one of my purposes in Hunnicutt, *Free Time*.

61. Brooks, "The Experience Economy."

62. H. Ford and S. Crowther, "Unemployment or Leisure," *Saturday Evening Post*, August 2, 1930, p. 19. See also Ford and Crowther, *Moving Forward* (New York: Doran, 1930), chap. 5.

63. Walter S. Gifford, "Prosperity," 1930, Yale University Libraries Special Collection, New Haven, CT.

64. Ibid.

65. Robert Whaples, "Where Is There Consensus among American Economic Historians? The Results of a Survey on Forty Propositions," *Journal of Economic History* 55, no. 1 (March 1995): 139–154.

66. Hunnicutt, *Kellogg's Six-Hour Day*, 13.

67. The economics of working less, and thereby "buying" one's own time, is discussed in Chapter 8.

68. Herbert Marcuse, *Eros and Civilization: A Philosophical Inquiry into Freud* (New York: Vintage, 1962), vii.

69. "With all else remaining unaltered"—that is, without the market's malfunctioning because of some normative or irrational agenda such as the continuing ascendancy of what Max Weber identified as the culture of wealth and work as ends in themselves (the new work-based fetish or religion); power-seeking, exploitative corporate

skullduggery; or government interventions designed to sustain Full-Time, Full Employment in perpetuity. Each of these is a very real possibility. See Max Weber, *The Protestant Ethic and the "Spirit" of Capitalism, and Other Writings* (New York: Penguin, 2002), 18, 25, 35, 153, 294–295.

CHAPTER 1

1. Benjamin Kline Hunnicutt, *Free Time: The Forgotten American Dream* (Philadelphia: Temple University Press, 2013).

2. See Karl T. Compton, "Science Makes Jobs," *Scientific Monthly* 38, no. 4 (1934): 297–300.

3. Joseph A. Schumpeter, *Capitalism, Socialism and Democracy* (1942; repr., New York: Routledge, 2013), 123.

4. Benjamin Franklin, *Works of the Late Dr. Benjamin Franklin: Consisting of His Life, Written by Himself* (New York: Samuel Campbell, 1794), 2:74.

5. In *Capital*, Marx famously observed, "The realm of freedom actually begins only where labour, which is determined by necessity and mundane considerations, ceases; thus in the very nature of things it lies beyond the sphere of actual material production. . . . Beyond begins that development of human energy which is an end in itself, the true realm of freedom. . . . The shortening of the working-day is its basic prerequisite." Karl Marx, *Capital: A Critique of Political Economy*, ed. Frederick Engels, trans. Ernest Untermann (Chicago: Charles H. Kerr, 1909), 954–955. Hegel, Kant, and other nineteenth-century philosophers often used the phrase "realm of freedom," but Marx and Engels grounded it in the historical process of shorter working hours. I have argued that workers in the United States understood that connection long before, beginning during their struggle for the ten-hour day in the United States. See Hunnicutt, *Free Time*.

6. John Danaher, *Automation and Utopia: Human Flourishing in a World without Work* (Cambridge, MA: Harvard University Press, 2019), 24.

7. Benjamin Kline Hunnicutt, *Work without End: Abandoning Shorter Hours for the Right to Work* (Philadelphia: Temple University Press, 1987), chap. 3.

8. Ibid.

9. J. B. Gilbert, *Work without Salvation: America's Intellectuals and Industrial Alienation, 1880–1910* (Baltimore: Johns Hopkins University Press, 1977), vii–xv, 31–66, 181. See also Hunnicutt, *Free Time*, 74.

10. Hunnicutt, *Work without End*, chap. 3.

11. Helen Nearing and Scott Nearing, *Living the Good Life: How to Live Sanely and Simply in a Troubled World* (New York: Schocken Books, 1970).

12. J. M. Keynes, "Economic Possibilities of Our Grandchildren," in *Essays in Persuasion* (London: Macmillan, 1931), 363, 367–368.

13. John H. Pencavel, *Diminishing Returns at Work: The Consequences of Long Working Hours* (Oxford: Oxford University Press, 2018), 18.

14. Certainly, some of FDR's make-work policies had been tried before in Europe—public works in Germany during Bismarck's chancellorship, for example.

15. Benjamin Hunnicutt, "Kellogg's Six-Hour Day: A Capitalist Vision of Liberation through Managed Work Reduction," *Business History Review* 66, no. 3 (Autumn 1992): 475–522.

16. Hunnicutt, *Work without End*, chap. 6.

17. See also Jean-Baptiste Michel et al., "Quantitative Analysis of Culture Using Millions of Digitized Books," *Science* 331, no. 6014 (2011): 176–182.

18. Hunnicutt, *Work without End*, 154.

19. In 1934, prominent scientists convened in New York City to defend themselves against charges that their new technologies were putting the nation out of work. In this defining moment, American scientists turned from an ideology that had always before directed their efforts (i.e., freeing humans with laborsaving devices) to one of "Science Makes Jobs," also the name of their national symposium. What influence this meeting had on the deliberations about unemployment going on at the same time in Washington is hard to determine. Roosevelt did communicate with the symposium; Owen D. Young played important roles in both the symposium and FDR's administration. Given the timing of the symposium, it is quite possible that American scientists' discovery that science makes jobs influenced the formation of Roosevelt's make-work strategy rather than the other way around. See "Science Defended as Makers of Jobs," *New York Times*, February 23, 1934, p. 1; and "Science Presses toward New Goals," *New York Times*, January 28, 1934, sec. 6, p. 60. For an account of the symposium, the scientists involved, its impact on Roosevelt's administration, and the subsequent "science makes jobs" campaign, see Hunnicutt, *Work without End*, chap. 10.

20. Rexford Tugwell, *The Industrial Discipline* (New York: Columbia University Press, 1933), 94.

21. With the exception of civil rights, it is hard to find a comparable domestic political issue.

22. See May Bulman, "German Workers Win Right to 28-Hour Week following Industrial Action," *The Independent*, February 11, 2018, available at https://www.independent.co.uk/news/world/europe/german-workers-right-28hour-week-trade-union-industrial-action-ig-metall-a8205751.html.

23. See Jefferson Chase, "Scrap 'Outmoded' 8-Hour Workday in Germany, Economic Experts Say," *DW*, December 11, 2017, available at http://www.dw.com/en/scrap-outmoded-8-hour-workday-in-germany-economic-experts-say/a-41346723.

24. Hunnicutt, *Work without End*, chap. 8; Hunnicutt, *Free Time*, chap. 7.

25. Charlotte McDonald, "How Many Earths Do We Need?" *BBC News Magazine*, June 16, 2015, available at https://www.bbc.com/news/magazine-33133712.

26. Hunnicutt, *Free Time*, 186–190.

27. Derek Thompson, "A World without Work," *The Atlantic*, July–August 2015, available at https://www.theatlantic.com/magazine/archive/2015/07/world-without-work/395294/.

28. Thomas Piketty, *Capital in the Twenty-First Century*, trans. A. Goldhammer (Cambridge, MA: Belknap Press, 2014).

29. Robert M. Hutchins, *The University of Utopia* (Chicago: University of Chicago Press, 1953), ix.

30. Gallup, "State of the American Workplace," 2013, p. 12, available at www.gallup.com/file/services/176708/State_of_the_American_Workplace_.

31. B. Joseph Pine II and James H. Gilmore, *The Experience Economy*, rev. ed. (Boston: Harvard Business Press, 2011), ix–xxii.

CHAPTER 2

1. B. Joseph Pine II and James H. Gilmore, *The Experience Economy*, rev. ed. (Boston: Harvard Business Press, 2011), ix.

2. Ibid., xii.

3. Ibid., ix; see also xx, xxvii, 17, 105, 241. See also B. Joseph Pine II and James H. Gilmore, "The Experience Economy: Past, Present and Future," in *Handbook on the Experience Economy*, ed. Jon Sundbo and Flemming Sørensen (Cheltenham, UK: Edward Elgar, 2013), 37. Pine and Gilmore add that "focusing on goods and services alone leads down the road of economic austerity. Experiences . . . hold the key to . . . economic prosperity" (22).

4. Pine and Gilmore, *The Experience Economy*, xxiv.

5. Predictions about the collapse or end of work, a jobless future, and a world without work seem to have grown to a crescendo over the last decades. See, for example, Clive Jenkins and Barrie Sherman, *The Collapse of Work* (London: Eyre Methuen, 1979); Stanley Aronowitz and William DiFazio, *Jobless Future: Sci-Tech and the Dogma of Work* (Minneapolis: University of Minnesota Press, 1994); and Edward Granter, *Critical Social Theory and the End of Work* (London: Routledge, 2016).

6. Jeremy Rifkin, *The Age of Access: The New Culture of Hypercapitalism, Where All of Life Is a Paid-for Experience* (New York: J. P. Tarcher/Putnam, 2000).

7. Derek Thompson, "A World without Work," *The Atlantic*, July–August 2015, available at https://www.theatlantic.com/magazine/archive/2015/07/world-without -work/395294. Rifkin's remedy is in the Keynesian tradition. He prescribes new public policies and additional government spending to expand employment opportunities in the public sector: community projects, service-based enterprises, and nonprofits that could reemploy those who have lost their service or transportation jobs.

8. Erik Brynjolfsson and Andrew McAfee, *The Second Machine Age: Work, Progress and Prosperity in a Time of Brilliant Technologies* (New York: W. W. Norton, 2014).

9. Tyler Cowen, *Average Is Over: Powering America beyond the Age of the Great Stagnation* (New York: Penguin, 2013).

10. Pine and Gilmore, *The Experience Economy*, 15; see also introduction.

11. Pine and Gilmore, "The Experience Economy," 22.

12. Pine and Gilmore, *The Experience Economy*, 292.

13. Dan Goldman, Sophie Marchessou, and Warren Teichner, "Cashing In on the US Experience Economy," McKinsey and Company, December 2017, available at https://www.mckinsey.com/industries/private-equity-and-principal-investors/our -insights/cashing-in-on-the-us-experience-economy.

14. Pine and Gilmore, *The Experience Economy*, xxvi.

15. W. W. Rostow, *The Stages of Economic Growth: A Non-Communist Manifesto* (Cambridge: Cambridge University Press, 1960).

16. Pine and Gilmore, *The Experience Economy*.

17. For a more in-depth discussion of the progression of economic values, see Chapter 3.

18. Rifkin, *Age of Access*, 7.

19. Jon Sundbo, "Innovation in the Experience Economy: A Taxonomy of Innovation Organisations," *Service Industries Journal* 29, no. 4 (2009): 431.

20. Ibid., 435.

21. Hélder Ferreira and Aurora A. C. Teixeira. "'Welcome to the Experience Economy': Assessing the Influence of Customer Experience Literature through Bibliometric Analysis," FEP Working Papers no. 481, January 2013, p. 15, available at http://wps.fep.up.pt/wps/wp481.pdf.

22. Ibid., 21–22.

23. Sundbo and Sørensen, *Handbook on the Experience Economy*, 7.

24. T. O'Dell and P. Billing, *Experiencescapes: Tourism, Culture and Economy* (Copenhagen: Copenhagen Business School Press, 2005). See also Anne Lorentzen and Hugues Jeannerat, "Urban and Regional Studies in the Experience Economy: What Kind of Turn?" *European Urban and Regional Studies* 20, no. 4 (2013): 363–369.

25. Gary Ellis and J. Robert Rossman, "Creating Value for Participants through Experience Staging: Parks, Recreation, and Tourism in the Experience Industry," *Journal of Parks and Recreation Administration* 26 (Winter 2008): 1–20.

26. Bernd Schmitt, "Experience Marketing: Concepts, Frameworks and Consumer Insight," *Foundations and Trends in Marketing* 5, no. 2 (2010): 55–122.

27. Joseph B. Pine and James H. Gilmore, "Welcome to the Experience Economy," *Harvard Business Review* 76 (1998): 97.

28. "Profiting from Experiences—Mark Cameron, Jaguar Land Rover," *YouTube*, November 22, 2013, available at https://www.youtube.com/watch?v=fk2L1EyRWmI.

29. See "Experience Drives," available at https://experience.landroverusa.com/?_ga=2.199416366.1439461234.1564004530-1528451527.1564004530 (accessed July 24, 2019).

30. Ibid.

31. "One Hour Experience," available at https://experience.landroverusa.com/experiences/one-hour-experience.html#choose (accessed July 24, 2019).

32. "California Owners' Days," available at https://experience.landroverusa.com/experiences/owners-days-summary.html (accessed October 19, 2019).

33. "Adventure Travel Moab," available at https://www.landroverusa.com/experiences/lr-experience-drives/adventure-travel-moab.html (accessed November 1, 2019).

34. Alex Brownsell, "Six Things Brands Should Know about Experience Marketing," *Campaign*, October 18, 2013, available at http://www.marketingmagazine.co.uk/article/1216926/six-things-brands-know-experience-marketing.

35. See the marketing video at https://www.youtube.com/watch?v=qZhbmlbfG5U.

36. Best Buy, "Come Explore the New Samsung Experience Shop," available at http://www.bestbuy.com/site/clp/samsung-experience-shop/pcmcat297800050005.c?id=pcmcat297800050005 (accessed July 25, 2019).

37. Jay Moye, "Dispensing Happiness: 12 Innovative Coca-Cola Vending Machines in Action," Coca-Cola, December 3, 2013, available at http://www.coca-colacompany.com/innovation/dispensing-happiness-12-innovative-coca-cola-vending-machines-in-action.

38. Robert Johnston and Xiangyu Kong, "The Customer Experience: A Road-Map for Improvement," *Managing Service Quality* 21, no. 1 (2011), available at https://pdfs.semanticscholar.org/cb45/befce6cca39749730c250449e7756df0f6d4.pdf. Hans Gelter notes, "The concept of experiences is still unclear and vaguely defined within

the Experience Economy." Hans Gelter, "Total Experience Management—a Conceptual Model for Transformational Experiences within Tourism," in *The Nordic Conference on Experience, 2008: Research, Education and Practice in Media*, ed. S.-B. Arnolds-Granlund and P. Bjork (Vaasa, Finland: Tritonia, 2010), 49, available at https://www.academia.edu/18229177/Total_Experience_Management_a_conceptual_model _for_transformational_experiences_within_tourism?auto=download. Susanne H. G. Poulsson and Sudhir H. Kale write, "The definition of an experience is nowhere to be found in marketing literature. . . . [T]here has been no attempt made to systematically define what exactly constitutes an Experience. [Consequently,] any meaningful research in this area is impossible, thus stymieing the emergence of even rudimentary theory." Susanne H. G. Poulsson and Sudhir H. Kale, "The Experience Economy and Commercial Experiences," *Marketing Review* 4 (2004): 267. Poulsson and Kale offer an operational definition of the experience phenomenon by including "elements of novelty, surprise, learning, and engagement" (267).

39. Anders Sørensen and Jon Sundbo, eds., *Cases from the Experience Economy* (Roskilde, Denmark: Roskilde University, 2010), 5; Jon Sundbo and Flemming Sørensen, "Introduction to the Experience Economy," in *Handbook on the Experience Economy*, ed. Jon Sundbo and Flemming Sørensen (Cheltenham, UK: Edward Elgar, 2013), 1.

40. Sørensen and Sundbo, *Cases from the Experience Economy*, 5. Others have commented on the confusion and wide range of definitions. See, for example, Paul Hekkert and Hendrik Schifferstein, eds., *Product Experience* (Amsterdam: Elsevier, 2008), 1–3. Ferreira and Teixeira note that "scholars from a wide range of fields, including marketing, philosophy, cognitive science, and management practice . . . have categorized experience in various ways, leading to a multiplicity of definitions, sometimes with seemingly circular references . . . but none of which were really able to cover its essence holistically." All of which "poses challenges to . . . [a] clear-cut understanding." See Ferreira and Teixeira. "Welcome to the Experience Economy,'" 4–6. See also J.M.C. Snel, "For the Love of Experience: Changing the Experience Economy Discourse" (Ph.D. diss., University of Amsterdam, 2011). Snel writes that "the experience economy is still theoretically ill-founded" (27) and that "when reviewing the business literature on experiences, it is difficult to extract a clear and concise definition of what exactly is an experience" (55). Consequently, "it is not clear what experiences are and what they are not" (57). Enrique Alcántara, Miguel A. Artacho, Natividad Martínez, and Tomás Zamora agree that "there is not a single and widely accepted definition of experience." See Enrique Alcántara, Miguel A. Artacho, Natividad Martínez, and Tomás Zamora, "Designing Experiences Strategically," *Journal of Business Research* 67 (2014): 1074–1080.

41. Johnston and Kong, "The Customer Experience." Johnston and Kong discuss the widespread, intuitive use of "the experience economy" and conclude, "The idea of the customer experience appears to have resonated with practitioners and academics alike and many managers and service researchers now talk about the customer experience" (5).

42. Joseph Pine and James Gilmore, *Welcome to the Experience Economy* (Boston: Harvard Business Review Press, 2011), 3. See also Pine and Gilmore, *The Experience Economy*, 3, 36. "The company . . . no longer offers goods or services alone but the resulting experience, rich with sensations, created within the customer. All prior eco-

nomic offerings remain at arm's length, outside the buyer, but experiences are inherently personal. They actually occur within any individual who has been engaged" (17). For the claim that in the marketplace-theater, an experience occurs "when a company intentionally uses services as the stage, and goods as props, to engage individual customers in a way that creates a memorable event," see Pine and Gilmore, *Welcome to the Experience Economy*, 17.

43. For a discussion of material versus nonmaterial, or immaterial, values, see Britta Timm Knudsen, Dorthe R. Christensen, and Per Blenker, eds., *Enterprising Initiatives in the Experience Economy: Transforming Social Worlds* (London: Routledge, 2015), 12.

44. Several writers have included one or more of these four components in their analyses of experiences. For example, Paul Hekkert and Hendrik Schifferstein emphasize "psychological consequences," defining "experience" as "the awareness of the psychological effects elicited by the interaction with a product, including [stimulation of the senses], the meanings and values we attach to the product, and the feelings and emotions that are elicited." See Hekkert and Schifferstein, *Product Experience*, 2. See also C. Cupchik and M. C. Hilscher, "Holistic Perspectives on the Design of Experience," in Hekkert and Schifferstein, *Product Experience*, 241–256. Cupchik and Hilscher stress the importance of the impression and memory left by an experience. See also Schmitt, "Experience Marketing," 60.

45. The European Commission pointed to "the lack of statistical tools available to measure the contribution of the cultural sector to the economy" as a factor in the lack of public support in Europe. See KEA European Affairs, "The Economy of Culture in Europe," October 2006, available at http://ec.europa.eu/culture/library/studies/cultural-economy_en.pdf.

46. Trine Bille, "The Nordic Approach to the Experience Economy—Does It Make Sense?" Creative Encounters Working Paper 44, January 2010, available at http://openarchive.cbs.dk/bitstream/handle/10398/8012/44_TB_The_Nordic_Approach_to_Experience_Economy_-_Does_it_make_Sense_Final.pdf?sequence=3.

47. Pine and Gilmore, *The Experience Economy*, 17. Trying to distinguish experiences from services, Pine and Gilmore write, "Although experiences themselves lack tangibility, people greatly desire them because the value of experiences lies within them, where it remains long afterward" (19).

48. Ibid., xxii.

49. For a discussion of the most common rhetorical methods of definition, including definition by continuum, by contrast and comparison, by negation, by function, by enumeration, by necessary condition, and by classification, see Douglas Ehninger and Wayne Brockriede, *Decision by Debate* (New York: IDEA, 2008), 216.

50. Pieter Desmet and Paul Hekkert, "Framework of Product Experience," *International Journal of Design* 1, no. 1 (2007), available at http://www.ijdesign.org/index.php/IJDesign/article/view/66/15.

51. Paul Hekkert and Hendrik Schifferstein, "Introducing Product Experience," in *Product Experience*, ed. Paul Hekkert and Hendrik Schifferstein (Amsterdam: Elsevier, 2008), 2.

52. Sundbo and Sørensen, *Handbook on the Experience Economy*, 4.

53. Johnston and Kong, "The Customer Experience."

54. Pine and Gilmore recognize the value of such methods. See Pine and Gilmore, *The Experience Economy*, 126.

55. Alcántara et al., "Designing Experiences Strategically," 1079.

56. Sundbo and Sørensen, *Handbook on the Experience Economy*, 3.

57. Peter Drucker, *Innovation and Entrepreneurship* (New York: Harper and Row, 1989). For the importance of innovation in the experience economy, see Sundbo, "Innovation in the Experience Economy."

58. Sundbo, "Innovation in the Experience Economy," 431.

59. Morris B. Holbrook, "Consumption Experience, Customer Value, and Subjective Personal Introspection: An Illustrative Photographic Essay," *Journal of Business Research* 59 (2006): 715.

60. For researchers using Pine and Gilmore's taxonomy, see, for example, Laetitia Radder and Xiliang Han, "An Examination of the Museum Experience Based on Pine and Gilmore's Experience Economy Realms," *Journal of Applied Business Research* 31, no. 2 (March–April 2015): 43–57; Aikaterini Manthiou, Seonjeong (Ally) Lee, Liang (Rebecca) Tang, and Lanlung Chiang, "The Experience Economy Approach to Festival Marketing: Vivid Memory and Attendee Loyalty," *Journal of Services Marketing* 28, no. 1 (2014): 22–35; and Mehmet Mehmetoglu and Marit Engen, "Pine and Gilmore's Concept of Experience Economy and Its Dimensions: An Empirical Examination in Tourism," *Journal of Quality Assurance in Hospitality and Tourism* 12, no. 4 (2012): 237–255. See also Tanja Kotro, Päivi Timonen, Mika Pantzar, and Eva Heiskanen, "The Leisure Business and Lifestyle," National Consumer Research Centre, January 2005, p. 3, available at http://www.academia.edu/4732195/The_Leisure_Business_and_Lifestyle. Kotro and colleagues use Pine and Gilmore's taxonomy, adding their own dimension—a continuum ranging from creative to hedonistic pleasures.

61. Pine and Gilmore, *The Experience Economy*, 45.

62. Ibid., 46 (emphasis added).

63. Ibid., 47.

64. Ibid., 48–49.

65. Peter Guttman, *Adventures to Imagine: Thrilling Escapes in North America* (New York: Fodor's Travel, 1997).

66. Pine and Gilmore, *The Experience Economy*, 50.

67. Comic-Con International, "About Comic-Con International," available at https://www.comic-con.org/about (accessed July 25, 2019).

68. Pine and Gilmore, *The Experience Economy*, 53.

69. Ibid. Lena Mossberg adds that people who buy an "entertainment experience like to feel." Those purchasing "an education experience like to learn." Those enjoying an "esthetic experience like to be there," and those interested in "an escapism experience like to do." Lena Mossberg, *Att skapa Upplevelser—Från OK till WOW!* [Creating experiences—From OK to WOW!] (Lund, Sweden: Studentlitteratur HÄFTAD, Svenska, 2003), 64.

70. Nathan Shedroff, *Experience Design* (Indianapolis, IN: New Riders, 2001), 2.

71. Pine and Gilmore, *The Experience Economy*, 22.

72. Ibid.

73. Ibid., 24.

74. The Comic-Con annual convention held in San Diego has spawned several other examples of "ing-ing" comics such as Phoenix Comic Fest, Brussels Comic Strip Festival, and the Festival of Comics and Games in Lodz, Poland.

75. Pine and Gilmore, *The Experience Economy*, 24 (emphasis in original).
76. Ibid., 338.
77. Duck Brand, "Duct Tape Crafts," available at https://www.duckbrand.com/craft-decor (accessed July 25, 2019).
78. See Eataly's website, at https://www.eataly.com.
79. Brownsell, "Six Things Brands Should Know about Experience Marketing."
80. Pine and Gilmore, "Welcome to the Experience Economy," 17.
81. Shedroff, *Experience Design*, 2.
82. Albert Boswijk, Thomas Thijssen, and Ed Peelen, *The Experience Economy: A New Perspective* (Amsterdam: Pearson Education, 2007), 169–172.
83. B. Joseph Pine II and Kim Korn, *Infinite Possibility: Creating Customer Value on the Digital Frontier* (Oakland, CA: Berrett-Koehler, 2011).
84. C. K. Prahalad and Venkat Ramaswamy, *The Future of Competition: Co-creating Unique Value with Customers* (Cambridge, MA: Harvard Business Press, 2013), ix.
85. Shedroff, *Experience Design*, 166.
86. Pine and Gilmore, "The Experience Economy, Past, Present and Future," 34.
87. "San Diego Comic Con International—San Diego, CA," *Meetup*, available at https://www.meetup.com/it-IT/ConnecticutCosplayNetwork/events/221861482 (accessed July 25, 2019). See also http://www.comic-con.org/cci/masquerade#sthash.oZLNZnet.dpuf.
88. Ehninger and Brockriede, *Decision by Debate*, 216.

CHAPTER 3

1. B. Joseph Pine II and James H. Gilmore, *The Experience Economy*, rev. ed. (Boston: Harvard Business Press, 2011), 242–243.
2. Hélder Ferreira and Aurora A. C. Teixeira, "'Welcome to the Experience Economy': Assessing the Influence of Customer Experience Literature through Bibliometric Analysis," FEP Working Papers no. 481, January 2013, p. 5, available at http://wps.fep.up.pt/wps/wp481.pdf.
3. Pine and Gilmore, *The Experience Economy*, 254. This assumption, fundamental to the transformation economy, finds strong support in the findings of positive psychologists, summed up by Martin Seligman's observation: "Human beings are often, perhaps more often, drawn by the future than they are driven by the past. . . . And so a science that measures and builds expectations, planning, and conscious choice will be more potent than a science of habits, drives, and circumstances." Martin E. P. Seligman, *Flourish: A Visionary New Understanding of Happiness and Well-Being* (New York: Simon and Schuster, 2012), 106.
4. Pine and Gilmore note, "Identifying this new offering [transformations] requires using words not normally associated with businesses and their economic output." Pine and Gilmore, *The Experience Economy*, 252.
5. Josef Chytry, *Unis vers Cythère: Aesthetic-Political Investigations in Polis Thought and the Artful Firm* (New York: Peter Lang, 2009), 140.
6. Pine and Gilmore, *The Experience Economy*, 252–254.
7. Ibid. Distinguishing transformations from services and experiences, Pine and Gilmore write, "While commodities are fungible, goods tangible, services intangible, and experiences memorable, transformations are effectual" (252).

8. Brian Solis, *What's the Future of Business: Changing the Way Businesses Create Experiences* (Somerset, NJ: John Wiley, 2013), 160.

9. Pine and Gilmore, *The Experience Economy*, 254.

10. J.M.C. Snel, "For the Love of Experience: Changing the Experience Economy Discourse" (Ph.D. diss., University of Amsterdam, 2011), 166–170.

11. Pine and Gilmore, *The Experience Economy*, 252.

12. Ibid., 8.

13. Ibid., 273; see also 297.

14. Albert Boswijk, Thomas Thijssen, and Ed Peelen write, "And so, we contend, transformations are the fifth and final offering." Albert Boswijk, Thomas Thijssen, and Ed Peelen, *The Experience Economy: A New Perspective* (Amsterdam: Pearson Education, 2007), 169.

15. These numbers are credible partly because Pine and Gilmore count "medical care services" as a "transformation industry." Pine and Gilmore, *The Experience Economy*, 272.

16. Josef Chytry notes, "If the experience economy was exemplified by Disneyland and Rainforest Cafes, the transformation economy resembles the long-term offerings of the martial arts, nutrition management, reading transformations, and higher education." Chytry, *Unis vers Cythère*, 140.

17. Frank Füredi, *Therapy Culture: Cultivating Vulnerability in an Uncertain Age* (New York: Psychology Press, 2004).

18. Tanja Kotro, Päivi Timonen, Mika Pantzar, and Eva Heiskanen, "The Leisure Business and Lifestyle," National Consumer Research Centre, January 2005, p. 14, available at http://www.academia.edu/4732195/The_Leisure_Business_and_Lifestyle. For more about Nordic fitness, see http://www.nordic-fitness.co.uk/aboutnordicfitness.html.

19. Jeffrey A. Kottler, *Travel That Can Change Your Life: How to Create a Transformative Experience* (San Francisco: Jossey-Bass, 1997), xi.

20. Rick Steves, "10 Tips for Traveling as a Political Act," Rick Steves' Europe, available at https://www.ricksteves.com/watch-read-listen/read/articles/10-tips-for-traveling-as-a-political-act (accessed July 25, 2019).

21. CoreCivic, "CoreCivic Community," available at http://www.corecivic.com/community (accessed July 25, 2019). See also CoreCivic, "CoreCivic Reentry," available at http://www.corecivic.com/reentry (accessed July 25, 2019).

22. Pine and Gilmore, *The Experience Economy*, xvii.

23. Ibid., 262.

24. Ibid., 64.

25. Compare this with positive psychology's "drawn by the future" (Seligman, *Flourish*, 106), discussed in Chapter 5.

26. Karl Marx, of course, expected that the proletariat would eventually seize ownership of the means of industrial production by revolution. The transformation economy suggests an alternative route through the natural progression of economic values taking place within the free marketplace.

27. Pine and Gilmore suggest, "By staging a series of experiences, companies are better able to achieve a lasting effect on the buyer than through an isolated event. . . . [A]ny experience can become the basis for a new offering that elicits a transformation." Pine and Gilmore, *The Experience Economy*, 244.

28. Ibid., 277.

29. J. Sundbo, "Innovation in the Experience Economy: A Taxonomy of Innovation Organisations," *Service Industries Journal* 29, no. 4 (2009): 433.

30. J. R. Bryson, "Arts, Dance, Cultural Infrastructure and City Regeneration: Knowledge, Audience Development, Networks and Conventions and the Relocation of a Royal Ballet Company from London to Birmingham," *Norwegian Journal of Geography* 61, no. 3 (2007): 98–110.

31. Sundbo, "Innovation in the Experience Economy, 433.

32. See Jon Sundbo and Flemming Sørensen, eds., *Handbook on the Experience Economy* (Cheltenham, UK: Edward Elgar, 2013), 3. Pine and Gilmore discuss *Erfahrung* in "The Experience Economy, Past, Present and Future," in Sundbo and Sørensen, *Handbook on the Experience Economy*, 32. Hans Gelter makes similar claims. See Hans Gelter, "Total Experience Management—a Conceptual Model for Transformational Experiences within Tourism," in *The Nordic Conference on Experience, 2008: Research, Education and Practice in Media*, ed. S.-B. Arnolds-Granlund and P. Bjork (Vaasa, Finland: Tritonia, 2010), 49, available at https://www.academia.edu/18229177/Total _Experience_Management_a_conceptual_model_for_transformational_experiences _within_tourism?auto=download.

33. Christian Jantzen, "Experiencing and Experiences: A Psychological Framework," in Sundbo and Sørensen, *Handbook on the Experience Economy*, 155.

34. Snel, "For the Love of Experience," 136–137.

35. Gelter, "Total Experience Management," 52.

36. Ibid., 47.

37. Jantzen, "Experiencing and Experiences," 151. Jantzen explains, "Our memory sets expectations guiding us toward certain events . . . [that] are motivating . . . experience-based knowledge frames such events" (151).

38. Kotro and colleagues report, "We have located two clusters that both produce a turnover of approximately 2,000 million Euros: the sports and outdoor activities cluster and the home and garden cluster." Kotro et al., "The Leisure Business and Lifestyle," 1.

39. Ibid., 1, 12 (emphasis added).

40. For Gelter's use of Dewey and developmental education theory, see H. Gelter, "Polar Tourist Experiences—Challenges and Possibilities for Transmodern Tourism," in *Polar Tourism: A Tool for Regional Development*, ed. A. Grenier and D. Müller (Québec: Presses de L'Université du Québec, 2001), 227–250.

41. Phil Graham, Michael Dezuanni, Andy Arthurs, and Greg Hearn, "A Deweyan Experience Economy for Higher Education: The Case of the Australian Indie 100 Music Event," *Cultural Politics* 11, no. 1 (March 2015): 111–125.

42. Gelter, "Total Experience Management," 59.

43. A. H. Maslow, "A Theory of Human Motivation," *Psychological Review* 50, no. 4 (1943): 370–396.

44. Sundbo, "Innovation in the Experience Economy," 436 (emphasis added).

45. Gelter, "Total Experience Management," 47. See also R. M. Rodriguez Magda, "Transmodernidad: Un Nuevo Paradigma," *Orbis Tertius* 1 (2007): 11–94.

46. Rolf Jensen, *The Dream Society: How the Coming Shift from Information to Imagination Will Transform Your Business* (New York: McGraw Hill, 1999).

47. Gelter, "Total Experience Management," 47. Patrick Newbery uses the term "aspirational value" but attaches it to customers' desire for luxury purchases rather than Maslow's hierarchy. Patrick Newbery, *Experience Design: A Framework for Integrating Brand, Experience, and Value* (Wiley, 2013), location 157.

48. See Chapter 5.

49. Gary Ellis and J. Robert Rossman, "Creating Value for Participants through Experience Staging: Parks, Recreation, and Tourism in the Experience Industry," *Journal of Park and Recreation Administration* 26, no. 4 (Winter 2008): 13 (emphasis added). See also James Robert Rossman and Barbara Elwood Schlatter, *Recreation Programming: Designing and Staging Leisure Experiences*, 6th ed. (Urbana, IL: Sagamore, 2011).

50. Seligman, *Flourish*, 106.

51. Jantzen, "Experiencing and Experiences," 147, 164.

52. Richard Toon, "Solitude and Reflection in Science Centers," *Journal of Museum Education* 25, nos. 1–2 (2000): 25–27.

53. Ibid., 27.

54. Pine and Gilmore, *The Experience Economy*, 254.

55. Snel, "For the Love of Experience," 17.

56. Jantzen, "Experiencing and Experiences," 146.

57. Enrique Alcántara, Miguel A. Artacho, Natividad Martínez, and Tomás Zamora, "Designing Experiences Strategically," *Journal of Business Research* 67 (2014): 1075. See also Boswijk, Thijssen, and Peelen, *The Experience Economy*; and C. K. Prahalad and V. Ramaswamy, *The Future of Competition, Co-creating Unique Value with Customers* (Boston: Harvard Business School, 2004).

58. Britta Timm Knudsen, Dorthe R. Christensen, and Per Blenker, eds., *Enterprising Initiatives in the Experience Economy: Transforming Social Worlds* (London: Routledge, 2015). 2. See also Alvin Toffler, *Third Wave* (New York: William Morrow, 1980), 282. Toffler was one of the first writers to predict the coming of the prosumer.

59. "All Eyes on the Sharing Economy," *The Economist*, March 9, 2013, available at https://www.economist.com/node/21572914.

60. Knudsen, Christensen, and Blenker, *Enterprising Initiatives in the Experience Economy*, i.

61. George Ritzer and Nathan Jurgenson, "Production, Consumption, Prosumption: The Nature of Capitalism in the Age of the Digital 'Prosumer,'" *Journal of Consumer Culture* 10, no. 1 (2010): 13.

62. Pine and Gilmore write, "What should be considered is the degree of control. . . . [W]e would welcome excellence in both dimensions [of customer and experience provider]." Pine and Gilmore, *The Experience Economy*, xxi.

63. Ibid., 244.

64. Selda Basaran Alagöza and Nezahat Ekici, "Experiential Marketing and the Vacation Experience: The Sample of Turkish Airlines," *Procedia—Social and Behavioral Sciences* 150 (September 2014): 500.

65. Pine and Gilmore, "The Experience Economy, Past, Present and Future," 376.

66. John Schouten, James McAlexander, and Harold F. Koenig, "Transcendent Customer Experience and Brand Community," *Journal of the Academy of Marketing Science* 35 (2007): 357.

67. Newbery, *Experience Design*, location 227.

68. Paul Hekkert and Hendrik Schifferstein, eds., *Product Experience* (Amsterdam: Elsevier, 2008), 2.

69. Marshall Lager, "Children Are the Currency," *CRM*, July 2011, p. 66.

70. Juliet B. Schor, *Born to Buy: The Commercialized Child and the New Consumer Culture* (New York: Scribner, 2005).

71. Pine and Gilmore, *The Experience Economy*, 283.

72. Ibid., 273.

73. Ibid., 271.

74. Ibid., xix, xx.

75. Ibid., 271.

76. Ibid., xv.

77. Ibid., 8.

78. Ibid., xvi.

79. Quoted in "In the Name of Experience," *The Economist*, November 23, 2000, available at https://www.economist.com/business/2000/11/23/in-the-name-of-experience.

CHAPTER 4

1. E. Cowdrick, "The New Economic Gospel of Consumption," *Industrial Management* 74 (October 1927): 208.

2. E. P. Thompson, "Time, Work-Discipline, and Industrial Capitalism," *Past and Present* 38 (December 1967): 95.

3. Ibid., 95, 96.

4. Cowdrick, "The New Economic Gospel of Consumption," 208.

5. Hoover and his administration used a report published in the summer of 1929 to refute claims that unemployment had become chronic. See Committee on Recent Economic Changes, *Recent Economic Changes* (Washington, DC: U.S. Government Printing Office, 1929). Wesley Mitchell at Columbia University was quick to rebut this "unscientific" idea of the new term "technological unemployment," pointing out that technology created more jobs than it replaced and would do so well into the future. Technology was not a threat to economic stability. See Wesley Mitchell, "Forces That Make for American Prosperity," *New York Times*, May 12, 1929, sec. 10, p. 3.

6. See Benjamin Kline Hunnicutt, *Work without End: Abandoning Shorter Hours for the Right to Work* (Philadelphia: Temple University Press, 1987), chap. 2. For the fear of overproduction, see G. Garrett, "Business," in *Civilization in the United States*, ed. H. Stearns (New York: Wentworth, 1922), 124–129, 414; J. A. Hobson, *Economics of Unemployment* (London: Allen and Unwin, 1922), 23; J. A. Hobson, *Incentives in the New Industrial Order* (London: L. Parsons, 1922), 50; J. A. Hobson, "The Limited Market," *Nation*, April 11, 1925, pp. 350–352; and F. J. Boland, *Wage-Rates and Industrial Depressions: A Study of the Business Cycle* (New York, 1924), 4–7, 75. See also W. M. Persons, "Crisis of 1920 in the United States," *American Economic Review* 12, suppl. no. 1 (March 1922): 5.

7. Vincent H. Gaddis and Mary O. Furner, *Herbert Hoover, Unemployment, and the Public Sphere: A Conceptual History, 1919–1933* (Lanham, MD: University Press of America, 2005), 30–31.

8. "Text of the Program for Business Recovery Presented by the Hoover Committee," *New York Times*, October 29, 1931, p. 18.

9. J. S. Mill, *Principles of Political Economy* (London: Routledge, 1923), 751.

10. Ibid. John Stewart Mill, noticing that belief in the "unlimited increase of wealth" was being accepted in some quarters as the definition of progress, objected, saying that perpetual economic growth would eventually destroy the natural world and all that made wealth desirable or possible. Ibid., 594.

11. John Kenneth Galbraith, *The Affluent Society* (New York: Houghton Mifflin, 1976), 118. Galbraith noted, "The doctrine of diminishing marginal utility . . . seemed to put economic ideas squarely on the side of the diminishing importance of production under conditions of increasing affluence" (118).

12. For a fuller historical review of economists who made the connection between declining marginal utility and the reduction of working hours, see Hunnicutt, *Work without End*, 30–40; and R. B. Ekelund and R. F. Hebert, *A History of Economic Theory and Method* (New York: McGraw-Hill, 1975), 590. See also A. Marshall, *Principles of Economics*, 5th ed. (London: Macmillan, 1907), 527–529, 681, 719; and G. S. Becker, "A Theory of the Allocation of Time," *Economic Journal* 75 (September 1965): 493–517. For a basic college text treatment of the subject, see R. L. Heilbroner, *The Economic Problem*, 7th ed. (Englewood Cliffs, NJ: Prentice-Hall, 1984), 453. For a good history of this theory, see W. S. Jevons, *Theory of Political Economy* (1870; repr., New York: Kelley and Millman, 1957), 11–19.

13. Galbraith, *The Affluent Society*, 243.

14. For a summary treatment of the topic, see G. B. Cutten, *The Threat of Leisure* (New Haven, CT: Yale University Press, 1926), 67–73. George Cutten was president of Colgate University when he wrote this book.

15. Hunnicutt, *Work without End*, 81. For over a century, labor pursued the "progressive shortening of the hours of labor."

16. See, for example, W. H. Grimes, "The Curse of Leisure," *Atlantic Monthly*, April 1928, pp. 355–360.

17. I try to provide a more complete catalog of the various hopes for the expanding "realm of freedom" in *Free Time: The Forgotten American Dream* (Philadelphia: Temple University Press, 2013).

18. Walt Whitman, *Democratic Vistas*, in *Prose Works, 1892*, vol. 2, ed. Floyd Stovall (New York: New York University Press, 1964), 410.

19. The Library of Congress has assembled a fine collection of manuscripts and publications from the 1920s titled *Prosperity and Thrift: The Coolidge Era and the Consumer Economy, 1921–1929*, available at http://memory.loc.gov/ammem/coolhtml/coolhome.html.

20. Benjamin Hunnicutt, "Luxury or Leisure: The Dilemma of Prosperity in the New Era" (Ph.D. diss., University of North Carolina, Chapel Hill, 1976), 57.

21. William H. Adams, *On Luxury: A Cautionary Tale, a Short History of the Perils of Excess from Ancient Times to the Beginning of the Modern Era* (Washington, DC: Potomac Books, 2012), 1.

22. Max Weber, *The Protestant Ethic and the "Spirit" of Capitalism: And Other Writings*, trans. Peter Baehr and Gordon C. Wells (New York: Penguin, 2002), 35.

23. "Realm of freedom" was a common nineteenth-century construct, employed by Friedrich Hegel and Karl Marx, among others. The idea was commonplace in the writings of Americans such as Walt Whitman well into the twentieth century.

24. Weber, *The Protestant Ethic*, 35 (emphasis in original).

25. According to a proposed Pigouvian Redistribution Club manifesto, "It is evident that any transference of income from a relatively rich man to a relatively poor man of similar temperament, since it enables more intense wants to be satisfied at the expense of less intense wants, must increase the aggregate sum of satisfaction. The old 'law of diminishing utility' thus leads securely to the proposition: Any cause which increases the absolute share of real income in the hands of the poor, provided that it does not lead to a contraction in the size of the national dividend from any point of view, will, in general, increase economic welfare." Mark Thoma, "Pigouvian Redistribution," *Economist's View*, November 14, 2006, available at http://economistsview.typepad .com/economistsview/2006/11/pigouvian_redis.html. Such analyses have reappeared in political debates in the United States, such as in Rep. Alexandria Ocasio-Cortez's proposal for a 70 percent tax on the income of wealthy individuals.

26. Daniel Rodgers, *The Work Ethic in Industrial America* (New Haven, CT: Yale University Press, 1973), 11.

27. Certainly, intelligentsia from Bernard Mandeville and Adam Smith and on through the nineteenth century, including John Stuart Mill and Frederick Engels, have discussed the possibility. The idea that private vices could be public virtue had a long history before 1920. But what was new in the twentieth century was the widespread endorsement of limitless economic growth, its institution as the foundation of a nation's well-being by organizations such as the National Association of Manufacturers and the U.S. Chamber of Commerce and then, during Roosevelt's administrations, its incorporation into federal government policy.

28. Hunnicutt, *Work without End*, chap. 2.

29. Committee on Recent Economic Changes, *Recent Economic Changes*, xv; see also xvii, 15, 52, 59, 80, 81, 578. Hoover put this committee together during his term as secretary of commerce under Calvin Coolidge. The committee brought the best and brightest economic minds in the nation together to consider the problems of unemployment and economic growth in an age when a host of new products, never seen before, were playing an increasingly vital role in the economy. See "Text of the Program for Business Recovery."

30. T. C. Cochran, *Two Hundred Years of American Business* (New York: Delacorte, 1977), 192. See also J. Dorfman, *The Economic Mind in American Civilization* (New York: A. M. Kelley, 1949), 5:593–594; and T. C. Cochran and W. Miller, *The Age of Enterprise: A Social History of Industrial America* (New York: Macmillan, 1961), 310–324.

31. H. E. Krooss, *Executive Opinion* (New York: Doubleday, 1970), 531.

32. D. N. Potter, *People of Plenty* (Chicago: University of Chicago Press, 1954), 173. See also Committee on Recent Economic Changes, *Recent Economic Changes*, 402, 424.

33. F. L. Allen, *Only Yesterday: An Informal History of the Nineteen-Twenties* (New York: Harper, 1964), 140. For additional accounts of the coming of consumerism during the 1920s, see C. H. Hession and H. Sardy, *Ascent to Affluence: A History of Economic Development* (Boston: Allyn and Bacon, 1969), 666; D. Riesman, *The Lonely Crowd* (New Haven, CT: Yale University Press, 1950), 74, 75, 96–98, 116–123, 150, 189–191, 227, 290; and W. Leuchtenburg, *Perils of Prosperity, 1914–32* (Chicago: University of Chicago Press, 1958), 278.

34. Dorfman, *Economic Mind*, 5:593–594.

35. The committee used "luxury" only once in its report, in a doubtful assertion: "We no longer look on food as a luxury or as a primary source of pleasure." Committee on Recent Economic Changes, *Recent Economic Changes*, xv.

36. C. Southworth, "Can There Be General Overproduction? No!" *Journal of Political Economy* 32 (December 1924): 722–723. See also M. Leven, H. Moulton, and C. Warburton, *America's Capacity to Consume* (Washington, DC: Brookings Institution, 1934), 115–117; and W. Foster and W. Catchings, "Business under the Curse of Sisyphus," *World's Work* 52 (September 1926): 503–511. More recently than these authors, Juliet Schor notes that the "biological determinist arguments of insatiable desire became dominant" in the 1990s. See Juliet Schor, "In Defense of Consumer Critique: Revisiting the Consumption Debates of the Twentieth Century," *Annals of the American Academy of Political and Social Science* 611 (May 2007): 16–30. See also James Twitchell, *Lead Us into Temptation* (New York: Columbia University Press, 1999).

37. Hoover's committee recognized the threat of leisure. In the preface to their two-volume report, the committee stated, "Closely related to the increased rate of production-consumption of products is the consumption of leisure." They explicitly rejected this possibility in favor of increased production and consumption of goods and services offered by the marketplace, calling on business to meet the threat by innovation and marketing. Committee on Recent Economic Changes, *Recent Economic Changes*, xvi.

38. Jean-Baptiste Say, *A Treatise on Political Economy*, ed. Clement C. Biddle, trans. C. R. Prinsep (Philadelphia: Lippincott, Grambo, 1855), 17, available at http://www.econlib.org/library/Say/sayT15.html.

39. As John Kenneth Galbraith observed, the twentieth century marks the beginning of an era in which "the productive process incorporates the means by which wants are created. . . . The most important and intrinsically most evident source of consumer demand is the advertising and salesmanship of those providing the product. First you make the good, then you make the market." Galbraith, *The Affluent Society*, 137.

40. For a thoroughgoing account, see Daniel Horowitz, *The Anxieties of Affluence: Critiques of American Consumer Culture* (Amherst: University of Massachusetts Press, 2004).

41. William Wordsworth, "Sonnet 33," in *The Poetry of William Wordsworth* (London: Edward Moxon, 1847), 203.

42. James Truslow Adams, *The Epic of America* (1931; repr., New York: Blue Ribbon Books, 1941), 406. The watershed for the applied sciences in the United States came in the 1930s when debate about the practical value of science and technology shifted from laborsaving devices to what Vannevar Bush declared to be the new purpose: "Science makes jobs." See "Leaders Deny Science Cuts Jobs," *New York Times*, February 23, 1934, p. 1. See also Waldermar Kaekpffert, "Science Presses On toward New Goals," *New York Times*, January 28, 1934, p. SM6.

43. Adams, *The Epic of America*, 412. See also James Truslow Adams, *Our Business Civilization* (New York: A&C Boni, 1929), 17.

44. S. Leacock, *The Unsolved Riddle of Social Justice* (New York: John Lane, 1920), 23, 24.

45. E. Sapir, "Culture; Genuine and Spurious," *American Journal of Sociology* 29 (January 1924): 417.

46. J. A. Ryan, *Declining Liberty and Other Papers* (New York: Macmillan, 1927), 173, 178. See also J. A. Ryan, "Experts Look at Unemployment: A Shorter Work Period," *The Commonweal*, October 23, 1920, pp. 636–637.

47. Weber, *The Protestant Ethic and the "Spirit" of Capitalism*, 35.

48. S. Strauss, "Things Are in the Saddle," *Atlantic Monthly*, November 1924, p. 582. See also S. Strauss, "Rich Men and Key Men," *Atlantic Monthly*, December 1927, pp. 721–734. "Consumptionism" and "consumerism" were rarely used, if at all, before 1920. Afterward and until the 1960s, both terms were used occasionally. After 1960, "consumerism" gained wide circulation as a description of the modern, widespread spending on luxuries—or on what Hoover and his committee called "optional consumption."

49. G. Alger, "Effects of Industrialism," *Atlantic Monthly*, April 1925, pp. 483–484.

50. Strauss, "Things Are in the Saddle," 582.

51. Thorstein Veblen, *Absentee Ownership: Business Enterprise in Recent Times* (1923; repr. London: Transaction, 1997), 307n, 308. Veblen made no mention of psychologists selling luxuries in his *The Theory of the Leisure Class* (New York: Macmillan, 1912); rather, he presented a class-based critique of luxuries, similar to what had issued from the labor movement and its leaders during the nineteenth century. For laborites, luxuries represented the unjust expropriation of workers' labor. Veblen added pecuniary emulation and status seeking to this traditional critique—a critique that remained influential during the rest of the twentieth century.

52. Quoted in Douglas Dowd, *Thorstein Veblen* (New Brunswick, NJ: Transaction, 2000), 109.

53. Veblen, *Absentee Ownership*, 310.

54. For an overview of criticisms about consumerism, see Daniel Horowitz, *The Anxieties of Affluence: Critiques of American Consumer Culture* (Amherst: University of Massachusetts Press, 2004).

55. Pierre Bourdieu, *Distinction: A Social Critique of the Judgment of Taste*, trans. Richard Nice (Cambridge, MA: Harvard University Press, 1984).

56. Vance Packard, *The Hidden Persuaders* (New York: David McKay, 1957); Vance Packard, *The Waste Makers* (New York: D. McKay, 1960). According to Google Books Ngram Viewer, the use of the word "consumerism" began to rise shortly after the publication of Packard's books and culminated at a two-hundred-fold increase by 2000.

57. Vance Packard, *The Hidden Persuaders* (New York: Pocket Books, 1970), 1.

58. Packard, *The Waste Makers*, 119.

59. Ibid., 119, 315.

60. Mark Crispin Miller, introduction to *The Hidden Persuaders*, by Vance Packard (Brooklyn, NY: Ig, 2007), 26. For another critique of consumerism, see Roland Marchand, *Advertising and the American Dream: Making Way for Modernity, 1920–1940* (Berkeley: University of California Press, 1985), chap. 3.

61. Hannah Arendt, *The Human Condition*, 2nd ed. (Chicago: University of Chicago Press, 1998), 4–5.

62. Theodor Adorno and Max Horkheimer, *Dialectic of Enlightenment* (1944; repr., New York: Herder and Herder, 1972).

63. Jürgen Habermas, *The Structural Transformation of the Public Sphere: An Inquiry into a Category of Bourgeois Society*, trans. Thomas Burger with the assistance of Frederick Lawrence (Cambridge, MA: MIT Press, 1993), 4.

64. Jürgen Habermas, *The Theory of Communicative Action*, vol. 2, *Lifeworld and System: A Critique of Functionalist Reason*, trans. Thomas McCarthy (Boston: Beacon Press, 1987), 325.

65. Ibid.

66. Jacques Rancière, *La Nuit des Prolétaires* (Paris: Fayard, 1981), trans. John Drury as *The Nights of Labor: The Workers' Dream in Nineteenth-Century France* (Philadelphia: Temple University Press, 1989).

67. Jacques Rancière, "Preface to the Hindi Translation of *The Nights of Labor*," in *Sarvahara Raatein: Unneesaveen sadi ke Frans mein Mazdoor Swapna*, trans. Abhay Kumar Dube (Delhi, India: Vani Prakashan, 2008), viii, available at http://hydrarchy .blogspot.com/2009/01/ranciere-2-new-preface-to-hindi.html. I argue in *Free Time* (chap. 2) that similar kinds of worker communities of discourse developed along with demands for the ten-hour and eight-hour day in the United States during the nineteenth and early twentieth centuries.

68. Habermas, *Structural Transformation of the Public Sphere*, 173–174n80.

69. Ibid., 215–216.

70. John Hemingway, "Emancipating Leisure: The Recovery of Freedom in Leisure," *Journal of Leisure Research* 28, no. 1 (1996): 27–43.

71. Andre Gorz, *Critique of Economic Reason*, trans. Gillian Handyside and Chris Turner (London: Verso, 1989).

72. For Silver's ideas, see Chapter 9.

73. B. Joseph Pine II and James H. Gilmore, *The Experience Economy*, rev. ed. (Boston: Harvard Business Press, 2011), 34.

74. Jeremy Rifkin, *The Age of Access: The New Culture of Hypercapitalism, Where All of Life Is a Paid-For Experience* (New York: J. P. Tarcher/Putnam, 2000), 7.

75. Ibid.

76. Recent debates about the rise of the "gig" economy provide new context to Rifkin's claims about jobs becoming more servant-like, with pros and cons being argued in the 2019 debate in California. See Miriam Pawel, "You Call It the Gig Economy: California Calls It 'Feudalism,'" *New York Times*, September 12, 2019, available at https://www.nytimes.com/2019/09/12/opinion/california-gig-economy-bill-ab5 .html.

77. Rifkin, *The Age of Access*, 9.

78. Ibid., 29.

79. Ibid., 145–146. Rifkin quotes Pine and Gilmore and concludes, "Now the totality of our existence is being commodified: the foods we eat, the goods we produce, the services we perform for one another, and the cultural experiences we share" (146).

80. Ibid., 173.

81. Ibid., 12.

82. Ibid., 255.

83. Ibid., 2.

84. For a summary of the literature on consumption, see Schor, "In Defense of Consumer Critique."

85. Michel Foucault, *The Foucault Reader* (New York: Pantheon Books, 1984), 78. "Gray detail" is the phrase Foucault used to describe aspects of his "genealogy" project, which he defined as the "union of erudite knowledge and local memories . . . a reactivation of local knowledges . . . in opposition to scientific hierarchisation of knowledges" (78). See also Michel Foucault, *Power and Knowledge: Selected Interviews and Other Writings, 1972–1977*, ed. C. Gordon, trans. C. Gordon, L. Marshall, J. Mepham, and K. Soper (New York: Pantheon Books, 1980), 83–85. Some critics of consumerism are Veblen, Rifkin, and Jean Baudrillard. For an example of Baudrillard's critiques, see Jean Baudrillard, *Selected Writings*, ed. Mark Poster (Stanford, CA: Stanford University Press, 2001).

86. Eric J. Arnould, "Should Consumer Citizens Escape the Market?" *Annals of the American Academy of Political and Social Science* 611 (2007): 100–101. See also Søren Askegaard and Linda Scott, "Consumer Culture Theory: The Ironies of History," *Marketing Theory* 13 (June 2013): 139–147.

87. Arnould, "Should Consumer Citizens Escape the Market?," 96–97.

88. Eric J. Arnould and Craig J. Thompson, "Consumer Culture Theory (CCT): Twenty Years of Research," *Journal of Consumer Research* 31, no. 4 (2005): 868–882.

89. Ibid., 868. CCT has its own website: http://cctweb.org.

90. Perhaps the most famous of such claims is found in Milton and Rose Friedman, *Free to Choose: A Personal Statement* (New York: Houghton Mifflin Harcourt, 1990), chap. 1. See also Deirdre McCloskey, *The Bourgeois Virtues: Ethics for an Age of Commerce* (Chicago: University of Chicago Press, 2006), 1–7.

91. David Steigerwald, "All Hail the Republic of Choice: Consumer History as Contemporary Thought," *Journal of American History* 93, no. 2 (2006): 385.

92. Kathy Peiss, *Cheap Amusements: Working Women and Leisure in Turn-of-the-Century New York* (Philadelphia: Temple University Press, 1986), 15; Lizabeth Cohen, *Making a New Deal: Industrial Workers in Chicago, 1919–1938* (New York: Cambridge University Press, 1990), 100; Vicki L. Ruiz, *From Out of the Shadows: Mexican Women in Twentieth-Century America* (New York: Oxford University Press, 1998), 33–50; George Sanchez, *Becoming Mexican American: Ethnicity and Acculturation in Chicano Los Angeles, 1900–1943* (New York: Oxford University Press, 1993), 171–203; Randy McBee, *Dance Hall Days: Intimacy and Leisure among Working-Class Immigrants in the United States* (New York: New York University Press, 2000).

93. Lizabeth Cohen, *A Consumers' Republic: The Politics of Mass Consumption in Postwar America* (New York: Knopf, 2003), 7. Even though Cohen maintains that consumption has provided women with a degree of choice and enabled some political activism, she concludes that, on balance, the consumers' republic produced restrictive, enervating consumer markets rather than freed individuals from them. While admitting that there were times when the merging of public life with consumption produced healthy forms of civic engagement, Cohen sees the attenuation of opportunities to escape and find alternatives to the market ultimately stultifying and restrictive. See also Steigerwald, "All Hail the Republic of Choice."

94. Arnould, "Should Consumer Citizens Escape the Market?" 106 (Arnould encloses "should" with quotation marks in the original for emphasis). See also C. K. Prahalad and Venktatram Ramaswamy, "The New Frontier of Experience Innovation," *MIT Sloan Management Review*, Summer 2003, pp. 12–18; and Stephen L. Vargo

and Robert F. Lusch, "Evolving to a New Dominant Logic for Marketing," *Journal of Marketing* 68 (January 2004): 1–17.

95. Robert Putnam, *Bowling Alone: The Collapse and Revival of American Community* (New York: Simon and Schuster, 2001), 20.

96. Michael Schudson, *Advertising, the Uneasy Persuasion: Its Dubious Impact on American Society* (New York: Routledge, 2013), 140. See also Michael Schudson, "Criticizing the Critics of Advertising," *Media, Culture and Society* 3 (1981): 3–12; and Michael Schudson, "Delectable Materialism: Second Thoughts on Consumer Culture," in *Consumer Society in American History: A Reader*, ed. Lawrence Glickman (Ithaca, NY: Cornell University Press, 1999), 249.

97. Eric J. Arnould, Linda L. Price, and Avinash Malshe, "Toward a Cultural Resource-Based Theory of the Customer," in *The Service-Dominant Logic in Marketing*, ed. Robert F. Lusch and Stephen L. Vargo (Armonk, NY: M. E. Sharpe, 2006), 91.

98. Caroline Tynan and Sally McKechnie, "Experience Marketing: A Review and Reassessment," *Journal of Marketing Management* 25, nos. 5–6 (2009): 501–517.

99. Pine and Gilmore, *The Experience Economy*, xx.

100. Thompson, "Time, Work-Discipline and Industrial Capitalism," 95 (emphasis added). The similarity between this Thompson quote and Max Weber's famous "iron cage" prediction in *The Protestant Ethic and the Spirit of Capitalism* is worth noting. Weber wrote, "No one knows who will live in this cage in the future, or whether at the end of this tremendous development entirely new prophets will arise, or there will be a great rebirth of old ideas and ideals, or, if neither, mechanized petrification, embellished with a sort of convulsive self-importance." Max Weber, *The Protestant Ethic and the Spirit of Capitalism*, trans. T. Parsons (New York: Charles Scribner's Sons, 1930), 182.

101. Arendt, *The Human Condition*, 4–5.

102. Adams, *Our Business Civilization*, 17.

103. Thompson, "Time, Work-Discipline and Industrial Capitalism," 96.

CHAPTER 5

1. Martin Seligman, *Flourish: A Visionary New Understanding of Happiness and Well-Being* (New York: Free Press, 2011), 121. See also Martin E. P. Seligman, Peter Railton, Roy Baumeister, and Chandra Sripada, *Homo Prospectus* (New York: Oxford University Press, 2016), xi, xii.

2. Seligman, *Flourish*, 121.

3. Mihaly Csikszentmihalyi, "Positive Psychology and a Positive World-View: New Hope for the Future of Humankind," in *Applied Positive Psychology: Improving Everyday Life, Health, Schools, Work, and Society*, ed. Stewart I. Donaldson, Mihaly Csikszentmihalyi, and Jeanne Nakamura (New York: Psychology Press, 2011), 205–213. See also John Bagnell Bury, *The Idea of Progress: An Inquiry into Its Origin and Growth* (London: Macmillan, 1920), 346. Bury wrote that progress was "a general article of faith" in the Western world in modern times. See also John Gray, "An Illusion with a Future," *Daedalus* 133, no. 3 (2004): 10–17.

4. Csikszentmihalyi, "Positive Psychology and a Positive World-View," 209.

5. Gregg Easterbrook, "Psychology Discovers Happiness: I'm OK, You're OK," *New Republic*, March 5, 2001, available at http://docplayer.net/40806856-Psychology -discovers-happiness-i-m-ok-you-re-ok.html.

6. Genna Rivieccio, "The Horrible and the Miserable: Why Woody Allen's Take on Humanity Is Astoundingly Accurate," *Culled Culture*, August 2, 2014, available at https://www.culledculture.com/the-horrible-and-the-miserable-why-woody-allens -take-on-humanity-is-astoundingly-accurate.

7. Csikszentmihalyi, "Positive Psychology and a Positive World-View," 209.

8. Seligman writes, "So a science that measures and builds expectations, planning, and conscious choice will be more potent than a science of habits, drives, and circumstances." Seligman, *Flourish*, 106.

9. Csikszentmihalyi, "Positive Psychology and a Positive World-View, 205.

10. Christopher Peterson and Martin Seligman, *Character Strengths and Virtues: A Handbook and Classification* (New York: Oxford University Press, 2004).

11. American Psychiatric Association, *Diagnostic and Statistical Manual of Mental Disorders* (Washington, DC: American Psychiatric Association, 2013).

12. Peterson and Seligman, *Character Strengths and Virtues*, 18. For a discussion of universal values, see S. W. Schwartz, "Universals in the Content and Structure of Values: Theoretical Advances and Empirical Tests in 20 Countries," in *Advances in Experimental Social Psychology*, ed. M. P. Zanna (San Diego, CA: Academic Press, 1992), 1–65.

13. Orlando Patterson makes a compelling historical case that slavery was the origin of the "idea of freedom" in the Western world. Concluding that the "valorization of personal liberty is the noblest achievement of Western civilization," he insists that slaves realized most intensely the constraints and burdens set on them by their masters and, conceiving of freedom as their release, first gave direction to human progress. Orlando Patterson, *Freedom in the Making of Western Culture* (New York: Basic Books, 1991), 402.

14. Richard Dawkins, *A Devil's Chaplain: Reflections on Hope, Lies, Science, and Love* (Boston: Houghton Mifflin, 2003), 120.

15. Csikszentmihalyi, "Positive Psychology and a Positive World-View," 210. Unfortunately, "meme" has become a cliché, popularly used without precision to mean simply an idea or cultural theme that has a sudden, wide Internet usage—that has gone viral.

16. Ibid., 210.

17. Ibid., 209.

18. Alasdair C. MacIntyre, *Dependent Rational Animals: Why Human Beings Need the Virtues* (Chicago: Open Court, 1999), 5 (emphasis added).

19. Lisa G. Aspinwall and Ursula M. Staudinger, *A Psychology of Human Strengths: Fundamental Questions and Future Directions for a Positive Psychology* (Washington, DC: American Psychological Association, 2003). Aspinwall and Staudinger see "adaptiveness or functionality" as important considerations in understanding well-being and suggest defining "functionality as balancing one's own good and the good of others" (10, 11). They also note that "human strengths may primarily lie in the ability to flexibly apply as many different resources and skills as necessary to solve a problem or work toward a goal" (13). See also Gregory Bateson, *Steps to an Ecology of Mind: Collected Essays in Anthropology, Psychiatry, Evolution, and Epistemology* (Chicago: University of Chicago Press, 1972).

20. Robert M. Hutchins, "The University and Character," *The Commonweal*, April 22, 1938, pp. 710–711. For a similar list of virtues ("courage, temperance, liberality, honor, justice, wisdom, reason and understanding—these are still the virtues"),

see Robert M. Hutchins, *No Friendly Voice* (Chicago: University of Chicago Press, 1936), 4.

21. Robert M. Hutchins, *The University of Utopia* (Chicago: University of Chicago Press, 1965), 56–62; James Richard Connor, "The Social and Educational Philosophy of Robert Maynard Hutchins" (master's thesis, University of Wisconsin, Madison, 1954), 26. See also Frank K. Kelly, *Court of Reason: Robert Hutchins and the Fund for the Republic* (New York: Free Press, 1981), 38.

22. Instead of elements of well-being, Morten Kringelbach and Kent Berridge offer the term "empirical features." See Morten L. Kringelbach and Kent C. Berridge, "The Neuroscience of Happiness and Pleasure," *Social Research* 77, no. 2 (Summer 2010), available at https://www.ncbi.nlm.nih.gov/pmc/articles/PMC3008658.

23. Mihaly Csikszentmihalyi, *Flow and the Foundations of Positive Psychology* (New York: Springer, 2014), xx.

24. John Neulinger, *The Psychology of Leisure: Research Approaches to the Study of Leisure* (Springfield, IL: C. C. Thomas, 1974); Seppo E. Iso-Ahola, *Social Psychological Perspectives on Leisure and Recreation* (Springfield, IL: C. C. Thomas, 1980); John T. Haworth and A. J. Veal, *Work and Leisure* (London: Routledge, 2004).

25. Mihaly Csikszentmihalyi, *Flow and the Foundations of Positive Psychology*, xv–xx. Csikszentmihalyi and Iso-Ahola also recognize in play the expression of a primordial and universal stimulus-seeking or sensation-seeking behavior. See Iso-Ahola, *Social Psychological Perspectives*. For fun as the paradigm for happiness, see Johan Huizinga, *Homo Ludens: A Study of the Play Element in Culture* (New York: Harper and Row, 1970), 3; see also chap. 1.

26. Richard Kraus, *Recreation and Leisure in Modern Society* (Burlington, MA: Jones and Bartlett, 2001), 15.

27. For discussion of the topic, see Ziva Kunda and Shalom H. Schwartz, "Undermining Intrinsic Moral Motivation: External Reward and Self-Presentation," *Journal of Personality and Social Psychology* 45, no. 4 (1983): 763.

28. Seligman, *Flourish*, 26.

29. Quoted in William C. Compton and Edward Hoffman, *Positive Psychology: The Science of Happiness and Flourishing* (Belmont, CA: Wadsworth, 2013), 34. See also R. M. Ryan and E. L. Deci, "Self-Determination Theory and the Facilitation of Intrinsic Motivation, Social Development, and Well-Being," *American Psychologist* 55, no. 1 (2000): 68. See also E. L. Deci, *Intrinsic Motivation* (New York: Plenum, 1975).

30. Ryan and Deci, "Self-Determination Theory." Ryan and Deci suggest that the term "autonomous motivation" may be preferable to "intrinsic motivation" and "controlled motivation" preferable to "extrinsic motivation." William Compton and Edward Hoffman agree: "Autonomous motivation is self-chosen and is congruent with one's true self, while controlled motivation is driven by external rewards or guilt and is not congruent with a person's core values." Compton and Hoffman, *Positive Psychology*.

31. Richard Ryan and Edward Deci, *Self-Determination Theory: Basic Psychological Needs in Motivation, Development, and Wellness* (New York: Guilford Press, 2017), vii; see also 3.

32. Ryan and Deci, "Self-Determination Theory," 68.

33. V. Chirkov, R. M. Ryan, Y. Kim, and U. Kaplan, "Differentiating Autonomy from Individualism and Independence: A Self-Determination Perspective on Inter-

nalization of Cultural Orientations and Well-Being," *Journal of Personality and Social Psychology* 84 (2003): 97–110.

34. Ryan and Deci, *Self-Determination Theory*, 11.

35. Ryan and Deci, "Self-Determination Theory," 68.

36. Ibid., 68. Self-determination theory has found that barriers or constraints often interfere with competency, autonomy, and relatedness. Constraints, while causing unhappiness and dissatisfaction, are also frequently motivators, often the source of inspiration and aspiration. As Orlando Patterson notes, few have a keener vision of what freedom means, or stronger desire to attain it, than slaves and the oppressed. Patterson, *Freedom in the Making of Western Culture*.

37. Edward Deci and Maarten Vansteenkiste, "Self-Determination Theory and Basic Need Satisfaction: Understanding Human Development in Positive Psychology," *Ricerche di Psicologia* 27, no. 1 (2004): 23, 24 (emphasis added). See also Ryan and Deci, "Self-Determination Theory."

38. Seligman, *Flourish*, 121.

39. Carl R. Rogers, *On Becoming a Person: A Therapist's View of Psychotherapy* (Boston: Houghton Mifflin, 1961), 185–186.

40. Ibid., 186.

41. Ibid., 187.

42. Ibid., 188.

43. Barbara L. Fredrickson, "The Broaden-and-Build Theory of Positive Emotions," *Philosophical Transactions of the Royal Society B: Biological Sciences* 359, no. 1449 (2004): 1367.

44. Martin E. P. Seligman, *Authentic Happiness: Using the New Positive Psychology to Realize Your Potential for Lasting Fulfillment* (New York: Free Press, 2002). In 2000, Csikszentmihalyi and Seligman wrote, "A science of positive subjective experience, positive individual traits, and positive institutions promises to improve quality of life. . . . [A]t the subjective level [the science] is about valued subjective experiences: well-being, contentment, and satisfaction (in the past); hope and optimism (for the future); and flow and happiness (in the present). At the individual level, it is about positive individual traits: the capacity for love and vocation, courage, interpersonal skill, aesthetic sensibility, perseverance, forgiveness, originality, future mindedness, spirituality, high talent, and wisdom. At the group level, it is about the civic virtues and the institutions that move individuals toward better citizenship: responsibility, nurturance, altruism, civility, moderation, tolerance, and work ethic." Martin E. P. Seligman and Mihaly Csikszentmihalyi, "Positive Psychology: An Introduction," *American Psychologist* 55, no. 1 (2000): 5.

45. Seligman, *Flourish*, 27.

46. Ibid., 30.

47. Ibid., chap. 1. See also Compton and Hoffman, *Positive Psychology*, 65–80; Fabian Gander, René Proyer, and Willibald Ruch, "The Subjective Assessment of Accomplishment and Positive Relationships: Initial Validation and Correlative and Experimental Evidence for Their Association with Well-Being," *Journal of Happiness Studies* 18, no. 3 (2017): 743–764; John Coffey, Laura Wray-Lake, Debra Mashek, and Brittany Branand, "A Multi-study Examination of Well-Being Theory in College and Community Samples," *Journal of Happiness Studies* 17, no. 1 (2016): 187–211; Dianne A. Vella-Brodrick and Nansook Park, "Three Ways to Be Happy: Pleasure,

Engagement, and Meaning—Findings from Australian and US Sample," *Social Indicators Research* 90, no. 2 (2009): 165–179; C. Peterson, Willibald Ruch, Ursula Beermann, Nansook Park, and Martin E. P. Seligman, "Strengths of Character, Orientations to Happiness, and Life Satisfaction," *Journal of Positive Psychology* 2, no. 3 (2007): 149–156; and Margaret L. Kern, Lea E. Waters, Alejandro Adler, and Mathew A. White, "A Multidimensional Approach to Measuring Well-Being in Students: Application of the PERMA Framework," *Journal of Positive Psychology* 10, no. 3 (2015), available at https://www.ncbi.nlm.nih.gov/pmc/articles/PMC4337659. Some make claims to universality. Philip Watkins writes, "I believe that the most significant achievement of the [Values in Action] project was to identify virtues and strengths that appear to transcend time and culture." Philip C. Watkins, *Positive Psychology 101* (New York: Springer, 2016), 98. (For a description of the VIA project, go to https://www.viafdn .org.) Research has also demonstrated that PERMA values are common across cultures. See L. Lambert D'raven and N. Pasha-Zaidi, "Using the PERMA Model in the United Arab Emirates," *Social Indicators Research* 125, no. 3 (2016): 905–933. D'raven and Pasha-Zaidi conclude, "The results [of this study] showed that the way in which happiness was described overlapped with the PERMA pathways in culturally consistent ways" (905). See also S. Leimkötter, "One Step Further in the Search of the Good Life? A Cross Cultural Application of the PERMA Model in Germany between Individualists and Collectivists in Describing What a Good Life Is to Them: A Qualitative Study" (BSc thesis, University of Twente, 2017).

48. Compton and Hoffman, *Positive Psychology*, 46.

49. Plutchik's primary bipolar emotions are joy-sadness, anger-fear, trust-disgust, and surprise-anticipation. Robert Plutchik, *Emotions and Life: Perspectives from Psychology, Biology, and Evolution* (Washington, DC: American Psychological Association, 2002).

50. Daniel Schacter, Daniel Gilbert, Daniel Wegner, and Bruce Hood, *Psychology* (Basingstoke, UK: Palgrave Macmillan, 2011), 373 (emphasis in original).

51. Ibid., 395.

52. Michel Cabanac, "What Is Emotion?" *Behavioral Processes* 60, no. 2 (2002): 69.

53. Paul T. P. Wong, "Toward a Dual-Systems Model of What Makes Life Worth Living," in *The Human Quest for Meaning: Theories, Research, and Applications*, ed. Paul T. P. Wong (New York: Routledge, 2012), 6.

54. Seligman, *Flourish*, 26.

55. Stephen Joseph, *Positive Psychology in Practice: Promoting Human Flourishing in Work, Health, Education, and Everyday Life* (Somerset, NJ: Wiley, 2015), 2. See also James M. Nelson and Brent D. Slife, "A New Positive Psychology: A Critique of the Movement Based on Early Christian Thought," *Journal of Positive Psychology* 12, no. 5 (2017): 459–467. Short, useful definitions are provided by Stewart Donaldson, Maren Dollwet, and Meghana A. Rao, "Happiness, Excellence, and Optimal Human Functioning Revisited: Examining the Peer-Reviewed Literature Linked to Positive Psychology," *Journal of Positive Psychology* 10, no. 3 (2015): 185–195. Donaldson and colleagues write, "The hedonic component (subjective well-being) . . . is conceptualized as the experience of positive emotions and the absence of negative emotions, as well as an overall evaluation of one's life satisfaction. . . . The eudaimonic component . . . is conceptualized as the search and attainment of meaning, self-actualization, and personal growth" (189). Michael Steger writes, "Hedonia is marked by self-centered

interest in immediate gratification and eudaimonia is marked by more collectively-oriented interest in enduring effort and contribution." See Michael F. Steger, "Hedonia, Eudaimonia, and Meaning: Me versus Us; Fleeting versus Enduring," in *Handbook of Eudaimonic Well-Being*, ed. Joar Vittersø (Cham, Switzerland: Springer, 2016), 175.

56. Steger, "Hedonia, Eudaimonia, and Meaning," 181.

57. Csikszentmihalyi, *Flow and the Foundations of Positive Psychology*, xx, 100. Focus of attention is one of the primary strategies for experience design suggested by positive psychologists' research.

58. Seligman, *Flourish*, 32.

59. Signature strengths, the set of abilities unique to an individual, is a key concept in the list of Values in Action that Peterson and Seligman propose in *Character Strengths and Virtues*, 18.

60. Csikszentmihalyi, *Flow and the Foundations of Positive Psychology*, 184.

61. Ibid.

62. M. Csikszentmihalyi and O. Beattie, "Life Themes: A Theoretical and Empirical Exploration of Their Origins and Effects," *Journal of Humanistic Psychology* 19, no. 1 (1979): 45–63.

63. Seligman, *Flourish*, 35. Other researchers agree: "Experiences that are shared produce greater happiness than those experienced alone." See Cassie Mogilner, Ashley Whillans, and Michael I. Norton, "Time, Money, and Subjective Well-Being," in *Handbook of Subjective Well-Being*, ed. E. Diener, S. Oishi, and L. Tay (NobaScholar, 2017), 6, available at https://www.nobascholar.com/chapters/29.

64. Richard Dawkins, *The Selfish Gene* (New York: Oxford University Press, 1976).

65. Seligman, *Flourish*, 35–38.

66. Ibid., 36. Seligman concludes that humans are, "emotionally, creatures of the hive . . . who ineluctably seek out positive relationships with other members of our hive. . . . Very little that is positive is solitary" (38).

67. Ibid., 32.

68. Michael F. Steger, "Meaning in Life," in *The Oxford Handbook of Positive Psychology*, 2nd ed., ed. Shane J. Lopez and C. R. Snyder (Oxford: Oxford University Press, 2009), 682, 680.

69. Compton and Hoffman, *Positive Psychology*, 77–78. See also Steger, "Meaning in Life."

70. Michael F. Steger, "Meaning in Life and Wellbeing," in *Wellbeing, Recovery and Mental Health*, ed. Mike Slade, Lindsay Oades, and Aaron Jarden (Cambridge: Cambridge University Press, 2017), 76.

71. Steger, "Meaning in Life."

72. Steger, "Meaning in Life and Wellbeing," 75.

73. Ibid.

74. Steger, "Meaning in Life and Wellbeing," 76. Steger finds that "seeking and having meaning are non-linearly related." See Steger, "Hedonia, Eudaimonia, and Meaning," 181. Michael F. Steger and colleagues define the search for meaning as "the strength, intensity, and activity of people's desire and efforts to establish and/ or augment their understanding of the meaning, significance, and purpose of their lives." Michael F. Steger, Todd B. Kashdan, Brandon A. Sullivan, and Danielle Lorentz, "Understanding the Search for Meaning in Life: Personality, Cognitive Style,

and the Dynamic between Seeking and Experiencing Meaning," *Journal of Personality* 76, no. 2 (2008): 200.

75. Compton and Hoffman, *Positive Psychology*, 77–78.

76. Steger et al., "Understanding the Search for Meaning in Life," 225. See also E. Klinger, "The Search for Meaning in Evolutionary Perspective and Its Clinical Implications," in *The Human Quest for Meaning: A Handbook of Psychological Research and Clinical Application*, ed. Paul T. P. Wong and Prem S. Fry (Mahwah, NJ: Lawrence Erlbaum, 1998), 27–50.

77. Compton and Hoffman, *Positive Psychology*; Steger et al., "Understanding the Search for Meaning in Life."

78. Steger et al., "Understanding the Search for Meaning in Life," 225.

79. Ibid. See also Matthew Gallagher and Shane J. Lopez, "Curiosity and Well-Being," *Journal of Positive Psychology* 2, no. 4 (2007): 236–248; and Todd B. Kashdan, Paul Rose, and Frank D. Fincham, "Curiosity and Exploration: Facilitating Positive Subjective Experiences and Personal Growth Opportunities," *Journal of Personality Assessment* 82, no. 3 (2004): 291–305.

80. V. E. Frankl, *Man's Search for Meaning: An Introduction to Logotherapy* (New York: Washington Square Press, 1963). See also Wong, "Toward a Dual-Systems Model of What Makes Life Worth Living."

81. Frankl, *Man's Search for Meaning*, 121, 212.

82. Steger et al., "Understanding the Search for Meaning in Life," 200.

83. Paul T. P. Wong, introduction to Wong, *The Human Quest for Meaning: Theories, Research, and Applications*, xliii.

84. Wong, "Toward a Dual-Systems Model of What Makes Life Worth Living," 4–6.

85. Clifford Geertz, *The Interpretation of Cultures: Selected Essays* (New York: Basic Books, 1973), 140.

86. Making a claim similar to Steger's and Geertz's that most people are motivated to search for meaning, Kashdan, Rose, and Fincham conceptualize curiosity "as a *positive emotional-motivational system* associated with the recognition, pursuit, and self-regulation of novel and challenging opportunities." They recognize that curiosity "overlaps" with positive affect and sensation seeking. Kashdan, Rose, and Fincham, "Curiosity and Exploration," 291.

87. Steger, "Meaning in Life," 78. See also Steger, "Hedonia, Eudaimonia, and Meaning."

88. Seligman, *Flourish*, 33.

89. Ibid., 19.

90. Margaret L. Kern et al., "A Multidimensional Approach to Measuring Well-Being in Students." Kern et al. conclude that, while "[student well-being is multidimensional] . . . life satisfaction remained significantly correlated with Positive emotion, Relationships, and Accomplishment and less Depression. For health variables, Positive emotion and Accomplishment related to better physical activity and vitality." Ibid. See also Fabian Gander, René T. Proyer, and Willibald Ruch, "Positive Psychology Interventions Addressing Pleasure, Engagement, Meaning, Positive Relationships, and Accomplishment Increase Well-Being and Ameliorate Depressive Symptoms: A Randomized, Placebo-Controlled Online Study," *Frontiers in Psychology*, May 20, 2016, pp. 1–12; and Paddy J. Steinfort, "Coaching Character: Winning on and off the Field,"

in *Future Directions in Well-Being: Education, Organizations and Policy*, ed. Mathew A. White, Gavin R. Slemp, and A. Simon Murray (Cham, Switzerland: Springer International, 2017), 147–151.

91. Ryan and Deci, "Self-Determination Theory."

92. Robert White, "Motivation Reconsidered: The Concept of Competence," *Psychological Review* 66, no. 5 (1959): 300.

93. Carol D. Ryff, "Psychological Well-Being in Adult Life," *Current Directions in Psychological Science* 4, no. 4 (August 1995): 102.

94. Paul Wong, "Big Money, Big Science, Big Names, and the Flourishing of Positive Psychology," review of *Flourish: A Visionary New Understanding of Happiness and Well-Being*, by Martin E. P. Seligman, December 7, 2011, available at http://www .drpaulwong.com/big-money-big-science-big-names-and-the-flourishing-of-positive -psychology.

95. Compton and Hoffman, *Positive Psychology*, 66.

96. Carol D. Ryff and Corey Lee M. Keyes, "The Structure of Psychological Well-Being Revisited," *Journal of Personality and Social Psychology* 69 no. 4 (1995): 727.

97. Peterson and Seligman, *Character Strengths and Virtues*, 18.

98. Alasdair MacIntyre, *The Tasks of Philosophy: Selected Essays*, vol. 1 (Cambridge: Cambridge University Press, 2006), viii. Competence and achievement both may be elements of positive subjective experiences and a positive individual trait.

99. Seligman, *Flourish*, 39.

100. Peterson and Seligman, *Character Strengths and Virtues*, 18.

101. Ibid., 21.

102. Ibid., 6. Nevertheless, Peterson and Seligman sometimes persist in essentialist claims, arguing that the six broad categories of virtue "are universal, perhaps grounded in biology through an evolutionary process that selected for these aspects of excellence as means of solving the important tasks necessary for survival of the species." Ibid., 25. Similar universals are the foundation for other deontological systems that purpose sets of rules derived from the inherent human condition.

103. Ibid., 22.

104. Ibid., 25.

105. Ibid., 12, 15, 16.

106. Ibid., 17.

107. Character strengths also have similarities to what G. W. Allport called "personal traits." G. W. Allport, *Personality: A Psychological Interpretation* (New York: H. Holt, 1937).

108. Peterson and Seligman, *Character Strengths and Virtues*, 19.

109. Ibid., 21.

110. Ibid. The remaining *Character Strengths and Virtues* criteria are somewhat technical and less promising in terms of practical applications: *Nonfelicitous Opposite* (the opposite of a strength cannot itself be a strength), *Traitlike* (a strength needs to be manifest in the range of an individual's behavior), *Distinctiveness*, the existence of *Paragons*, the existence of *Prodigies*, the existence of people who show *Selective Absence* of a particular strength, and the larger society provides *Institutions* and associated *Rituals* for cultivating strengths.

111. Ryan and Deci, *Self-Determination Theory*, 11.

112. Shalom H. Schwartz, "An Overview of the Schwartz Theory of Basic Values," *Online Readings in Psychology and Culture* 2, no. 1 (2012), available at https://scholarworks.gvsu.edu/cgi/viewcontent.cgi?article=1116&context=orpc.

113. Ryan and Deci, *Self-Determination Theory*, 11 (emphasis added).

114. Seligman, *Flourish*, 19.

115. Florencia M. Sortheix and Shalom H. Schwartz, "Values That Underlie and Undermine Well-Being: Variability across Countries," *European Journal of Personality* 31 (2017): 187–201.

116. Schwartz, "An Overview of the Schwartz Theory of Basic Values," 3.

117. Ibid. Schwartz's ten "basic personal values" are self-direction, stimulation, hedonism, achievement, power, security, conformity, tradition, benevolence, and universalism. (See Table 7.1 for comparisons with other theorists.)

118. Sortheix and Schwartz, "Values That Underlie and Undermine Well-Being," 187.

119. Schwartz, "An Overview of the Schwartz Theory of Basic Values," 6.

120. Joseph, *Positive Psychology in Practice*, 103. See also Ryan and Deci, "Self-Determination Theory," 68.

121. M. Bobowik, N. Basabe, D. Páez, A. Jiménez, and M. A. Bilbao, "Personal Values and Well-Being among Europeans, Spanish Natives and Immigrants to Spain: Does the Culture Matter?" *Journal of Happiness Studies* 12 (2011): 401–419. However, Sortheix and Schwartz show that the associations between power and achievement and well-being are more complex than previous research has appreciated, demonstrating that the "value–[subjective well-being] relations depend on the combination of dynamic motivations that underlie each value and their trade-offs," that "these motivations interact with cultural characteristics of the context," and that "Cultural Egalitarianism moderates the value–[subjective well-being] associations." Sortheix and Schwartz, "Values That Underlie and Undermine Well-Being," 28.

122. Richard Easterlin, "Does Economic Growth Improve the Human Lot? Some Empirical Evidence," in *Nations and Households in Economic Growth: Essays in Honor of Moses Abramovitz*, ed. Paul A. David and Melvin W. Reder (New York: Academic Press, 1974), 90–124.

123. Ed Diener and Martin E. P. Seligman, "Beyond Money: Toward an Economy of Well-Being," *Psychological Science in the Public Interest* 5, no. 1 (2004): 1. The *Character Strengths and Virtues* handbook also discusses "the diminishing returns of material wealth for increasing subjective well-being" (21).

124. For Gossen's law, see Jürgen G. Backhaus, ed., *Modern Applications of Austrian Thought* (London: Routledge, 2007), 60. See also Chapter 8. Galbraith argues that this is also true with goods in general, vis-à-vis working hours, because the decline in working hours during the first part of the twentieth century reflected "a tacit but unmistakable acceptance of the declining marginal urgency of goods. There is no other explanation." Galbraith, *The Affluent Society*, 243.

125. Diener and Seligman, "Beyond Money," 1.

126. Andrew Oswald, "The Hippies Were Right All Along about Happiness," *Financial Times*, January 8, 2006, available at https://www.ft.com/content/dd6853a4-8853-11da-a25e-0000779e2340.

127. In addition to social comparison, researchers suggest that the "hedonic treadmill" is part of the reason that income and subjective well-being have fewer positive

correlations in wealthier nations. The "hedonic treadmill" suggests that most people soon return to a set happiness point after both positive and negative life events. Moreover, not only does the happiness associated with new purchases diminish, rising income prompts rising expectations, hence the "treadmill" on which we have to keep running just to stay even with others and our own expectations. Shane Frederick, "Hedonic Treadmill," in *Encyclopedia of Social Psychology*, ed., Roy Baumeister and Kathleen D. Vohs (Thousand Oaks, CA: Sage, 2007), 419–420.

128. Thomas Gilovich and Amit Kumar, "We'll Always Have Paris: The Hedonic Payoff from Experiential and Material Investments," in *Advances in Experimental Social Psychology*, ed. James M. Olson and Mark P. Zanna (Cambridge, MA: Academic Press, 2015), 147.

129. Elizabeth Weil, "Happiness Inc.," *New York Times*, April 19, 2012, available at http://www.nytimes.com/2013/04/21/fashion/happiness-inc.html. See also Daniel Kahneman, Alan Krueger, David Schkade, Norbert Schwarz, and Arthur Stone, "Would You Be Happier If You Were Richer? A Focusing Illusion," *Science* 312, no. 5782 (June 2006): 1908–1910.

130. Ed Diener, *The Science of Well-Being: The Collected Works of Ed Diener* (New York: Springer Science and Business Media, 2009), 103.

131. F. Cheung and R. E. Lucas, "Income Inequality Is Associated with Stronger Social Comparison Effects: The Effect of Relative Income on Life Satisfaction," *Journal of Personality and Social Psychology* 110, no. 2 (February 2016): 332 (emphasis added).

132. Ibid., 332 (emphasis added). Cheung and Lucas conclude, "In sum, research on perceived relative income has yielded generally consistent findings, suggesting subjective ranking of income compared to others is associated with life satisfaction" (333).

133. Betsey Stevenson and Justin Wolfers, "Economic Growth and Subjective Well-Being: Reassessing the Easterlin Paradox," *Brookings Papers on Economic Activity* 39, no. 1 (Spring 2008): 1. See also M. Hagerty and R. Veenhoven, "Wealth and Happiness Revisited—Growing National Income Does Go with Greater Happiness," *Social Indicators Research* 64 (2003): 1–27.

134. Stevenson and Wolfers, "Economic Growth and Subjective Well-Being," 1.

135. Edsel L. Beja Jr., "Income Growth and Happiness: Reassessment of the Easterlin Paradox," *International Review of Economics* 61 (2014): 329.

136. Yannis Georgellis, Nicholas Tsitsianis, and Ya Ping Yin, "Personal Values as Mitigating Factors in the Link between Income and Life Satisfaction: Evidence from the European Social Survey," *Social Indicators Research* 91, no. 3 (2009): 329–344.

137. Ibid., 329. Georgellis, Tsitsianis, and Ping Yin also confirm other findings about social comparison: "Reference or comparison income exerts a strong negative influence" on life satisfaction (329).

138. Ibid., 329. See also M. Rojas, "Heterogeneity in the Relationship between Income and Happiness: A Conceptual-Referent Theory Explanation," *Journal of Economic Psychology* 28 (2007): 1–14.

139. Georgellis, Tsitsianis, and Ping Yin, "Personal Values as Mitigating Factors," 329. For subjective well-being and intrinsic versus extrinsic values and orientation, see L. Sagiv, S. Roccas, and S. Oppenheim, "Values and Well-Being," in *Positive Psychology in Practice*, 2nd ed., ed. S. Joseph (New York: Wiley, 2015), 103–121.

140. Tim Kasser, Katherine L. Rosenblum, Arnold J. Sameroff, Edward L. Deci, Christopher P. Niemiec, Richard M. Ryan, Osp Árnadóttir, Rod Bond, Helga Dittmar,

Nathan Dungan, and Susan Hawks, "Changes in Materialism, Changes in Psychological Well-Being: Evidence from Three Longitudinal Studies and an Intervention Experiment," *Motivation and Emotion* 38 (2014): 20. Kasser et al. write, "Cross-cultural studies show that self-transcendent values and intrinsic goals . . . are consistently antipodal to self-enhancing values and extrinsic goals for money, status, wealth, etc." They conclude, "People's well-being improves as they place relatively less importance on materialistic goals and values, whereas orienting toward materialistic goals relatively more is associated with decreases in well-being over time." They suggest that "researchers and practitioners might begin to develop interventions, and to support public policies, that encourage people to place relatively more importance on self-transcendent and intrinsic aims in life, rather than the accumulation of more wealth and possessions" (20).

141. Thomas C. Mann and Thomas Gilovich, "The Asymmetric Connection between Money and Material vs. Experiential Purchases," *Journal of Positive Psychology* 11, no. 6 (2016): 649.

142. Andrea Gaggioli, Giuseppe Riva, Dorian Peters, and Rafael A. Calvo, "Positive Technology, Computing, and Design: Shaping a Future in Which Technology Promotes Psychological Well-Being," in *Emotions and Affect in Human Factors and Human–Computer Interaction*, ed. Myounghoon Jeon (Amsterdam: Elsevier, 2017), 485. See also T. Kasser and R. M. Ryan, "Further Examining the American Dream: Differential Correlates of Intrinsic and Extrinsic Goals," *Personality and Social Psychology Bulletin* 22 (1996): 280–287; and Georgellis, Tsitsianis, and Ping Yin, "Personal Values as Mitigating Factors."

143. Helga Dittmar, Rod Bond, Megan Hurst, and Tim Kasser, "The Relationship between Materialism and Personal Well-Being: A Meta-analysis," *Journal of Personality and Social Psychology* 10 (November 2014): 879.

144. Assigning a high value to the pursuit of money and valuing life choices primarily in monetary terms, "a monetizing mindset," is detrimental to well-beings on its own. See Mann and Gilovich, "The Asymmetric Connection between Money and Material vs. Experiential Purchases," 647.

145. Todd B. Kashdan and William E. Breen, "Materialism and Diminished Well-Being: Experiential Avoidance as a Mediating Mechanism," *Journal of Social and Clinical Psychology* 26, no. 5 (2007): 534.

146. Ryan T. Howell and Graham Hill, "The Mediators of Experiential Purchases: Determining the Impact of Psychological Needs Satisfaction and Social Comparison," *Journal of Positive Psychology* 4, no. 6 (2009): 511.

147. Mann and Gilovich, "The Asymmetric Connection between Money and Material vs. Experiential Purchases," 65. Mann and Gilovich conclude, "Viewing the world through a monetary lens has been shown to be injurious to psychological well-being. . . . Anything that consistently calls a person's attention to price and induces a monetary mindset can thus threaten happiness, satisfaction, and joy" (65).

148. Ibid.; Travis J. Carter and Thomas Gilovich, "The Relative Relativity of Material and Experiential Purchases," *Journal of Personality and Social Psychology* 98, no. 1 (2010): 146–159; Dittmar et al., "The Relationship between Materialism and Personal Well-Being."

149. Jesse Walker, Amit Kumar, and Thomas Gilovich, "Cultivating Gratitude and Giving through Experiential Consumption," *Emotion* 16, no. 8 (2016): 1127.

150. Jia Wei Zhang, Ryan T. Howell, and Peter A. Caprariello, "Buying Life Experiences for the 'Right' Reasons: A Validation of the Motivations for Experiential Buying Scale," *Journal of Happiness Studies* 14, no. 3 (June 2013): 817.

151. Thomas Gilovich, Amit Kumar, and Lily Jampol, "A Wonderful Life: Experiential Consumption and the Pursuit of Happiness," *Journal of Consumer Psychology* 25, no. 1 (2015): 152–165.

152. L. Van Boven and T. Gilovich were among the first to examine the relation between subjective well-being and material versus experiential purchases. Their original definitions still provide some precision. Material purchases are "made with the primary intention of acquiring a material good: a tangible object that is kept in one's possession." Experiential purchases are made "with the primary intention of acquiring a life experience." See L. Van Boven and T. Gilovich, "To Do or to Have: That Is the Question," *Journal of Personality and Social Psychology* 85 (2003): 1194. See also Peter Caprariello, Harry Reis, and Eliot Smith, "To Do, to Have, or to Share? Valuing Experiences over Material Possessions Depends on the Involvement of Others," *Journal of Personality and Social Psychology* 104, no. 2 (2013): 199–215; Carter and Gilovich, "The Relative Relativity of Material and Experiential Purchases," 146–159; T. J. Carter and T. Gilovich, "I Am What I Do, Not What I Have: The Differential Centrality of Experiential and Material Purchases to the Self," *Journal of Personality and Social Psychology* 102 (2012): 1304–1317; Howell and Hill, "The Mediators of Experiential Purchases"; A. Kumar and T. Gilovich, "Some 'Thing' to Talk About? Differential Story Utility from Experiential and Material Purchases," *Personality and Social Psychology Bulletin* 41 (2015): 1320–1331; A. Kumar and T. Gilovich, "To Do or to Have, Now or Later? The Preferred Consumption Profiles of Material and Experiential Purchases," *Journal of Consumer Psychology* 26 (2016): 169–178; A. Kumar, M. A. Killingsworth, and T. Gilovich, "Waiting for Merlot: Anticipatory Consumption of Experiential and Material Purchases," *Psychological Science* 25 (2014): 1924–1931; L. Nicolao, J. R. Irwin, and J. K. Goodman, "Happiness for Sale: Do Experiential Purchases Make Consumers Happier than Material Purchases?" *Journal of Consumer Research* 36 (2009): 188–198; and P. Pchelin and R. T. Howell, "The Hidden Cost of Value-Seeking: People Do Not Accurately Forecast the Economic Benefits of Experiential Purchases," *Journal of Positive Psychology* 9 (2014): 322–334.

153. Carter and Gilovich, "The Relative Relativity of Material and Experiential Purchases."

154. Gilovich and Kumar, "We'll Always Have Paris," 147.

155. T. Carter and T. Gilovich, "Getting the Most for the Money: The Hedonic Return on Experiential and Material Purchases," in *Consumption and Well-Being in the Material World*, ed. M. Tatzel (Dordrecht, Netherlands: Springer, 2014), 49–62.

156. Mann and Gilovich, "The Asymmetric Connection between Money and Material vs. Experiential Purchases."

157. Walker, Kumar, and Gilovich, "Cultivating Gratitude and Giving through Experiential Consumption," 1127.

158. Gilovich, Kumar, and Jampol, "A Wonderful Life," 152.

159. Howell and Hill, "The Mediators of Experiential Purchases," 520.

160. Gilovich and Kumar, "We'll Always Have Paris," 148.

161. Sara J. Solnicka and David Hemenway, "Is More Always Better? A Survey on Positional Concerns," *Journal of Economic Behavior and Organization* 37 (1998): 373–

244 / NOTES TO CHAPTER 5

383. A number of researchers have cited this example, including Carter and Gilovich, "The Relative Relativity of Material and Experiential Purchases." See also Cheung and Lucas, "Income Inequality Is Associated with Stronger Social Comparison Effects."

162. Bruce Headey, "Life Goals Matter to Happiness: A Revision of Set-Point Theory," *Social Indicators Research* 86, no. 2 (2008): 213–231.

163. Gilovich and Kumar, "We'll Always Have Paris."

164. Mann and Gilovich, "The Asymmetric Connection between Money and Material vs. Experiential Purchases," 647.

165. R. T. Howell, P. Pchelin, and R. Iyer, "The Preference for Experiences over Possessions: Measurement and Construct Validation of the Experiential Buying Tendency Scale," *Journal of Positive Psychology* 7 (2012): 57.

166. Zhang, Howell, and Caprariello, "Buying Life Experiences for the 'Right' Reasons." Zhang and colleagues contrast autonomous spending on experiences with spending on experiences for controlled or amotivated reasons.

167. Gilovich and Kumar, "We'll Always Have Paris," 162.

168. Carter and Gilovich, "I Am What I Do, Not What I Have," 1304.

169. Mann and Gilovich, "The Asymmetric Connection between Money and Material vs. Experiential Purchases," 647.

170. Howell, Pchelin, and Iyer, "The Preference for Experiences over Possessions," 68.

171. Carter and Gilovich, "The Relative Relativity of Material and Experiential Purchases," 147, 158.

172. Kashdan and Breen, "Materialism and Diminished Well-Being," 524.

173. Ibid., 524.

174. Mogilner, Whillans, and Norton, "Time, Money, and Subjective Well-Being."

175. Ashley Whillans, "Exchanging Cents for Seconds: The Happiness Benefits of Choosing Time over Money" (Ph.D. diss., University of British Columbia, 2017), iii. Research showing that buying time increases happiness includes A. V. Whillans, E. W. Dunn, P. Smeets, R. Bekkers, and M. I. Norton, "Buying Time Promotes Happiness," *Proceedings of the National Academy of Sciences* 114, no. 32 (2017): 8523–8526; H. E. Hershfield, C. Mogilner, and U. Barnea, "People Who Choose Time over Money Are Happier," *Social Psychological and Personality Science* 7, no. 7 (2016): 697–706; and A. V. Whillans, A. C. Weidman, and E. W. Dunn, "Valuing Time over Money Is Associated with Greater Happiness," *Social Psychological and Personality Science* 7, no. 3 (2016): 213–222.

176. Whillans, Weidman, and Dunn, "Valuing Time over Money," 213. See also Mogilner, Whillans, and Norton, "Time, Money, and Subjective Well-Being," 1.

177. Mogilner, Whillans, and Norton, "Time, Money, and Subjective Well-Being," 2.

178. Erica Mina Okada, "Justification Effects on Consumer Choice of Hedonic and Utilitarian Goods," *Journal of Marketing Research* 42, no. 1 (2005): 51. Okada suggests that guilt associated with spending for hedonic goods may be a strong reason for the preference. But one may assume that other reasons must be involved that future research, or the marketplace, may reveal.

179. F. Gino and C. Mogilner, "Time, Money, and Morality," *Psychological Science* 25, no. 2 (2014): 414–421.

180. Quoted in Cassie Mogilner, Hal E. Hershfield, and Jennifer Aaker, "Rethinking Time: Implications for Well-Being," *Consumer Psychology Review* 1, no. 1 (2018): 47.

181. Mogilner, Whillans, and Norton, "Time, Money, and Subjective Well-Being," 7.

182. Mogilner, Whillans, and Norton, "Time, Money, and Subjective Well-Being," 3. The activation of time versus money was accomplished in varied ways: having test subjects complete a scrambled-word test in which temporal words were found, asking how much time was "spent on" a product. To activate money versus time, questions about money were asked or word clues about money were given.

183. Whillans, Weidman, and Dunn, "Valuing Time over Money," 213.

184. Cassie Mogilner and Michael Norton, "Time, Money, and Happiness," *Current Opinion in Psychology* 10 (2016): 13.

185. Cassie Mogilner and Jennifer Aaker, "The Time vs. Money Effect: Shifting Product Attitudes and Decisions through Personal Connection," *Journal of Consumer Research* 36, no. 2 (2009): 277–291.

186. Mogilner, Whillans, and Norton, "Time, Money, and Subjective Well-Being," 4 (emphasis added).

187. Ibid.

188. Jesse Walker, Amit Kumar, and Thomas Gilovich, "Cultivating Gratitude and Giving through Experiential Consumption," *Emotion* 16, no. 8 (2016): 1126–1136.

189. Mogilner, Whillans, and Norton, "Time, Money, and Subjective Well-Being."

190. Compton and Hoffman, *Positive Psychology*, 70–71.

191. Mogilner and Aaker, "The Time vs. Money Effect," 288. It is important to note that psychologists' sumptuary advice and "should" language are, of course, of the hypothetical variety, "If you want to be happy, you *should* do *x*," rather than the rule-based, deontological variety.

192. Ibid.

193. Ibid.

194. Donaldson, Dollwet, and Rao, "Happiness, Excellence, and Optimal Human Functioning Revisited."

195. Mogilner and Aaker, "The Time vs. Money Effect."

196. Mogilner, Whillans, and Norton, "Time, Money, and Subjective Well-Being."

197. Whillans, Weidman, and Dunn, "Valuing Time over Money Is Associated with Greater Happiness."

198. Whillans, "Exchanging Cents for Seconds," ii.

199. Ibid., iii. This is Gary Becker's claim as well. See Chapter 7 and G. S. Becker, "A Theory of the Allocation of Time," *Economic Journal* 75 (September 1965): 493–517.

200. Whillans, "Exchanging Cents for Seconds," 114. Her findings are consistent with Okada's claim that people prefer to spend their time rather than their money on experiences. See Okada, "Justification Effects on Consumer Choice of Hedonic and Utilitarian Goods."

201. Whillans, "Exchanging Cents for Seconds," 3. See also Whillans et al., "Buying Time Promotes Happiness."

202. Economists have long proposed that there are opportunity costs in the mutually exclusive alternatives of work versus leisure. Choosing additional leisure may be

understood to have a price, an opportunity cost, determined by the amount of potential wages lost by not working. Becker, "A Theory of the Allocation of Time."
   203. Whillans, "Exchanging Cents for Seconds," 115.

CHAPTER 6

   1. Daniel J. Siegel, *Pocket Guide to Interpersonal Neurobiology: An Integrative Handbook of the Mind* (New York: W. W. Norton, 2012), 243.
   2. Christopher Peterson and Martin Seligman, *Character Strengths and Virtues: A Handbook and Classification* (New York: Oxford University Press, 2004).
   3. Daniel J. Siegel, *Mindsight: The New Science of Personal Transformation* (New York: Bantam Books, 2010), 301. See also Daniel J. Siegel, *Pocket Guide to Interpersonal Neurobiology: An Integrative Handbook of the Mind* (New York: W. W. Norton, 2012), 12.
   4. Gardiner Morse, "The Science behind the Smile, Interview with Daniel Gilbert," *Harvard Business Review* 90, nos. 1–2 (January–February 2012): 85.
   5. Edward O. Wilson, *Consilience: The Unity of Knowledge* (New York: Knopf, 1998). Research and theoretical advances from these fields have contributed to the consilience: anthropology, biology (developmental, evolution, genetics, zoology), cognitive science, computer science, developmental psychopathology, economics, linguistics, neuroscience (affective, cognitive, developmental, social), mathematics (game and systems theory), mental health, physics, psychiatry, psychology (cognitive, developmental, evolutionary, experimental, of religion, social, attachment theory, memory), sociology, and systems theory (chaos and complexity theory).
   6. Siegel, *Mindsight*, 301. See also Siegel, *Pocket Guide to Interpersonal Neurobiology*, 12; Stefan Klein, *The Science of Happiness: How Our Brains Make Us Happy and What We Can Do to Get Happier* (Cambridge, MA: Marlowe, 2002); and Richard Layard, *Happiness, Lessons from a New Science* (New York: Penguin Books, 2005), 10.
   7. I hope to contribute to Siegel's larger project with this book's defense of the commercial marketplace.
   8. Wilson, *Consilience*, 8. Consilience is one of the purposes of the Norton Series on Interpersonal Neurobiology. See "The Norton Series on Interpersonal Neurobiology," available at https://www.drdansiegel.com/books/ipnb_series/ (accessed October 22, 2019). For an introduction to positive neuroscience, see University of Pennsylvania, "Positive Neuroscience," https://www.authentichappiness.sas.upenn .edu/learn/positiveneuroscience (accessed July 8, 2019). Martin Seligman began the Positive Neuroscience Project in 2008 at the Pennsylvania Positive Psychology Center at the University of Pennsylvania.
   9. Joshua D. Greene, India Morrison, and Martin E. P. Seligman, *Positive Neuroscience* (Oxford: Oxford University Press, 2016).
   10. Morten L. Kringelbach and Kent C. Berridge, "The Functional Neuroanatomy of Pleasure and Happiness," *Discovery Medicine* 9, no. 49 (2010): 579–587. Morten Kringelbach and Kent Berridge offer the term "the neuroscience of happiness and pleasure" as an alternative to "positive neuroscience." See Morten L. Kringelbach and Kent C. Berridge, "The Neuroscience of Happiness and Pleasure," *Social Research* 77, no. 3 (2010): 659–678. Penn State's web page on authentic happiness quotes Seligman as saying, "Research has shown that positive emotions and interventions can bolster health, achievement, and resilience, and can buffer against depression and anxiety.

And while considerable research in neuroscience has focused on disease, dysfunction, and the harmful effects of stress and trauma, very little is known about the neural mechanisms of human flourishing. Creating this network of positive neuroscience researchers will change that." See University of Pennsylvania, "Authentic Happiness," available at https://www.authentichappiness.sas.upenn.edu/learn/positiveneuroscience (accessed July 29, 2019).

11. University of Pennsylvania, "Authentic Happiness."

12. Siegel, *Mindsight*, 74.

13. Kringelbach and Berridge, "The Neuroscience of Happiness and Pleasure," 660.

14. Siegel, *Mindsight*, 86.

15. Siegel, *Pocket Guide to Interpersonal Neurobiology*, 360.

16. Siegel, *Mindsight*, 110.

17. Mihaly Csikszentmihalyi describes humans as fundamentally self-aware and self-reflective (see Chapter 5). Mihaly Csikszentmihalyi, "Positive Psychology and a Positive World-View: New Hope for the Future of Humankind," in *Applied Positive Psychology: Improving Everyday Life, Health, Schools, Work, and Society*, ed. Stewart I. Donaldson, Mihaly Csikszentmihalyi, and Jeanne Nakamura (New York: Psychology Press, 2011), 205–213.

18. A. Pascual-Leone, A. Amedi, F. Fregni, and L. B. Merabet, "The Plastic Human Brain Cortex," *Annual Review of Neuroscience* 28 (2005): 377–401. Seligman notes that, together with psychology, neuroscience concentrated on diseases, trauma, and the like until the last few decades, neglecting to investigate the "neural mechanisms of human flourishing." See University of Pennsylvania, "Authentic Happiness."

19. Siegel, *Mindsight*, 27.

20. Daniel J. Siegel, *The Neurobiology of "We": How Relationships, the Mind, and the Brain Interact to Shape Who We Are*, read by the author (Louisville, CO: Sounds True Audio Learning Course, 2011). See also Patty de Llosa and Daniel Siegel, "The Neurobiology of 'We': Relationship Is the Flow of Energy and Information between People, Essential in Our Development," available at https://charterforcompassion.org/defining-and-understanding-compassion/the-neurobiology-of-we-relationship-is-the-flow-of-energy-and-information-between-people-essential-in-our-development (accessed July 29, 2019).

21. Rick Hanson, *Hardwiring Happiness: The New Brain Science of Contentment, Calm, and Confidence* (New York: Harmony Books, 2016), 11.

22. Ibid., 10.

23. Ibid., 127.

24. For a stricter, medical definition of neuroplasticity and its relation to experiences, see Christopher Ariel Shaw and Jill C. McEachern, *Toward a Theory of Neuroplasticity* (Philadelphia: Psychology Press, 2013), 85.

25. Siegel, *Mindsight*, 268.

26. Siegel, *Pocket Guide to Interpersonal Neurobiology*, 315. Siegel continues, "In *developmental* terms we can state that interpersonal patterns of communication that are integrative stimulate the activity and growth of integrative fibers in the *brain*. And it is the integrative fibers in the brain that enable self-regulation because they are the circuits responsible for coordination and balancing the internal and interpersonal elements of the individual" (315).

27. Hanson, *Hardwiring Happiness*, 65.

28. Siegel, *Pocket Guide to Interpersonal Neurobiology*, 93.

29. Rick Hanson, "The Next Big Step: What's Ahead in Psychotherapy's Fascination with Brain Science?" *Psychotherapy Networker*, January–February 2014, available at https://www.questia.com/read/1P3-3193759481/the-next-big-step-what-s-ahead-in-psychotherapy-s.

30. Siegel, *Pocket Guide to Interpersonal Neurobiology*, 58.

31. Ibid.

32. Hanson, *Hardwiring Happiness*, 10.

33. Dan Siegel, "The Healthy Mind Platter," available at https://www.drdansiegel.com/resources/healthy_mind_platter/ (accessed October 22, 2019).

34. Hanson, *Hardwiring Happiness*, chap. 5.

35. Ibid., 91.

36. Martin E. P. Seligman and Mihaly Csikszentmihalyi, "Positive Psychology: An Introduction," *American Psychologist* 55, no. 1 (2000): 13.

37. Rick Hanson, *Buddha's Brain: The Practical Neuroscience of Happiness, Love, and Wisdom* (Oakland, CA: New Harbinger, 2009).

38. Mark Twain, *What Is Man? And Other Philosophical Writings* (Berkeley: University of California Press, 1973), 40.

39. Benjamin Hunnicutt, "Leisure and Play in Plato's Teachings and Philosophy of Learning," *Leisure Science* 12, no. 2 (1990): 211–227.

40. There are hazards to this teaching method. Plato feared "unlawful" play and emphasized that play needed to be guided. Experiential educators stress the importance of reinforcing experiences with word-based follow-ups in the classroom.

41. Christian Jantzen, "Experiencing and Experiences: A Psychological Framework," in *Handbook on the Experience Economy*, ed. Jon Sundbo and Flemming Sørensen (Northampton, MA: Edward Elgar, 2013), 155.

42. J.M.C. Snel, "For the Love of Experience," 17; J.M.C. Snel, *Valuable and Meaningful Experiences* (Amsterdam: European Centre for the Experience Economy, 2005), 4.

43. Sundbo and Sørensen, *Handbook on the Experience Economy*, 3. For a discussion of *Erfahrung* versus *Erlebnis*, see Jantzen, "Experiencing and Experiences," 151.

44. Daniel Siegel, "Play, Well-Being, and the Mind," *Mindsight Digital Journal*, no. 2 (June 2015), available at https://www.mindsightinstitute.com/system/files/digital_journal/Mindsight%20Digital%20Journal,%20Issue%20No.%202%2%20June%202015.pdf. Jaak Panksepp understands *"MindBrain"* as a top-down process, in which structures developing later (e.g., the cortex) influence structures developing earlier (e.g., the subcortex), and *"BrainMind"* as the opposite, bottom-up process. See Theresa A. Kestly, *The Interpersonal Neurobiology of Play: Brain-Building Interventions for Emotional Well-Being* (New York: W. W. Norton, 2014), 44.

45. Eugen Fink, "The Ontology of Play," *Philosophy Today* 4, no. 2 (1960): 98.

46. Johan Huizinga wrote that play "contains its own course and meaning. . . . Play creates order, is order." Johan Huizinga, *Homo Ludens* (Boston: Beacon Press, 1971), 9. Joseph Pieper agreed that play has meaning only in its own terms and that it epitomizes purposefulness in itself. It has the inner quality of being meaningful in itself. Josef Pieper, *Leisure: The Basis of Culture*, trans. Alexander Dru (New York: New American Library, 1952), 42.

Eugen Fink saw play establishing its own "imminent meaning." For Fink, play is a "serene 'presence'" with a purpose "sufficient to itself. . . . [Play] is not directed as [are] other activities of man toward a supreme end. The activity of play has only internal finalities which do not transcend it . . . it is self-sufficient." Fink also distinguished between "the intrinsic meaning of play—the meaningful bond between things, actions and played relations—and the external meaning, the meaning of play for those who initiate it and take part in it, as well as the meaning it is supposed to have for the spectators," including critics and objective researchers. Fink, "The Ontology of Play," 102. See also Eugen Fink, *Oase des Glücks Gedanken zu einer Ontologie des Spiels* (Buchausstittung: Hanspeter Schmidt, Riehen-Basel, Herder-Druck Freiburg im Breistau, 1957).

Hans-Georg Gadamer agreed, making claims about play that anticipate Siegel's systems-based theories. Play is the "transformation into a structure . . . not simply transformation into another world. Certainly it is in an 'outside,' separate world in which play takes place. But inasmuch as it is a structure, it has . . . found its measure in itself and measures itself by nothing outside it. . . . [It] exists absolutely as something that rests within itself. It no longer permits of any comparison with reality as the secret measure of all copied similarity. It is raised above all such comparisons and hence above the question whether it is all real—because a superior truth speaks from it. . . . What unfolds before one is for everyone so lifted out of the continuing progression of the world and so self-enclosed as to make an independent circle of meaning that no one is motivated to go beyond it to another future and reality." Hans-Georg Gadamer, *Truth and Method* (London: Continuum, 1975), 113.

47. Huizinga, *Homo Ludens*, chap. 1.

48. Jaak Panksepp, "The Primary Process Affects in Human Development, Happiness, and Thriving," in *Designing Positive Psychology: Taking Stock and Moving Forward*, ed. Kennon M. Sheldon, Todd B. Kashdan, and Michael F. Steger (New York: Oxford University Press, 2011), 64–65.

49. Daniel Siegel, "Play, Well-Being, and the Mind," *Mindsight Digital Journal*, no. 2 (June 2015), available at https://www.mindsightinstitute.com/system/files/digital_journal/Mindsight%20Digital%20Journal,%20Issue%20No.%202%20June%202015.pdf.

50. Diana Fosha, Daniel J. Siegel, and Marion Solomon, *The Healing Power of Emotion: Affective Neuroscience, Development and Clinical Practice* (Boston: W. W. Norton, 2009), 16.

51. Kestly, *The Interpersonal Neurobiology of Play*, xiv. See also Siegel, "Play, Well-Being, and the Mind."

52. Eugen Fink, "The Ontology of Play," in *Sport and the Body: A Philosophical Symposium*, ed. Ellen Gerber and William J. Morgan (Philadelphia: Lea and Febiger, 1979), 76.

53. Kestly reports that several researchers conclude that "*emotional calibration . . . how to manage your emotions . . . is the primary purpose of play.*" Kestly, *The Interpersonal Neurobiology of Play*, 180 (emphasis in original).

54. Bessel van der Kolk, *The Body Keeps the Score: Brain, Mind, and Body in the Healing of Trauma* (New York: Penguin, 2014), 78.

55. Panksepp, "The Primary Process Affects in Human Development," 64–65.

56. Stephen Porges, *The Polyvagal Theory: Neurophysiological Foundations of Emotions, Attachment, Communication, and Self-Regulation* (New York: W. W. Norton, 2011), 276.

57. Kestly, *The Interpersonal Neurobiology of Play*, 34. See also Theresa A. Kestly and Franc Hudspeth, "Presence and Play: Why Mindfulness Matters," *International Journal of Play Therapy* 25, no. 1 (2016): 14–23.

58. Daniel Siegel, *The Mindful Therapist: A Clinician's Guide to Mindsight and Neural Integration* (New York: W. W. Norton, 2010), 155, 177.

59. Kestly, *The Interpersonal Neurobiology of Play*, viii.

60. Hans Gelter, "Total Experience Management—a Conceptual Model for Transformational Experiences within Tourism," in *The Nordic Conference on Experience, 2008: Research, Education and Practice in Media*, ed. S.-B. Arnolds-Granlund and P. Bjork (Vaasa, Finland: Tritonia, 2010), 49, available at https://www.academia.edu/18229177/Total_Experience_Management_a_conceptual_model_for_transformational_experiences_within_tourism. Jantzen writes, "*Erfahrungen* are not only outcomes of *Erlebnisse*, they are also sources of *Erlebnisse*. Our memory sets expectations guiding us toward certain events . . . [that] are motivating. . . . [E]xperience-based knowledge frames such events." Jantzen, "Experiencing and Experiences," 151.

61. Siegel, *Pocket Guide to Interpersonal Neurobiology*, 375.

62. Siegel, "Play, Well-Being, and the Mind."

63. Siegel, *Mindsight*, 86.

64. Frank Fujita and Ed Diener, "Life Satisfaction Set Point: Stability and Change," *Journal of Personality and Social Psychology* 88, no. 1 (January 2005): 158–164.

65. Terry Marks-Tarlow, Marion Solomon, and Daniel J. Siegel, *Play and Creativity in Psychotherapy* (New York: W. W. Norton, 2018), 16.

66. Huizinga, *Homo Ludens*, first page of the foreword.

67. Gregory Bateson, "Theory of Play and Fantasy," in *Steps to an Ecology of Mind: Collected Essays in Anthropology, Psychiatry, Evolution, and Epistemology* (Northvale, NJ: Jason Aronson, 1972). In his "Theory of Play and Fantasy" Bateson suggested that symbol use and language originate as and develop through play, both for individuals and for our species. Symbol use takes place on several levels of abstraction. The first and simplest is the denotative level. A sound or gesture comes to stand for something else—for example, a mood sign. However, the beaver slapping the water with his tail, the deer flashing the white of his tail signaling danger do not recognize and have no way to talk about these elemental, denotative acts of communication.

The second level of abstraction, the metalinguistic, has to do with the recognition of symbols as symbols. Humans and some animals begin to use symbols to refer to other symbols. The distinction between "map" and "territory," realizing that the symbol is not the thing the symbol stands for, seems simple minded; however, the ability to recognize that symbols are symbols and to call attention to this fact is vital for communication more complex than simple mood signs.

The metalinguistic level of abstraction is followed by the metacommunicative, the level in which symbols and signs are employed to *change* and *modify* other signs and symbols. The *way* what is said is the issue, and the reference is to the relationship between speakers and the social context of the language. The metacommunicative is the most complex level of abstraction and just as vital as the first two for human communication. We automatically use various verbal and nonverbal strategies to meta-communicate. Tone of voice, body language, posture, and the physical place where the symbol originates all modify the meaning of our words. Change the tone of voice or add different gestures and the meaning of the most ordinary of statements changes dramatically. Just imagine how many ways "please" can be said.

Syntax in writing does the same things. Learning how sentences are constructed to shade meanings—how some words can be used close to others to alter the sense of both—is a skill honed over a lifetime. An entire group of essential words, common to all human languages, depend on the ability to bend symbols easily. These words, "de-ictics," change depending on who is speaking and where the speaker is located. Vital, ordinary words such as "I," "you," "in front of," and "behind" fall in this category.

Of special importance for Bateson is the metacommunication "This is play." This metacommunication is special on several counts. In the first place it occurs before language acquisition. Animals metacommunicate "This is play" by body signals, or mood signs. Bateson believes the signal "This is play" first involves the recognition (meta-linguistic) that signals are signals and thus establishes the precondition in evolution as well as in individual development for the acquisition of language and "*all the complexities of empathy, identification, projection*, etc. . . . and the possibility of communicating at the multiplicity of levels of abstraction" (184; emphasis added).

Moreover, "This is play" generates a paradox, the understanding of which is at the heart of all human communication. In "This is play" we violate the logical principles outlined in Bertrand Russell's theory of logical types in the sense that we mix together levels of abstraction. See Alfred North Whitehead and Bertrand Russel, *Principia Mathematica* (Cambridge: Cambridge University Press, 1925). As a consequence, as we play we communicate in the middle of Epimenides's paradox (formally known as "the Liar"). As Bateson saw it, fantasy play's form is "These actions in which we now engage, do not denote what would be denoted by these actions which these actions denote." Bateson, "Theory of Play and Fantasy," 185. The playful nip denotes the bite but does not mean the same thing as it does outside the play frame. The meaning of "bite" or "growl" has changed because the players have agreed through the use of symbols ("let's play" signs) to change their meaning. These things are relatively easy to understand and negotiate. But what about the metacommunication within the play frame—for example, "Let's stop playing," or "Tarzan would never do that," a play within a play? How are these to be understood except as paradoxical? More generally, how does one, in the middle of the game, refer to the reality that "this is playing" without falling victim to "the Liar," becoming the pariah of all games, the spoilsport?

Whereas Russell would banish such self-referencing from pure mathematics, children practice and use the play paradox regularly in fantasy play, practicing skills useful in ordinary communication (e.g., deictics). Learning about the existence of the levels of abstraction and how to negotiate them, communicating in the middle of Epimenides's paradox is a vital language skill.

According to Bateson, play sets the stage for language acquisition phylogenetically and ontogenetically and continues to function to develop metacommunication skills, which increase in complexity from "This is play" to "Is this play?" (teasing), to formal-ized games, and on to ritual (188).

68. In some of the earlier somatic theories of emotions, William James and oth-ers maintained that physiological responses to subcortical impulses (such as increased

heart rate and facial expressions) were signs interpreted by the conscious mind as emotions. Long subject to criticism, this theory of emotions has recently been restored to a measure of respectability.

69. Gregory Hickok, *The Myth of Mirror Neurons: The Real Neuroscience of Communication and Cognition* (New York: W. W. Norton, 2014). "I am playing" is also self-referential. While playing, the first player must not only be aware that he or she is playing but must also recognize the existence of the other player and that he or she is playing. The first player must also realize that the other player recognizes that the first player is present and is playing, otherwise the game would fail—no play bite would be possible. In such recognitions, self-awareness and the awareness of the existence of other selves form and are reenforced. Bateson, "A Theory of Play and Fantasy."

70. Kerry Mildon, "Modeled Symbolic Play and Language Development in Autistic Children" (Ph.D. diss., University of Iowa, 1989).

71. Bateson, "A Theory of Play and Fantasy," 184.

72. Marks-Tarlow, Solomon, and Siegel, *Play and Creativity in Psychotherapy*, 15.

73. See Douglas R. Hofstadter, *Godel, Escher, Bach: An Eternal Golden Braid* (New York: Basic Books, 1979), 642. One of the leading theorists of artificial intelligence, Douglas R. Hofstadter writes about the role of fantasy in the creation of theory much as Bateson talked about the role of play in the formation and use of language. Hofstadter suggests that, using our imaginations, we "manufacture subjunctive worlds" (643). We take what we see in the world and play with it—imagining the ways that things could be different, gaining an intangible perspective on reality. Through these sorts of what-if imaginings, we bring new worlds and possibilities to mind, so that, as Seligman writes, we are "drawn by the future." Play is the practice of imagination.

74. V. W. Turner, *From Ritual to Theatre: The Human Seriousness of Play* (New York: Performing Arts Journal, 1982).

75. Victor Turner, *Blazing the Trail: Way Marks in the Exploration of Symbols*, ed. Edith Turner (Tucson: University of Arizona Press, 1992), 132.

76. Turner, *From Ritual to Theatre*, 23.

77. Ibid., 33.

78. Turner, *Blazing the Trail*, 56–57.

79. Turner, *From Ritual to Theatre*, 28. Turner also observed, "Liminal phenomena are . . . often subversive, representing radical critiques of the cultural structures and proposing utopian alternative models. . . . [L]iminal and liminoid phenomena constitute metalanguages (including nonverbal ones) devised for the purpose of talking about the various languages of everyday, and in which mundane axioms become problematic, where cherished symbols are . . . reflected upon, rotated, and given new and unexpected valences." Turner, *Blazing the Trail*, 57.

80. Turner, *Blazing the Trail*, 54–55. For an explanation of flow, see Mihaly Csikszentmihalyi, *Flow: The Psychology of Optimal Experience* (New York: Harper Collins, 2009). Turner and Csikszentmihalyi were colleagues at the University of Chicago.

81. Huizinga, *Homo Ludens*, chap. 1.

82. Turner, *From Ritual to Theatre*, 28.

83. Huizinga, *Homo Ludens*, 12; Turner, *Blazing the Trail*, 59. See also Mihaly Csikszentmihalyi, introduction to *Optimal Experience: Psychological Studies of Flow in Consciousness*, ed. Mihaly Csikszentmihalyi and Isabella Selega Csikszentmihalyi (Cambridge: Cambridge University Press, 1988).

84. Turner bases many of his conclusion about play and the liminal state on his and his wife's research of pilgrimages in Ireland. Turner, *Blazing the Trail*, 43–47.

85. Csikszentmihalyi, introduction to *Optimal Experience*, 9.

86. Victor Turner, *Dramas, Fields, and Metaphors: Symbolic Action in Human Society* (Ithaca, NY: Cornell University Press, 1975), 274.

87. Edith Turner, prologue to Turner, *Blazing the Trail*, xiii.

88. Ibid.

89. Edith Turner, *Communitas: The Anthropology of Collective Joy* (New York: Springer, 2012), 3.

90. Kestly, *The Interpersonal Neurobiology of Play*.

91. Stuart Brown and Christopher Vaughan, *Play: How It Shapes the Brain, Opens the Imagination and Invigorates the Soul* (New York: Avery/Penguin, 2009), 63, 148.

92. Bonnie Badenoch and Theresa Kestly, "Exploring the Neuroscience of Healing Play at Every Age," in *Play Therapy: A Comprehensive Guide to Theory and Practice*, ed. D. A. Crenshaw and A. L. Stewart (New York: Guilford Press, 2014), 524–538.

93. Siegel, *Pocket Guide to Interpersonal Neurobiology*, 374. For the general importance of adult play, see Crenshaw and colleagues, *Play Therapy*, 374, 453.

94. Siegel, "Play, Well-Being, and the Mind."

95. Ibid. Siegel makes a distinction between "rule-bound" games and freer, healthier forms of exploratory play.

96. Marks-Tarlow, Solomon, and Siegel, *Play and Creativity in Psychotherapy*, 69.

97. K. R. Ginsburg, "The Importance of Play in Promoting Healthy Child Development and Maintaining Strong Parent-Child Bonds," *Pediatrics* 119 (2007): 182–191.

98. Alexander Burgemeester, "Jean Piaget's Theory of Play," *Psychologized*, available at https://www.psychologized.org/jean-piagets-theory-of-play (accessed July 29, 2019).

99. M. Parten, "Social Participation among Preschool Children," *Journal of Abnormal and Social Psychology* 27, no. 3 (October 1932): 243–269. Following Piaget, Parten saw play as a primary way that children develop social skills, learning both differentiation and integration. As discussed above, adults may also develop social skills through play experiences. Kestly, *The Interpersonal Neurobiology of Play*, xv.

100. Roger Caillois, *Man, Play, and Games*, trans. Meyer Barash (1961; repr., Urbana: University of Illinois Press, 2001), 12.

101. B. Joseph Pine II and James H. Gilmore, *The Experience Economy*, 2nd ed. (Boston: Harvard Business Press, 2011), xiv; P. Gray, "Play as a Foundation for Hunter-Gatherer Social Existence," *American Journal of Play* 1 (2009): 476–522; P. Gray, *Free to Learn: Why Unleashing the Instinct to Play Will Make Children Happier, More Self-Reliant, and Better Prepared for Life* (New York: Basic Books, 2013).

102. Kestly, *The Interpersonal Neurobiology of Play*, xv.

103. Ibid., xvi.

104. Ibid.

105. Huizinga, *Homo Ludens*, 211.

106. Josef Pieper, *Leisure: The Basis of Culture* (San Francisco: Ignatius Press, 2009), 20.

107. From the time that Daniel Patrick Moynihan championed the cause, I have spent decades supporting guaranteed minimum annual incomes. I have also supported

government-guaranteed vacations for working people, tried to recall laborites back to their old shorter-hours struggle, and sought support for public spaces, programs, and facilities (in public parks and recreation programs). I have tried to encourage the schools to return (at least a little) to education for leisure and freedom. I worked with Senator Eugene McCarthy during his 1992 presidential bid (reducing work hours as an unemployment strategy was one of his top issues). See Benjamin Hunnicutt, "Work Redistribution vs. New Jobs Creation: A Reconsideration of Depression Employment Policies and Depression Views of Economic Advance," a position paper prepared at the request of Senator Eugene McCarthy's 1992 Presidential Campaign Staff, published and circulated by the McCarthy Campaign, in author's possession. However, I am more than a little disillusioned by what has happened politically and in public institutions over the last decades. I certainly do not rule out the role of government, but I also remember my bitter experience while with the McCarthy campaign. At one of the Iowa caucuses, I was shouted down and called a yahoo for trying to introduce a resolution supporting McCarthy's plea for shorter hours. I also know that today a simple suggestion in an article written for *Politico* that work hours might be reduced by public policy creates an eruption of outrage and death threats. Benjamin Kline Hunnicutt, "Why Do Republicans Want Us to Work All the Time?" *Politico*, February 7, 2014, available at https://www.politico.com/magazine/story/2014/02/jobs-leisure-republicans-want-us -to-work-all-the-time-103282. Such experiences reinforce my conviction that the free market is the last, best hope for higher progress and should at least be given a chance and encouraged.

108. According to Peterson and Seligman, one of positive psychology's three priorities is "institutions that enable positive experiences and positive traits." What more important institution is there than the marketplace? Peterson and Seligman, *Character Strengths and Virtues*, 5. See also Seligman and Csikszentmihalyi, "Positive Psychology," 5.

CHAPTER 7

1. Christopher Peterson and Martin Seligman, eds., *Character Strengths and Virtues: A Handbook and Classification* (New York: Oxford University Press, 2004), 18.

2. Ibid., 12–19; B. Joseph Pine II and James H. Gilmore, *The Experience Economy*, rev. ed. (Boston: Harvard Business Press, 2011), 279.

3. Peterson and Seligman, *Character Strengths and Virtues*, 5.

4. See Chapter 3 for these developments.

5. Martin Seligman, *Flourish: A Visionary New Understanding of Happiness and Well-Being* (New York: Free Press, 2011), 121. See also Martin E. P. Seligman, *Homo Prospectus* (New York: Oxford University Press, 2016).

6. B. Joseph Pine II and James H. Gilmore, *The Experience Economy*, rev. ed. (Boston: Harvard Business Press, 2011), 254.

7. Josef Chytry, *Unis vers Cythère: Aesthetic-Political Investigations in Polis Thought and the Artful Firm* (New York: Peter Lang, 2009), 140.

8. Seligman, *Flourish*, 106.

9. See Rick Hanson, *Hardwiring Happiness: The New Brain Science of Contentment, Calm, and Confidence* (New York: Harmony Books, 2016), chap. 5; and James

Hamblin, "Buy Experiences, Not Things," *The Atlantic*, October 7, 2014, available at https://www.theatlantic.com/business/archive/2014/10/buy-experiences/381132.

10. William C. Compton and Edward Hoffman, *Positive Psychology: The Science of Happiness and Flourishing* (Belmont, CA: Wadsworth, 2013), 90–91. See Chapter 5 for a discussion of psychological views of the frequency versus intensity of experiences. A caveat must be added to the assumption of rational behavior. Psychologists such as Daniel Kahneman remind us that our memories are fallible and that we are often thoughtless and do not always act rationally in the marketplace. Daniel Kahneman, "Economics Discovers Its Feelings: Not Quite as Dismal as It Was," *The Economist*, December 19, 2006, available at https://www.economist.com/special-report/2006/12/19/economics-discovers-its-feelings.

11. Thomas Gilovich and Amit Kumar, "We'll Always Have Paris: The Hedonic Payoff from Experiential and Material Investments," in *Advances in Experimental Social Psychology*, ed. James M. Olson and Mark P. Zanna (Cambridge, MA: Academic Press, 2015), 148.

12. Pine and Gilmore, *The Experience Economy*, 254.

13. Enrique Alcántara, Miguel A. Artacho, Natividad Martínez, and Tomás Zamora, "Designing Experiences Strategically," *Journal of Business Research* 67 (2014): 1075. See also Albert Boswijk, Thomas Thijssen, and Ed Peelen, *The Experience Economy: A New Perspective* (Amsterdam: Pearson Education, 2007); C. K. Prahalad and V. Ramaswamy, *The Future of Competition, Co-creating Unique Value with Customers* (Boston: Harvard Business School, 2004); and S. Zuboff and J. Maxmin, *The Support Economy: Why Corporations Are Failing Individuals and the Next Episode of Capitalism* (New York: Viking, 2002).

14. Britta Timm Knudsen, Dorthe R. Christensen, and Per Blenker, eds., *Enterprising Initiatives in the Experience Economy: Transforming Social Worlds* (New York: Routledge, 2015), 2. See also Alvin Toffler, *Third Wave* (New York: William Morrow, 1980), chap. 20.

15. George Ritzer and Nathan Jurgenson, "Production, Consumption, Prosumption: The Nature of Capitalism in the Age of the Digital 'Prosumer,'" *Journal of Consumer Culture* 10, no. 1 (2010): 13.

16. Albert Boswijk, Ed Peelen, and Steven Olthof, *Economy of Experiences*, trans. Christene Beddow, 3rd ed. (Amsterdam: European Centre for the Experience and Transformation Economy, 2012), 297.

17. Ibid., x.

18. Ibid., 9–11. See also Jon Sundbo and Flemming Sørensen, eds., *Handbook on the Experience Economy* (Cheltenham, UK: Edward Elgar, 2013), 173.

19. See especially Gary Ellis and J. Robert Rossman, "Creating Value for Participants through Experience Staging: Parks, Recreation, and Tourism in the Experience Industry," *Journal of Park and Recreation Administration* 26, no. 4 (Winter 2008): 1–20. Ellis and Rossman see the relevance of Mihaly Csikszentmihalyi's flow to experience staging. See also J. Robert Rossman and Barbara Elwood Schlatter, *Designing and Staging Leisure Experiences*, 6th ed. (Urbana, IL: Sagamore, 2011); Philip L. Pearce and Jan Packer, "Minds on the Move: New Links from Psychology to Tourism," *Annals of Tourism Research* 40, no. 1 (2012): 386–411; Sebastian Filep and Philip Pearce, eds., *Tourist Experience and Fulfilment: Insights from Positive Psychology* (Abingdon,

UK: Routledge, 2014); and Michael Morgan, Jörgen Elbe, and Javier de Esteban Cu-
riel, "Has the Experience Economy Arrived? The Views of Destination Managers in
Three Visitor-Dependent Areas," *International Journal of Tourism Research* 11 (2009):
201–216. Pine and Gilmore mention the work of psychologists such as Mihaly Csikszentmihalyi, Travis Carter, and Thomas Gilovich but only in passing and as supporting their conclusions about a taxonomy of experiences and as backing up their claims
that experiences are more strongly correlated with happiness than buying traditional
products. They quote Travis Carter and Thomas Gilovich, "The Relative Relativity of
Material and Experiential Purchases," in Pine and Gilmore, *The Experience Economy*,
19, 302, 304, 305.

20. See Christian Jantzen and Mikael Venter, "Oplevelsens Psykologiske Struk-
tur," in *Oplevelsesøkonomi—Produktion, Forbrug, Kultur*, ed. Jørgen Ole Bærenholdt
and Jon Sundbo (Copenhagen: Samfundslitteratur, 2007), 27–50; and Christian Jantzen and Tove Rasmussen, "Oplevelsesøkonomiens Historiske Og Psykologiske Forud-
sætninger," in *Oplevelsesøkonomi: Vinkler På Forbrug*, ed. Christian Jantzen and Tove
Rasmussen (Aalborg, Denmark: Aalborg Universitetsforlag, 2007), 11–20. See also
Sundbo and Sørensen, *Handbook on the Experience Economy*, 7; and Knudsen, Christensen, and Blenker, *Enterprising Initiatives in the Experience Economy*.

21. B. Schmitt, "Experience Marketing: Concepts, Frameworks and Consumer
Insights," *Foundations and Trends in Marketing* 5, no. 2 (2010): 55–112.

22. For an excellent collection of case studies, see Anders Sørensen and Jon
Sundbo, eds., *Cases from the Experience Economy* (Nykøbing Falster, Denmark: CELF
(Center for Leisure Management Research); Roskilde, Denmark: Roskilde University,
2008), http://citeseerx.ist.psu.edu/viewdoc/download?doi=10.1.1.575.9069&rep=rep1
&type=pdf.

23. Joseph Schumpeter sees a similar bottom-up formation of meaning, writing
about the marketplace as a "matrix of logic." See Joseph Schumpeter, *Capitalism, Socialism, and Democracy* (1942; repr., New York: Harper Perennial, 2008), 123.

24. Brian Chesky, "Open Letter to the Airbnb Community about Building a
21st Century Company," Airbnb Newsroom, January 25, 2018, available at https://
press.airbnb.com/brian-cheskys-open-letter-to-the-airbnb-community-about-building
-a-21st-century-company.

25. Charlie Aufmann, "Designing for Trust: Observations from My First Year at
Airbnb," Airbnb, available at https://airbnb.design/designing-for-trust (accessed July
29, 2019).

26. Leslie Hook, "Airbnb Marks First Full Year of Profitability in 2017,"
Financial Times, January 25, 2018, available at https://www.ft.com/content/
96215e16-0201-11e8-9650-9c0ad2d7c5b5.

27. See "Trust and Safety," Airbnb, available at https://www.airbnb.com/trust (accessed July 29, 2019).

28. See "What Is the Airbnb Service Fee?" Airbnb, available at https://www
.airbnb.com/help/article/1857/what-is-the-airbnb-service-fee (accessed July 29, 2019).

29. Carlo Motta, "'Airbnb and YouTube Are Two Great Examples of Crowd Based
Capitalism': Key Stakeholders Outline the Boundaries of the 4th Industrial Revolution in Davos," *European Sting*, January 26, 2016, available at https://europeansting
.com/2016/01/26/voices-from-the-digital-world-how-new-platforms-are-changing-our
-economies-and-our-lives.

30. Chesky, "Open Letter to the Airbnb Community."

31. The word "amateur" (originally, one who does something more for the love of it than for the money) has been a casualty of the modern trivialization of leisure.

32. Leigh Gallagher, *The Airbnb Story: How Three Ordinary Guys Disrupted an Industry, Made Billions . . . and Created Plenty of Controversy* (New York: Houghton Mifflin, 2017), 216.

33. Chesky, "Open Letter to the Airbnb Community."

34. Brian Chesky, "Belong Anywhere," *Medium*, July 16, 2014, available at https://medium.com/@bchesky/belong-anywhere-ccf42702d010.

35. Gallagher, *The Airbnb Story*, 85. Airbnb's logo represents people, places, love, and Airbnb (ibid.).

36. Chesky, "Belong Anywhere."

37. David Passiak, "Belong Anywhere—the Vision and Story behind Airbnb's Global Community," *Medium*, January 30, 2017, available at https://medium.com/cocreatethefuture/belong-anywhere-the-vision-and-story-behind-airbnbs-global-community-123d32218d6a.

38. Gallagher, *The Airbnb Story*, 85.

39. Aufmann, "Designing for Trust."

40. Gallagher, *The Airbnb Story*, 215, 212.

41. Shirin Ghaffary, "The Experience Economy Will Be a 'Massive Business,' According to Airbnb CEO Brian Chesky," *Recode*, May 30, 2018, available at https://www.recode.net/2018/5/30/17385910/airbnb-ceo-brian-chesky-code-conference-interview.

42. Gallagher, *The Airbnb Story*, 215.

43. Ghaffary, "The Experience Economy Will Be a 'Massive Business.'"

44. The reliability of user-generated ratings in the sharing economy has been investigated, producing mixed preliminary results. See, for example, Judith Bridges and Camilla Vásquez, "If Nearly All Airbnb Reviews Are Positive, Does That Make Them Meaningless?," *Current Issues in Tourism* 21, no. 18 (2018): 2057–2075. See also Georgios Zervas, Davide Proserpio, and John A. Byers, "First Look at Online Reputation on Airbnb, Where Every Stay Is Above Average," *SSRN*, January 28, 2015, available at https://ssrn.com/abstract=2554500.

45. The use of the word "sharing" to describe the experience might predispose a respondent to have a more positive view of the experience.

46. Edith Turner, *Communitas: The Anthropology of Collective Joy* (New York: Springer, 2012), 3.

47. Mihaly Csikszentmihalyi, introduction to *Optimal Experience: Psychological Studies of Flow in Consciousness*, ed. Mihaly Csikszentmihalyi and Isabella Selega Csikszentmihalyi (Cambridge: Cambridge University Press, 1988), 9.

48. Johan Huizinga, *Homo Ludens: A Study of the Play Element in Culture* (London: Routledge, 1948), 12.

49. Seligman, *Flourish*, 106.

50. Hans Gelter, "Total Experience Management—a Conceptual Model for Transformational Experiences within Tourism," in *The Nordic Conference on Experience, 2008: Research, Education and Practice in Media*, ed. S.-B. Arnolds-Granlund and P. Bjork (Vaasa, Finland: Tritonia, 2010), 47, available at https://www.academia.edu/18229177/Total_Experience_Management_a_conceptual_model_for_transformational_experiences_within_tourism?auto=download.

51. "Handmade Pasta with Grandma," Airbnb, available at https://www.airbnb.com/experiences/55449 (accessed October 22, 2019).

52. Ibid.

53. See Chapter 8 for a discussion of intrinsically motivated productive consumption.

54. Huizinga, *Homo Ludens*, 12.

55. Turner, *Communitas*, 3.

56. See their respective websites, at https://dancewithmeusa.com, https://arthurmurray.com, and https://www.fredastaire.com.

57. See the website of USA Dance, at https://usadance.org.

58. Robert Putnam, *Bowling Alone: The Collapse and Revival of American Community* (New York: Simon and Schuster, 2001).

59. M. Grodzins, *The American System* (Chicago: Rand McNally, 1966), 41.

60. See the Tru website, at http://tru3.hilton.com/en/index.html. See also Hilton, "Hilton Worldwide Changes the Game with a Revolutionary New Midscale Brand," January 25, 2016, available at https://newsroom.hilton.com/embassy/news/hilton-worldwide-changes-the-game-with-a-revolutionary-new-midscale-brand.

61. Nick Friedman, "Dinner and a Movie: 10 of the Greatest Dine-In Theaters in America," *The Credits*, February 12, 2014, available at https://www.mpaa.org/2014/02/dinner-a-movie-10-of-the-greatest-dine-in-theaters-in-america.

62. See, for example, the website of Pinot's Palette, at https://www.pinotspalette.com. See also Laura M. Holson, "Forget a Fast Car: Creativity Is the New Midlife Crisis Cure," *New York Times*, July 14, 2018, available at https://www.nytimes.com/2018/07/14/sunday-review/creativity-midlife-crisis-cure.html.

63. Ken, "By the Numbers: UK vs the Rest of the World," *Exit Games*, September 14, 2017, available at http://exitgames.co.uk/blog/2017/09/14/by-the-numbers-uk-vs-the-rest-of-the-world.

64. Will Levith, "Former President Obama Joins the Global 'Escape Room' Craze," *Inside Hook*, March 17, 2017, available at http://www.realclearlife.com/adventure/former-president-obama-escape-room-global-craze.

65. For a historical account of deskilling and a bibliography, see Benjamin Kline Hunnicutt, *Work without End: Abandoning Shorter Hours for the Right to Work* (Philadelphia: Temple University Press, 1987), 85.

66. The show's website is available at http://www.woodsmithshop.com.

67. IKEA, "IKEA Ideas," available at https://www.ikea.com/hk/EN/ideas (accessed October 28, 2019).

68. Michael Norton, Daniel Mochon, and Dan Ariely, "The IKEA Effect: When Labor Leads to Love," *Journal of Consumer Psychology* 22 (September 2011): 453–460; Richard N. Landers, "Unfolding the IKEA Effect: Why We Love the Things We Build," *NeoAcademic*, September 22, 2011, available at http://neoacademic.com/2011/09/22/unfolding-the-ikea-effect-why-we-love-the-things-we-build.

69. Tyler Tervooren, "Ikea Effect: Make People Happy by Putting Them to Work," *Riskology*, available at https://www.riskology.co/ikea-effect (accessed July 29, 2019).

70. Barbara L. Fredrickson, "The Broaden-and-Build Theory of Positive Emotions," *Philosophical Transactions of the Royal Society B: Biological Sciences* 359, no. 1449 (2004): 1367–1378.

71. Tervooren, "Ikea Effect."

72. See the discussion of consumer culture theory in Chapter 4.

73. "Global DIY Tools Market Is Forecast to Grow to USD 13.9 Billion by 2021: Technavio," *Business Wire*, January 5, 2017, available at http://www.businesswire.com/news/home/20170105006255/en/Global-DIY-Tools-Market-Forecast-Grow-USD.

74. Omri Barzilay, "With 66M Monthly Visits, HomeTalk Is on Its Way to Become the Next Houzz," *Forbes*, August 15, 2017, available at https://www.forbes.com/sites/omribarzilay/2017/08/15/with-66m-monthly-visits-hometalk-is-on-its-way-to-become-the-next-houzz/#25d012921e74.

75. Ibid.

76. Sanjeev Kumar Singh, *Human Resource Development* (New Delhi, India: Atlantic, 2007), 3.

77. John Maynard Keynes wrote, "We have been expressly evolved by nature with all our impulses and deep instincts for the purpose of solving our economic problem." J. M. Keynes, *Essays in Persuasion* (New York: Norton, 1931), 366.

78. Ibid.

79. On the basis of this reasoning, Keynes predicted that before the twentieth century was over, humans would be working less than three hours a day. Keynes, *Essays in Persuasion*, 365. In the nineteenth century, economists such as John Stuart Mill and his follower in America, Simon Patten, made similar arguments. See Hunnicutt, *Work without End*, 31–39.

80. See the discussion of postmaterialism in the Introduction.

81. Keynes, *Essays in Persuasion*, 368.

82. J. M. Keynes, "Economic Possibilities of Our Grandchildren," in *Essays in Persuasion* (London: Macmillan, 1931), 365–373; E. P. Thompson, "Time, Work-Discipline and Industrial Capitalism," *Past and Present* 38 (December 1967): 95.

83. See Hunnicutt, *Work without End*, 262.

84. Ernst Friedrich Schumacher, *Small Is Beautiful: Economics as If People Mattered* (New York: Harper and Row, 1973).

85. National Center for Appropriate Technology, "The History of NCAT," available at https://www.ncat.org/history.

86. John Ruskin, *Unto This Last: Four Essays on the First Principles of Political Economy* (New York: Wiley, 1881), 125.

87. Jay Sorenson, *The Life and Death of Trade Unionism in the USSR, 1917–1928* (New Brunswick, NJ: Aldine Transaction, 2010), 138.

88. The web page of International Development Enterprises is available at http://www.paulpolak.com/business-solution-to-poverty-ideas/international-developement-enterprises.

89. See Hunnicutt, *Work without End*, 262.

CHAPTER 8

1. McKinsey and Company reported in December 2017 that "over the past few years, personal-consumption expenditures on experience-related services . . . have grown more than 1.5 times faster than overall personal-consumption spending and nearly 4.0 times faster than expenditures on goods." Dan Goldman, Sophie Marches-

sou, and Warren Teichner, "Cashing In on the US Experience Economy," McKinsey and Company, December 2017, available at https://www.mckinsey.com/industries/private-equity-and-principal-investors/our-insights/cashing-in-on-the-us-experience-economy.

2. Will Kenton, "Utility," *Investopedia*, March 29, 2019, available at https://www.investopedia.com/university/economics/economics5.asp.

3. Staffan Burenstam Linder, *The Harried Leisure Class* (New York: Columbia University Press, 1970), 147. In a move anticipated by the Nobel Prize winner Gary Becker, Linder concluded that utility, U, is a function of things that are purchased, Q (number of units of consumption goods, services, etc.), and the number of hours needed to use, consume, or experience them, T_c. Among the most basic of economic reasoning, familiar to students in any econ 101 class reading about consumer theory, the relation is expressed $U = f(Q, T_c)$. If one assumes a diminishing rate of marginal substitution, the familiar indifference curve may be drawn:

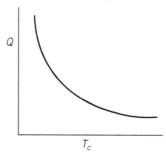

A less precise, more commonsense way of illustrating such ideas is to assume that time is the commodity being economized and that the more a person chooses to work for income, the less leisure he has; and the more leisure a person chooses, the less income she earns:

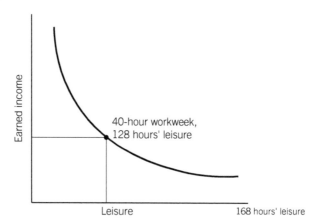

Time is, uniquely, the one limited human resource, however: We all have just so much (thus the *x*, or leisure, axis terminates at 168 hours per week).

4. Before the 1980s, in support of their century-long shorter-hours campaign that saw working hours cut nearly in half, the American labor movement advanced a commonsense version of the theory. As the economy grows, people will need both more money to buy all the things they are producing and more time to use and enjoy them—the more workers are able to buy, the more time they would need. The sluggish growth of leisure would slow both consumption and economic growth and cause unemployment as surely as inadequate spending. See Benjamin Kline Hunnicutt, *Work without End: Abandoning Shorter Hours for the Right to Work* (Philadelphia: Temple University Press, 1987), chap. 3.

5. Linder, *The Harried Leisure Class*, 9.

6. Linder begins *The Harried Leisure Class* with this: "We had always expected one of the beneficent results of economic affluence to be a tranquil and harmonious manner of life, a life in Arcadia. What has happened is the exact opposite. . . . It used to be assumed that, as the general welfare increased, people would become successively less interested in further rises in income. And yet in practice a still higher income growth rate has become the overriding goal of economic policy in the rich countries, and the goal also of our private efforts and attitudes. . . . In practice, not even those endowed with the necessary intellectual and emotional capacity have shown any propensity for immersing themselves in the cultivation of their minds and spirit. The tendency is rather the reverse" (1).

7. Ibid., 83.

8. Ibid., 2, 4.

9. Ibid., 2.

10. B. Joseph Pine II and James H. Gilmore, *The Experience Economy*, rev. ed. (Boston: Harvard Business Press, 2011), xv.

11. Ibid.

12. John Owen writes, "Most modern economic analysis of the determination of hours of work or leisure time has been in terms of the influence of the wage rate." John Owen, *The Price of Leisure: An Economic Analysis of the Demand for Leisure Time* (Montreal: McGill-Queen's University Press, 1970), 16.

13. Economists define a "normal good" as one having a positive income elasticity—when incomes increase, more of a normal good is demanded in the market.

14. J. K. Galbraith, *The Affluent Society* (1958; repr., New York: Houghton Mifflin Harcourt, 1998), 119.

15. Lionel Robbins, "On the Elasticity of Income in Terms of Effort," *Economia* 10 (June 1930): 123–129. Robbins argued against the inevitability of the income effect, but he also summarized the case in the affirmative made by writers such as Hugh Dalton, Dennis Robertson, and Philip Wicksteed, as well as Knight and Pigou.

16. Robbins, "On the Elasticity of Income in Terms of Effort." Gary Becker writes, "The effect of an uncompensated increase in earnings on hours worked would depend on the relative strength of the substitution and income effects. The former would increase hours, the latter reduce them; which dominates cannot be determined a priori." Gary Becker, "A Theory of the Allocation of Time," *Economic Journal* 75, no. 299 (1965): 502.

17. Robbins, "On the Elasticity of Income in Terms of Effort," 127. "Forgone earnings" is Becker's term. Becker, "A Theory of the Allocation of Time," 502.

18. John Owen was a member of Gary Becker's original Labor Workshop at Columbia University, which introduced "the cost of time systematically into decisions about non-work activities." Becker, "A Theory of the Allocation of Time," 494.

19. Owen, *The Price of Leisure*, 18; see also 62–67. For the claim that there had been no increase in leisure for American workers since World War II, see J. D. Owen, "Workweeks and Leisure: An Analysis of Trends, 1948–75," *Monthly Labor Review* 99 (August 1976): 3–8. See also J. M. Keynes, *Essays in Persuasion* (New York: Norton, 1931), 365–373.

20. Linder, *The Harried Leisure Class*, 53.

21. Juliet Schor, "The (Even More) Overworked American," in *Take Back Your Time: Fighting Overwork and Time Poverty in America*, ed. John de Graaf (San Francisco: Berrett-Koehler, 2003), 6–11.

22. See, for example, Tim Kreider, "The 'Busy' Trap," *New York Times*, June 30, 2012, available at https://opinionator.blogs.nytimes.com/2012/06/30/the-busy-trap.

23. Eduardo Porter and Mary Williams Walsh, "Retirement Turns into a Rest Stop as Benefits Dwindle," *New York Times*, February 9, 2005, available at https://www.nytimes.com/2005/02/09/business/retirement-turns-into-a-rest-stop-as-benefits-dwindle.html. The *Monthly Labor Review* reported in 2008 that "over the past dozen or so years, older men—especially those 65 years or older—have increased their labor force participation and full-time employment, thereby reversing long-run declines; increases for older women also have occurred and have been proportionately greater." See Murray Gendell, "Older Workers: Increasing Their Labor Force Participation and Hours of Work," *Monthly Labor Review* 131, no. 1 (2008): 41.

24. Catherine Rampell, "Paid Vacation's Decline," *New York Times*, September 3, 2013, available at https://economix.blogs.nytimes.com/2013/09/03/paid-vacations-decline.

25. "Leisure Time Distortion: Study Finds Americans Put Work First, TV Second, Family Third in Order of Time Priorities," *Business Wire*, January 22, 2004, available at https://www.businesswire.com/news/home/20040122005357/en/Leisure-Time-Distortion-Study-Reveals-Americans-Put.

26. Katrina Onstad, "The Concept of the Weekend Is Dying," *Think*, November 3, 2017, available at https://www.nbcnews.com/think/opinion/concept-weekend-dying-ncna817131.

27. Andrew Curry, "Today American Society Is Dominated by Work: But There Was a Time When People Could Have Made a Different Choice," *U.S. News and World Report*, February 24–March 3, 2003, p. 50.

28. Schor, "The (Even More) Overworked American"; Joe Robinson, *Work to Live: The Guide to Getting a Life* (New York: Berkley, 2003), 3.

29. No one has claimed that the work-reduction process remains as robust as it once was or as central to the national debate, however. The *historical* end of shorter hours remains crystal clear. The progressive shortening of the hours of labor, organized labor's century-long cause, has disappeared. Widespread expectations about the coming of an age of mass leisure, the eventual subordination of work, and fulfillment of Walt Whitman's dream of higher progress that characterized the nineteenth and much of the twentieth centuries, have ended. More work, not less, is now the hope for the future and the foundation of much public policy. One may agree with economists such as

Valerie Ramey and Neville Francis that some preference for leisure taking may remain, hidden from the public, most of whom think that we have a time famine. Ramey and Francis's work, however, encourages the hope that leisure still has the potential for positive income elasticity, without which the experience and transformation economies' prospects are dim indeed. Ramey and Francis's research may reveal pockets of leisure preferences that are potential targets for experience-economy marketing. Such pockets may be the places for the renewal of the old dreams of mass leisure and higher progress. See Valerie Ramey, "Time Spent in Home Production in the Twentieth-Century United States," *Journal of Economic History* 69, no. 1 (March 2009): 1–47; and Valerie Ramey and Neville Francis, "A Century of Work and Leisure," *American Economic Journal: Macroeconomics* 1, no. 2 (July 2009): 189–224. See especially John Robinson and Geoffrey Godbey, *Time for Life: The Surprising Ways Americans Use Their Time* (University Park: Penn State Press, 1999).

30. John Owen notes that as the cost of complementary spending associated with leisure increases, the price of leisure increases. For a similar example, consider that as the cost of tires increases, the price of automobiles increases. Owen, *The Price of Leisure*, 62–67.

31. See Hunnicutt, *Work without End*, 4–5; Owen, "Workweeks and Leisure; and J. D. Owen, *Working Hours: An Economic Analysis* (Lexington, MA: Lexington Books, 1979), especially chap. 3.

32. Hunnicutt, *Work without End*.

33. Pierre-André Chiappori and Arthur Lewbel, "Gary Becker's A Theory of the Allocation of Time," *Economic Journal* 125 (March 2015): 493–517.

34. Becker, "A Theory of the Allocation of Time," 496.

35. Ibid., 514. Becker wrote, "The substitution towards goods induced by an increase in the relative cost of time would often include a substitution towards more expensive goods" (514).

36. Ibid.

37. Stephen Hill, "Time at Work: An Economic Analysis," in *Time, Work and Organization*, ed. Paul Blyton, John Hassard, Stephen Hill, and Ken Starkey (New York: Routledge, 2017), 71. Writing about tourist behavior, Tommy Anderson agrees: "Tourists that have well-paid and interesting work may limit their leisure time but make their holidays more 'experience efficient' by spending more during a shorter time." Tommy Anderson, "The Tourist in the Experience Economy," *Scandinavian Journal of Hospitality and Tourism* 7, no. 1 (2007): 56. For a discussion of the "psychology of time vs. money," see Ashley Whillans, "Exchanging Cents for Seconds: The Happiness Benefits of Choosing Time over Money" (Ph.D. diss., University of British Columbia, 2017), chap. 5; see also A. V. Whillans, A. C. Weidman, and E. W. Dunn, "Valuing Time over Money Is Associated with Greater Happiness," *Social Psychological and Personality Science* 7, no. 3 (2016): 213–222.

38. Becker, "A Theory of the Allocation of Time," 517 (emphasis added).

39. Hill, "Time at Work," 64 (emphasis added).

40. Becker, "A Theory of the Allocation of Time," 506.

41. The possibility that shortening hours remains viable as a continuing historical process is also supported by the work of Mark Agular, Erik Hurst, Valerie Ramey, Neville Francis, and others who suggest leisure time is still growing. See Mark Agular

and Erik Hurst, "Measuring Trends in Leisure: The Allocation of Time over Five Decades," *Quarterly Journal of Economics* 122, no. 3 (August 2007): 969–1006; and Ramey and Francis, "A Century of Work and Leisure." If, as most economists agree, the choice between income and leisure is indeterminate, it is theoretically possible for the income effect to swamp the substitution effect, and as people move increasingly into the experience and transformation economies, they may be willing to exchange existing income for increasing leisure, unprompted by wage increases. Amy Salzmann reported on this phenomenon in *Downshifting: Reinventing Success on a Slower Track* (New York: HarperCollins, 1992).

42. Becker, "A Theory of the Allocation of Time," 516.

43. Ibid., 496 (emphasis added).

44. James Heckman notes that before Becker's time allocation theories appeared, economists tended to assume that all nonmarket time can be aggregated into a single composite, "leisure." James J. Heckman, "Introduction to a Theory of the Allocation of Time by Gary Becker," *Economic Journal* 125 (March 2015): 403–409.

45. According to Adam Arvidsson, "productive consumption" involves "practices [that] generally unfold beyond the direct control of markets, . . . [and] are based on a blurring of consumption and production, . . . [in which] participants play an important role." Adam Arvidsson, "The Potential of Consumer Publics," *Ephemera: Theory and Politics in Organization* 13, no. 2 (2013): 370.

46. To the extent that our day jobs remain a cost incurred, as the marginalists would say, they may be said to have an opportunity cost in their relation to IMPC, which has much less, or zero, cost incurred and may be more productive. Until our day jobs become as much play as our IMPC (the socialist's dream), Becker's opportunity costs must be at least recalibrated.

47. Roc Morin, "How to Hire Fake Friends and Family," *The Atlantic*, November 7, 2017, available at https://www.theatlantic.com/family/archive/2017/11/paying-for-fake-friends-and-family/545060.

48. Pierre-André Chiappori and Arthur Lewbel note that "what Becker does uniquely is to merge goods consumption with time use in the production of household utility. Previous models of labour supply considered consumption and leisure as distinct goods that separately provide utility." Becker's original distinction between productive consumption (time used in the production of household utility) and other forms of leisure breaks down when productive consumption displays leisure's one distinguishing feature, intrinsic motivation. Chiappori and Lewbel, "Gary Becker's A Theory of the Allocation of Time," 410.

49. Arvidsson, "The Potential of Consumer Publics." Theorists, including Karl Marx, have used the term "productive consumption" for various purposes. See Karl Marx, "Production, Consumption, Distribution, Exchange (Circulation)," 1859, available at https://caringlabor.wordpress.com/2010/07/30/karl-marx-production-consumption-distribution-exchange-circulation.

50. Arvidsson, "The Potential of Consumer Publics, 369.

51. Clay Shirky, *Cognitive Surplus: Creativity and Generosity in a Connected Age* (New York: Penguin Press, 2010). See also Robert Putnam, *Bowling Alone: The Collapse and Revival of American Community* (New York: Simon and Schuster, 2001).

52. Arvidsson, "The Potential of Consumer Publics, 369. Arvidsson agrees with Clay Shirky about cognitive surpluses. See Shirky, *Cognitive Surplus.*

53. Compare with G. Hardin, "The Tragedy of the Commons," *Science* 162 (December 1968): 1243–1248.

54. Shirky, *Cognitive Surplus.* See also Steven Johnson, "The Internet? We Built That," *New York Times*, September 21, 2012, available at https://www.nytimes.com/2012/09/23/magazine/the-internet-we-built-that.html. The legal scholar Yochai Benkler and Helen Nissenbaum have called this phenomenon "commons-based peer production." See Yochai Benkler and Helen Nissenbaum, "Commons-Based Peer Production and Virtue," *Journal of Political Philosophy* 14, no. 4 (2006): 394–419.

55. Arvidsson, "The Potential of Consumer Publics," 371.

56. Ibid., 368.

57. Owen, *The Price of Leisure*, 66.

58. Becker, "Theory of the Allocation of Time," 517.

59. Pine and Gilmore observe, "Time is the currency of experiences." Pine and Gilmore, *The Experience Economy*, xv.

60. William C. Compton and Edward Hoffman, *Positive Psychology: The Science of Happiness and Flourishing* (Belmont, CA: Wadsworth, 2013), 71.

61. The Kellogg Company women I interviewed in the 1980s and 1990s pointed out that of course a good deal of housework and childcare was burdensome—things they would prefer to have others do. However, most were able to make distinctions, finding other household duties, such as gardening, canning vegetables, and reading to their children, enjoyable, constituting the best rewards of their six-hour day at Kellogg's. When I asked about how they used their "extra time," the women often talked about such IMPC as the best part of their leisure. Benjamin Hunnicutt, "Kellogg's Six-Hour Day: A Capitalist Vision of Liberation through Managed Work Reduction," *Business History Review* 66, no. 3 (Autumn 1992): 475–522.

62. Stewart I. Donaldson, Maren Dollwet, and Meghana A. Rao, "Happiness, Excellence, and Optimal Human Functioning Revisited: Examining the Peer-Reviewed Literature Linked to Positive Psychology," *Journal of Positive Psychology* 10, no. 3 (2015): 185–195.

63. Linder, *The Harried Leisure Class*, 83.

64. James Gleick, *Faster: The Acceleration of Just about Everything* (New York: Pantheon, 2000).

65. D. Guex and O. Crevoisier, "A Comprehensive Socio-Economic Model of the Experience Economy: The Territorial Stage," in *Spatial Dynamics in the Experience Economy*, ed. A. Lorentzen, L. Schröder, and K. Topsø Larsen (Abingdon, UK: Routledge, 2015), 1–17.

66. Arianna Huffington, "America's Real Deficit Crisis," *Huffington Post*, July 2, 2013, available at https://www.huffingtonpost.com/arianna-huffington/americas-real-deficit-crisis_b_3204683.html.

67. See the Introduction for a discussion of postmaterialist values.

68. A negative income elasticity of demand is associated with *inferior goods*; an increase in income will lead to a fall in the demand and may lead to substitutes. A positive income elasticity of demand is associated with *normal goods*; an increase in income will lead to a rise in demand.

69. Eventbright observed, "Our increased preference for live experiences is being driven by a strong desire to connect with people, our communities, and the world—and there's no doubt that the current political climate is contributing to this uptick. . . .

When Americans consider the future of our country, they say that two things are essential to promoting positive change: Connecting with one another in real life, and the resulting expansion of perspective." Eventbrite, "The Experience Movement: How Millennials Are Bridging Cultural and Political Divides Offline," 2017, p. 2, available at https://s3.amazonaws.com/eventbrite-s3/marketing/landingpages/assets/pdfs/Eventbrite+Experience+Generation+report-2017.pdf.

70. Ibid. I argue in "Kellogg's Six-Hour Day" that among the reasons that the six-hour day ended in Battle Creek was a change in values attached to work vis-à-vis leisure. What I saw there was the reverse of the coming of postmaterialism: for decades after the Great Depression, work was in ascendancy and leisure trivialized.

71. Amy Adkins, "Majority of U.S. Employees Not Engaged despite Gains in 2014," Gallup, January 28, 2015, available at http://news.gallup.com/poll/181289/majority-employees-not-engaged-despite-gains-2014.aspx.

72. Jaison R. Abel, Richard Deitz, and Yaquin Su, "Are Recent College Graduates Finding Good Jobs?" *Current Issues in Economics and Finance* 20, no. 1 (2014): 1–8. See also Jessica Lutz, "The Underemployment Phenomenon No One Is Talking About," *Forbes*, July 21, 2017, available at https://www.forbes.com/sites/payout/2017/07/21/the-underemployment-phenomenon-no-one-is-talking-about/#2b7817655a01.

73. Compton and Hoffman, *Positive Psychology*, 90–91. See Chapter 5 for a discussion of psychological research concerning the frequency versus intensity of experiences.

74. Compton and Hoffman, *Positive Psychology*, 99. Compton and Hoffman include several supporting studies. See also Tim Kasser and Kennon Sheldon, "Time Affluence as a Path toward Personal Happiness and Ethical Business Practice: Empirical Evidence from Four Studies," *Journal of Business Ethics* 84, suppl. 2 (January 2009): 243–255.

75. Benjamin Hunnicutt, *Free Time: The Forgotten American Dream* (Philadelphia: Temple University Press, 2013), 52, 112.

76. John de Graaf and David K. Batker, *What's the Economy for, Anyway? Why It's Time to Stop Chasing Growth and Start Pursuing Happiness* (New York: Bloomsbury Press, 2012).

77. "Happiness and Economics: Economics Discovers Its Feelings," *The Economist*, December 19, 2006), available at https://www.economist.com/special-report/2006/12/19/economics-discovers-its-feelings.

78. Chiappori and Lewbel, "Gary Becker's A Theory of the Allocation of Time," 412.

79. F. H. Knight, *Risk, Uncertainty, and Profit* (1921; repr., Minola, NY: Dover, 1964), 117 (emphasis in original).

80. Keynes, *Essays in Persuasion*, 365.

81. G. A. Laing, *Toward Technocracy* (Los Angeles: Angelus Press, 1933), 31.

82. Galbraith, *The Affluent Society*, 119.

83. Jesse Walker, Amit Kumar, and Thomas Gilovich, "Cultivating Gratitude and Giving through Experiential Consumption," *Emotion* 16, no. 8 (2016): 1127.

84. Thomas Gilovich, Amit Kumar, and Lily Jampol, "A Wonderful Life: Experiential Consumption and the Pursuit of Happiness," *Journal of Consumer Psychology* 25, no. 1 (2015): 152.

85. Christopher Peterson and Martin Seligman, *Character Strengths and Virtues: A Handbook and Classification* (New York: Oxford University Press, 2004), 21.

86. See Anders Hayden, *Sharing the Work, Sparing the Planet: Work Time, Consumption and Ecology* (London: Zed Books, 1999). See also Donella H. Meadows and the Club of Rome, *The Limits to Growth: A Report for the Club of Rome's Project on the Predicament of Mankind* (New York: New American Library, 1974).

87. Anna Coote, Jane Franklin, and Andrew Simms, "21 Hours: Why a Shorter Working Week Can Help Us All to Flourish in the 21st Century," New Economics Foundation, February 2010, available at https://web.archive.org/web/20160209144546/http://b.3cdn.net/nefoundation/f49406d81b9ed9c977_p1m6ibgje.pdf. See also Heather Stuart, "Cut the Working Week to a Maximum of 20 Hours, Urge Top Economists," *The Guardian*, January 8, 2012, available at https://www.theguardian.com/society/2012/jan/08/cut-working-week-urges-thinktank; and David Rosnick, "Reduced Work Hours as a Means of Slowing Climate Change," Center for Economic and Policy Research, February 2013, available at http://cepr.net/documents/publications/climate-change-workshare-2013-02.pdf.

88. C. N. Lombardo, "Shorter Workweek in a Tough Economy," *Wisconsin Employment Law Letter*, February 4, 2010, available at https://hrdailyadvisor.blr.com/2010/02/04/shorter-workweek-in-a-tough-economy; Philip L. Rones, Randy E. Ilg, and Jennifer M. Gardner, "Trends in Hours of Work since the Mid-1970s," *Monthly Labor Review*, April 1997, available at https://www.bls.gov/opub/mlr/1997/04/art1full.pdf; Harvey Schachter, "Save the World with a 3-Day Work Week," *Globe and Mail*, February 10, 2012, available at https://web.archive.org/web/20160505185931/http://www.theglobeandmail.com/report-on-business/careers/management/morning-manager/save-the-world-with-a-3-day-work-week/article2332609; Dean Baker, "Pass the Stimulus—Then Help Shorten the Work Week," *New York Daily News*, January 28, 2009, available at https://www.nydailynews.com/opinion/pass-stimulus-shorten-work-week-article-1.425158; T. Abate, "Get to Work: Want More Jobs? Shorten the Workweek," *San Francisco Chronicle*, July 11, 2010, p. D3. Most of these recommendations depend on government regulations to reduce working hours.

89. Jennifer Sumner and Heather Mair, "Sustainable Leisure: Building the Civil Commons," *Leisure/Loisir* 41, no. 3 (2017): 281–295; Nicole Vaugeois, Pete Parker, and Yufan Yang, "Is Leisure Research Contributing to Sustainability? A Systematic Review of the Literature," *Leisure/Loisir* 41, no. 3 (2017): 297–322. This entire issue of *Leisure/Loisir* (vol. 41, no. 3) was devoted to leisure and sustainability. See also Hayden, *Sharing the Work, Sparing the Planet*.

CHAPTER 9

1. Mihaly Csikszentmihalyi, "Positive Psychology and a Positive World-View: New Hope for the Future of Humankind," in *Applied Positive Psychology: Improving Everyday Life, Health, Schools, Work, and Society*, ed. Stewart I. Donaldson, Mihaly Csikszentmihalyi, and Jeanne Nakamura (New York: Psychology Press, 2011), 205.

2. Csikszentmihalyi writes that some sources of past wisdom that inform positive psychology are: First, "Christian theological virtues (1. Corinthians 13:13): hope (refraining from despair), faith (steadfastness in belief), [and] charity (selfless, voluntary loving-kindness)." Second, Zoroastrianism, which maintains that "order and disorder are in constant conflict in the universe. Each individual needs to actively participate in life through good thoughts, good words, and good deeds to ensure happiness and

keep chaos at bay. This active participation is a central element in Zoroaster's concept of free will." Zoroastrianism stresses "responsibility for the environment: Zoroastrians prayed each evening to express their gratitude to the air, the water, the plants, and the earth, and asked forgiveness from each for the harm that the person might have done during the day to each of them (conservation psychology)." And third, Buddhism, which promotes "control of attention—mindfulness, savoring"—and the "eightfold path: (1) right view, (2) right intention, (3) right speech, (4) right action, (5) right lifestyle, (6) right effort, (7) right mindfulness, [and] (8) right concentration." Csikszentmihalyi, "Positive Psychology and a Positive World-View," 212.

3. Ibid., 211.

4. Ibid.

5. Using similar reasoning, Siegel describes interpersonal neurobiology as a field that "examines the parallel findings from independent disciplines to uncover their common principles," including the parallel findings from historical sources—philosophers, sages, traditions, and so forth. Siegel goes on to acknowledge the 1998 book by Edward O. Wilson, *Consilience: The Unity of Knowledge* (New York: Knopf), agreeing that "consilience enables us to push the boundaries of our knowledge forward by moving beyond the usual constraints of academic fields' often isolated attempts to describe reality." Daniel J. Siegel, *Mindsight: The New Science of Personal Transformation* (New York: Bantam Books, 2010), 279; see also 149–151, 301.

6. Christopher Peterson and Martin Seligman, *Character Strengths and Virtues: A Handbook and Classification* (New York: Oxford University Press, 2004), 50.

7. Ibid., 51.

8. Ibid., 59.

9. Csikszentmihalyi, "Positive Psychology and a Positive World-View," 205.

10. Benjamin Hunnicutt, *Free Time: The Forgotten American Dream* (Philadelphia: Temple University Press, 2013).

11. Benjamin Hunnicutt, *Work without End: Abandoning Shorter Hours for the Right to Work* (Philadelphia: Temple University Press, 1987), 78.

12. There is evidence that Hegel influenced Whitman in his view of history as the unfolding of freedom and of higher progress as history's and freedom's capstones. See Benjamin Kline Hunnicutt, "Walt Whitman's 'Higher Progress' and Shorter Work Hours," *Walt Whitman Quarterly Review* 26, no. 2 (2008): 92–109.

13. Walt Whitman, *Democratic Vistas*, in *Prose Works 1892*, ed. Floyd Stovall (New York: New York University Press, 1964), 410.

14. Ibid., 369.

15. Walt Whitman, *Leaves of Grass: The 1892 Edition* (New York: Bantam Books, 1983), 127.

16. Walt Whitman, *Democratic Vistas*.

17. Martin Seligman, *Flourish: A Visionary New Understanding of Happiness and Well-Being* (New York: Free Press, 2011), 106.

18. There were exceptions: Bertrand Russell's essay "In Praise of Idleness," *Harper's*, October 1932, pp. 552–559, and the popularity of hoboes in the twentieth century.

19. Peterson and Seligman, *Character Strengths and Virtues*, 59.

20. Whitman, *Democratic Vistas*, 381.

21. Whitman, *Leaves of Grass*, 22.

22. Benjamin Kline Hunnicutt, "Walt Whitman's 'Higher Progress' and Shorter Work Hours," *Walt Whitman Quarterly Review* 26, no. 2 (2008): 92–109.

23. Hunnicutt, *Free Time*.

24. Jonathan Edwards, *A Narrative of Many Surprising Conversions in Northampton and Vicinity* (Worcester, MA: Moses W. Grout, 1832), 136. Edwards reported, "[During the Great Awakening] our public praises were then greatly enlivened. God was then served in our psalmody, in some measure, in the beauty of holiness. It has been observable, that there has been scarce any part of divine worship, wherein good men amongst us have had grace so drawn forth, and their hearts so lifted up in the ways of God, as in singing his praises. Our congregation excelled all that ever I knew in the external part of the duty before, the men generally carrying regularly and well, three parts of music, and the women a part by themselves: But now they were evidently wont to sing with unusual elevation of heart and voice, which made the duty pleasant indeed. . . . A great delight in singing praises to God and Jesus Christ, and longing that this present life may be, as it were, one continued song of praise to God; longing, as the person expressed it, *to set and sing this life away*" (136; emphasis added).

25. Hunnicutt, *Free Time*, 15–17. See also Jonathan Edwards, *The Works of President Edwards in Ten Volumes* (Boston: Carvell, 1829), 5:148.

26. Rick Hanson comes close to "disinterested benevolence" with his wish for good things to happen to other people. Rick Hanson, *Hardwiring Happiness: The New Brain Science of Contentment, Calm, and Confidence* (New York: Harmony Books, 2016), 91.

27. W. E. Channing, *The Works of William E. Channing* (Boston: American Unitarian Association, 1891), 19–20, 111 (emphasis added).

28. Robert T. Rhode, "Culture Followed the Plow, However Slowly," *Kentucky Philological Review* 15 (2001): 49–56. See also A. Lincoln, "Address to the Wisconsin State Agricultural Society, Milwaukee, Wisconsin, Sept. 30, 1859," reprinted in Andrew Delbanco, ed., *The Portable Abraham Lincoln* (New York: Penguin, 2009), 181. Nineteenth-century visionaries who endorsed higher progress include Charles Sumner, Karl Heinzen, William E. Channing, Gerrit Smith, Josiah Abbott, and William Lloyd Garrison. See Hunnicutt, *Free Time*.

29. Hunnicutt, *Work without End*, 361.

30. H. Ford and S. Crowther, "The Fear of Overproduction," *Saturday Evening Post*, July 12, 1930, p. 3.

31. E. Cowdrick, "The New Economic Gospel of Consumption," *Industrial Management* 74 (October 1927): 208.

32. Hunnicutt, *Work without End*, 269. See also Rexford Tugwell and Leon Keyserling, eds., *Redirecting Education* (New York: Columbia University Press, 1934).

33. Robert Hutchins, *The Great Conversation: The Substance of a Liberal Education* (Chicago: Encyclopedia Britannica, 1955), 29–30. Hutchins wrote, "The revolt against the classical dissectors and drillmasters was justified. So was the new interest in experimental science. The revolt against liberal education was not justified. Neither was the belief that the method of experimental science could replace the methods of history, philosophy, and the arts. As is common in educational discussion, the public had confused names and things. The dissectors and drillmasters had no more to do

with liberal education than the ordinary college of liberal arts has to do with those arts today" (29–30).

34. Robert M. Hutchins, *Education for Freedom* (Baton Rouge: Louisiana State University, 1943), 89.

35. Robert M. Hutchins, *The Higher Learning in America* (New Haven, CT: Yale University Press, 1936), 5.

36. John Maynard Keynes, "Economic Possibilities for Our Grandchildren," in *Essays in Persuasion* (1931; repr., London: Palgrave Macmillan, 2010), 326.

37. Robert M. Hutchins, *The University of Utopia* (Chicago: University of Chicago Press, 1953), vii, ix.

38. Robert M. Hutchins, "Something New in Education," *Rotarian*, February 1933, pp. 7, 8.

39. "Education: Chicago's Adjustment," *Time*, January 4, 1932, p. 22; "Education: Report Card," *Time*, December 29, 1952, p. 42.

40. Robert M. Hutchins, "The Public Library: Its Place in Education," *Library Quarterly* 20, no. 3 (1950): 186. See also Robert M. Hutchins, "The University and Character," *The Commonweal*, April 22, 1938, pp. 710–711. A list of virtues ("courage, temperance, liberality, honor, justice, wisdom, reason, and understanding—these are still the virtues") is in Robert Hutchins, *No Friendly Voice* (Chicago: University of Chicago Press, 1936), 4. Ordinarily, social virtues were taught by the church and family. With the rise of "Salvation by Work" and the increased secularization of modern life, however, Hutchins believed that the schools needed to take more responsibility to teach such things. Hutchins, *The University of Utopia*, ix.

41. The three criteria for inclusion in the Great Books set were contemporary relevance, readability, and representations of the "great ideas," such as the enduring virtues, classical and religious. Hutchins, *The Great Conversation*, 78.

42. Hutchins, "The Public Library," 183.

43. Benjamin Hunnicutt, "Leisure and Play in Plato's Teaching and Philosophy of Learning," *Leisure Sciences* 12, no. 2 (1990): 211–227.

44. Hutchins, *The Great Conversation*, 70.

45. Hutchins, *The University of Utopia*, ix.

46. Hutchins, *The Great Conversation*, 1. Adult education had always been central to Hutchins's vision of the coming age of leisure. See Mary Ann Dzuback, *Robert M. Hutchins: Portrait of an Educator* (Chicago: University of Chicago Press, 1991), 234. During the 1930s when the Black-Connery thirty-hour workweek bill was making headlines across the country, Hutchins wrote, "We know that the shorter day and the shorter week are going to be with us long after the depression is over. . . . We may be quite confident that the present trend toward a shorter day and shorter week will be maintained. Whether the six-hour day comes this year or next, whether it comes by legislation or not, we may be sure it will come. . . . [Therefore] there is one great and pressing [need], adult education." See Hutchins, *No Friendly Voice*, 104–105. See also Robert Hutchins, *Some Observations on American Education* (Cambridge: Cambridge University Press, 1956), 93, 118; and Robert Hutchins, "A Letter to the Reader," in *Gateway to the Great Books*, ed. Robert Hutchins, Mortimer Adler, and Clifton Fadiman, vol. 1, *Introduction, Syntopical Guide* (Chicago: Encyclopedia Britannica, 1963). Hutchins was fond of saying that education was popularly seen as something for young people to get over, like a case of the measles.

47. Hannah Arendt, *The Human Condition* (Chicago: University of Chicago Press, 1958), 129.

48. Robert Hutchins and Mortimer Adler, "Wealth and Happiness," in *The Great Ideas Today: Work, Wealth, and Leisure* (Chicago: Encyclopedia Britannica, 1965), 90. Throughout history, wealth had most often been seen as a subordinate value—a means to the more important end of human happiness. Wisdom was the ability to recognize when a person or a nation had enough and to move on to better things. Quoting from great books that made this point—among them Karl Marx's observation that economic progress is valuable because it lays the "real basis of a higher form of society, a society in which the full and free development of every individual forms the ruling principle"—Hutchins and Alder concluded that "wealth holds the lowest place among the necessary means" of life (90).

49. Hutchins and Adler, "Wealth and Happiness," 103; see also 2, 3, 90–92.

50. William Ellery Channing, "On the Elevation of the Laboring Classes," in *The Works of William E. Channing*, 58.

51. "Education: Trouble in Chicago," *Time*, May 1, 1944, pp. 56–58. See also Milton Mayer, *Robert Maynard Hutchins: A Memoir* (Berkeley: University of California Press, 1993), 295, 340, 408. The faculty's list of grievances included Hutchins's proposal to form an Institute of Liberal Studies that some faculty feared would reorganize the school's graduate program around the Great Books, his streamlining of undergraduate education, and his emphasis on adult education. Mayer writes that in February and March of 1944, Hutchins faced something of an uprising by senior faculty who wrote to him, "Toward the close of your speech of January 12 you state that 'the purpose of the University is nothing less than to procure a moral, spiritual, and intellectual revolution throughout the world' and you refer later to 'the crusade to which we are called' and 'the revolution which must come if men are to live together in peace,' a revolution which you say must involve 'a reversal of the whole scale of values by which our society lives.'" The group thought this was a bit much. Most of all they were concerned by his suggestion that the doctorate "might well be so redefined as to make it a degree primarily for the teachers . . . needed to discover and introduce liberal education for all" (340). This episode was the beginning of a rebellion at Chicago that would culminate with Hutchins's resignation eight years later.

52. Lloyd Wendt, "Renaissance in the Midwest: The Story of the Great Books Course," *Chicago Tribune*, October 20, 1946, p. 11.

53. The Great Books Foundation began offering the Great Books classes, taking over from the University of Chicago, and published a set of sixteen inexpensive books in 1947 (60 cents each, $7.50 for the set). "Education: Culture C.O.D.," *Time*, June 16, 1947. p. 54.

54. Ibid.

55. T. Lacy, *The Dream of a Democratic Culture: Mortimer J. Adler and the Great Books Idea* (New York: Palgrave Macmillan, 2013).

56. "Services: Cashing In on Culture," *Time*, April 20, 1962, p. 96. See also "Education: Culture C.O.D." I grew up in the countryside, just outside Raleigh, North Carolina, in the 1950s, and my father was a postal worker. I was nevertheless surrounded by good books and encouraged to read and talk about them. While we did not have Chicago's Great Books, we did have, and read, several of the Charles Eliot's Harvard Classics, including works of Plato and Aristotle. Olivia Raney Library's

bookmobile that delivered books to country folks and WUNC public television also helped convince me that the life of the mind was within my reach—that I could go study at Chapel Hill and seek out Bernard Boyd, who lectured on biblical archeology and the German higher critics on public TV, and challenge him, as he had challenged me. And I did.

57. "Education: New Job for a Salesman," *Time*, January 1, 1951, p. 97.

58. See, for example, Hutchins and Adler, *The Great Ideas Today*, 2, 3.

59. Paint and Sip Studio #197 advertises, "Looking for a fun night out? We've got the answer for you! Unleash your creative side with Painting with a Twist! Painting With A Twist is a BYOB art studio where you bring your favorite beverage, your favorite food & your favorite people and we'll take care of the rest. Our talented team of instructors guides you every step of the way as you eat, drink and paint your way to a finished work of art. You'll be amazed before the night is over! You just might discover your inner artist!" See the studio's website, at https://www.paintingwithatwist.com/studio/asheville.

60. Aldo Leopold, *A Sand County Almanac: With Essays on Conservation from Round River* (1949; repr., New York: Random House, 1990), 238.

61. Keynes, "Economic Possibilities for Our Grandchildren." Of course, Keynes was British. But his influence in the United States was widespread.

62. For Keynes, "in the long run . . . *mankind is solving its economic problem.*" Ibid., 327 (emphasis in original).

63. Ibid., 326.

64. Ibid.

65. John A. Ryan, *Distributive Justice: The Right and Wrong of Our Present Distribution of Wealth* (Auckland, New Zealand: Floating Press, 2013), 370. See the discussion of economics of abundance, declining utility, and the demand for leisure in Chapter 4.

66. Deirdre McCloskey, *Bourgeois Equality: How Ideas, Not Capital or Institutions, Enriched the World* (Chicago: University of Chicago Press, 2016), 443. McCloskey has not yet emphasized leisure's importance.

67. For a history of "humane and moral progress," see Hunnicutt, *Free Time*, 65.

68. Ibid., 14.

69. Kenneth Cmiel, "Whitman the Democrat," in *A Historical Guide to Walt Whitman*, ed. David S. Reynolds (Oxford: Oxford University Press, 2000), 227.

70. McCloskey, *Bourgeois Equality*, 443, 674, 675. I am not a purist defender of the free market. Rather, I am more persuaded by McCloskey's nuanced and brilliant "Apology." Maintaining that "capitalism can . . . be virtuous," she argues that "American capitalism needs to be inspirited, moralized, completed," noting that "one of the ways capitalism works 'pretty well' . . . is to nourish the virtues," which is a position in keeping with the tradition of economic liberalism. Sounding the themes reminiscent of those of the positive psychologists, she warns, "I think a worse 'tragedy' . . . would be to accept the pessimistic view and abandon the daily task of moralizing capitalism." I have been intrigued by her vision from the time that I knew her at the University of Iowa and am heartened by her invitation: "A democratic but cultured and creative capitalism is possible, and to our good. It needs to be worked on. You come, too." My willingness to give the free market a chance and my hope that the eudaimonic technology may "nourish" the virtues in the experience and transformation economies are, in part, the

result of accepting her invitation. Deirdre McCloskey, "Apology," in *The Bourgeois Virtues: Ethics for an Age of Commerce* (Chicago: University of Chicago Press, 2006), 3, 13. See also Deirdre McCloskey, "Avarice, Prudence, and the Bourgeois Virtues," in *Having: Property and Possession in Religious and Social Life*, ed. William Schweiker and Charles Mathewes (Grand Rapids, MI: Wm. Eerdmans, 2004): 312–336.

71. Keynes, "Economic Possibilities for Our Grandchildren," 326.

72. Ibid.

73. Karl Marx, *Capital: A Critique of Political Economy*, ed. Frederick Engels, trans. Ernest Untermann (Chicago: Charles H. Kerr, 1909), 954–955.

74. Herbert Marcuse, *Eros and Civilization: A Philosophical Inquiry into Freud* (Boston: Beacon Press, 1966), 152–153.

75. Keynes, "Economic Possibilities for Our Grandchildren," 326.

76. Ibid., 328.

77. Keynes, "Economic Possibilities for Our Grandchildren," 327. For a more complete historical treatment of what people, from 1920 until the 1970s, called the "problem of leisure," see Hunnicutt, *Work without End*, 261–264.

78. Keynes, "Economic Possibilities for Our Grandchildren," 328.

79. Peterson and Seligman, *Character Strengths and Virtues*, 59.

80. Keynes, "Economic Possibilities for Our Grandchildren," 327.

81. Ibid.

82. Ibid., 332.

83. Ibid., 329.

84. Ibid., 331.

85. Ibid., 329.

86. Ibid., 371.

87. E. P. Thompson, "Time, Work-Discipline and Industrial Capitalism," *Past and Present* 38 (December 1967): 95 (emphasis added). See also Max Weber, *The Protestant Ethic and the Spirit of Capitalism*, trans. T. Parsons (New York: Charles Scribner's Sons, 1930), 181–182.

88. Thompson, "Time, Work-Discipline and Industrial Capitalism," 95; Keynes, "Economic Possibilities for Our Grandchildren," 330.

89. Thompson, "Time, Work-Discipline and Industrial Capitalism," 96.

90. Hunnicutt, *Free Time*, chap. 5.

91. Cynthia Estlund, fearing with Joseph Pine and James Gilmore and many others that "the current wave of labor-replacing technology might lead to net job losses, sharper labor market polarization, or both," proposes "a three-dimensional response to a future of less work." She explains that "the idea of reducing working hours, standing alone, does not pretend to solve the present or future problems of workers. . . . The shorter hours strategy only works in tandem with some plan for increasing incomes at the bottom of the income distribution." Her "three-dimensional strategy" involves implementing government policy necessary for job creation, spreading work and leisure, and raising the floor on material living standards. Cynthia Estlund, "Three Big Ideas for a Future of Less Work and a Three-Dimensional Alternative," *Law and Contemporary Problems* 82, no. 3 (2019): 40, 32.

Still, being intrigued by public policy solutions, I see Estlund's as certainly one of the best-reasoned around. But the likelihood of selling her "three-dimensional strategy" politically is slim at best. Having been a professor of leisure studies for forty-four years, I can testify that, in particular, convincing people to support increasing leisure through government policy is nearly inconceivable. The religion of work forecloses that possibility. Therefore, I am betting on the marketplace and the eudaimonic technology as being more realistic shorter-hours strategies.

92. Arendt, *The Human Condition*, 129.

93. Joseph Pieper, *Leisure: The Basis of Culture* (New York: New American Library, 1963), 21.

94. Jacques Ellul, "L'ideologie du travail," *Foi et Vie* 4 (1980), available at https://lesamisdebartleby.wordpress.com/2016/12/11/jacques-ellul-lideologie-du-travail (my translation).

95. Paul Tillich, *Systematic Theology* (Chicago: University of Chicago Press, 1973), 1:64.

96. Hutchins, *The University of Utopia*, ix.

97. Barth shared Saint Anselm's starting point: "For I do not seek to understand in order to believe; I believe in order to understand." Saint Anselm, *Basic Writings*, trans. and ed. Thomas Williams (Indianapolis, IN: Hacket, 2007), 81. Pointing out that all knowledge, including the sciences, have their starting points in belief—in assumptions (presuppositions, paradigms) about the world that are not "provable" by the systematic application of those assumptions, Barth starts his arguments with the basic tenants of the Christian faith—such as Christ's incarnation—and reasons systematically from there, gradually constructing a larger view of the world built on Christianity's foundational beliefs.

98. Karl Barth, *Church Dogmatics*, vol. 3, *The Doctrine of Creation*, trans. G. T. Thompson (New York: Scribner, 1955), 522.

99. Ibid., 521.

100. Ellul, "L'ideologie du travail."

101. Keynes, "Economic Possibilities for Our Grandchildren," 329.

102. Ellul, "L'ideologie du travail."

103. Felix Cohen, "The Blessing of Unemployment," *American Scholar* 2 (April 1933): 206–207. Cohen concluded, "If work is a curse, unemployment is a blessing. How to increase this blessing of unemployment and distribute it more fairly is the fundamental problem of modern civilization" (207).

104. Arendt, *The Human Condition*, 4, 5.

105. See Bertrand Russell, "In Praise of Idleness," *Harper's*, October 1932, pp. 552–559.

106. Keynes, "Economic Possibilities for Our Grandchildren," 330.

107. Aldous Huxley, *The Perennial Philosophy: An Interpretation of the Great Mystics, East and West* (1945; repr., New York: Harper Perennial, 2012), 21.

108. Psalm 100.

109. Nurit Bird-David, "The Giving Environment: Another Perspective on the Economic System of Gatherer-Hunters," *Current Anthropology* 31, no. 2 (April 1990): 189–196.

110. Huxley, *The Perennial Philosophy*. "Hubris, which is the original sin, consists in regarding the personal ego as self-sufficient" (190).

111. Frederick Engels, "The Part Played by Labour in the Transition from Ape to Man," trans. Clemens Dutt (Moscow: Progress, 1934).

112. Hannah Arendt, *The Life of the Mind* (San Diego, CA: Harcourt, 1978), 215.

113. James M. Demske, *Being, Man, and Death: A Key to Heidegger* (Lexington: University Press of Kentucky, 2015), 22.

114. Benjamin K. Hunnicutt, "Walter Kerr's Utopia of Re-creation," in *Hope and Longing for Utopia: Futures and Illusions in Theology and Narrative*, ed. Daniel Boscaljon (Cambridge, UK: James Clarke, 2015), 119–136.

115. Walter Kerr, *The Decline of Pleasure* (New York: Time, 1962), 306. See also Walter and Jean Kerr papers, Wisconsin Historical Society Library Archives, Madison, Wisconsin.

116. Kerr, *The Decline of Pleasure*, 307.

117. Ibid., 305–306.

118. Ibid., 288–289.

119. Ibid.

120. Alasdair C. MacIntyre, *Dependent Rational Animals: Why Human Beings Need the Virtues* (Chicago: Open Court, 1999), 5.

121. Josef Pieper, *Leisure: The Basis of Culture*, trans. Alexander Dru (New York: New American Library, 1952), 33.

122. Michael Naughton, "Teaching Note on Josef Pieper's *Leisure the Basis of Culture*: An Integration of the Contemplative and Active Life," available at https://www.stthomas.edu/media/catholicstudies/center/ryan/curriculumdevelopment/theologicalethics/NaughtonTeachingNote.pdf (accessed July 30, 2019).

123. The Quran recognizes the biblical Sabbath, but most Muslims have replaced seventh-day observances with *jumu'ah*, Friday prayers and day of rest.

124. A. H. Silver, "Leisure and the Church," *Playground* 20 (January 1927): 539.

125. Ibid. See also A. H. Silver, *Religion in a Changing World* (New York: R. R. Smith, 1930), 143.

Index

Benjamin Kline Hunnicutt is a historian and professor at the University of Iowa. He is also the author of *Kellogg's Six-Hour Day*, *Work Without End: Abandoning Shorter Hours for the Right to Work*, and *Free Time: The Forgotten American Dream* (all Temple).